FROM **UNDERESTIMATED** TO
UNSTOPPABLE

ASCD MEMBER BOOK

Many ASCD members received this book as a
member benefit upon its initial release.

Learn more at: **www.ascd.org/memberbooks**

FROM **UNDERESTIMATED** TO **UNSTOPPABLE**

8 Archetypes for Driving Change in the Classroom and Beyond

ASHLEY LAMB-SINCLAIR

ascd

Arlington, Virginia USA

2800 Shirlington Rd., Suite 1001 • Arlington, VA 22206 USA
Phone: 800-933-2723 or 703-578-9600 • Fax: 703-575-5400
Website: www.ascd.org • Email: member@ascd.org
Author guidelines: www.ascd.org/write

Penny Reinart, *Chief Impact Officer;* Genny Ostertag, *Managing Director, Book Acquisitions & Editing;* Susan Hills, *Senior Acquisitions Editor;* Julie Houtz, *Director, Book Editing;* Jamie Greene, *Editor;* Thomas Lytle, *Creative Director;* Donald Ely, *Art Director;* Melissa Johnston, The Hatcher Group, *Graphic Designer;* Kelly Marshall, *Production Manager;* Christopher Logan, *Senior Production Specialist;* Keith Demmons, *Senior Production Designer;* Valerie Younkin, *Senior Production Designer;* Shajuan Martin, *E-Publishing Specialist*

PAPERBACK ISBN: 978-1-4166-3149-1   ASCD product #123017
PDF EBOOK ISBN: 978-1-4166-3150-7; see Books in Print for other formats.
Quantity discounts are available: email programteam@ascd.org or call 800-933-2723, ext. 5773, or 703-575-5773. For desk copies, go to www.ascd.org/deskcopy.

ASCD Member Book No. FY23-1 (Sep 2022 PSI+). ASCD Member Books mail to Premium (P), Select (S), and Institutional Plus (I+) members on this schedule: Jan, PSI+; Feb, P; Apr, PSI+; May, P; Jul, PSI+; Aug, P; Sep, PSI+; Nov, PSI+; Dec, P. For current details on membership, see www.ascd.org/membership.

Library of Congress Cataloging-in-Publication Data
Names: Lamb-Sinclair, Ashley, author.
Title: From underestimated to unstoppable : 8 archetypes for driving change in the classroom and beyond / Ashley Lamb-Sinclair.
Description: Arlington, VA : ASCD, [2022] | Includes bibliographical references and index.
Identifiers: LCCN 2022024888 (print) | LCCN 2022024889 (ebook) | ISBN 9781416631491 (paperback) | ISBN 9781416631507 (pdf)
Subjects: LCSH: Educational change.
Classification: LCC LB2806 .L26 2022 (print) | LCC LB2806 (ebook) | DDC 371.2—dc23/eng/20220810
LC record available at https://lccn.loc.gov/2022024888
LC ebook record available at https://lccn.loc.gov/2022024889

30 29 28 27 26 25 24 23 22   1 2 3 4 5 6 7 8 9 10 11 12

For my Dad, who always believed in me. And for my Mom,
who never let me settle. Thank you both.

FROM **UNDERESTIMATED** TO **UNSTOPPABLE**

8 Archetypes for Driving Change in the Classroom and Beyond

INTRODUCTION

On a frosty winter morning, I shuffled through a slushy parking lot into a large boardroom in the state department of education building. I had only been in the room once before, when it was empty, and that was not at all like the situation I found myself in now: a very formal state education board meeting stuffed to the brim with education leaders, legislators, the general public, and the media. I wore pantyhose in a valiant if misguided attempt to dress the part of the very-important-professional-woman I thought I needed to be to enter the room.

I was there in my capacity as the first "teacher in residence" at the state department of education. It was an ambiguous, made-up title meant to give me a peek behind the proverbial curtain while I represented the educators in my state as best I could. Prior to entering this board meeting, my journey as teacher in residence had been tumultuous, and my confidence came in fits and starts. I leaned into the opportunity as best I could, primarily by relying on my oldest talent: writing. I wrote essays and articles for a variety of publications, discussing everything from educator leadership to education policy—and let's just say that those pieces were not always well received by colleagues who'd hoped I might toe the company line a bit more.

I sat quietly in a back row, listening attentively. When a team of education leaders presented a proposal for a program that I vehemently disagreed with (and that I knew many of my colleagues around the state would also disagree with), I felt myself fill with resentment. This team had not spent any time collaborating with classroom educators on the proposed program yet was bringing it up for a vote before the state board. I shuffled in my seat as the team spoke, searching the faces around me for some indication of fellow disapproval. As the presentation concluded, the board members took the opportunity to pose questions and comments about the proposed program. The first comments were verbal pats on the back ("Such a great plan!") from board members with no education background. My face flushed with fury as it became clear this program would get the votes it needed and be implemented before state educators knew what hit them.

Then, out of nowhere, another board member spoke. "As I listen to your proposal, I am reminded of an article I recently read by Ashley Lamb-Sinclair," the board member said. "She says many educators feel frustrated when decisions like these are made without their insight, and I am concerned that voting for this program would be doing exactly that."

I couldn't believe it: someone in a traditional position of power, with a shiny gold nameplate in front of her, was speaking *for* me. A thoughtful debate then ensued among board members as to whether the designers had spent enough time collaborating with classroom educators to develop the program effectively. Eventually, the proposal was dismissed and the team behind it was forced back to the drawing board.

As I exited that fancy boardroom in a haze of elation, I ran into the board member who had spoken for me and thanked her. As it turned out, I had actually taught this woman's niece for several years. Because her niece had felt inspired by my class and spoke frequently of me at home, the board member had decided to read my article when she saw my byline attached to it.

An invisible trail of impact had struck a big, visible chord. I thought, "What if every time a program was created or a vote passed, the voice of an educator rang through the room?" This was the moment I realized that my actions as an educator could create a chain reaction that might actually lead to broader change. Since then, I have been on a determined mission to figure out how to do it on purpose rather than by accident—and how to help other educators do the same.

I am not an organizational psychologist, an academic researcher, an expert sociologist, or an anthropologist. I've got a handful of degrees and certificates, but those particular titles do not don them. I do, however, have a diverse range of professional experience, a spongelike curiosity for learning in all forms, and some tried-and-true tools and tricks that have continually worked for me and others I know. Furthermore, I know there are others just like me—thinkers, learners, and questioners who want to make the world around us better but who may struggle to find the confidence to do it.

The information, tools, and resources in this book come from my own changemaking experience, a rabid passion for collecting stories and interesting ideas, and years of collaborating with inspiring change agents both in and out of the traditional education system. My 14 years in the classroom taught me when and how to navigate the red tape of bureaucracy—and when to push beyond it. My four years as an edtech founder taught me how to question assumptions and pivot quickly—and how to walk away when necessary. In the years since, I have learned how to rally toward a cause and persistently press on across systems ranging from large school districts to state agencies to national networks and global nonprofits. I have spent a decade and a half as a mashup of educator, storyteller, and social entrepreneur, constantly deepening my learning.

My unique perspective and tendency to take creative risks have led me to support a variety of change efforts from inception to closure. This book is inspired by those efforts, as well as by the efforts of dear friends and colleagues who have helped me cultivate an understanding of the four key points that serve as a catalyst for this book: (1) Human beings, regardless of job title or place of work, can offer unique insights and pathways for creating change for themselves and those around them, but (2) most people don't always see their own gifts, insights, and capacity clearly, and because (3) many organizations—especially in education—tend to ignore or misunderstand these individuals and their innate gifts, (4) the narrative moves forward without its most vital characters.

In the months between March and September of 2020, when so much was uncertain for educators, I reached my own personal pinnacle of perception on these matters. During this period, I was not teaching students but rather spinning many educational plates at the local, state, and national levels, which provided me with an illuminating perspective as the winds of change blew. In my role at National Geographic Education, I spent time listening to a global collective of educators who offered crucial insights into the similarities and differences of their experiences.

At the state and local level, I collaborated with a network of educators to propose and implement solutions to problems exacerbated by the COVID-19 pandemic.

Because almost everyone I know is an educator of some kind, I spent much of this time engaging in long, thought-provoking conversations about what it means to be an educator, what it means to be a student, and how the system does or does not support the 2020-and-beyond realities of those identities. Interestingly, I had many conversations with educators who were rethinking their own career paths because they felt the work they wanted to do—this lifelong mission of supporting the growth and development of young people—no longer aligned with what was being asked of them by the world at large.

For some, the problem was systemic: *I don't know that our systems do what they claim to do, and I don't know that I want to be part of it anymore.* For others, it was about agency: *I have ideas for moving forward and try to share them, but no one in a position of authority seems to listen.* For others still, it was highly personal: *I can't manage my work and support my own well-being simultaneously.*

Whatever the message, I listened. And I understood. I know the intimate struggle of navigating the call for change along one's career path because I have taken big, terrifying leaps when the opportunities arose. I also intimately know the eternal, sometimes Sisyphean task of trying to rally multiple stakeholders toward a call for change and encouraging the mindsets and actions necessary to actually create it. I could hear this same struggle in the voices of educators, and it is out of that recognition that this book emerged.

I know we're on the precipice of change, but I fear the human beings we need most right now to create it—boundless educators in every form—could lose steam or hope; worse, they might not see the power they hold to shape that change into what's best for young people rather than what's best for systems. As Alice Walker once said, "The most common way people give up their power is by thinking they don't have any" (quoted in Martin, 2004). My dearest hope is that the words in this book will help educators who may feel powerless see the lightning bolts of lasting change only they can wield.

1

WRITING YOUR CHANGE STORY

There is no greater agony than bearing an untold story inside you.

—Maya Angelou (1969)

As of this writing, so much of our world continues to be shaken by the COVID-19 pandemic. For educators at every level, this shaking up has given rise to questions that had always lain beneath the surface. Questions about the work we do and how or even why we do it beg to be asked anew. The answers that have propelled us forward for so long now give many of us pause. There is a rumbling beneath our feet, and calls for change surround us.

Yet for many educators, change can be daunting. It's no secret that many of us have initiative fatigue in the best of times. When you layer global crises on top of work that is already difficult, thinking about reinvention—new initiatives, new strategies, new goals, possibly new purpose—can cause even the most dedicated change agent to collapse into a heap of stress.

The thing about change, though, is that whether we invite it or not, it comes. It is a universal human truth, and if we take a magnifying glass to our beloved field of educating young people, we can't deny that change is long overdue. We've talked about it for decades. Thought leaders on the subject abound. Technology, programs, pilots, organizations, and initiatives of every kind have been created to finally—*finally*—bring that change about. Yet, we dabble. We get tired. We lose steam. Or the various attempts at change are ill-advised, ill-informed, and ill-fated.

But this time, the change that's coming is different from what's come before. I know this because I am actively working toward it, and I know others like me who will refuse to take *no* for an answer this time around.

The thing about creating change is that there is no one-size-fits-all approach. It usually goes something like this: a flashy trend comes down from on high. Education leaders talk about it, think about it, speak about it, and write about it. Other leaders get super excited and decide, "We're going to do this!" They meet around tables, they create strategies and plans, they tell classroom educators all about it and how it's the best new thing and everything will be awesome and amazing when said plan is implemented. Some educators agree and get excited. Some educators join the cause. Some roll their eyes and ignore it. Some are so focused on the human beings in front of them that the great new plan falls flat in the face of the real needs of those humans. So change doesn't come in any real way. The plan doesn't work. The trend fades, and another enters the scene. Thus the cycle continues.

I have personally lived through countless versions of this process. If I'm honest, I've even perpetuated a few of them. But I see the flaws in this cycle now more than ever. If we ask ourselves some hard questions about how positive change occurs, we'll see that the answer is actually very personal; we are the protagonists of our change journeys. Sometimes we play the role of the invisible hero, accomplishing something private that turns on a little light inside of us. Other times we play the hero who is loud and vocal, with light on full display. Still other times, we play the collective hero who brings others along, making the journey communal and creating waves that ripple far beyond us—a million individual actions that amount to a sea change.

For many educators, it may not feel that way right now. So many of my dearest friends and colleagues feel worried, tired, or hopeless. Still, whether we know it or not, each of us is crafting our own personal change story that is contributing toward a broader vision of what education might become in the years ahead. We are all at different points along the journey, and we all have varying philosophies and approaches, but we are collectively building toward something. If we build with intention, we could actually build something quite revolutionary if we so choose.

Cathedral Thinking

In 2019, Greta Thunberg told the European Parliament: "It... will take cathedral thinking. To do your best is no longer good enough. We must all do the seemingly impossible" (Rankin, 2019). Educators everywhere are embracing *cathedral thinking* whether we call it that or not, simultaneously laying the foundation for and constructing the ceilings of a new educational construct. We are all contributing to this collective shift, even if it feels as if we're merely surviving.

If you're familiar with habit theory, you know that small habits over time lead to unconscious routines that in turn lead to sustainable change (Godoy & Douglis, 2021). What if we woke up to the individual contributions we make to collective change—held them up to the light and harnessed their power? What if the many contributions you make every day just by being your dedicated self could become cathedrals of impact both for you and for the collective?

Carl Jung once said, "The privilege of a lifetime is to become who you truly are" (1933/2001). I think we owe it to ourselves to build systems that illustrate this notion. Most educators come into the profession with a strong personal drive and idealistic pull toward something greater than themselves. Yet that idealism gets twisted into a beaten-down version of itself and we find ourselves asking for permission more than we ever imagined we might. Joining a cause larger than our individual selves doesn't mean we have to become cogs in a machine. As Seth Godin quips, "The machine has enough cogs. What it needs instead is you" (2018). So why not offer the most authentic "you" to help build a better machine?

How Do *You* Lead? How Do *You* Create Change?

As an English teacher, I loved to send my students home for the weekend with this little riddle attributed to John Gardner: "There are only two kinds of stories in the universe: a hero takes a journey or a stranger comes to town" (Metcalf, 2007). I used to challenge students to find a story that proved this theory wrong, but I've yet to see it disproved. Similarly, you might say there are only two kinds of change stories: a person creates change from inside out or change influences a person from the outside in.

Think about a time when something changed for you in your work as an educator. Either you decided to proactively make the change (e.g., try a new strategy, redesign your unit, take on a new role) or change was thrust upon you (e.g., a district reorganization, your principal leaves for another school, assessment mandates change). Either way, your path has changed and ripples onto the paths of others. Even when the change was thrust upon you by some external force, your reaction to the change created, inspired, or influenced the reactions of those around you.

I used to teach my students a simple formula for analyzing and developing a character's journey through a story that we can also apply to creating change stories in our lives. It goes like this: *Character illustrates motivational drive, drive leads to conflict, conflict fuels the plot, and setting shapes the action.* Our motivations, or drives, define us; for example, if I look back over my professional experiences, I see a consistent drive for *autonomy, creativity,* and *validation.* I am motivated by freedom to explore ideas, and I want others to value those ideas and their impact.

Drive also dictates the kinds of conflict we find ourselves experiencing over and over again. In my case, my desire for creative freedom tends to lead me to swim upstream against the status quo by refusing to follow a school mandate or by going my own way when collaborating with colleagues. Because I also desire to be valued and validated, I often experience the internal conflict of feeling alone or misunderstood.

Time and again, my professional life has followed a formula: *Rebel to preserve creative autonomy. Upset others. Feel misunderstood because others are upset. Rebel again and upset others some more.* But once I captured the formula, I learned to both embrace it and reshape it to become more effective at moving my own story forward. You could probably create your own formula by asking yourself these questions:

- What consistently motivates you?
- What problems consistently arise from the actions you take?
- How has this pattern created a story or journey in your professional life?
- How has the context around this pattern shifted from setting to setting?

Creating change for yourself and others is like writing a story and living it out. In the realm of social science, this is called *narrative identity.* Narrative identity is an internalized and evolving story we tell ourselves and project outward to make meaning in our lives (Schwartz et al., 2012). Your drive defines your story. If you're the kind of character who is motivated by autonomy, the narrative you create will be different from that of a character who is motivated by collaboration. Your character drive also lets you know the kinds of obstacles you tend to face when creating change, allowing you to plan for them in advance. You control the plot of your own narrative when you root it in character; otherwise, the plot might control you.

Allow me to illustrate.

A few years ago, I was fresh out of the classroom and enthusiastic about a new gig as an instructional coach. But the school where I worked already *had* an instructional coach who had worked long and hard over many years to create the systems and culture I was blindly walking into. I had been hired on the spot to "help teachers innovate." The principal had picked up on my freedom-loving, no-holds-barred creative drive, and I guess he thought I might infect some of the staff with the same kind of energy. However, there were a few problems with this theory:

- For the most part, his staff didn't want to be "infected" with this particular kind of bug.
- His admin team—including the other instructional coach—hadn't signed up for my style of coaching.
- Change doesn't happen like this anyway.

As a result, my pattern unfolded. I enthusiastically set about creating a schoolwide innovation plan because, as you'll recall, I am driven to create and tend to act autonomously when I do. Because I am also driven by validation from others, I was heartbroken when my plans fell short in the eyes of some of my new colleagues—especially the other coach. Never mind that I never bothered to collaborate with her in a way that suited her character and drive. But I wasn't as effective in creating the collective change I had hoped for and I created a lot of frustration and angst for myself and some of my peers along the way.

Now imagine I had entered this situation with a clear understanding of the pattern I display when navigating change. I also might have taken the time to understand the other coach's character and drive before charging full speed ahead. Maybe then I wouldn't have felt so alone when I needed validation but didn't receive it. If I had paid more attention to how my own drive interacted with the needs of the school, I could have been a more successful change agent by better understanding myself and how I might interact best with those around me—and maybe I wouldn't have left the role after one year. With the passage of time and a few other similar experiences under my belt, I now understand how I might have created the kind of change I wanted to see and support through more self-awareness—and saved myself a whole lot of heartache to boot. We can lead change most effectively when we focus on *who* we are, *what* we want, and *how* we seek to achieve those desires.

Character: What Role Do You Play?

We've all sat through enough rounds of "faculty meeting bingo," "what's your color" quizzes, and hair-raising "icebreakers" to be skeptical about anything resembling a personality profile or "get to know you" activity. I'll not do that to you again, but there *is* a nugget of universal wisdom we can pull from these kinds of profiles: the importance of archetypes. At the heart of most personality profiles is an *archetype*—a recurring pattern or motif—that repeats for you time and time again. The concept of archetypes is validated by social science, going back at least as far as Carl Jung's archetypal understanding of personality (Jung, 2014) and influencing many fields even beyond psychology today.

Think of archetypes this way: imagine a prehistoric bird. Many ancient bird species were giant, resembling dinosaurs more than the birds who build nests outside our windows today. When our prehistoric ancestors thought of a bird, what they saw in their mind's eye was likely very different from what we see now. Even today, depending on where you are in the world and your own lived experiences with birds, each of us will imagine a different picture—ducks, pigeons, penguins, swans, doves, cranes, eagles, swallows, parrots—you get the idea. Yet, the essence of *bird* will remain the same. There is a common thread even when the details shift. If we layer this idea of *bird* with pop culture or mythological images and symbols—the phoenix, wise old owls, the Quetzalcóatl, Donald Duck, Toucan Sam, or the Mockingjay from *The Hunger Games* trilogy—the form shifts, but the essence is the same— they're all bird *archetypes*.

Regardless of whatever personality or profile lens we're looking through, at the heart of them all, we will find an archetype that repeats time and again. Knowing our archetypes and how to put them to use to lead change can empower us to do so with authenticity and intention. In my work, I have seen many colleagues display archetypal patterns when they have led change efforts in education. Reflecting on these inspiring colleagues and the work they do, I distilled these patterns down to the eight primary change archetypes that are the focus of this book (see Figure 1.1). When compiling this list of change archetypes, it was critical that they be dynamic and not static because that is the reality of how human beings behave. A *change archetype* in particular is both consistent and malleable, providing space for boundless growth within whatever context we may find ourselves.

Conflict: What Drives Us?

These eight change archetypes are also motivated by specific drives. Understanding what drives our behaviors helps us better understand what we want and how we can most effectively go about getting it. Just as the archetype of a bird may change over time and space but is essentially the same at heart, these change archetypes function in the same way. In storytelling, underlying drives lead characters (archetypes) into specific types of conflict, and the same is true in real life.

Anyone who has ever worked in a school understands how a school environment is similar to a story that unfolds with many characters interacting and various subplots connecting over time. The science educator who is a passionate Champion of environmental conservation will likely be motivated to *advocate* for that cause with their students and colleagues. The school counselor who is a committed Guardian will likely be motivated to *connect* with young people and nurture their well-being. The principal who is a thoughtful Inventor will likely be motivated to *generate* novel approaches to solving problems for the school they lead. So within this school story, many drives intersect all the time, which inevitably leads to conflict.

However, conflict is not inherently a bad thing. Later in this book, we will discuss how it can inspire action and move the plot of our change stories forward. We need many characters leading with a variety of drives to create the kind of conflict necessary for change. Figure 1.2 shows the four core drives for the eight change archetypes we'll explore throughout this book. When we take the time to understand what motivates people, we are better able to embrace both our own humanity and the

Figure 1.1

Likert Scale for Change Archetypes

ARCHETYPE	LEADS...	CREATES CHANGE...	HOW DOES THIS ALIGN WITH MY PATTERNS? (Circle where you land for now, 0 being not aligned at all and 5 being very aligned)
Diplomat	by building relationships	through an objective sense of fairness and integrity	0—1—2—3—4—5
Champion	through passionate defense of a cause	through advocacy of ideals and people	0—1—2—3—4—5
Creative	with divergent thinking and process-oriented instincts	through novelty and ingenuity	0—1—2—3—4—5
Storyteller	with thoughtful attention to detail	through discernment and clear communication	0—1—2—3—4—5
Inventor	with insightful detachment and a forward-thinking approach	through free experimentation and self-possessed initiative	0—1—2—3—4—5
Sage	with perceptive insight and persuasive guidance	with dignified expertise and wise counsel	0—1—2—3—4—5
Investigator	with analytical curiosity	by asking probing questions and conducting thorough research	0—1—2—3—4—5
Guardian	with compassion for and in service to others	by nurturing and protecting the humanity of others	0—1—2—3—4—5

The change archetype that most resonates for me right now is:

humanity of others. Getting back to the essential humanity of the teaching and learning experience is essential to rebuild—and to disrupt.

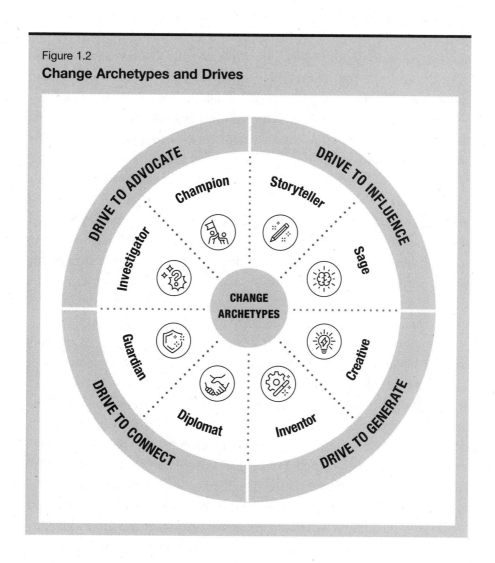

Figure 1.2

Change Archetypes and Drives

What Do Archetypes Have to Do with Creating Change?

When I served as an instructional coach, I realized that leading a school-wide effort was not ideal because of the competing drives involved, so I decided to develop a small cohort of educators who wanted to lead change of some kind. I thought creating a mini-community of change agents would be an opportunity to cultivate grassroots innovation. I developed the vision, pitched it to my principal, and got the greenlight to recruit educators.

I will never forget a conversation I had with a third-year art teacher—an inspiring Investigator—who approached me in the hallway after I shared the vision with the faculty. "This sounds like a really awesome opportunity," she said, "and I have a ton of ideas for what I would want to do, but I just don't think I'm cool enough for something like this."

I was floored. Here was a talented educator wanting to try something new but worried she didn't fit a certain "type." I told her of course she was "cool enough" and promptly recruited her to the cohort. She became one of the most inspiring and creative leaders of that effort, completely revamping her classroom into a student-centered visual art studio. She also influenced how educators outside the cohort approached their own classroom practice as word of her success spread and her peers came to her for input on their own ideas for change. Seeing everything she accomplished (and continues to accomplish well beyond that year) reminds me of an essential truth: *We sometimes have to be convinced of our own power in order to embrace it.*

When most of us think of the term *change agent*, we think of amazing leaders like Malcolm X or Malala Yousafzai. But for every Malcolm or Malala, there are thousands of other change agents whose names we will never know—Diplomats who facilitated conversations behind the scenes, Sages who offered wise counsel, Storytellers who effectively communicated a vision. We have to understand that *we are all cool enough* to lead change; in fact, we *must* do so. First, though, we need to recognize our strengths and take the steps to lead *authentically*.

Whether you want to follow in the footsteps of my art educator friend and change an approach to your craft, start a schoolwide program, implement new district policy, develop a new role for yourself, or inspire your colleagues to embrace a new instructional method, when you begin with your individual strengths, navigate according to your own drives, develop your own approaches to managing tension, and keep your bold vision clear, you can rely on the map in Figure 1.3 as a guide along the way. We will unpack all the elements of this map step by step throughout this book, but know that your goal is to chart this map for yourself and for your vision of the profession. If you aren't the one to create the change you hope to see, then who is?

Figure 1.3
Writing a Change Story

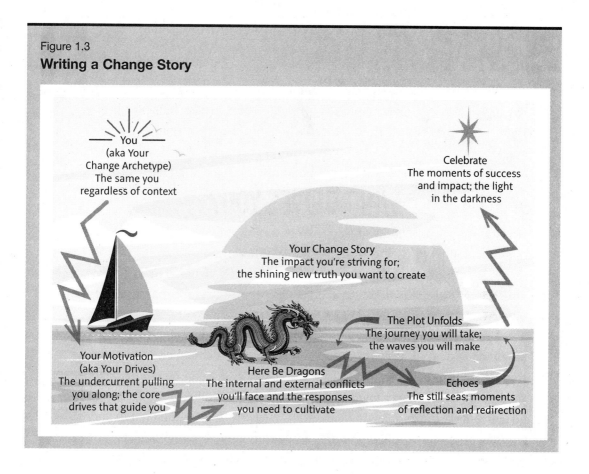

I truly believe that each of us has great influence, but it is also the responsibility of organizations and systems to lead widespread change, especially as it pertains to inequities, oppression, and any harm to individuals. As you read this book and chart ways to lead change, you will likely hit a few systemic obstacles that will require systemic effort to overcome. We will discuss situations like these as best we can, but if you are a leader in a position of hierarchical power at an organizational level, I hope you will embrace the strengths each individual brings while addressing systemic problems. Most importantly, I hope you will listen to their wisdom and let them lead when they embrace their own strengths too. By doing so, we may free each other from outdated bounds that have limited all of us for far too long.

Now, whatever role you play, let's write your change story…

2

WHAT DRIVES YOU?

Find out who you are and do it on purpose.

—Dolly Parton (2015)

Along the edge of a pinewood forest close to a nearly abandoned mountain town, golden-mantled ground squirrels spend their days collecting nuts and seeds, perching on rocks, and digging burrows underground. Scientists come from around the world to work at a research center here, including Jaclyn Aliperti, whose mission was to understand how knowledge of squirrel behavior might lead to new pathways for wildlife conservation. For three years, Aliperti and her team studied the squirrels nearby—marking individual squirrels, mapping their whereabouts, and collecting data to make sense of one main question: *What role does individual personality play in shaping an ecosystem* (Aliperti et al., 2021)?

Let's consider two particular squirrel characters Aliperti came to know over the course of her study. Let's call them Coy and Maverick. (Animal personality is a hard science, and researchers like Dr. Aliperti would not give names to the animals in their studies. I am choosing to do so in this case because I am an English educator who likes witty character names, so please forgive the indulgence.) Each day the researchers would explore the field station noting the specific home range of the individual squirrels they tracked in the study. Coy tended to be very difficult to locate. For days on end, she would evade the humans stomping around her habitat. When the researchers did eventually locate her, she was quick to flee, barely allowing them an inch toward her before jetting back to her safety zone. Attempting to trap her briefly in a box to record her reaction was an unending chase. Dr. Aliperti had to experiment with a series of increasingly more gourmet snacks before Coy was finally enticed to step into the box, where she quickly snatched the goods and bolted. Over the course of three years, Coy never wavered as a master evader and frequent flyer.

Maverick, however, couldn't get enough of the humans. This was his time to shine. When Aliperti approached him, he would get so close she almost stepped on his toes. When they opened the box to see how he would respond to a novel environment, he inspected every inch while leisurely nibbling his snack, and when the researchers opened it for him to leave, he stood firm. They shooed him out and he scampered back in. Aliperti estimates that on one memorable day, Maverick was trapped at least 40 times. Another time, while making her rounds to check on all the study subjects, she happened to glance sideways into the window of a cabin where Maverick was sitting on the kitchen counter (presumably snacking) peering out the window at her as she passed.

Clearly, Coy and Maverick are very different, although they are the same species living in the same ecosystem. But while Coy behaves coyly in almost any situation, Maverick boldly bounces into whatever catches his whim. Aliperti found that squirrels show their personalities through four main traits: boldness, aggressiveness, activity level, and sociability. We may ask why squirrel personality matters, but she believes that understanding how these traits influence the animals' behaviors can support conservation efforts by shedding light on how the squirrels both influence and respond to their environment. If a new competitor, resource, or even a human-powered bulldozer came for Maverick's home range, his response would be very different than if any of those things came for Coy's. Their actions would have consequences for their habitats and their species. Even among our animal kingdom cohorts, individual personality influences choices, which influence behavior over time and ultimately the overall environment.

Aliperti's research is the first of its kind for golden-mantled ground squirrels but not within the study of animal personality. After decades of research by scientists like her, we now know things like how the social networks of individual lizards can be mapped over decades, how mother bluebirds can adjust the rotation of eggs in their nest to incline their hatchlings toward more boldness, and how the stress levels of elk can be measured relative to an individual's bravery when they approach new objects. These are not singular moments in time that can be written off as flukes of nature. In fact, the study of animal personality is actually defined as the consistency in the behavior that individuals exhibit over time: *an archetype.*

Although we all (humans and animals alike) may behave differently depending on the context, our core tendencies mostly stay the same. We may behave differently at the dentist than we would at a dinner party, but there are some traits that follow us from place to place. We each bring a consistent part of our individual selves to the spaces we occupy, just as Coy and Maverick do. That consistent part—our archetype—is rooted in specific motivations or drives.

Let's put this into an educational context. Let's say Coy and Maverick are collaborating educators teaching math together in a school. They are planning an upcoming unit on fractions and meet on a Saturday morning at their favorite coffee shop to collaborate. Coy arrives early, orders an iced espresso for Maverick (having memorized their preferred order) and a flat white for themself, unloads a stack of meticulously organized binders from past fraction units, and waits contentedly near a window away from the bustle of the order counter. Maverick arrives 10 minutes late with no materials, spends another four minutes chitchatting with other customers along the path from the door, plops down on a seat at the table by the window, thanks Coy generously for the coffee, and boldly announces, "I can't wait to tell you my outrageous idea for inspiring students to love fractions!"

Coy listens quietly to Maverick's idea. Coy is anxious about trying something so new and concerned about how disconnected Maverick's idea seems to be from the skills and content necessary for students to learn fractions. Coy is driven to influence student learning by focusing on a detailed, proven path of skill development. When Maverick finishes sharing, Coy shares their concern.

Now it's Maverick's turn to listen. Maverick is worried that their bold and exciting idea may get watered down and that Coy's vision for the unit will focus too much on skills and not enough on engagement, and they really want to excite students about learning fractions. Maverick is driven to generate lessons that excite their students.

Depending on how aware each of these educators is of their own motivations and how well they have learned to communicate them, this scenario could end in several different ways:

- Neither Maverick nor Coy reflect on their motivations, so they don't communicate what they feel or what they really want. They argue about who is "right" and decide to each teach the unit alone. Students never get the benefit of an authentic collaboration between their styles, and their refusal to collaborate ripples across the school culture. Neither of them grows from working with the other.

- Maverick does not realize they are driven by ideas, so they stumble when advocating for their vision after hearing Coy's concerns, which are valid. Maverick lets Coy's vision dominate the unit plan and follows the lessons dispassionately, feeling frustrated and burned out.

- Coy does not realize they are driven by detailed evidence, so they stumble when advocating for their vision after hearing Maverick's concerns, which are also valid. Coy lets Maverick's vision dominate the unit plan and follows the lessons dispassionately, feeling frustrated and burned out.

- Maverick knows exciting ideas drive them, and they communicate this to Coy. Coy knows they need a research-backed plan, so they communicate this to Maverick. Coy wants Maverick's ideas to work, so they agree to look through past lessons for ways to integrate Maverick's vision. Maverick wants to support Coy's vision for an evidence-based learning path, so they agree to research lessons from reliable sources that root their big ideas in practical skill development. Their collaborative unit is more solid and innovative, students are engaged and learn more than they ever have in past fraction units, Coy and Maverick both grow as educators by challenging their respective approaches to teaching, and each of them is so energized by their work that their colleagues are inspired by them.

Notice that in the last scenario, neither educator is required to relinquish authenticity. They challenge each other's approaches, but not their core drives. Everyone benefits when we protect and communicate our core drives.

Too often, we conflate collaboration with imitation. As shown in the second and third scenarios, this leads to frustration and burnout for those who have to give up what drives them. Worst of all, when we don't see our core drives in ourselves *or* others, we cannot communicate what motivates us, so we react to surface-level issues rather than the heart of the matter. In so many collaborative planning scenarios, I have found myself lingering on this level, overly focused on my teaching partner's work style or preferred methods. Upon reflection, I now see that if I had better understood my own drives and those of my colleagues, I wouldn't have dwelt so much on these relatively minor issues.

Figure 2.1 shows how each of the eight change archetypes introduced in Figure 1.1 might respond to a variety of scenarios like Coy's and Maverick's. Read along and make note of the response that most aligns with how you might respond in each scenario. Then read the detailed descriptions about the archetypes and their core drives and determine which one resonates most with you.

After considering all the scenarios in Figure 2.1, note which letter you chose most often in your responses. If you selected...

- A: The Storyteller most resonates with you, and your core drive is to influence.
- B: The Inventor most resonates with you, and your core drive is to generate.
- C: The Diplomat most resonates with you, and your core drive is to connect.
- D: The Guardian most resonates with you, and your core drive is to connect.
- E: The Creative most resonates with you, and your core drive is to generate.
- F: The Champion most resonates with you, and your core drive is to advocate.
- G: The Sage most resonates with you, and your core drive is to influence.
- H: The Investigator most resonates with you, and your core drive is to advocate.

Figure 2.1

Change Archetype and Core Drives Assessment

Scenario	Responses	Response Most Aligned with You
You and a collaborator are working together on a project, but you have conflicting visions for how to approach the work. Your approach to developing collaborative projects tends to be…	A. You are practical and detail-oriented when developing projects, so you prefer to rely on tried-and-true methods. You refuse to cut corners. B. You are open to and curious about lots of different ideas, so you love to consider many options. You also love to experiment, so failure does not often faze you. C. You believe that every voice should be heard when collaborating, so you go out of your way to include everyone's ideas and mitigate conflict. You also love to bring others beyond the original team into projects you develop. D. You want to know and trust your collaborators as people first and professionals second. Once you connect on a personal level, you will try your hardest to understand another's point of view—even if it is contradictory to your own. E. You never approach a project in the same way as the last one, so you love to start from scratch. You love the messiness of the process and don't mind the starts and stops along the way. F. You are decisive and action-oriented because if you signed up to do any kind of project, you are likely already deeply passionate about it and know exactly where to take the work. If you are forced into the project, you will resist wholeheartedly. G. You like to work with an audience in mind, knowing that the best projects create more impact when people care about them. You love to explore many perspectives and move forward with the combined wisdom of others. H. You prefer to develop projects with deep subject-matter expertise and an analytical approach. You are inquisitive and love to dive deeply into a topic before taking any action.	
You have a great idea for a solution to a problem that your leader wants the staff to address. What would you do first?	A. Meticulously plan exactly what you will say and how you will communicate your idea before you approach your leader. B. Pilot your solution with a small-scale experiment on your own, then share your solution with your leader along with the results of your pilot. C. Share your idea with your network, get lots of feedback from trusted collaborators, refine your idea, then approach your leader. D. Connect with trusted colleagues or students first to better understand how your proposed solution might benefit them, then present your idea to your leader.	

continued

Figure 2.1 (*continued*)

Change Archetype and Core Drives Assessment

Scenario	Responses	Response Most Aligned with You
	E. Present your idea to your leader before the idea is fully formed, but your energy for the idea is high. Volunteer to try the solution out yourself or lead the effort with a select few to learn as you go before approaching the entire staff. F. Get straight to work on your solution on your own, then share the idea with your leader when you reach a roadblock and need their support. G. Develop a beautiful presentation outlining your solution from start to finish, then use it to persuade your leader to adopt it. H. Conduct deep research on the topic and outline evidence-based reasons for adopting your proposed solutions, citing each source in detail.	
You get negative feedback from a colleague. You...	A. Repeat back to them what you hear them saying, so you can be sure you fully understand. B. Ask them how they would resolve the issue if it were them in your shoes. C. Avoid engaging in a conflict with them at the moment, but try to listen to their opinion in order to address the issue later after discussing it with others. D. Determine if your actions were harmful to others; readily take accountability if so, respond with thoughtful consideration of their opinion if not. E. Address your mistakes, but defend your ideas. F. Address your mistakes, but defend your cause. G. Respond the way you think they would want you to. H. Ask a series of questions to get to the true basis of their opinion	
Your leadership makes a decision that you disagree with. You...	A. Write a direct, concise, and well-crafted email to your leader detailing your opinion and recommending adjustments. B. Provide a logical argument to change their mind, while also offering ideas for better options they may not have considered. C. Conduct a poll among your colleagues about the decision and present the results to your leadership. D. Engage in a handful of meaningful conversations with trusted colleagues about how the decision may affect them or others, then discuss what you learn from them privately with your leadership (while keeping your colleagues anonymous).	

Your leadership makes a decision that you disagree with. You…	E. Speak with your leadership about how the decision may negatively impact current projects or processes. F. Speak with your leadership about how the decision may negatively impact causes important to the organization. G. Calmly advise your leader of potential outcomes of their decision they may not see but you can because of your perspective. H. Provide a well-reasoned, evidence-based, and logical argument to change their mind. Send them additional resources to further encourage them to adjust.	
A colleague makes a mistake and asks for your advice. You say…	A. "Tell me exactly what happened, play by play." B. "Let's brainstorm some ideas for fixing it." C. "Let's go ask [trusted colleague] for advice." D. "Oh you must feel terrible. How can I help?" E. "So what would happen if you [idea for addressing the mistake]?" F. "Okay, here's what you do [strong opinion for addressing the mistake]." G. "If I were you, here's what I would [persuasive advice]." H. "Let's start at the beginning and get to the bottom of it."	
Something out of anyone's control changes the scope of a project you have been leading. You…	A. Try to understand all the details of the change, then communicate those details clearly to everyone affected. B. Zoom out to understand the big picture, then develop a logical approach to adjusting. C. Tap all your connections across your network for advice before adjusting your plan. D. Reach out to the people most affected by the change in support of them; then adjust with their needs in mind. E. Get frustrated at the loss of the ideas you had for the old plan, then get excited about developing new ones. F. Determine if the cause at the heart of your project is affected. If so, advocate for maintaining the cause. If not, adjust quickly to the changes. G. Quickly assess the variety perspectives surrounding the change, then persuade those affected to move forward accordingly. H. Use the opportunity to analyze the details and ask questions, then respond with thoughtful consideration of the evidence.	

continued

Figure 2.1 *(continued)*

Change Archetype and Core Drives Assessment

Scenario	Responses	Response Most Aligned with You
You're leading a group of people toward a goal and realize that the direction you have taken needs major adjusting. What would you do first?	A. Clearly and concisely share your reasoning for the changes to your team. B. Explain the bigger picture of your decision logically to your team. C. Ask for input from everyone, including those on the team and off. D. Ask your team how they would feel about changing direction before making any decisions. E. Come up with a host of ideas for changing direction and present them to your team as options. F. Make the decision quickly, then passionately communicate it to the team with the main goal in mind. G. Determine the best path, then persuade your team to align with your view. H. Present research and evidence for the change and let the team determine how to move forward with facts in mind.	
	TOTALS	# of As: # of Bs: # of Cs: # of Ds: # of Es: # of Fs: # of Gs: # of Hs:

Both versions of Coy and Maverick—squirrels and educators alike—make unique contributions to their immediate environment and overall ecosystem. They are unique because of their traits and the choices they make as a result—choices that affect the whole community. Now more than ever in the world of education, deepening our understanding of who we are as individuals—our drives, patterns, and choices—can support our collective efforts to move the profession forward, both for ourselves and for the young people we serve.

Let's now explore the core change drives and archetypes in depth. Take time to read about each one, highlighting lines that resonate with you, and respond to the reflection questions that follow. You may discover that more than one archetype aligns with your traits and patterns. This is perfectly normal. People are complex, and although personality quizzes across the internet and even in professional spaces may try to lump people neatly into boxes, we will try to avoid that tendency here. That said, the purpose of archetypes is to have a consistent model on which we can rely. They are as complex as people are, and noting that one resonates with you most across time periods and contexts does not mean that others don't resonate with you, too. To paraphrase Walt Whitman (1885), *we all contain multitudes*. But leaning into a single archetype will help you examine your approach to leading and creating change.

So, who are you? Let's find out.

3

ARCHETYPES DRIVEN TO CONNECT

I am a part of all that I have met.

—Alfred, Lord Tennyson (1850)

People who are driven to connect value relationships more than anything else. Even though relationships are relevant to the overall human condition, for these individuals they are uniquely vital to how they operate. They would never make a life choice without consulting others whose opinions they value, and they would never make a leadership decision without considering how their actions might affect their community. If they are feeling isolated at work, do not have a strong team, or lack a collaborative culture, then they will burn out very quickly. They need the support of others to thrive, and they need others to rely on their support. The plot of their lives will often include many other characters who wind their way through the story and influence the behavior of this connection-driven protagonist. You may spot them as the heart of the team, the voice of the collective, or the mediator of a conflict. They will use the word *we* more than they use the word *me,* and it will be genuine when they do. The two change archetypes driven to connect are the Diplomat and the Guardian.

Are You Driven to Connect?

Although everyone will seek connective experiences in their lives, think about your first instincts and gut reactions when considering the following questions about your own core drive:

- In a tense discussion, does your initial focus tend to be on the feelings of others or repairing relationships?
- In a new environment, do you initially seek camaraderie with others?
- When starting a new project, do you begin by asking for advice or support from others?
- Do you struggle with too much autonomy or independence?
- Do you feel like you're your best self when on a team?

The Diplomat

In the 1960s, a social psychologist named Stanley Milgram ran an experiment where he asked 300 participants in Kansas to mail a package to a target person in Boston. He wanted to understand how many links strangers in different communities would have between them. What he discovered has become something of modern lore (with quite a bit of interesting scientific research to back it up now) called "the small world experiment." Better known to most of us as "six degrees of separation." Milgram discovered that in fact, there was an average of six degrees between the sender and the receiver of the packages that made it from Kansas to Boston (Ouellette, 2012). This study has been analyzed, critiqued, and replicated quite a bit since. For example, in 2011, with the advent of social media and the ability to literally connect a large percentage of people around the world, a study of Facebook connections for approximately 721 million users found that the average distance between most people on earth is actually now less than six degrees. That study revealed that it may be closer to four, and as time goes on, the number will likely continue decreasing (Cuthbertson, 2016).

With their desire and willingness to expand their networks, Diplomats do a lot to skew these numbers, and we all benefit from being in community with them. We all probably know a Diplomat. They are actually quite easy to spot because they are usually everywhere and connected to everyone. Here are a few Diplomats I have had the pleasure of knowing along my own journey:

- The "edu-Twitter" aficionado who follows tons of other educators, participates in Twitter chats, and uses social media to gather great ideas and advice.
- The music educator who serves on a local committee to connect musicians and music educators through community programs.
- The calm voice of reason who mediates when a team is struggling to get along.

The Diplomat's Leadership Style

Diplomats are the leaders who really want to understand other people. It is not inauthentic when they ask you how your day is going; they truly do want to know. Knowing and understanding other people brings them joy, but they can also be loyal empathizers during times of stress. They care about people, and they lead from a sense of genuine concern for everyone. Diplomats will certainly build and value close relationships around them, but they care for and value relationships far beyond their immediate environment as well. If you tell a Diplomat that you have an interest in growing as a writing instructor, before the day is up, you'll get an email connecting you to a writing program facilitator they know. If a Diplomat asks you for advice, know that you are likely the third or fourth person they have asked and will likely not be the last. If you are ever in the market for a new gig, find your closest Diplomat and use them as a reference. They will likely already know your interviewer or at least be a few degrees separated from them through one of their many networks. Their leadership is rooted in connecting people, opportunities, and ideas.

The Diplomat's Approach to Change

Because Diplomats love connecting across broader networks, they have a knack for big-picture thinking, which means they like to take the broad view on most issues and can be objective in times of conflict. They move people forward by providing insight beyond what is right in front of them. If a team is suffering from tunnel vision, bring in the nearest

Diplomat. They are usually able to jolt everyone out of their narrow perspectives.

Diplomats serve important roles as innovators in communities by bringing new ideas from connections they've made elsewhere. They may not always be the ones to implement those ideas, but they seed them everywhere they go. Because people tend to trust them, they can be vital in moving new ideas forward.

Diplomats are most effective at leading change when they

- Connect with lots of people in lots of places.
- Can approach issues with objective distance.
- Can share new insights, ideas, opportunities, and connections with others.
- Feel respected and trusted by others.

The Diplomat's Challengers

People who generally dislike others will irritate a Diplomat. The Diplomat doesn't last long around too much gossip or complaining. Diplomats also prefer collaborative environments, so working with individuals who are highly autonomous by nature may frustrate them because they will have a hard time nailing down these kinds of individuals. People who prefer to "do their own thing" may be difficult for a Diplomat to collaborate with closely because the Diplomat will not be able to function as they do best—through connection. Engaging in healthy discussion and the exchange of ideas makes a Diplomat excited to get up every morning.

The Diplomat's Allies

Few things bring Diplomats more joy than a new connection with someone who inspires them. They get energy from new people and new ideas, so surrounding themselves with interesting, innovative thinkers is good for them. They collaborate well when they feel inspired but most prefer working with easygoing people. They like to collaborate in situations where ideas flow freely, people connect effortlessly, and progress is smooth. Although Diplomats do make great mediators, they will feel burnt out if they are constantly in mediating mode, so being around people who get along is critical to helping them thrive.

The Diplomat in Real Life: Meet Kip

Though he began his career as a guidance counselor, after one year Kip decided that he could do more counseling as a classroom educator—where he'd have more opportunities to build relationships with students. Eventually, he became a Spanish educator. In high school, he fell in love with Spanish culture and language; after living abroad in Mexico, he fell in love more broadly with the quest to understand other cultures. He feels that his passion for teaching Spanish is really about connecting young people to other cultures.

Kip's professional journey is rooted in relationships and connection.

One day, about 10 years into his career, Kip opened an email describing an opportunity for a statewide fellowship connecting education policy to classroom practice. He decided to take the leap and apply, and he says everything opened up after he was accepted.

The opportunity that Kip jumped on was dedicated to connecting educators and policymakers with the hope of building stronger relationships and policy.

Kip had no prior experience with education policy, but he did have a great mentor in the fellowship who inspired him as a learner. He says that although he was initially intimidated, he built confidence through support from others and learned how to jump on opportunities, share resources, and connect across networks.

Diplomats learn best from the guidance of others.

One day, Kip went with a handful of people to the state capitol to experience an education committee session. He watched a world-language bill pass into law in a mere seven minutes. His mentor said to him, "What do you think of your profession changing in seven minutes?" Kip looked around and realized there were no world-language educators present. It was then that he understood how the relationships between educators and legislators could be mutually beneficial for both parties. He knew he could have gotten angry, but he instead decided to embrace the opportunity to build relationships and connect the dots between people who wanted the same things but were maybe going about it in different ways.

Kip has learned through educator leadership that what matters is what we do with all the experiences and opportunities we have to move others forward. Within his network, Kip connects people, relationships, and experiences from his past to his current community. He connects his principal with national experts he has met along his path. "Teacher leadership was never really about me or about what I could specifically do for myself or even my own classroom," he says. "It was about leading from behind and sharing opportunities with others to expand the power of influence."

After a host of experiences across the education spectrum, Kip is now driven to connect his colleagues to opportunities he is often offered himself or that he knows about through relationships he has cultivated.

"I think many teachers come into the profession in isolation," Kip continues. "When I started, I felt very much thrown into survival mode, which is not fair to teachers or students. After 17 years in the profession, I look back to the beginning and realize that I did my students a disservice by not connecting to others the way I do now.

"Survival mode is detrimental for everyone. I didn't realize at the time that being such a connector is so critical to my path as an educator. The fellowship I joined forced me to embrace a mission of connecting educators to each other and to others outside of the profession in order to improve everyone's work. When I reached the point that I felt proficient with my own classroom craft, I really started to see the power of connecting my experiences and opportunities to others who needed those connections and opportunities as well.

"None of us should have to survive alone in isolation. Now I love to find out what makes other teachers tick and what inspires them, then connect them with colleagues I have 'collected' over time. I love to see how it all expands beyond me and beyond a single person's world."

A Diplomat's best-kept secret and superpower is knowing how to truly listen. Diplomats want to expand their world and the worlds of others, as Kip illustrates through his philosophy of "leading from behind" and his practice of connecting others to opportunities to expand their worlds just as his has been expanded.

Are You a Diplomat?

If you…

- Feel driven to connect with a large network of people,
- Prefer collaboration to debate,

- Are inspired by others and joyful when learning from new people,
- Would rather cooperate than compete, and
- Find that others rely on you for advice about new ideas or opportunities,

   … then you might be a Diplomat.

The Guardian

Few things in the world are more human than hugs. In fact, there is scientific evidence that frequent hugging can boost the immune system, lower blood pressure and heart rates, dull the pain of chronic conditions, and even change our brain chemistry over time (Cleveland Clinic, 2020). Many researchers believe that the social bonds and sense of belonging that hugs represent may lie behind their power (Edelson, n.d.).

Few understood the power of hugs more than Elizabeth Laird, a U.S. Air Force veteran from Texas who acquired the endearing moniker "The Hug Lady" due to her passion for handing out hugs to army recruits at Fort Hood. Over 12 years, Laird hugged nearly 500,000 soldiers. For many, she was the only person to connect personally with them. When Laird's health took a turn for the worse, the soldiers repaid her in kind, lining up outside her hospital room door to hug her back in her own time of need. "When they enter the room, they give me a hug and then we talk about anything from their family to what it was like overseas or if they got a civilian job upon returning," she said (Stump, 2015). The exchanges between Laird and many of the soldiers she hugged both at the airport terminal and in the hospital represented far more than a simple gesture. The hug itself may have been the initial contact, but Laird wanted to listen. She wanted to connect with the soldiers she met as human beings, and when they came to her before she passed after a long battle with breast cancer, they too wanted to provide a small moment of humanity for a person in need (Itkowitz, 2021).

Much like Elizabeth Laird, Guardians recognize the power of human connection. For them, little matters more than centering people in all they do. It is their superpower. You may recognize Guardians such as these in your own community:

- The department chair or team leader who listens thoughtfully to even the most minute complaints from colleagues and shares relevant concerns anonymously with leadership on their behalf.
- The calm but stern voice during a team meeting who redirects a colleague complaining unfairly about a student.
- The drama educator who knows a student well enough and has a strong enough relationship with them to encourage them to apply their lived experience to a lead role in the school play.

Guardians are the glue that holds a community together. They are the fierce protectors of humanity when we most need it. They are powerful nurturers who lead from the heart, cultivate strong relationships, and connect with people during critical moments of need.

The Guardian's Leadership Style

Guardians lead through compassionate action, working to help those around them better serve one another's humanity. They lead by listening first, but they will also act in response to what they hear. A Guardian leading a team toward a common goal will want to know each team member's feelings, ideas, and concerns about the plan in place before moving the group forward. This does not mean Guardians are pushovers; in fact, because they take the time to show everyone how much they value people, they are especially well equipped to lead tough conversations. Guardians hand out genuine praise without reservation, but they can also be tough critics. They are trustworthy leaders who will come to the defense of others swiftly and offer loyal support without question.

The Guardian's Approach to Change

People are always at the center of Guardians' change efforts. Unless an issue directly affects someone close to them, they may not have a strong opinion about it. However, once they recognize that the issue is affecting those they care about, just try to stop them from stepping up.

Guardians approach solutions based on what they know about how people operate. The Hug Lady gave out hugs not because she understood the science of hugging but because she understood the feelings of soldiers in a state of transition.

Guardians lead change by cultivating support and protecting the humanity of others. They genuinely know people and build authentic relationships within a common community, taking the time to ask real questions and truly listen to the answers. Guardians like to redirect focus from issues to people. They're the type to always ask how new policies will affect their students or their colleagues, and they will offer solutions that others may not have considered because they look at all problems through the lens of humanity first.

Guardians protect themselves as well as they protect others, recognizing that service to others does not mean sacrificing one's own needs, desires, or ambitions. Guardians are our mirrors; we see our best selves through their eyes, which is how they inspire us to move forward. They do us all a service by honoring themselves as much as they honor others. We can support the Guardians around us by honoring their boundaries and supporting their self-care.

The Guardian's Challengers

People who complain often, behave rudely, or are disagreeable without reason will eventually wear on Guardians. They care about people, and they listen openly to the feelings of others, but they also have strict principles about behaviors they will tolerate from others. They do not take kindly to people who abuse or exploit their community, including through harsh gossip or extended negativity. People who refuse to engage as active community members also bug them. Distancing or detaching oneself from people and issues that matter for the collective is a quick way to lose a Guardian's support and collaboration.

Guardians prefer to work in communities that aren't overly hierarchical, where people are working toward a collective mission and care about one another's roles toward the larger vision. They want to be in communities where every single person's exit is felt because each individual matters to the whole. They will feel uncomfortable in organizations where people are replaceable.

The Guardian's Allies

If Guardians disagree with others, they will still find a way to work with them as long as they are kind and human-centered. For this reason, Guardians are great bridge-builders in any community. They are not bothered by differences of opinion as long as people are motivated by what's best for students and educators—and they are quick to jump into protective mode if they believe students or educators are being harmed or neglected. A Guardian works well with a team of passionate people who care about others and treat one another with respect. Any other problems are surmountable if those basic principles are met.

The Guardian in Real Life: Meet Mili

As an undergraduate, Mili was an intern at the Indiana Statehouse during the 2005 General Assembly. "I was smitten with the democratic process, I would stay late to watch debates and come early to see democracy in action," she says. "I believed that the political work being done in that building was sacred; there was something beautiful in the purported equality of 'one person, one vote.'"

Notice how Mili was inspired by a principle rooted in people: "One person, one vote."

One day, while interning, Mili saw two opposing rallies take place: one against new taxes to fund public schools and another—made up mostly of students and teachers—in favor. The first group had access to lawmakers inside the warm building; the other was denied entry and remained outside in the cold.

"It was then we heard noises from outside the building while standing in the rotunda," Mili says. "Music? Drums? Chanting? I went with the other interns to investigate. Many students had instruments (one trombone had frozen into a block of ice), some carried artwork, others were in athletic uniforms, many carried homemade signs that said 'Save the Arts' and 'Fund Our Schools.' Outside, the frosty students, families, and educators spoke of collective need. Their lexicon was inclusive: *our* schools, *our* kids, *our* communities. Meanwhile, inside a building that I knew as 'The People's House,' the comfortably warm legislators spoke exclusively of '*my* money, *my* community,' without a thought to the children outside."

Mili notices individuality, but she also recognizes collective needs and wisdom. She identifies the students as athletes and artists by paying attention to how they showed up that day. She expresses a protective concern for how cold they were, noting the trombone felt like a block of ice even though she herself did not carry it. Mili also innately understands the juxtaposition of these individual students and their teachers against the larger issue of school funding. She is drawn to the collective mission, noting the use of our *versus* my, *and is appalled by the lack of recognition those on the inside are giving to those outside.*

Mili's path shifted dramatically that day. She thought, "In this intern work that I was doing, who and what was I standing for?" A young girl handed her a green bracelet that had *Save Our Schools* written on it. That night, Mili applied to Teach for America. She no longer wanted to field phone calls from angry taxpayers who didn't want their money to go to equity in education. She wanted to teach children like those marching around the capitol.

Recognizing how people were being affected (or neglected) by the work she was doing shifted Mili's direction. Like a true Guardian, she was spurred to lead change by a single person. This moment of human connection was enough for Mili to alter her career path.

Today, Mili is an outspoken advocate for menstrual equity. "This journey came to me," she says. "A student bled through their clothes and was horribly bullied for it. Fresh from my experience leading our Gay Straight Alliance, I helped students organize menstruation stations on campus to provide anyone with supplies. We met with our state representative to write a menstrual equity bill for our state. For the last two years, our bills have failed, but we'll be introducing a bill again this year and hope the third time's a charm."

Often, Guardians will find that they are guided toward causes by other people. If a person they care about at any level comes to them with a problem, Guardians will go as far as trying to change the law to find a solution.

Mili's impact is felt beyond her own connections. "I *love* that I get emails from people around the country asking me how to start 'menstruation stations' in schools," she says, "and I hope to get around to creating a how-to guide for other educators as well."

A true Guardian, Mili illustrates how human-centered leadership can influence collective action.

Are You a Guardian?

If you...

- Feel driven to connect with a close group of trusted people,
- Prefer authentic conversation to small talk,

- Feel empathetic toward others and drawn to supporting them,
- Seek to nurture others, and
- Find that others rely on you for support when they are struggling,
    … then you might be a Guardian.

4

ARCHETYPES DRIVEN TO ADVOCATE

When the world is silent, even one voice becomes powerful.

—Malala Yousafzai (Yousafzai et al., 2015)

Those who are driven to advocate value a set of ideals and will view most other issues through the lens of these ideals. For the Champion, this ideal is a cause near and dear to the heart; for the Investigator, it is objective truth. Champions are heart-driven advocates, and Investigators are mind-driven advocates, but the essence of their motivation is the same.

Those who are driven to advocate cannot thrive in environments where they cannot operate from the foundation of their ideals and purpose. People who are driven to advocate lead with conviction, so they tend to attract followers—and detractors—wherever they go. For this reason, the plot of their lives may include battles waged, as well as subplots of redemption and resilience. You may spot these individuals as authors of editorials, spokespeople in meetings, or the first to raise an inquisitive hand. Their ideals will always come before their egos, so if they rise, their ideals will rise with them.

Are You Driven to Advocate?

Everyone may find themselves as advocates at some point in their lives, but think about your first instincts and gut reactions when considering the following questions about your own core drive:

- In a tense discussion, will your initial focus be grasping the larger purpose of the conflict?
- In a new environment, will you initially seek a clear purpose you can align with?
- When starting a new project, will you first ask probing questions to better align yourself with the work?
- Do you struggle when you feel a lack of purpose in your work?
- Are you your best self when you understand the bigger picture?

The Champion

In 1872, Sitting Bull, Crazy Horse, and other Lakota Sioux happened upon a survey party who had been sent as scouts for the U.S. government. The U.S. government planned to construct the Northern Pacific Railway directly through the last of the great Sioux buffalo hunting grounds, but in an act of resistance, Sitting Bull and other Lakota leaders attacked the survey party, catching the soldiers by surprise. As both sides attacked the other across the plains, Sitting Bull calmly walked to the middle of the battle, sat down where he stood as bullets blazed past him, and proceeded to smoke his pipe until the tobacco was spent. Ignoring the shots firing at him, Sitting Bull cleaned his pipe, slowly and deliberately, then rose and walked back to join the others in battle (Andrews, 2015).

Such an act of staunch, unapologetic bravery seems like a fictional account from a book of myths, yet the story is true. Sitting Bull's life was dedicated to the cause of resisting colonization, and he refused to waver from who he was and what he stood for. Over the course of his life, he resisted American pilfering of Dakota, Lakota, and Nakota territory and culture, refusing to convert to Christianity as commanded or fall in line with U.S. antibigamy laws (in typical Lakota tradition, Sitting Bull had two wives). He once famously said, "I would rather die an Indian than live as a white man." He advocated for his tribe's right to freedom and against its oppression until his death (A&E Networks Television, 2021).

Though Sitting Bull may have been exceptional, Champions like him are dedicated advocates for causes that matter to them. They will take risks in defense of their cause without question. In schools or other educational contexts, Champions will often carve their causes into the work they do. For example, consider some of these Champions I have met along my own path:

- The tech enthusiast who applies for a grant to acquire the best technology for students and lobbies the district budget officer to purchase better technology for all schools.
- The environmentalist who develops and leads a school sustainability program.
- The social justice advocate who never fails to raise a hand in meetings to question policies that may lead to inequities and who takes action to see the required changes through.

The Champion's Leadership Style

Champions lead through passionate defense of a cause. Remember that passion can manifest in both calm and dramatic ways. Champions will lead with decisive action and unrelenting dedication, all while keeping a cool head. This calm foundation comes from knowing their cause is an honorable one. They are passionate about their advocacy, and they move forward with a firm sense of integrity. Though they may at times find themselves narrowly focused on the causes they lead or at odds with those around them who may not share their passion, they are also willing to listen to others with whom they have mutual respect.

The best way to gain the support of Champions is to illustrate your respect for their cause. Once you show you have a basic sense of honor for the cause they are advocating, Champions will listen with an open heart, even to opinions very different from their own. Their cause is the front door to collaboration with them.

The Champion's Approach to Change

Champions can move change forward by rallying others around a common issue, presenting arguments with multiple perspectives in mind, and advocating for people who are affected by the cause they treasure.

Champions are most effective when they have others behind them. They can find these allies by slowing down and canvassing people around them so when they address the issue with a larger community, they can integrate many viewpoints into their discussion.

Advocating for people who are affected by a cause means moving beyond the abstract to the concrete. Champions will often see and understand their causes in both intimate and visionary ways. They have a deep understanding of the complexity of the issue writ large, but they also understand the implications of the issue's impact on individual people. They may be tempted only to focus on the former, but they are wise to lead with a people-first approach when they can.

The Champion's Challengers

Champions have two nightmares: apathy and indecision. Because they care so much, they may lack tolerance for more apathetic colleagues. They are also quick decision makers, so they won't align well with those who drag decisions out or spend too much time debating before acting. Champions can address these pet peeves by communicating them effectively to others before collaborating.

If others around them tend toward indecisiveness, Champions can also try finding thoughtful ways to take ownership of decision making. For example, if they are collaborating with a team on an upcoming unit but find themselves frustrated with a lack of consensus, Champions may volunteer to outline the unit for the team while individuals fill out the lessons according to their needs. Finding ways to take action will suit Champions better than languishing in environments where they feel their hands are tied where they will inevitably become resentful.

The Champion's Allies

Even if a Champion is the only advocate for a specific cause in their community, they will find peace of mind if they are surrounded by open-minded people who listen well. They care less that everyone agrees with them and more that others are willing to listen and understand. Feeling that others do not listen to them can be a Champion's kryptonite. They also love collaborating with action-oriented colleagues. People who move forward without much fuss will make a Champion's heart sing. Nothing makes them happier than seeing an impact on an issue they love, so an impact-focused team will be a powerful momentum-builder for a Champion.

The Champion in Real Life: Meet Lauren

Lauren majored in zoology and decided to become an educator because, as she says, "I get to share my passion [for ecology] daily and help ignite similar passions in my students. One person alone cannot change the world, but as an educator I can form a collaborative of passionate thinkers with my students, and we can work together to gain knowledge and hopefully disrupt systems."

Notice how what Lauren loves most about her role as an educator is sharing her passion with her students. She even describes her classroom environment as a "collaborative of passionate thinkers." She is also visionary and action-driven, focusing on a future of "disrupting systems."

Lauren says her goal as an educator is to "get people fired up about what we are doing to this Earth so we can work together to fix what's broken. My hope is to share the knowledge about what sustainable action is and how we can each be a part of that action. I want to ensure that all students in my classes know how science matters to them because sometimes they think they don't like science—but really, they just don't like how science is taught."

Lauren's cause since she started her career has been environmental education. Champions' causes may shift some throughout their careers, but they often remain firmly rooted. Here, Lauren considers how to make her cause relevant to her students. By taking this approach, she better ensures that her cause will be more readily adopted by others.

When asked what impact Lauren has seen from her change efforts over the years, she says, "I have had several students decide to major in environmental science as a consequence of my course. I have seen students be creative in ways they didn't think they were able to. I have had students create and collaborate in ways they wouldn't expect to in school. I've had students win awards and get grant money based on their ideas that I only facilitated."

Lauren measures her success by her students' success. As a Champion, she roots her efforts in people rather than concepts alone. Because Champions are action-oriented, measuring meaningful impact helps them see the results of their actions and inspires them to keep going.

Lauren has struggled at times to align her ideals with her environment, but she has navigated moments like these by finding like-minded cohorts both in person and virtually. "I had the opportunity to design my own course, and as a result I was able to branch out and collaborate with people outside of my school and in the community," she says. "This allowed me to think very differently about how content could be applied to real-world situations and how we could solve real-world problems."

Relying on the support and insight of others who care about a Champion's cause is incredibly important for a Champion's motivation and sense of well-being. Notice how Lauren acted autonomously to create the environment she needed by designing her own course, but she also reached out to educators and experts beyond her immediate environment for support. She also adjusted her approach over time thanks to inputs from her wider network, which helped her better advocate for her cause.

Are You a Champion?

If you…

- Feel driven to advocate for a cause,
- Prefer action to debate,
- Feel passionately connected to issues that transcend your own life or personal experience,
- Would rather see results than progress, and
- Are relied on by others to speak or lead around collective issues,
  … then you might be a Champion.

The Investigator

In Elizabeth Bishop's beautiful poem "The Fish," the narrator catches a battered old fish "speckled with barnacles… and infested with tiny white sea-lice" (Bishop, 2011). The fish doesn't put up a fight when the narrator catches it, giving the impression that it is too tired and beaten to even try. "I saw that from his lower lip… hung five old pieces of fish-line," says the narrator, who realizes this fish has fought many battles with fishing lines before—and won every time. It's not old and worn after all but resilient and wise. The narrator ultimately decides to let the fish go, satisfied that it has earned its freedom.

Investigators are like this narrator, but truth itself is the fish they hope to catch. Just as the narrator ultimately lets the fish go, so too will Investigators. Although the fish represents the search for truth and Investigators have an insatiable need to seek it, the chase can be just as alluring as the catch for them. They love studying trends and patterns, thoughtfully puzzling together insights, and advocating for the new truths they discover along the way.

How might we identify the Investigators among us? Here are a few I have come across myself:

- The reading educator who is curious about how children best learn to read and enrolls in a doctorate program to become immersed in the latest research on literacy education.
- The educator who wants to understand how to teach coding in creative ways, so they collaborate with educators outside their discipline to learn to apply coding across content.
- The educator who raises a hand to ask "why?" in literally every meeting they have ever attended.

The Investigator's Leadership Style

Investigators lead with analytical curiosity. This means they will always start any project by asking questions to better understand the heart of the matter. Like Champions, Investigators are driven to advocate, but in their case, it's for knowledge—not issues. As leaders, this means they will not make decisions until they have a clear understanding of both the whole picture and the minute details. They will not tolerate decisions that aren't rooted in evidence.

Like the narrator who lets the fish go when they understand it in a new way, Investigators will also change their minds readily if they gain new insight that justifies it. They are among the most open-minded leaders and colleagues. They strongly value objective truth. Investigators lead others wisely by listening to many perspectives, getting to the bottom of things, and making logical decisions based on the information they acquire. They love newly discovered insights and cutting-edge research, so a good entry point for collaborating with Investigators is to provide them with information they haven't yet learned. Engage them with a spirited Socratic dialogue, and you will have a friend for life.

The Investigator's Approach to Change

The change efforts of Investigators are always in response to the true problem at hand rather than an assumed one. When Albert Einstein reportedly said, "If I had an hour to solve a problem, I'd spend 55 minutes thinking about the problem and 5 minutes thinking about solutions," he was channeling the essence of an Investigator. Whereas Champions take action quickly and decisively, Investigators will ponder an issue for a long time, taking time to research it in depth and ask probing questions. Their solutions have a strong chance of succeeding if they have the time and space to develop them, which is why many people are drawn to Investigators when issues are especially complex.

Investigators are most effective at leading change when they

- Have the time and space to research an issue in depth.
- Are at liberty to be inquisitive.
- Feel respected for their expertise.
- Can elicit multiple perspectives on an issue.
- Approach change efforts like puzzles to be solved.
- Feel curious and enthusiastic about exploring a topic in depth.
- Operate in an environment that embraces open-mindedness.
- Have opportunities for sharing information readily with others.

The Investigator's Challengers

People who do not question the world around them will drive an Investigator mad. It is very hard for them to interact with people who blindly accept the state of things without deeper analysis. Collaborating on a team with colleagues who rely on static information, outdated research, or flimsy evidence is incredibly challenging for Investigators because it prevents them from advocating for knowledge and truth. They are better off finding a willing audience and building a coalition among them.

People who tend toward passivity will frustrate quick-thinking, thirsty-for-knowledge Investigators. Like their Champion counterparts, Investigators also value taking strong action; they just want time to explore the problem in detail first.

The Investigator's Allies

Investigators can thrive if they are surrounded by people who value thorough research and analysis. They pair well with colleagues who want to learn from them and will readily change their minds and adjust accordingly as they learn new information. Because they love to be relied on for their analytical skills, having Investigators lead committees or initiatives that take on complex problems are great ways to engage them. Leaders who find opportunities for Investigators to learn, research, analyze, share their knowledge with others, and lead efforts aligned to their inquiries will be their best collaborators.

The Investigator in Real Life: Meet Shawn

Shawn began his career as a job coach for adults with disabilities but soon shifted gears. "I kept seeing that individuals with disabilities faced far more barriers to finding meaningful employment than their peers without disabilities," he shares. "I felt they were being interviewed differently and had to answer discriminatory kinds of questions in interviews. I wanted to get ahead of that and decided to pursue my master's in special education so I could work with high school students with disabilities and help better prepare them for careers and postsecondary education."

Shawn's Investigator qualities are clear from the very start of his career. The phrase "I kept seeing" is the mark of an analyst; he noticed a pattern and wanted to get to the root of it. Among the evidence for his analysis were "discriminatory kinds of questions." Investigators are drawn to questions; they like asking them and pay attention to the kinds of questions others are asking as well. Like a true Investigator, Shawn took action to get to the heart of the matter—he "wanted to get ahead of that."

Shawn had a pivotal moment early in his career while sitting in the teacher's lounge. He "heard a respected colleague and veteran teacher on the phone with her college-age child," he says. "She said, 'Don't [choose teaching as a job]. The pay is too low, you won't be respected, and you're smart enough to do something else.' I thought to myself, *What a terrible sales pitch!* At that moment, I realized that public education desperately needed a public relations makeover. Teachers needed tools to better advocate for the profession, and that was the change catalyst that launched my shift into education advocacy."

Shawn illustrates a contradiction that bothered him. What his colleague was saying on the phone didn't seem to align with Shawn's perspective of the truth—namely, that there is in fact value in becoming an educator. Contradictions will bother an Investigator but also inspire their curiosity. Shawn also calls out here how he wanted to help teachers gain better tools for advocacy. Because Investigators are driven to advocate, they are also driven to support the advocacy of others.

After this moment of change, Shawn went on to create a nonprofit organization called Teach Like Me to address teacher recruitment and retention efforts in his state. "We set out to redefine the teaching profession for the public and legislators," he says. "Teach Like Me allowed me to engage with educators across the country about issues ranging from teacher pay to whether or not educators should be armed at school."

Redefine is an excellent Investigator word. Shawn founded Teach Like Me with the goal of "redefining" the profession within the minds of the public. He was driven to advocate for a new understanding of what educators do not only for young people but also for society. Shawn notes here how much he learned by inquiring into the opinions and experiences of other educators, illustrating the importance he places on asking critical questions to better understand different perspectives on an issue.

Shawn is currently serving as his school district's director of governmental affairs to combat poor education policy, which is what he says gets him "up in the morning." As a result of his efforts in this new role, Shawn says he "knows that my district's elected officials are more responsive to our needs, which is critical now more than ever. I also feel that our educators are more aware of the legislative issues that impact their work.... At the end of the day, it's about ensuring I can navigate the complex and changing waters of education policy in a way that will ultimately benefit my students and teachers."

Shawn's new role is an Investigator's dream. He gets to advocate for a collective truth each time new legislation is proposed by seeking input from educators and collaborating with legislators to better understand the issues. More importantly, Shawn is highly effective in a role that amplifies his investigative skills, as demonstrated by the impact he describes having. "Navigating complex and changing waters" is an opportunity to get curious, adapt, learn, and grow—essential ingredients for an Investigator's success.

Are You an Investigator?

If you…

- Feel driven to advocate for facts, reason, and evidence,
- Prefer analysis to debate,
- Feel drawn to puzzling out solutions to complex problems,
- Would rather build initiatives from clear data than interesting ideas, and
- Are relied on by others to ask critical questions or offer insight on nuanced issues,

… then you might be an investigator.

5

ARCHETYPES DRIVEN TO GENERATE

I dwell in Possibility.

—Emily Dickinson (1890/2005)

Those who are driven to generate value possibility. For them, the world of *what if* is far more interesting than the world of *what is.* This doesn't mean they don't live in the present; in fact, the present is of vital importance to them because they love the process of generation as much as they love the results.

For Creatives, the drive to generate is emotional. What they create and how they engage in the process of creation are rooted in emotion and passion. They are as committed to their ideas as they are to themselves. By contrast, Inventors maintain a distance from their ideas. These individuals thrive when they can follow their curiosity and do not feel overly pressured to produce. People who are driven to generate view deadlines as mere suggestions and established protocols as flimsy guardrails. You may find them sketchnoting during meetings, lost in thought mid-conversation, trying novel approaches, or offering an insight others may have never considered. They would rather be wrong than bored—or reinvent the drum before marching to another's beat.

Are You Driven to Generate?

Even though most people have the instinct to generate, think about your first instincts and gut reactions when considering the following questions about your own core drive:

- In a tense discussion, will your initial focus be on offering ideas and solutions?
- In a new environment, will you initially seek opportunities to experiment or explore ideas?
- When starting a new project, will you first get to work right away on your own ideas before connecting with others on theirs?
- Do you struggle when you feel constrained by the ideas of others?
- Are you your best self when creating or experimenting?

The Creative

The first time young Jimi Hendrix heard Muddy Waters playing the guitar on the radio, it "scared the hell out of him." He couldn't believe a sound like that could exist. As his brother Leon Hendrix remembers, he was so blown away by the sound, "Jimi took a radio apart, trying to find the music inside it." Eventually, his father procured a guitar for him. However, he was left-handed and the guitar was for right-handed players, so he flipped it upside down and restrung it "the wrong way up, dulling the high notes and brightening the low ones," setting the stage for a lifetime of radical experimentation (Wenner & Wolman, 1968).

Jimi would become famous for playing the guitar backward, upside down, between his legs, and with his teeth. He was the first person to ever set his guitar on fire on stage. Audiences flocked to see him play live, including other musical icons like Paul McCartney. Hendrix literally changed how music was played, producing novel sounds due to the innovative way he had restrung his right-handed guitar (Harbeck, 2013). He also applied an obscure blues technique of wrapping his thumb around the neck of the guitar to play the bass notes, freeing up the rest of his fingers to jump around the treble notes. Everything about Jimi Hendrix—from his obsession with the sound of a guitar, to his love of innovative performance, to his offbeat approach to songwriting—was unique and unorthodox; he was the definitive Creative.

The Creatives among us are driven to generate new ideas and approaches. Maybe you recognize a few people such as these:

- The science educator who enthusiastically leads a district committee to re-create science curriculum from the ground up.
- The educator who arrives at school each morning with a new lesson idea they came up with the night before or during their commute.
- The instructional coach who is a coveted brainstorming partner among staff when they want to reinvigorate outdated lessons.

The Creative's Leadership Style

Jimi Hendrix was the epitome of a divergent thinker: someone who can generate creative ideas by exploring many possible solutions. He could have simply learned to play guitar right-handed, but by restringing his guitar the way he did, he was able to produce sounds so unique they changed the face of music. Creatives lead with divergent thinking. They are driven to generate ideas, and they find joy in seeking solutions from different perspectives. If Creatives find themselves in a tight spot, especially with others relying on them, they will usually find their way out of it in an unexpected way.

Creatives find inspiration literally anywhere, so when they lead a project, their team may get used to phrases like "I was watching [insert Netflix show] last night and it made me think..." or "On a long walk this weekend, I saw a [insert yard sign, rambling brush, bold squirrel] and decided we should...." Collaborating with a Creative is like living inside a psychedelic Hendrix lyric or an M. C. Escher painting; there is no telling where the next turn of phrase or metaphorical staircase may lead.

The Creative's Approach to Change

Creatives create change through novel approaches and ingenuity. They love to transform *what is* into *what if?* Rather than accept things the way they are, they seek opportunities to shift the world around them to suit their imaginations.

By embracing their strengths as divergent thinkers, Creatives own their need to engage with lots of ideas without necessarily knowing their immediate usefulness. They may frustrate others (or even themselves) because their minds tend to wander and their interests change frequently. They may not know why they are drawn to a particular topic or concept, but they will benefit themselves and others when they take the time and space to explore it freely.

Creatives will be most effective as change leaders when they understand how to translate their wandering ideas clearly to others. Balancing autonomy with collaboration and learning how to quickly express the who, what, when, where, why, and how of any new idea will result in a goldmine of impact for a Creative.

Creatives may struggle to implement ideas as readily as they generate them. Ideas are the air they breathe, and they are full of joy during the brainstorming phase of any effort. However, their interest may naturally wane when it comes time to roll up their sleeves and move along the ups and downs of seeing an idea through. Creatives will grow as change leaders when they push themselves to engage as fully when implementing ideas as they do when generating them.

The Creative's Challengers

Creatives feel personally attached to their ideas, so people who perpetually burst their bubbles will feel like mortal enemies to them. They have a hard time separating themselves from their ideas, so they struggle when collaborating with individuals who are highly critical by nature. Creatives will also struggle in teams that value efficiency over exploration. Nothing will drive a Creative madder than a lack of time to brainstorm. They work best with collaborators who also value the time and space it takes to find inspiration. Even if that freedom comes within a frame, Creatives will appreciate colleagues who embrace idea generation.

The Creative's Allies

Creatives love the process of creating, and they appreciate colleagues who want to get lost in the process with them. If a Creative can find someone to pick up where they leave off mid-sentence or mid-idea, they will be content. At any given time, a Creative will have text or email threads going where colleagues toss them ideas and they volley ideas back. Creatives love being the go-to thought partner for others. It warms their heart and energizes their mind when people come to them in search of new methods or insights. Even though Creatives might not always love the jarring moment when a brainstorm is redirected toward efficiency, they will benefit from colleagues who know how to find the balance between exploration and implementation.

The Creative in Real Life: Meet Tim

Tim began his career as a camp counselor. He fell in love with the daily experience of immersing himself in curiosity and play with young people. "It all came very naturally," he says. "I felt I was skilled at encouraging young people to become independent thinkers and to enjoy and question the world around them."

Creatives love to find joy in play, so it's no surprise that this is what drew Tim to teaching in the first place. Curiosity, play, and joyful exploration lead to the novelty and ingenuity that fuel a Creative's will to drive change.

The first years of Tim's career as a formal educator were illustrative of his natural tendency to observe and act on creative instinct. " I enjoyed the whole process of learning how a school functions," he says. "It was fresh and new. I learned quickly how to get the most out of students and began to notice and enjoy how their natural curiosity creeped into their learning. It was something I was keen to explore more and eventually utilize."

Notice how Tim loved the newness of his first years as a classroom educator. The process of learning how a school works interested him, and coming into the profession as a blank slate allowed him to lead in the way he felt most comfortable—from square one. Creatives thrive when they are in an open space that enables their generative nature to flourish. Tim also started to see natural opportunities for building around his students' curiosity, which a Creative loves to do.

Tim's natural inclination toward play led him to teach physical education, which was a boon to his Creative spirit. He shares a particularly catalytic moment: "The community had organized a flag relay connecting local schools. I orchestrated the whole ceremony on our playground involving 500 kids and 50 staff. It was colorful, noisy, and chaotically brilliant. As we left the school to continue the relay, the entire playground was chanting, 'Mr. Black! Mr. Black! Mr. Black!' I found it really emotional. I loved that I had a role in making memories for me, the students, and the school."

"Colorful, noisy, and chaotically brilliant" could serve as an excellent motto for Creatives. Tim happily describes his moment of change as chaotic, which is not as scary for Creatives as it might be for others. In the chaos, he could see that he was helping offer a memorable experience for those involved. Creatives instinctively understand that some of the most important memories and lessons often arise through messy processes. They do not fear these opportunities, which is why they can use them to their advantage when they want to lead change. Creatives will dive headfirst into chaos excited to see what may come as a result.

What followed Tim's moment of change was not as joyful or exciting for him: expectation. "Responsibility came my way in the form of leadership roles, observations, mentoring, inspection, student teachers, and curriculum design," he says. "But the more responsibility I gained, the more I burned out. It all became very monotonous, and I could not see how that might change."

Because Creatives lead through novelty, extreme routines can get in the way of their growth. They don't fear risk but need new experiences to feed their curiosity. Notice that the more responsibility Tim gained, the less happy he became, as he grew further and further away from the playful joy that defined his happiest moments as an educator. The expectations placed on him by those responsibilities compounded this unease. It's not that Creatives don't or can't handle responsibility; it's that they need responsibility that allows their generative nature to thrive. If they step into responsibilities with limited or predetermined pathways of leadership, they may struggle.

As time went on, Tim lived through terrorist attacks in Paris, natural disasters, and the COVID-19 pandemic when he started to feel a pull toward more global thinking. "After the terrorist attacks, so much changed within our school community and I started to feel it on a personal level," he says. "When the pandemic came, I really felt the loneliness in teaching in a way I had not before. When I felt that loneliness, I recognized that I wasn't happy teaching at my school any longer. I think we have big work to do right now to get people charged up for the next stage of education, and no one is doing any good if they feel stale in their teaching jobs and stay despite wanting to try something else. I always felt boxed in by teaching in a school, and now that I am working outside of one, I feel more liberated."

Tim leaned into his newfound passion for global education by creating a program called BitesizeSDGs, which helps educators integrate the United Nations Sustainable Development Goals and other global citizenship principles into their work. He has cultivated a new global community and is happy getting back to a blank slate from which he can build his ideas.

Although Creatives love autonomy, they still need thought partners with whom to share ideas. The second Creatives begin to feel lonely in their existing environment, they will seek community elsewhere. When Tim took the leap into a new open space that represented a growing passion for him, he felt "more liberated." Freedom to explore curiosities, passions, and fresh ideas is critical to a Creative's ability to lead change.

Are You a Creative?

If you…
- Feel driven to generate original ideas,
- Prefer process over product,
- Feel inspired by a lot of different, even contradictory, ideas,
- Would rather ideate than curate, and
- Are relied on by others to offer novel approaches or innovative insights,

    … then you might be a Creative.

The Inventor

Bette Nesmith Graham was a terrible typist, and electric typewriters, which were introduced when she worked as a secretary in the 1950s, only amplified her mistakes. The new carbon ribbons smudged relentlessly at any attempt to correct errors, and one small typo could invalidate hours of work—or even put her job at risk. For Graham, a divorced single mother, correcting typos became a make-or-break issue (Mejia, 2018).

One day, while watching a painter work on a display outside a bank window, Graham noticed how the painter would simply paint over any errors with white and begin afresh. She headed to the library, searched for a recipe for water-based tempera paint, then whipped it up that evening in her kitchen blender. She poured her blended white paint into an empty nail-polish bottle and snuck it into work the next day. Graham hid the bottle in her desk and began to covertly correct typos by painting over them, letting the paint dry briefly, then retyping over the white space. Suddenly being a terrible typist didn't seem like such a big problem (Bellis, 2019).

Word got out among Graham's colleagues, who started clamoring for their own bottles of what Graham had coined "Mistake Out." After a while, she was giving away hundreds of little bottles of her homemade correcting concoction. Eventually, to keep up with the demand, she decided to charge for them, and she put her son and his friends to work in their garage filling up the bottles. Graham even assembled her own production team—an office supply dealer, her son's chemistry teacher, and a paint manufacturer—to improve the formula. Eventually, they renamed the product "Liquid Paper" and sought a patent for it. Years later, Graham would sell her company for $42 million and start two non-profits to support single mothers and female entrepreneurs like herself (Chow, 2018).

A true Inventor, Bette Nesmith Graham transformed a limitation into opportunities for herself and others. Inventors lead innovation by approaching problems as challenges rather than limitations. You may be familiar with Inventors like these in your life:

- The playful optimist who turns last-minute class disruptions into learning opportunities for students.
- The fearless experimenter who takes the initiative to try out new methods before others are ready for them.
- The open-minded educator who consistently asks for student input, accepts it openly, and applies it with willing curiosity.

The Inventor's Leadership Style

Rather than just lament her poor typing skills, Bette Nesmith Graham zoomed out and approached the problem from multiple angles. Inventors like Graham have the ability to detach themselves from the problems they face. Whereas Creatives can become personally attached to the problems they are solving, Inventors tend to approach problems from a distance. Doing so frees them up to consider future possibilities others may not recognize and to perceive failures as opportunities. For Inventors, mistakes are tiny journeys of curiosity they get to follow.

Their leadership can be empowering for others because Inventors don't judge their colleagues when they too make mistakes. Although others may offer judgment or advice, Inventors will experiment with the problem as if it were their own—even if only in their minds. It is as if Inventors are constantly in "pilot mode," wanting not simply to learn about things but to try them out for themselves. They offer a unique type of empathy based on trying to figure out how others view the world. Inventors are driven to generate not only ideas but also experiences and insights; therefore, they lead by bringing others along with them as they follow a curiosity.

The Inventor's Approach to Change

Inventors can become single-minded when they are problem solving, which gives them a focused approach to change. Graham adjusted her formula over and over for years; had she not, Liquid Paper may not have stood the test of time. Inventors like Graham can see steps ahead of others and have no problem taking the initiative themselves. Because they are not deterred by past failure or perceived impossibility, they can be the optimistic visionaries of change efforts. Inventors are rolling up their sleeves to take on change before the rest of us even understand it's necessary.

Inventors are most effective at leading change when they

- Take ownership of the problems they want to solve.
- Methodically embrace experimentation.
- Feel empowered to take initiative to solve problems.
- Have opportunities to adjust plans freely if they recognize the need to do so.
- Feel valued as visionaries and ideators within the community.
- Can generate ideas and offer insights that others acknowledge.
- Have opportunities to follow their own insights and share what they learn with others.
- Are encouraged to pilot new initiatives before others.
- Work in an environment that values a growth mindset and embraces mistakes as learning opportunities.

The Inventor's Challengers

Anybody who uses "because it's always been done this way" as an excuse can make an enemy of an Inventor. Dogmatic thinking is incredibly frustrating for Inventors, who love reimagining the world around them. Because they are able to personally detach themselves from problems, Inventors may struggle with people who can't look beyond their personal connections or existing limits to solve them.

The Inventor's Allies

Inventors love curious, open-minded collaborators. They like to ask questions and apply the answers, so they will ask their colleagues or students for input. They also offer colleagues a safe space for freethinking because they are more curious than judgmental. Inventors work best with people who are open to experimentation, even if they themselves are doing the bulk of the experimenting.

The Inventor in Real Life: Meet Brad

Brad started out as an elementary school substitute teacher with no student teaching experience and no real preparation for managing the responsibilities of being a teacher. "I had no clue how bad a teacher I was and how ill-prepared I was for interacting with high-touch parents of gifted and talented students," he says. Nevertheless, Brad had great relationships with students. The more intense their giftedness and curiosity, the more intriguing he found them.

"We were curious together," he says. "After traditional lesson planning failed my students, I realized that to teach them, I had to be the lead learner and learn with them, not teach at them. I didn't have the language then that I do now, but I co-designed learning experiences with my students. It was super messy. I was disorganized. My ideas were all over the place and lacked focus and intentionality. There was a lot of strife that first year. I was feeling my way around a dark room, trying to make sense of complex things without the lights on."

Inventors thrive while "feeling their way around dark rooms" as Brad did. Even though Brad struggled and experienced his own share of failures like any first-year educator, notice that he seems to have moved on from them. He is playful in his approach and sees failures as opportunities to do better. Inventors love the blank page—and they also love crumpling it up and throwing it into the trash can.

After a few years, Brad grew through a crash-and-burn strategy of learning what not to do and slowly found a method in the chaos. At this point, he had developed skills as an instructional designer and learned how to co-design beautiful learning experiences alongside his students.

"The really difficult thing about co-designing learning with young people is that it is really hard to predict what will happen in the future," he says. "I hated the tension then, but now I can see that it was healthy for my professional growth. I had to build a system for communicating academic, social, emotional, and lifelong-learning skill development because it didn't exist in my context yet."

"Crash-and-burn strategy" and "method in the chaos" are common concepts for Inventors. Breaking a process apart in order to rebuild it is how they learn and grow. Brad also mentions how he had to build a system to address a lack he observed. Creating new systems from a blank slate allows Inventors to thrive and prove their strengths to both themselves and their community.

A major turning point in Brad's career came when he joined a fellowship focused on connecting classroom practitioners with policymaking at the state level. "I was in the first cohort of fellows and was able to co-design nearly all the programmatic elements of the fellowship for our state and as the fellowship expanded to other states," he says. "Much of this I did while still a classroom teacher. As the fellowship expanded rapidly, I eventually stepped into the role of state director, supporting other educators who would learn similar skills."

Inventors find change enticing when it is presented as an opportunity to develop new skills or create new processes. Taking leaps into the unknown is easier for Inventors than other archetypes, but they will only jump if they can be generative on the other side. If the opportunity offers more of the same, they will be less tempted to leap—or bore very quickly if they do.

"I love taking a host of complex, seemingly disconnected information and finding patterns in the complexity," Brad says. "These patterns typically reveal some new insight that informs the next step. It is much easier to understand and make sense of rich, complex things when you have many voices sharing their observations from different vantage points, backgrounds, and experiences."

Brad admits that he will pilot anything. "I love failing small and fast," he says. "I think everything is iterative. I enjoy taking a good idea and making it great or helping someone realize how great their idea is or could be. In my experience, the curious get further faster when you are working on far-off goals or visions of the possible. Having all the answers only works when the task to be accomplished is right in front of you."

Inventors make great thought partners, but they also need thought partners of their own. Brad's language illustrates so much about how Inventors think and what they love to do: "pilot," "iterative," "visions of the possible," "the curious get further faster." Inventors are also highly adept at juggling; in fact, they thrive when they have many balls in the air. What Brad learns on one project, he will apply to another. He leads change by cross-pollinating ideas and skills that otherwise may have remained siloed.

Are You an Inventor?

If you…

- Feel driven to generate new approaches to existing problems,
- Prefer small tweaks to big leaps,
- Feel inspired by the challenge of perceived limitations,
- Would rather experiment than examine, and
- Are relied on by others to take initiative,

    … then you might be an Inventor.

6

ARCHETYPES DRIVEN TO INFLUENCE

Influence is when you are not the one talking and yet your words fill the room; when you are absent and yet your presence is felt everywhere.

—TemitOpe Ibrahim (quoted in Schultz, 2021)

People driven to influence value mastery and perspective. They want to truly understand something, and once they do, they want to lead others toward understanding. People who are driven to influence thrive when they have opportunities to learn and to teach. They would make excellent chiefs of staff and often serve a version of that role even in one-on-one relationships. They are among the first people approached for guidance during a crisis, and they like being the reliable voice of wisdom for others. They view challenges they've faced as lessons learned that can help others. You may spot them behind the scenes or in front of the room, but you recognize their influence whether or not you know for sure they are behind it. When the dominoes of change fall one by one, look to these individuals to understand the tipping point. The two change archetypes driven to influence are the Storyteller and the Sage.

Are You Driven to Influence?

Even though everyone has the power to influence others, think about your first instincts and gut reactions when considering the following questions about your own core drive:

- In a tense discussion, is your initial focus on understanding the multiple perspectives at play?
- In a new environment, do you initially seek clear goals?
- When starting a new project, do you first seek clear understanding and open lines of communication?
- Do you struggle when you lack clarity?
- Are you your best self when sharing wisdom with others?

The Storyteller

Remember the Magic Eye craze in the 1990s? Engineer Tom Baccei and graphic artist Cheri Smith co-created colorful, two-dimensional images that, when looked at hard enough and in a certain way, could shift into recognizable three-dimensional images (Stinson, 2019). Those moments feel truly magical; your perspective shifts and suddenly you can see a boat or a fish or a rocket ship project off the page. Yet, by one estimate, up to 50 percent of people could not see the hidden images, no matter how hard they tried or how thoroughly they were coached (Rossen, 2020). If a picture is worth a thousand words, then a Magic Eye picture must be worth a thousand curse words.

Meanwhile, others seem to have a preternatural ability to pick up the hidden pictures. These are the Storytellers among us: people who know to look beyond what is right in front of us, can see clearly what is hidden, and can tell the rest of us what they have seen. Storytellers innately understand that if a picture is worth a thousand words, then a metaphor is worth a thousand pictures. They are the world's most powerful poets. A Storyteller can communicate in a single sentence what most of us need coaching to learn to do, and they are driven to influence the rest of us to notice what we may not be able to on our own. Storytellers perceive what others may not, and they can influence others to shift their perception as well. They love to capture details the rest of us may miss, and they use the power of discernment and communication to elevate collective understanding. You may recognize Storytellers among you such as these:

- The early childhood educator who crisply and effectively explains a complex topic to young children, then receives knowing nods and wide eyes in response.
- The social studies educator who reads between the lines and applies a storytelling approach to the classroom so students learn history beyond what is written on the page.
- The educator who gives a rousing speech to students when approaching a difficult task or topic.

The Storyteller's Leadership Style

Storytellers tend to care quite a bit about details—both gathering and sharing them. Details help them grasp hidden images more easily and craft metaphors more effectively, providing clarity for others. Colleagues will want to approach Storytellers with as many details as possible within any given situation so they can best apply their talents for perception and communication. Storytellers are among the most communicative and organized leaders, but they may keep their cards close to the chest if they do not have all the details they need yet and will wait to communicate until they do.

Storytellers take a storytelling approach to leadership; they are driven to influence how people think by telling stories that elicit images for an audience. For this reason, Storytellers make excellent pinch hitters when all other methods of communication have failed. A Storyteller will tell the right story with the right details at just the right time.

The Storyteller's Approach to Change

Being a lover of details also means that Storytellers are adept at discerning which ones matter and which ones do not. Storytellers know what not to look at as well as what's worth paying attention to. They lead change by prioritizing what matters and listening beyond the noise that distracts everyone else. When creating change, Storytellers disregard what is irrelevant and communicate clear priorities to their collaborators. They will struggle in environments that lack transparency.

Storytellers are most effective at leading change when they

- Are given opportunities to speak, write, or communicate.
- Feel valued as organizers and influencers within the community.
- Can shape the outcomes of an effort by influencing the perceptions and actions of others.
- Approach change efforts with a discerning eye.
- Feel safe enough to openly ask clarifying questions.
- Have opportunities to take on complex challenges and distill them for others.
- Have access to all the details of an issue.
- Work in an environment that values transparency.

The Storyteller's Challengers

Collaborators who operate in secret will frustrate a Storyteller who wants to make sense of all the details. They dislike being kept in the dark. Storytellers will also clash with people who are consistently vague. Teammates who feel like puzzles to them will eventually wear thin, because perceiving beyond the Magic Eye is a gift, and Storytellers will resent when it becomes an obligation.

A Storyteller needs a willing audience, so they like to collaborate with people who listen attentively. If a Storyteller is speaking during a meeting, the people with their laptops out will get a stern eye of disapproval. Storytellers want to be surrounded by people who are alert and focused because they cannot influence others when they are not heard.

The Storyteller's Allies

Storytellers like to work with people who speak honestly, openly, and directly. They function best when people are clear and concise. At the same time, they love tough conversations that may be unclear at first but are clarified by details. Their struggles arise when knowledge, insight, or motives are intentionally hidden. Storytellers like to be in situations where the truth can always be revealed, even if it takes some time—and because they love to share details with others, they want to be surrounded by willing listeners. They can find common ground with most people because of their desire to understand, with the one exception of those who refuse to listen openly to others.

The Storyteller in Real Life: Meet Sarah

The early days of Sarah's teaching career were hard because she hadn't been trained as an educator. She was an alternative certification teacher, which meant she started teaching right after graduating with an undergraduate degree while simultaneously taking her first education courses. A critical moment came during that first rough year.

"One student wrote me a note saying that I had taught her 'what writing was for,' whereas she had previously just written 'anything that came into [her] head,'" Sarah says. "Now she could imagine an audience and writing as a tool of communication. She wrote about her mother who had passed away and said that her writing helped her remember and record details about her mother that were precious and she didn't want to forget. I wondered too if writing had also helped her process the loss."

For a Storyteller, communication in all forms is a path to influence, as it was for Sarah during that first year. Influencing her student by helping her to "imagine an audience" and apply writing as a "tool of communication" solidified Sarah's choice to continue teaching despite the difficulties. Sarah also notes her student's realization of the power of "remember[ing] and record[ing] details," illustrating the weight Storytellers place on a detail-oriented approach to the world around them.

Sarah continued to focus on helping students find their own voices, while finding her own path in the process. "I realized teaching is about making meaning alongside students," she says, "and for me and the young people in my classes, that meaning-making would come through writing."

Though Storytellers are communicators, they do not necessarily need to be writers. Because of her early experiences working with young writers in her classroom, Sarah saw the influential power of writing and embraced it wholeheartedly. Other Storytellers may take different routes, but their goal remains the same: to seek clarity, perceive details, and share those details with others in hopes of influencing them.

"While I continued to learn as a teacher, I craved opportunities to expand and broaden my impact as a leader. [I discovered] the National Writing Project, [which] gave me permission to write. We were encouraged to submit all types of writing for publication. I realized quickly that my love of writing was a clear way I might be able to effectively advocate for my students. There were many issues in education that I was passionate about because I saw how they affected my individual students. I began submitting work to various state and national syndicates. As my work was accepted, I started to realize I did in fact have value as a voice for change and the ability to influence change for my students in public education."

Sarah's sphere of influence grew when she leaned into her strengths and her drive for change. Writing began as a tool for her to make meaning alongside her students, but it became a pathway for policy change at a local, state, and national level. She wrote (and helped other educators write) several pieces that shifted perception on several contentious issues. Sarah became a reliable voice for others. Both her educator colleagues and the public appreciated her ability to clarify the role of educator and advocate for students.

"After I began writing about issues of education, I felt more empowered as a teacher leader," Sarah says. "There were times when I would read about education issues or hear them discussed online, and I would not agree with the way the issues were presented. Now I realized I could write from a teacher's perspective to explain the complexities as they were presented at the school and district level. My work became about sharing stories in a way that is honest, authentic, and clear to folks who work outside public education."

Sarah exemplifies a Storyteller's strengths here when she notes how she wanted to "explain the complexities" of education for the larger public. Storytellers want to make complex issues clear for others, as if the issues are the swirly colors of a Magic Eye and the world needs their coaching to see the reality behind them. Sarah also says her work "became about sharing stories," illustrating a Storyteller's secret power in action.

"I believe leading through writing has actually kept me in the profession, because it has given a larger purpose or gravitas to my work in that it increased my impact without ever taking me out of the classroom or away from the students in my building," Sarah says. "I wanted to continue working directly with students in a single school, but I also wanted to have an impact beyond my school building. Leading through writing gave me that opportunity."

Even though Sarah has found bright spots after a rocky start to her career, she also recognizes the ongoing difficulties each new school year brings for educators. Relying on her strength as a Storyteller has kept her in the profession, as she says. Embracing the strengths of our archetype can help us move change forward within the larger system and sustain a sense of our own capacity for change.

Are You a Storyteller?

If you ...

- Feel driven to influence how people perceive the world around them,
- Prefer details to broad strokes,
- Feel inspired by stories and are drawn to telling them,
- Would rather communicate than demonstrate, and
- Are relied on by others to communicate what is unclear,
    ... then you might be a Storyteller.

The Sage

"It lowers the understanding of what poetry actually can do," said U.S. poet laureate Billy Collins. "*Hallmark cards* has always been a common phrase to describe verse that is really less than poetry because it is sentimental and unoriginal" (Matthews, 2003, para. 7). Collins was criticizing fellow poet Dr. Maya Angelou, who had chosen to collaborate with Hallmark on a line of products. Angelou was 72 years old at the time and had lived a rich and successful life, yet she still faced criticism for this decision. Penning greeting cards and tchotchkes was apparently beneath Billy Collins—but for Maya Angelou, it was necessary.

"If I'm the people's poet, then I ought to be in the people's hands," she said (Matthews, 2003, para. 11). And that includes people who would never buy a book.

Maya Angelou wanted her words to matter to people; criticism mattered little to her when people's hearts were at stake. Customers who purchased items from Angelou's collection told Hallmark that her words had carried them through joblessness, divorce, and health scares. Angelou's poetry landed in the hands of people who needed to hear it. She—and her words—provides the inspiration to others to love life and persevere through all of its challenges.

Angelou went on to produce other works that might reach people who don't typically read poetry, including two cookbooks. Her second cookbook is inscribed, "If this book finds its way into the hands of bold, adventurous people, courageous enough to actually get into the kitchen and rattle pots and pans, I will be very happy" (Angelou, 2011).

Angelou's lifelong pursuit to inspire and influence people took shape across many formats and platforms. She is known as the "godmother of hip-hop" because of the role she played mentoring and inspiring young artists. She famously brought a young Tupac Shakur to tears when she told him, "Don't you know how important you are?" (Weisman, 2014). Beyond hip-hop, Angelou also mentored Oprah Winfrey and advised comedians such as Richard Pryor and Dave Chappelle. "At the beginning of her literary career, readers viewed Angelou as friend, sister, and mentor," explains literature scholar Cheryl A. Wall. "By the end, she assumed the status of elder, teacher, and guide" (quoted in Hardison, 2021, para. 8).

There will only ever be one Dr. Maya Angelou, but plenty of others have similar gifts of wisdom and persuasion, drawing others to them and serving as mentors. These are the Sages among us. You may recognize a few in your own life, or in yourself:

- The department leader who offers tough love exactly when it is needed to redirect a colleague toward a better outcome.
- The math educator who patiently guides young mathematicians through a challenging unit of study and celebrates their successes along the way.
- The kind mentor who offers wise counsel to a struggling young educator.

The Sage's Leadership Style

Whereas Storytellers want to understand and clarify the details of life, Sages are more concerned with the bigger picture. They often have vast life experiences that give them a valuable perspective they can offer others; for example, Maya Angelou was an actor, a director, an activist, and a world traveler who spoke six languages.

Sages do not need to be advanced in age; I have personally been guided by many a young Sage along my own professional path. Because Sages have a wise nature, people tend to respond to what they say. I would be willing to bet that the best nugget of wisdom you have at your disposal during trying times likely originated with a Sage. Their guidance often transcends the moment they share it, and others may find themselves passing it along.

The Sage's Approach to Change

True Sages will reveal themselves as such by never claiming to be experts or to need the limelight. As Maya Angelou said, "I've learned that I still have lots to learn." A Sage's wisdom comes from knowing that a single person can never know everything. However, they do see the world differently than those around them—and knowing this makes them patient with others. Ignorance does not bother them as much as a refusal to learn. Wisdom, rather than knowledge, is their personal goal, and they value wisdom in others as well. This recognition of the difference between the two is what gives the Sage's expertise dignity and allows them to move others along. They are not afraid to try new things, take risks, or embrace a beginner's mindset. The Sage wants to soak up experiences for the sake of sharing them with others later.

Sages are most effective at leading change when they

- Take chances and opportunities as they arise.
- Embrace new ideas and even failure as they come.
- Feel empowered to mentor or advise others.
- Have opportunities to speak or present.
- Feel valued as advisors within the community.
- Can influence the opinions and actions of others.
- Have opportunities to understand new challenges and guide others through them.
- Are encouraged to explore new interests or opportunities to learn something new.
- Work in an environment that values a beginner's mindset.

The Sage's Challengers

People who are closed off to new opportunities, ideas, or experiences will frustrate a Sage. For them, the world is a learning buffet. They cannot understand people who choose to remain stuck in fixed mindsets. Sages love to serve as mentors and guides for others, but they have limited patience for people who refuse to grow and change. At the same time, although Sages know they are wise, they are not know-it-alls. Real know-it-alls will irritate them to no end because a Sage can see straight through any flimsy facade.

The Sage's Allies

A Sage's favorite collaborators are smart and open-minded. As much as Sages like to guide others, they love to learn from others too. People who challenge their thinking or offer new insights will satisfy the Sage's desire for knowledge and experience. Sages also thrive with collaborators who inspire them, who offer diverse perspectives, and who have a growth mindset. They thrive when they have the chance to bring out the best in the people around them, so they collaborate well with those who want to grow and improve. The best colleague a Sage could hope for is someone who both offers new insights and has a desire to improve.

The Sage in Real Life: Meet Natalie

"I have always played the role of an educator in my private life, so it seemed like a no-brainer to make it my job as well," says Natalie. "I enrolled in the education program a few days after a colleague suggested it would be a good fit."

"My first year of teaching was like constantly joining a conversation that was already in progress," she adds. Natalie noticed that new teachers have to learn the culture of the classroom, school, and community as well as the expectations that accompany all of those. "I didn't want to burden anyone," she says. "At the same time, I wasn't always sure what I needed, so when wonderful colleagues told me to let them know if I needed anything, I said 'okay' and journeyed on. That's why I am so thankful for the educators that I still consider my mentors. They were able to help me harness my whirling mind in such a way that I became a stronger educator."

Notice that Natalie says, "I have always played the role of educator in my private life, so it seemed like a no-brainer." Sages often play the role of educator and mentor outside the classroom. Natalie also describes her reluctance to "burden" others during her first year, though she found solace in mentors herself. Sages may find it difficult to be on the mentee side of a situation at first, but the experience of not knowing and finding support from others only fuels their ability to support others later.

When Natalie reached a point of personal breakdown, she reassessed exactly what type of person she wanted to be. Though she was habitually busy, she never felt productive or particularly competent. "It wasn't until I felt like I was completely losing myself that I learned to harness, focus, and exert my energy properly," she says. "This skill (which I'm still working to master) trickles into working with students and educators. We find out why we're doing things. We want our motives to be right so that we aren't spending precious time on things that don't work for us or don't matter to our main goals."

Sages catalogue their own experiences as lessons learned that they can impart to others later. They move through the experience of feeling lost thoughtfully so they can help others do the same. Notice how she uses words like mastery *and* motives—*developing skills for mastery and working toward a central purpose support a Sage's drive to influence others by understanding themselves first.*

Natalie is now aware not only of what she can and cannot control but also of what she should and should not control. Working on purpose allows her to see more clearly where the lines are between her passion, mission, vocation, and profession. "Honestly, it has made me a better educator and leader because I started allowing other people to be great," she says. "What is *your* passion? What do *you* want to master? How can *you* be put in a position to excel? My job is to launch people into their greatness."

"My job is to launch other people into their greatness." More Sage-like words were never said.

Natalie says she has seen her students responding positively to instruction and stepping up to the challenges set before them because they trust they will be supported. She says her colleagues are doing the same. "It's always great when teachers stop me in the hallway to tell me how things are working in their classrooms," she says. "They are all trying new things that make them uncomfortable sometimes, but when they feel supported, they give it their all. Everyone benefits from support that's rooted in love. It had to start with me, though. I couldn't give what I didn't have. When I started taking care of myself, the people around me started to benefit from the growth."

When Sages are unable to support and guide others, they feel off-center and ineffective (even if it isn't true). "Everyone benefits from support that's rooted in love," Natalie says, illustrating clearly how a Sage can come into their own sense of their power over time. Notice that Natalie plays a central role in her school as an advisor. Her colleagues seek her out, and she thrives as much by seeing their successes as by experiencing her own. This is why Sages need an audience; they require feedback loops rooted in the growth and strength of others.

"Teaching is a gift that I have," Natalie says. "It is not the totality of who I am. What I do for work increases in quality when who I am as a person increases in quality. With that being said, I don't hide in my work anymore. It does me no good to dedicate every waking moment of my life to work. It does more good when the time that I spend doing work is focused and intentional. I'm better because I rest and play and notice and experience the fullness of life. That means I have to leave work at work as often as I can."

Sages love to support and mentor others, but they also thrive in novel environments. By embracing her need to "leave her work at work" and spend time resting and playing, Natalie is fueling her needs as a Sage to learn as much as she teaches.

Are You a Sage?

If you…

- Feel driven to influence the growth and mindsets of others around you,
- Prefer exploration to established routines,
- Feel inspired by learning new things and drawn to sharing what you learn with others,
- Would rather advise than assist, and
- Are relied on by others to offer counsel or mentorship,
   … then you might be a Sage.

❈ ❈ ❈

Each of the archetypes discussed in the past few chapters is vital to every educational ecosystem. Recognizing our own archetypes and those of our colleagues can help all of us move forward effectively. Now we will take the next step in our journey: identifying the archetypal lens you apply when responding to conflict. As we move into the following chapters, my hope is that you can better understand how to apply what you know about yourself and others in the effort to create better school and organizational communities for everyone.

7

RESPONDING TO CONFLICT

You will recognize your own path when you come upon it, because you will suddenly have all the energy and imagination you will ever need.

—Jerry Gillies (1978)

We know the boldest squirrels will remain bold whatever the situation, and the shyest will remain shy. A bold squirrel may fight; a shy one may run. The plot will unfold differently for each, even as the character remains the same. Even though a bold squirrel in the mountains of Colorado might encounter a new predator as it expands its terrain, a bold squirrel near an urban area might find itself stuck in the middle of traffic with a very different kind of predator. Their basic traits and core drives may be the same, but each situation presents new problems. We all—squirrels and people alike—have to manage difficult situations from time to time, and each comes with a unique set of conflicts to navigate based on our individual behaviors and context. Understanding our change archetype and those of our colleagues can help us negotiate stressful circumstances at work, as well as indulge in those opportunities that bring out the best in each of us.

Traditionally, there are two types of conflict—*internal* and *external*—although most conflicts in life offer a bit of both. Change never comes without struggle from both inside *and* out. Consider an assistant principal Guardian who knows she must have a tough conversation with an educator she is close to. Internally, she fears hurting the relationship with a colleague because she is driven to connect. Externally, she knows this person she cares for needs to make an adjustment for the sake of the school and students, which of course the Guardian also values.

We weigh moments like these so often and so seamlessly that we may not even notice them as we navigate the day to day. Dr. Guardian, EdD, may not have had the time during her busy schedule as an assistant principal to pause and fret about the conversation she needed to have. She may have called the educator in, carried on with the conversation expertly, then packed up her bags and gone home, but some part of her will carry that conversation with her until she goes to sleep that night. This conversation exemplifies a microscopic drop in the ocean of internal and external conflict educators carry day in and day out within the interconnected system of a school. The conversation may have gone well, but the issue that led to it still lingers. The relationship may have remained intact, but the Guardian will worry about how to sustain relationships like these when big issues loom.

Even though we cannot avoid conflict, we can learn ways to *respond* rather than react based on our personal patterns. Reacting is what we do when we don't slow down long enough to remind ourselves of who we really are; responding is what we do when we know that the person we are in the midst of any conflict is the same person we will be when the conflict has subsided. Response requires self-awareness.

In his book *The Big Leap* (2010), Gay Hendricks provides a handy model for responding in work environments that I also think is a helpful starting point for thoughtful response to conflict when leading change. Hendricks's model is based on what he calls the four "zones of function":

- **Zone of Incompetence:** This is what we do not understand, do not do well, and do not really want to do well.
- **Zone of Competence:** This is what we can do well but not better than most. We don't stand out in this zone, and it doesn't particularly bring us joy or energy. We spend an inordinate amount of time in this zone when we are in systems that do not value individual strengths.
- **Zone of Excellence:** This is what we can do very well, standing out as a particularly skilled leader. We likely practiced this skill

and gained mastery over time. This zone can be the ladder that helps us climb to new heights—but it can also be the dungeon we find ourselves trapped inside.

- **Zone of Genius:** This is what Hendricks pushes us to aspire toward. Think of this zone as the place where our abilities are such that we are in a state of *flow*. We'll discuss this in detail further, but essentially our zone of genius is the place where our talents live far beyond the skills of others.

In addition to Hendricks' four zones, there are three types of conflict that can serve as opportunities for deeper self-awareness and professional growth:

1. Managing energy
2. Maintaining boundaries
3. Balancing tension with flow

In this chapter, you'll learn about how the four zones intersect with these three types of conflict and how you can leverage these intersections toward effective change. (See Figure 7.1 for a snapshot of the zones, types of conflict, and associated supports.)

Managing Energy

Educators have to juggle many tasks all day long. Every one of these tasks can feel monumental as pressure comes from both outside ourselves and within us to execute them perfectly. I once accidentally gave zeros in place of 10 points in the gradebook and within hours had received piles of emails from parents and students alike. It was a simple oversight that I quickly corrected, but I dwelled on the message those emails seemed to send for days on end: *Don't mess up again.*

What kind of messages are we berating ourselves with every day, and how do they affect our energy to lead change? Forgot to call in attendance one morning? (You're now the forgetful one.) Misplaced some paperwork? (You're now the unorganized one.) Spoke out of turn in a meeting? (You're now the difficult one.) Rushed out of the building as the bell rang for an appointment? (Your dedication is lacking.) On and on these thoughts go.

These anxiety-inducing messages are minor ones among thousands over a classroom career, but moments such as these can easily pile up,

Figure 7.1

Zones of Competence and Conflict

Zone	Type of Conflict	Tools of Supports
Zone of incompetence	Managing energy	Energy management challenge
Zone of competence		Energy inventory
Zone of excellence	Maintaining boundaries	Boundary naming
Zone of genius	Balancing tension with flow	Context and coping

bury us, and prevent us from ever moving forward. We place such undue pressure on ourselves and one another that it can zap us of more energy than our actual work does.

The stress we feel when burdened by these moments is associated with our zones of competence and incompetence. Think about it: you're probably adequate at best when it comes to checking off daily tasks such as taking attendance, completing paperwork, or attending meetings. Speaking for myself, I readily acknowledge that these kinds of tasks are within my own zone of incompetence, yet these are exactly the kinds of things we beat ourselves (and one another) up about. Trust me, no one loathed me more than our school attendance clerk—or so I thought. The energy we expend expecting perfection within our zones of competence and incompetence could power a major city.

I bet if you kept a running log of your energy levels day to day over the course of your work life, you would find that your energy is especially low during certain occasions and especially high during others. Once we can identify these patterns, we can start to unpack how to manage both our own energy and the collective energy of our organizations. So often, we expect new initiatives to gain momentum without properly understanding the energy needed to ignite *and* sustain them. If an opportunity for change comes with loads of tasks that most people will find within their zone of competence at best, then we are setting everyone up to eventually lose energy—no matter how worthwhile the endeavor may be.

Understanding energetic patterns provides a strong foundation for change work because it illustrates how our own behaviors might align (or not) with the collective patterns of our community or organization. The more organizations think energetically, the better position everyone will be in to engage in positive transformation work. Otherwise, educators will burn out before they get a real chance to begin, or communities won't have the right energy for the change they are trying to create. By examining our patterns and behaviors, we can illuminate invisible energetic patterns that may prevent honest and authentic progress. To begin, undertake the following energy management challenge:

Personal Energy Management Challenge

1. Document your energy lows and highs for an entire workweek.
2. Note which zones of function you were in during the lows and highs.
3. At the end of the week, respond to the following reflection questions.

   - What zone of function tends to drain you the most? Why do you believe this is?
   - How might you shift your energy from this zone into another that elevates your energy more?
   - What zone of function tends to elevate you the most? Why do you believe this is?
   - How might you create more opportunities to function within this zone and elevate your overall energy? For example, could you ask a teammate to switch roles if they seem drained by a task that lifts you? Could you turn a task from a drain to a lift by finding a way to apply more of your genius to it?
   - How might your archetype influence how you manage your energy?
   - How might your approach to change be influenced by the way you manage your energy?

Try to engage in this challenge several times during the school year if you can. Use any insights to better understand the nuances of your own energy and how your energy levels align to your zones of function and to consider how you might shift your energy to better meet the needs of your school community.

Of course, there is no magic wand for elevating your energy. I will not Pollyanna the fact that being an educator means operating in many different zones whether we want to or not. Nevertheless, there is hope in the form of self-awareness. By knowing who we are, the roles we play, the conflicts we encounter, and the ways we respond to those conflicts, we can take back our energy and use it how we see fit. If an entire organization slowed down long enough to acknowledge how different individuals respond to different situations, we all might stop expecting perfection from everyone and everything. Leaders who recognize that some collective tasks are energy drains on large groups of educators should consider shifting how those tasks are done—or cutting them out completely.

Understanding our energy patterns tells us when we are our most authentic selves. Of course, what lifts or drains a Guardian may be vastly different from what lifts or drains a Sage. Figure 7.2 provides an energy inventory for each archetype. These are jumping-off points, not landing stations; hopefully, they will inspire you to build your own personal energy management toolkit. When you feel drained or lifted, notice what is happening within and around you, and use your insights to adjust accordingly based on what you know about your personal energy needs. You'll need a firm energetic foundation to maintain the marathon of working toward sustainable change in education going forward.

Maintaining Boundaries

When we are in our zone of competence, we can become complacent or bored. When we are in our zone of incompetence, we can become easily frustrated. But when we are in our zone of excellence, we tend to enjoy ourselves—not always, but most of the time. The Diplomat who excels at social media will probably enjoy the upcoming edchat on Twitter and feel a rush of energy to participate and share new insights from the experience with colleagues. The Investigator who excels at research will likely love reading up on the latest trends in learning science and feel an energetic high when sharing what they learned with a colleague.

Figure 7.2

Energy Inventory Tool

 THE DIPLOMAT

Energetic Blueprint	**Energy Drains**	**Energy Lifts**
Relationships rooted in equality and fairness give me energy. Isolation, inequality, and codependence deplete my energy.	• Too much screen time • Overstimulation from others • Too much time alone or surface-level socializing • Hamster-wheel thinking about issues of injustice or unfairness • Neglecting one's own feelings	• Authentic conversation with a trusted colleague • Cultivating gratitude and seeking bright spots • Sharing personal feelings with trusted people • Sitting outdoors with loved ones

Energy Inventory:

- Have I focused on my own needs lately?
- Am I aimlessly socializing out of boredom?
- How many hours have I spent in front of a screen?
- Have I had authentic conversations with trusted people?
- Am I focusing too much on an injustice or something that is unfair to the detriment of my own mental health?

 THE CHAMPION

Energetic Blueprint	**Energy Drains**	**Energy Lifts**
Advocating for a worthy cause gives me energy. Feeling defeated, lacking agency, and feeling unheard deplete my energy.	• Fear of failure or defeat • Inability to rest • Consistent interaction with toxic news or toxic people • Feeling undervalued or unheard • Inability to create and see the results of those efforts • Having hands tied	• Naps or still time • Consistent progress or achievement • Heartwarming news stories • Feeling gratitude from others • Taking inventory of successes

Energy Inventory:

- Am I getting enough rest?
- Am I spending enough time and energy with people who support my mission?
- Am I spending too much time and energy with people who do not see eye to eye with my personal causes?
- Do I feel appreciated by others?
- Am I focusing on my successes more than my perceived failures?

continued

Figure 7.2 (*continued*)
Energy Inventory Tool

 ### THE CREATIVE

Energetic Blueprint	**Energy Drains**	**Energy Lifts**
Losing myself in my creative process gives me energy. A lack of understanding or validation from others depletes my energy.	• Escapist behaviors • Anxiety • Being too busy with rote or unfulfilling tasks • Boredom • Overly focusing on outcomes rather than processes	• A creative outlet • Purposeful tasks • Opportunities to explore new ideas or information • Validation • Being present

Energy Inventory:

- Do I have opportunities to think divergently in my work?
- Do I make time for creative outlets (both personal and professional)?
- Am I bored with a facet of my work? How can I reinvigorate this component of my work life?
- Do I feel a sense of purpose with the tasks I'm required to complete?
- Do I feel misunderstood or invalidated for my ideas?
- Do I have ample opportunity to explore my process, unencumbered by expected outcomes?

 ### THE STORYTELLER

Energetic Blueprint	**Energy Drains**	**Energy Lifts**
Clear and thoughtful communication gives me energy. A lack of clarity or sense of groundedness depletes my energy.	• Excessive criticism, especially self-criticism • Messiness (physical, mental, and emotional) • Vagueness • Rambling and excessive chatting • Wasted time, energy, or words	• Authentic praise from respected colleagues and leaders • Attention to detail • Intentional conversations with a purpose • Feeling of use • Feeling respected and heard

Energy Inventory:

- Am I being too hard on myself or others?
- Am I surrounded by clutter (physical, mental, or emotional)?
- Am I unclear of the expectations of myself or my work?
- Do I feel valued and respected by my colleagues and leaders? Have they verbalized my value to me?
- Do I feel that my time is spent on purposeful tasks?
- Do I feel a sense of order in my work and environment?

THE INVENTOR

Energetic Blueprint

Freedom to experiment and opportunities to take the long view give me energy. Rigid requirements and an excessive attention to detail deplete my energy.

Energy Drains

- Lack of insight
- Rigid rules and expectations
- "Can't see the forest for the trees" thinking from others
- Forced, purposeless tasks
- Unyielding adherence to systems, processes, or approaches that are no longer working
- Required networking or icebreakers

Energy Lifts

- Big-picture, what-if thinking
- Considering future possibilities or outcomes
- Free exploration of ideas
- Opportunities to pilot or implement ideas quickly
- Pivoting freely when new solutions present themselves
- Collaborative opportunities that also embrace independence

Energy Inventory:

- Have I zoomed out on an idea, issue, or process today?
- Do I feel restricted in my environment?
- Do I have opportunities to experiment?
- Am I surrounded by open-minded thinkers?
- Do I have opportunities to build toward a future vision or ideal?
- Do I feel a healthy sense of detachment from my work environment?

THE SAGE

Energetic Blueprint

Providing wise counsel and authentic opportunities to share my expertise and insights gives me energy. Feeling unheard, unseen or undervalued depletes my energy.

Energy Drains

- Few opportunities to share expertise
- Feeling inadequate
- Giving advice that is not received or acted upon
- Feeling invisible
- Feeling stunted as a learner

Energy Lifts

- Performative exercises or experiences
- Mentoring others
- Advising colleagues, leaders, or committees
- Opportunities to expand knowledge and wisdom
- Being viewed as a "someone you can talk to" by colleagues

Energy Inventory:

- Do I have opportunities to counsel or mentor others?
- Do leaders provide me with opportunities to advise?
- Do I feel adequately prepared to lead and advise others in my current environment?
- Do I feel heard and seen by colleagues and leaders?
- Do I have opportunities to speak, lead, or perform?
- Do I have opportunities to learn and grow?

continued

Figure 7.2 (*continued*)
Energy Inventory Tool

 THE INVESTIGATOR

Energetic Blueprint	**Energy Drains**	**Energy Lifts**
Opportunities to probe tough questions, implement thoughtful research, and explore my own curiosity gives me energy. Superficiality and an unwillingness to analyze ideas, issues, and experiences depletes my energy.	• Stagnation • Surface-level thinking • Refusal to explore issues in depth • Lack of curiosity • Relying on assumptions rather than evidence • Feeling unable to ask tough questions	• A new problem to tackle or a new approach to tackling an old problem • Fresh ideas and opportunities • Seeking and implementing evidence-based solutions • Deep conversations • Exploration of nuance • Open-question cultures

Energy Inventory:

- Do I have opportunities to explore my curiosity?
- Do I feel fresh and invigorated in my work?
- Do I have opportunities to research and solve problems?
- Do I have opportunities to engage in deep conversations with others?
- Do I feel free to ask tough questions?
- Do I feel empowered to research and implement new ideas or methods?

 THE GUARDIAN

Energetic Blueprint	**Energy Drains**	**Energy Lifts**
People-first mindsets, systems, and processes give me energy. A lack of compassion or unwillingness to nurture and care for others depletes my energy.	• Leaders and colleagues who do not nurture one another • Cold and distant colleagues or culture • Overextending oneself in service to others • Excessively defending oneself or others • Isolation • Toxic culture or lack of community	• Human-centered design • Opportunities to build community • Opportunities to counsel or nurture the well-being of others • Authentic relationships based upon mutual trust and support • Compassionate leadership • Warm and inviting social networks

Energy Inventory:

- Have I taken care of myself physically, emotionally, mentally, and spiritually?
- Do I have opportunities to guide and nurture others?
- Do I work in a compassionate, warm community?
- Do I feel a sense of belonging and support?
- Do I often feel the need to defend others at work?
- Do I feel that everyone's humanity is valued at work?

Though we feel buoyed when we have opportunities to explore our talents and share our accomplishments with others, we must also create and maintain strong boundaries in these situations so our high energy is not exploited by others. We do want to create organizations that cultivate individual strengths, but we also want to be careful not to abuse them. Since our zone of excellence is composed of the tasks and situations that we are so good at, others will want us to stay in this zone for their own benefit if we let them. If we do, we can never achieve our genius—and genius is where change lives.

Case in point: as a Creative, I love (like *love, love*) creating graphics and websites. My years dabbling in the world of edtech gave me the opportunity to develop these skills in ways that my time in the classroom did not. Over time, I have built up this skill enough that it sits squarely in my zone of excellence. In fact, this skill has been critical to many of the change efforts I have joined and co-led. Time and time again I have volunteered to apply my own zone of excellence skills to change efforts alongside talented colleagues, filling me with purpose and energy. Inevitably, I reach a point where I want to apply my zone of genius to these efforts and get stuck moving widgets at 2 in the morning or dealing with username and password drama when I would rather be creating something.

It took a long while, but I eventually learned how to create boundaries around my skills. If the team wants a website, I will get us started and then teach others how to take it from there. Or I will design the branding and then teach others how to use tools to control the color scheme and font choices. I am a Creative, and my joy is in the creating; everything else is an opportunity to teach and learn. My boundaries are firmly drawn at the moment I start to feel that my role as creator shifts to that of IT support.

When the need to protect your zone of excellence arises, consider using a boundary motto to anchor yourself. For example, let's say a dedicated Champion has worked hard for more than a decade teaching middle school social studies and is well respected by colleagues and students alike. Now let's say the school district decides to roll out a new program to redesign the social studies curriculum that this Champion has spent years developing and eliciting buy-in from colleagues to support. Figure 7.3 shows how we might use an empathy map—a tool for gaining deeper insight into how human beings might feel, think, want, or fear—to analyze this situation.

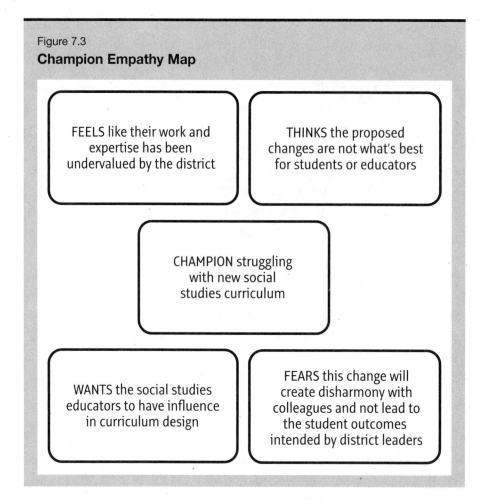

Figure 7.3

Champion Empathy Map

FEELS like their work and expertise has been undervalued by the district

THINKS the proposed changes are not what's best for students or educators

CHAMPION struggling with new social studies curriculum

WANTS the social studies educators to have influence in curriculum design

FEARS this change will create disharmony with colleagues and not lead to the student outcomes intended by district leaders

The strife this Champion faces is rooted in the cause and the outcomes they have worked toward for years, which are now being upended by external forces beyond their control. This Champion has worked hard to lead others using the existing curriculum and has proven an excellent leader when it comes to developing and cultivating support for new curriculum. Inevitably, the Champion will be asked to lead this change effort as they have before, even if their own needs and desires differ from that of leadership.

To create boundaries in this situation, the Champion should start with a boundary motto: *Advocating for a worthy cause gives me energy. Feeling defeated, lacking agency, and feeling unheard deplete my energy.*

The cause the Champion has advocated for in the past may be under threat from forces beyond their control, but they *can* control their own energy and investment through boundaries.

A motto is meant to remind us of who we are and what we value most. The Champion knows that feeling a lack of voice and agency is draining for them and what they need is to get behind a cause they find worthy. To determine what cause is worthy, they must take the time to better understand the new curriculum and decide whether they want to advocate for it, against it, or somewhere in between. They also need to remind themselves of their proven excellence as a leader, then find the stakeholders (colleagues, leadership, families) who will listen to them in order to take back their agency. Otherwise, they may choose to politely decline to lead this time, instead focusing their efforts on a cause they do find worthy with people who value their expertise.

For another archetype in the same situation, the situation and necessary motto will be different. An Investigator might want to understand the evidence-based research to support the new curriculum and feel stress learning that the research shows mixed results. A Storyteller will want concrete plans and effectively communicated strategies and will feel pained when these are lacking. The boundary motto is an anchor, reminding us of how we best operate and giving us insight into the actions we must take within a given situation in order not to lose ourselves when the winds of change blow.

Boundary Naming

The word *boundaries* has almost lost all meaning because it is used so frequently in vague contexts. In the workplace, though—and especially in education—it is essential to have real boundaries that matter. These boundaries should provide us with clarity in times of anxiety. Giving boundaries a name can help remind us why we have them and suggest practical ways to apply them. Use the following example boundary names I have created as a guide for naming the boundaries you find you need to protect your own zone of excellence.

Invisible Fence Boundaries

Visible only to the boundary creator. I have a person in my life whom I cannot escape, even though they cause me lots of personal stress. We are kind of stuck with each other, for better or worse. After years of running into similar conflicts with this person, I decided to build an invisible fence boundary, meaning this person has no idea the boundary is in place, but I do. For example, I recognized that when I give advice to this person's complaints, our conflicts with each other become more frequent and my energy is zapped unnecessarily. Consequently, I made a personal rule that I will no longer give this person advice, even if they go on and on about a problem seemingly in search of guidance. Now I just let them talk, and I merely listen. They don't know this boundary is in place because it wasn't necessary to discuss it. I recognized a negative pattern and interrupted it with an invisible fence boundary to protect my own energy.

Invisible fence boundaries can be incredibly helpful in education settings, too. For example, I have a dear colleague who is an incredibly talented Black educator and often finds herself in facilitation roles with mostly white educators. This colleague has invisible fences in place for these situations. Coaching white educators through the start of their antiracism journeys is emotionally burdensome for my colleague. Though such coaching would be within her zone of excellence, she has learned to take measures to protect her own energy. One way she does this is by refusing to engage in the emotional work of coaching white educators through the *why* of antiracism. She only supports white educators on their journeys once those educators understand the *why* and are deep into the work of *how,* attempting to decenter themselves from the process.

My colleague doesn't announce this boundary or even acknowledge it to others. She simply changes the subject, works with another educator, or asks a colleague to take over when the boundary risks being crossed.

Recipe Boundaries

Practical lists for negotiating interactions. Recipe boundaries are quick, practical, easily implemented, and rooted in daily experience. For example, one recipe boundary I have for the difficult person in my life is not to pick up the phone if they call me past 10 pm. I have learned that as soon as I answer a late-night call from this person, the conversation will be one-sided, volatile, and difficult to end. I came to realize that this person was exploiting my skills of empathy and open-minded listening. As soon as I noticed this pattern, I realized that a quick recipe boundary would solve my problem. The person remains difficult and inescapable, but at least I have some control over my energy.

Recipe boundaries are great with colleagues, too. Teammate complains constantly during afterschool planning sessions? Insist on a hard stop at 4:30. Know-it-all colleague constantly shares unsolicited advice? Tell them you just had that conversation with so-and-so and have figured it out. Recipe boundaries are quick and easy one-liners you can establish for yourself to efficiently address conflicts before they grow into more difficult problems.

Hedge Boundaries

Loose boundaries that support more defined ones. Hedge boundaries are the sparse shrubbery planted around a protected area. They have no immediate consequences attached to them, and we can be looser about protecting them, but if we don't pay attention, over time they can get bent and beaten as outsiders push their way through.

For example, a very kind Investigator I know is relied on by colleagues to help with all things technological. Whenever a new update or program needs installing, his coworkers pop in unannounced seeking guidance. The Investigator enjoys learning about new programs and mostly doesn't mind supporting others, but the pop-ins can become a frustrating distraction over time. When the Investigator grows tired of the interruptions, he might create a hedge boundary: establishing office hours for tech support one day a week, for example, or sending out a weekly tech newsletter that offers solutions to common issues. Just as a visitor can still peek into the other side of a hedge, a hedge boundary is ultimately one where the part you love can still be preserved, but the part that drains you can be kept at a distance.

Cafeteria Boundaries

Interactive exchange boundaries that are mutually beneficial for everyone. This might get confusing because schools have actual cafeterias, and we are talking metaphorical Cafeteria (capital *C*) boundaries, which take place in the mind and likely have fewer food fights. Cafeterias are places where you have options, where socializing and opportunities are free-flowing, and where occasionally you find yourself shunned to a table by yourself and in need of a new place to eat. Cafeteria boundaries are similar in that these are needed within mutually beneficial spaces of social or professional exchange—think of grade-level or content departments,

professional learning communities, or subcommittees. These are helpful environments and can offer incredible support during times of
change; however, they can also be situations that require boundary-
setting as well.

Imagine you're a Storyteller who creates phenomenal presentations
for students and your colleague is a Sage who loves to present to the
faculty or at district professional development sessions. The two of you
have a Cafeteria boundary with each other; you love creating thoughtful
presentations, and your colleague loves giving them. You dislike presenting to large groups, and your colleague loves it. You have an eye for
detail, and your colleague looks for the big picture.

It's a match made in heaven—that is, until your colleague gives a
presentation without crediting you for your work. The presentation is a
hit, and your colleague is offered a paid opportunity to give the presentation to other groups of educators. What was once a mutual exchange
has become one-sided; the boundary has been crossed.

Cafeteria boundaries are often socially enforced, sometimes covertly.
The best way to navigate these boundaries is to uphold them for others.
Someone at the "cool kids table" may take responsibility for calling
out the Sage's mistake and bringing the Storyteller back to the club.
Meaning: there are valuable social contracts within schools connecting
us with an invisible net to our colleagues. When boundaries are crossed
for one person, they will inevitably be crossed for others, which is when
environments that should be supportive risk becoming toxic instead. A
thriving Cafeteria with well-kept boundaries provides an energetic equi-
librium for everyone.

Although some of these boundary types may resonate with you more
than others, their essential purpose is to illustrate specific opportunities
for setting boundaries and protecting your energy and skills. Consider
how creating names for the boundaries you may need to set might offer
insight into the conflicts you navigate day to day.

Balancing Tension with Flow

A few years ago, I directed a lively, talented, sometimes dysfunctional
group of middle schoolers in a couple of school plays. I have zero background in theater, but because my principal knew that most "artsy" tasks

fit neatly into my zone of excellence, I was "volun-told" to take it on. As it turned out, those plays represent some of my best memories from the classroom.

I decided to task the students with writing and producing the plays they performed, and they rose to the occasion with thoughtful scripts about abandonment, bullying, and young love. Because I had so little theater experience, I empowered the students as not only the writers but also the directors, actors, musicians, costume designers, stage technicians, and makeup artists. The students, not I, produced those plays.

Most people who attended opening night of our first play might have viewed it as an utter mess. Our stage sat between the gym and the cafeteria, so the acoustics were abysmal. We had no stage curtains, so I bought yards of cheap black speaker fabric, which I stapled instead of sewed and hung with shower curtain rings. I bought industrial clamp lights from Home Depot, and students whisper-screamed lighting directions across the stage at the exact moment the actors stopped speaking. To the theater-trained eye, it was a disaster.

However, the students involved in that play were students who had never had a chance to take part in theater before. Trenton, a class clown who had a reputation for lacking motivation, showed up to every rehearsal without fail, shushing his peers and leading his castmates in making on-the-spot changes to the script because "it suited his character" more. Marion, a shy but gifted singer who flinched when teachers called on her in class, belted out Taylor Swift's "You Belong to Me" so beautifully that she received a standing ovation. Jake, who couldn't sit still in any class, directed his "lighting team" just as seriously as if he were a lighting manager on Saturday Night Live. The performance might have looked like a disaster, but it was a massive success from the perspective of the young people who felt agency and autonomy at school for the first time in their lives.

The experience also provided me with a window into my own zone of genius. I didn't have the basic skills or experience to produce and direct plays, so on the surface it may seem like I was struggling with tasks in my zone of incompetence—and I certainly was at times. Nevertheless, my zone of genius lies in *getting out of the way* and empowering others to take ownership and lead. I could avoid my zone of incompetence by leaning into my zone of genius. I didn't know enough to do it intentionally at the time, but in hindsight, I see clearly that I was operating at my highest potential even when I appeared to lack the basic skills for the task at hand.

That is not to say that everything was sunshine and Popsicles. Some days were rough. Like when students didn't have their lines memorized or when I needed support from my colleagues or leadership and realized my "volun-told" position was a very lonely one. But the difference between rough days in our lower zones and rough days in our zone of genius is *flow*.

Flow Theory

Flow theory has existed in a variety of contexts for thousands of years but gained prominence in the 1970s and 80s from studies led by Hungarian researcher Mihaly Csikszentmihalyi. Here is his definition of *flow:*

> Flow is when you are completely involved in an activity for its own sake. The ego falls away. Time flies. Every action, movement, and thought follows inevitably from the previous one, like playing jazz. Your whole being is involved, and you're using your skills to the utmost. (2009)

Every teacher who has experienced a truly magical day with students might relate to this definition of *flow*. Teaching is tough, but there are days when your lesson is beautifully designed, students are steadily engaged, and community relationships are thriving. You go home feeling like a million bucks, remembering exactly why you paid the tuition for a teaching certificate in the first place. Flow is most often described in terms of singular moments in time—the athlete, artist, writer, or scientist who is "in the zone" and loses all sense of self while engaged in their process. In the context of teaching and learning, I believe flow can best be described as consistent energetic highs over time that outweigh the lows. This kind of flow can only arise when we are operating within our zone of genius.

Flow occurs in that sweet spot between being skilled enough not to feel anxious and feeling challenged enough not to feel bored. Though I didn't know the first thing about stage lighting or blocking a scene when I was helping students produce plays, I had proven myself entrepreneurial enough to seek the information and skills I didn't already have in order to get the task done; my abilities within my zone of excellence brought the opportunity to me. If I hadn't leaned into my genius as a Creative who sees the creativity in every student, the challenge might have been more of a burden. Producing those plays alongside my students never felt like a burden, no matter how tense the situation became. In order to find flow over a period of time while leading or engaged in a project, we have to know who we are at our most genius and embrace the balance of tension between comfort and challenge. Challenges will always arise, so we cannot expect to embark on any kind of change effort without acknowledging the inevitability of tension.

Tension can provide us with opportunities to stretch ourselves. Of course, it can also be uncomfortable, so we do not want to live with it all the time. In unhealthy environments, it can be a drain on energy. Likewise, a continual state of comfort may feel good, but it doesn't necessarily push us to grow. Flow occurs when we are stretched but skilled and energetic enough for the task at hand. Because my genius as a classroom educator is empowering students to create and lead, when the DIY speaker-fabric stage curtains came down for the nth time, I didn't collapse into a heap as I may have in a different situation. Instead, I had cultivated a community with students who also took ownership of that situation. My genius buoyed me when I would have otherwise sunk. We can find flow within our zones of genius because we feel enough purpose and meaning to be challenged by tension rather than exhausted by it.

Every organization has a multitude of archetypal combinations. It is our responsibility as individuals to know our own zones of genius, flow states, and energetic drains, and it is the responsibility of organizations to establish a culture that encourages individual awareness and engagement. Figure 7.4 shows each archetype's best context for flow, tension triggers, and coping tactics. These are not definitive; we are all individuals, and though archetypes give us a starting point, we must still each ask ourselves, "How can I operate within my zone of genius more often?" I hope this information will help you start to craft a change story founded on your genius.

We have unpacked how to manage our energy, create boundaries, and balance tension. We cultivate these skills for two reasons. First, we are human and have a finite amount of mental, physical, emotional, and psychological energy; and second, we have work to do. Contrary to problematic superhero teacher myths, though, we cannot do everything.

Figure 7.4

Tension and Flow

Archetype	Best Context for Flow	Tension Triggers	Coping Tactics
Diplomat	• Strong and authentic relationships with colleagues and ample time to engage with them • Collaborative experiences rooted in mutual respect and shared values • Overall school climate and culture rooted in a sense of fairness and integrity	• Petty gossip and cliques • Protocols or procedures not backed by clear explanations • Leaders who directly or indirectly create hostile work environments • Feeling communication blocks with others	• Approaching problem head on, especially when the conflict is external • Befriending "enemies" or "petty tyrants" who may be connected to the conflict • Reflecting upon the ways in which one could be projecting unfairly onto others
Champion	• A cause to fight for • Respected colleagues to fight alongside (preferably with an underdog to root for) • A sense of achievement toward a goal	• When the chosen cause is not valued by others or within the environment • Forced alignment with causes • Not feeling valued or validated • Bullying and prejudice	• Waiting 24 hours to engage any colleague or leader when tension is high • Seeking bridges with others and their causes rather than building barriers • Taking time to understand the reasons behind any impulse to engage in conflict
Creative	• Opportunities to understand issues from a global perspective • Thought partners who believe in the power of big ideas • Trusted leaders who validate one's ideas and insights • autonomy to try ideas freely as they come and dismiss them when new insights develop	• Forced alignment to status quo methods • When others take credit or ownership for one's original ideas, especially without gratitude or humility • Systemic bastardizing of original ideas for the sake of the status quo • Forced collaboration with those with limited imagination	• Creating boundaries and being direct with others when generating ideas or collaborating • Journaling as a consistent practice • Being present and focusing on humility

Archetype	Best Context for Flow	Tension Triggers	Coping Tactics
Storyteller	• Concrete collective agreements and objectives • Clear and direct communication • Transparency and honesty from everyone all the time • Opportunities to edit, improve, evaluate, and present ideas to others	• Sloppiness or a lack of pride in one's craft • Vague communication • Lack of opportunities to grow or improve oneself or one's work • Dishonesty or sneakiness	• Consistently reflecting on one's locus of control • Mental empathy-mapping from the perspectives of others when annoyed or frustrated • Engaging often in new experiences or opportunities to learn
Inventor	• Autonomy and freedom to experiment with new ideas and methods • Strong collaborators who indulge curious explorations or no collaborators at all • Environment free from distracting opinions, gossip, rumors, and minutiae	• Close-mindedness • A lack of freedom and autonomy • Clutter, distractions, wasted time, and meaningless tasks • Forced collaboration	• Cultivating many projects at once • Creating distraction-free work zones and times • Finding trusted thought partners and collaborators with whom to share new ideas
Sage	• Opportunities to advise or mentor others (ideally those in need of counsel or those in leadership positions) • A platform from which to educate others, tell stories, or offer perspective • Respect from one's peers and response to one's advice	• Unwillingness of others to learn • Silencing of any kind • Feelings of unworthiness • Rejection	• Cultivating opportunities to shine in and outside of work • Engaging in thinking exercises like "if/then" statements • Mentoring or advising others who need and are open to it

continued

Figure 7.4 (*continued*)
Tension and Flow

Archetype	Best Context for Flow	Tension Triggers	Coping Tactics
Investigator	• Opportunities to question concepts, ideas, and processes privately and openly • Data to inspire further research and from which to unearth new insights • An open and willing audience with which to share findings, insights, and ongoing questions	• Lack of curiosity or opportunities to be curious • Environments closed off to questioning • Operating from assumptions	• Establishing side hustles, passion projects, and outside courses relevant to personal interests simply for the sake of learning or doing • Building an online or in-person community separate from colleagues with whom to discuss ideas, ask questions, and share insights • Diagramming or webbing from multiple perspectives
Guardian	• Leaders who show their own vulnerability and their care as well as their compassion for others • A "people first" environment and collective guiding principles that amplify this perspective • Opportunities to care for and nurture the well-being of others	• Environments lacking in compassion for others • Overextending support without opportunities to recharge or expressions of appreciation • Verbal arguments or tense conflict	• Carving out consistent, intentional time for oneself • Writing down feelings (especially when in conflict with others) as they come, without self-editing • Learning direct communication strategies

It would be lovely to eliminate all the situations within the zones that drain our energy, but we can't always do that within systems that increasingly demand more and more from us. It would be helpful if we didn't create and sustain cultures that require the need for establishing boundaries in the first place, but our ongoing need to diligently protect our individual boundaries is more critical now than ever. Even though an ideal state would be for everyone to operate all the time within their zones of genius and for school to be a place of flow for students and adults alike, it is difficult to maintain this ideal in a system that depends on conformity rather than individuality. These are conflicts that require our immediate and ongoing response.

In the final chapters of this book, we will explore how to move the plots of our change stories toward a climactic conclusion that you, your colleagues, your students, and our systems desperately need and deserve. As we do, we'll hear the change stories of educators around the world who have taken ownership of their influence to move change forward for themselves, their colleagues, and their students. In the spirit of the discussion around educator well-being we have just had, let's begin with Renee, the Guardian.

Change Story Case Study: Renee, the Guardian

"Collaborating with other educators in my state, we launched a statewide mental health and wellness initiative for educators," says Renee. "The initiative began organically; we simply came together at the height of the pandemic to consider how we could support our colleagues across the region at such a tense time. We asked ourselves what we thought educators truly needed and we kept coming back to this idea of educator well-being and what that really meant practically.

"We began by creating a podcast, feeling that short, practical, expert-led conversations on various well-being topics would be useful for educators and contribute to a more well-rounded conversation about educator well-being overall. So many of us lamented how, in our own schools, educator well-being came down to meditation videos and inspirational messages in the teachers' lounge. We wanted to dig deeper into the systemic elements of the issue. The podcast led to the publication of an article, which led to a virtual listening session, which led to a series of professional learning workshops we hosted around the state.

"I feel like this work is needed and appreciated. My hope is that the more we talk openly about mental health and well-being, the more we can destigmatize these conversations for educators who can then keep more open minds when students struggle with mental health. We are seeing increased interest in our initiative; for example, we are building relationships with education organizations in our state that are interested in the conversation we are leading. Other educators have joined the cause over time and are creating new community projects in their districts connecting students with community resources for well-being. More educators are choosing to be vocal and advocate for their needs because they see us paving the way for destigmatizing well-being conversations. We have even seen student journalists build on ideas of educator well-being and offer additional insight on the topic through articles and interviews.

"I spent 12 years trying to impact change in education before leaving the classroom to work for government organizations and nonprofits where I hoped to impact change on what I felt was a bigger level. Ultimately, I returned to the classroom, where I felt I could see daily progress impacting students. Twenty-four years in, I still haven't given up hope for big changes. Now, my mission is about humanity and well-being, because I believe individuals are the most important aspect in need of our attention in education."

8

PLOT: MOVING YOUR STORY FORWARD

There are only so many plots in the world. It's how they unfold that makes them interesting.

—Lauren Beukes (2020)

For the past 26 years, Ken Strahan has been researching bushfires in Australia—including the "megafire" bushfires of 2019–20, known collectively as "Black Summer." Dr. Strahan's research primarily revolves around seven bushfire evacuation archetypes that, he says, display "universally recognizable, fundamentally human characteristics… from 457 householders who had recently experienced a bushfire." Strahan's seven archetypes "characterize the diverse attitudes and behavior of typical groupings of householders faced with making a protective decision during a bushfire" (Strahan et al., 2018).

Strahan shared with me stories of people he has met who represent these archetypes at some of the most vulnerable moments of their lives. One couple lived on a small plot of land when a bushfire approached a few years ago. They sought the advice of a neighbor a few doors down who was a volunteer firefighter. As the three of them were talking, they remembered another neighbor who lived alone, so they all went to see him together. Soon enough, the entire neighborhood had come together, listening to the radio, seeking information on the internet, and consulting one another. When the fire was close, they all convoyed together out of the hazardous zone. Strahan calls the couple that started this chain of neighborly support "community guided," meaning they look to the advice and guidance of their community before acting.

More recently, Dr. Strahan interviewed a man who built his own house out of steel on a protected plot of land surrounded by fire resistant plants. He had an independent water supply, so he could pump his own water should a bushfire approach. He had generators to maintain electricity in case of a power outage and sprinklers on the walls that would be triggered in case of fire. When a major bushfire approached his land, he chose to stay and defend rather than evacuate because he had prepared to do so. For hours, he and his neighbor fought the fire as it roiled through his home, including one ember that came through the toilet vent above the wooden ceiling into the kitchen below. Strahan calls this man an "experienced independent," meaning he is self-reliant, well prepared, and committed to defending his property.

Another of Strahan's archetypes is the "threat denier"—the person who refuses to believe a threat exists at all. One person who fits this archetype told Strahan that his home was 150 years old and had stood the test of time through countless bushfires, so there was no way a fire could threaten it. He and his wife were having lunch when a bushfire was about a kilometer away. Fire services had blocked the roads and issued an evacuation order, but he refused to budge. In the end, the fire just missed the edge of his house, by which time he had finally evacuated to safety.

Story after story, Strahan listened and learned from people who had unique perspectives, attitudes, and behaviors around bushfires. People who struggled to evacuate because of their dependents, such as elderly parents or even animals like horses or sheep. People who needed to evacuate but wanted to stick to their routines, such as the family who spent their Saturdays watching their children play cricket and refused to acknowledge the bushfire approaching their home. People who felt the emergency services should handle everything, believing that preparation for bushfires was not their responsibility at all. Strahan understands from conversations with people like these that leaving one's home as a bushfire approaches is not a straightforward endeavor. Transforming these interviews into a set of seven archetypes may seem like simplification, but it actually allows for the complexity of such moments to be factored into policy and practice.

One of Strahan's collaborators is John Gilbert, who leads a research and evaluation unit at the Country Fire Authority (CFA) in Victoria, Australia. When Strahan and Gilbert first began their collaboration, Gilbert says, "We weren't seeing the change we wanted to see, so we realized we needed to change our approach and tailor our work toward the particular needs of the people in our communities. We started to look at things differently and consider who these individuals are and what their real needs might be." As a result of their collaboration, CFA Victoria has redesigned community education programming to align more with an archetypal approach to bushfire safety. Emergency safety educators teach the community about the archetypes, help them see themselves and their neighbors within them, then design plans accordingly.

When it comes to such matters of life and death, an archetypal approach to changing behavior and systems works—and it can also work in education.

So far in this book, we have considered who we are, what drives us, and how those two things influence our responses to conflict. These three elements work together to propel the plot of our change stories. When we make our change stories human-driven, as John Gilbert and Ken Strahan are doing at CFA Victoria, we are more capable of developing character-driven plots when climatic events present themselves.

"Some plots are moved forward by external events and crises," says Professor Jules Hilbert in the movie *Stranger Than Fiction*. "Others are moved forward by the characters themselves. If I go through that door, the plot continues. The story of me through the door. If I stay here, the plot can't move forward; the story ends" (Doran & Helm, 2006). In the movie, the protagonist, Harold Crick, takes Hilbert's advice and tries to determine the plot of his life by either taking action to move it forward or taking none at all to see what happens. He realizes that he is the protagonist of a plot that has been railroading him, but he chooses to change the nature of his plot and become the driver of it as best he can. Some things remain outside of his control—as they do for all of us—but rather than blindly fall into events as they happen, he chooses to step beyond the bounds of the plot created for him and take ownership of his own path.

How do we take control of the plot of the story of our work lives? In the following chapters, we'll walk through how to plot the change stories you hope to write. We will also gain insight from case studies where others like you have moved their own stories forward by leaning into their strengths and integrating some of the tools we will unpack in the pages that follow.

Character-Driven Stories Begin with You

To create a character-driven change story that is founded on the needs and desires of actual humans, you must first start with yourself. This can feel counterintuitive in a mission-driven, service-oriented profession, but you will not maintain the strength, energy, drive, persistence, and resilience needed to see your story through unless you're at the heart of it. So how do we build a change story rooted with ourselves? We've already begun, actually. Let's review.

Are You Giving Yourself an Opportunity to Apply Your Zone of Genius?

Where do your talents and abilities shine beyond those of others? Where do you find yourself most often in a state of flow? These are important reminders as you decide what change to seek for yourself and the systems around you. Too often, we offer our energy to people and situations that may not best serve our ability to shine or grow. When opportunities for change arise or when you're hoping to create them for yourself, consider first how to apply your genius to the situation. If your genius is coaching others, begin there. If it's data analysis, begin there. Whatever it may be, pause to ask yourself before any change endeavor: "Am I giving myself the best chance to prove my genius in this situation?" If the answer is no, renegotiate the situation to better suit your strengths.

What Drives You?

The eight change archetypes discussed in this book are driven by four main motivations: to connect, to generate, to advocate, and to influence. What we want most determines the choices we make, and the choices we make determine the conflicts in which we find ourselves. If a Diplomat who is driven to connect inadvertently creates a situation in which they do not have collaborators or a network of thought partners they respect and enjoy working with, they will lose steam no matter how urgent or purposeful the work. Simply pausing to ask yourself if an opportunity to create change presented to you actually motivates you or not can prevent you from taking a wrong turn before the journey even begins. If the driving force that motivates you will not be satisfied, the opportunity is not for you. Choosing to operate from your core drive empowers you to move forward with opportunities that motivate you from the inside out. You'll save yourself a lot of heartache by committing to this rule.

How Do You Lead and Create Change?

Because archetypes find themselves coming back to the same leadership patterns again and again, you might remind yourself of these patterns as you move your plot forward. A Champion should not embark upon a journey without a cause they believe in, nor would a Storyteller embrace a vague, wishy-washy opportunity to lead just because it is there. Remembering your essence as a leader and change agent can serve as a touchstone throughout your change journey. Pause now and remind yourself of your archetype's leadership and change patterns, and keep these patterns front and center when opportunities present themselves.

How Do You Want to Contribute?

Before embarking on a change story, you must ask yourself what your contribution to others and to the system will be. For example, let's say you're asked to help roll out a new program at your school. Maybe you're fine with the new program as is and already have the systems in place in your classroom to implement it effectively, so you decide not to contribute much more than by using the program with your students as requested by leadership. In that case, the subplot ends and you can save your energy for another endeavor.

However, let's say you are already implementing a similar program of your own design and seeing results with your students, so you might decide to contribute in a different way. Maybe you are a Guardian with a strong team of trusted colleagues and advisors who encourage you to offer your insights to the leadership team before rolling out the new program. Maybe you are an Inventor and want to compare the results of your program with the new one, so you propose to pilot the new program in your classroom first and present your findings to the leadership team before implementing the program schoolwide. Maybe you are an Investigator who wants to understand what the research says about the new program and may even decide to advocate against its implementation if there's not enough evidence to support its efficacy. Whatever contribution you decide to make to this change effort, you can place yourself into the story in a way that suits your needs and desires.

What Do You Want to Gain?

You deserve to gain something from the energy you expend and expertise you share. That gain may be financial, such as requesting extra pay for the time you give to a committee, for example, but benefits come in many shapes and sizes and may not even be explicitly stated. You may decide to contribute to a change effort because you want to learn a new skill or gain insight into the workings of some facet of your organization you didn't understand before. You may desire a connection with a new network or collaboration with a new colleague. Maybe your time and energy will lead to new opportunities down the road. Giving more than we receive contributes to burnout, so being intentional about what we hope to gain when we offer our time and energy is not selfishness but self-preservation. If we are motivated to contribute to any change effort, then we should expect to gain something from it as well.

Change Story Case Study: Heidi, the Inventor

"I am an Inventor," says Heidi. "For many years, I had to put my science curriculum together piecemeal. As a young teacher, I was the only science teacher in my building, which afforded me the ability to build inventive lessons that, for the most part, captured students' attention. I joined the curriculum teams early on and was excited to be a part of helping vet the potential next material set.

"Unfortunately, those chosen materials never really seemed to fit with my hopes for my science students. After many frustrating meetings, subpar in-services, and very expensive curriculum, I decided to seek out professional learning opportunities for myself and immediately began embedding the lessons and resources from training sessions into my course. Once, I drove myself 900 miles to attend a mapping training in southern California. For the first time in my career, I felt like I was with my people—geographers and scientists. When I returned, I shared what I had learned with students and staff. Students flourished; because who *wouldn't* want to do *real* science and geography as opposed to cracking open a dust-covered, 500-page textbook?

"Then came a chance to be a 'Geo-Inquiry ambassador' for National Geographic. I trekked across the country, made friends for life, and left invigorated to share the resources. It was a slow implementation with hesitant and tired peer teachers, but I persisted in my goal of bringing quality professional development opportunities to rural Colorado.

"The next two years had me feeling like Katniss Everdeen from *The Hunger Games,* trying to push for more innovative lessons within my school and district. I decided to start an afterschool STEM professional development course for teachers in my building. Each month, the educators would learn new skills and subjects to use with their students. Sometimes I taught the lessons, and sometimes my students would teach the educators.

"Slowly, educators started asking me to teach professional development, because what our poor and broken system offered for educators was not cutting it. Teachers felt helpless, worn out, and underpaid. My focus then morphed to ensure that my peers, and more importantly their students, felt a sense of hope. I knew they deserved the best! Through various entities, I began writing grants to bring better professional learning to my staff through weekend institutes that garnered local news coverage. When area teachers started asking for programming, I spent afternoons, evenings and many weekends trying to bring empowering learning to a system saturated with overwhelmed leadership and exhausted teachers in one of the lowest-funded areas of the country.

"My last year in the classroom, I helped seven teachers earn their National Geographic Educator certifications and asked to be a part of national teacher teams with the National Geographic Teacher Advisory Council and 100Kin10. What I learned from all these experiences is how important it is to feel OK with finding those who bring joy to teaching— those I refer to as 'jumpers' as opposed to stumpers and dumpers who drain your energy. Little did I know that all this would lead me to serve teachers not only from within my school or district but also as a teacher trainer with my own office, at my local makerspace, and under my own business name. The company name, STEM is My Future, is perfectly aligned to my vision and mission for those I teach. Like Mahatma Gandhi once said, 'You must be the change you wish to see in the world,' and for me that comes with a smidge of that inventive Katniss Everdeen reminding me of who I am and what I am capable of doing."

✳ ✳ ✳

When the fire rolls over the hill toward us, our particular character determines how we will respond and what actions we will take. There is never one monolithic story propelling a community or organization; rather, there are many interwoven plots driven by each person who plays a role. Centering your own needs, strengths, and desires during times of change can provide you personally with a stronger sense of control over your own destiny. Organizations centered around the actual human beings who comprise it will always fare better when change comes from the outside—and they will be better positioned to lead change from within.

9

SETTING: POSITIONING YOURSELF WITHIN YOUR STORY

So much of design is context.

—Steve Madden (Holson, 2013)

Once you are clear about your role as a character within any change story, you can start to grasp the setting, scene, and actions the story requires. For example, a connection-driven Diplomat who thrives when building a network may feel confined in an isolated situation. The context of our work determines how we choose to lead change just as the setting of a novel determines how a character advances the story. We each have the ability to contribute and gain according to our own desires, but there are still factors beyond our control—or even our knowledge. Although you may be required to attend professional development for a certain amount of time each year, you may not have any knowledge of or influence over the bill passed in state legislation that required those hours—or access to the vendors who approach the purchasing department at your district office to offer professional development services or products. This doesn't mean that you *can't* know or influence these things. In fact, if that is where your motivation and intended contributions lie, then step beyond outdated bounds into those situations if you want. Whatever path you decide to take, it can be helpful to grasp the larger setting within which your story is taking place. Knowledge, after all, is power.

Leverage Points

Leverage points are the places within any organization or system where opportunity lies to achieve a result. Leverage points exist at both the macro and micro levels of education. The micro level includes the local environment and context surrounding young people, educators, and schools. The macro level includes the broader education industry, such as organizations, legislation, policy, and systems. Knowing where these levers are allows us to pull them when and how we choose.

Leverage Points from the Macro Perspective

Founding. Education is an industry. From my personal experience, this statement can make educators feel a little uncomfortable, myself included. It's true nonetheless. Let's imagine your school district adopts "Reading Program ABC." Reading Program ABC was created by an organization, possibly for-profit or nonprofit, that may or may not have done adequate research before, during, or after its implementation. In addition, it may or may not have consulted with a classroom educator during its creation or implementation. Having sat around the table when educational products and services were being developed at the early stages of a company's founding, I can attest that many of these products and programs are founded without adequate educator insight, then land in classrooms where educators are expected to put them to use with students. Some I would have happily put to use as a classroom educator, and others I would have loathed to consider.

I also do not believe, by the way, that these companies or the products they create are part of an evil conspiracy to destroy the lives of educators and students. Having met many education organization founders and leaders with good intentions for creating change within education—just like many educators I know—I am simply offering here the knowledge of their existence. While there are of course educators who found organizations—nonprofit and for-profit alike—entering this leverage point may also look like serving as an advisor for founders who do not have backgrounds in education or collaborate with programs that support education startups or nonprofits, such as accelerators or fellowships.

The opportunity is certainly there for those change agents who want to insert themselves into this particular setting of the larger story.

Funding. This is another tricky leverage point that may cause some discomfort, but understanding it can be empowering. Organizations need funding to operate and scale. They get this funding most often from investors or grantmakers. Alternatively, they could charge school districts or individuals for their products or services. Many integrate some combination of both. Like it or not, this is a leverage point within the macro system of education. Who gets funding determines which products and programs are competitive enough to land an account as a vendor with a district or gain access to an educator's email to promote their products. The decision-makers at the table when these dollars are allocated have hold of a specific lever. They can move the story one way or another. For example, Reading Program ABC, which districts may have spent millions of dollars purchasing, could make a significant difference in a student's particular reading outcomes or how much (and whether) they love reading at all.

I know some educators who want to sit at the tables where these decisions are made—and I do know educators who have become venture capitalists at major education investment groups or program officers at grantmaking organizations and therefore have the opportunity to create change based on their investment choices for products and programs. I also know educators who serve on committees or advisory boards to pull the levers at this point in the system. I know educators who have become organizers within their unions or other organizations to take on issues such as educational funding in these capacities and create change in that way. Even educators whose futures don't involve venture capital or legislation can still benefit by understanding the role of funding within the educational ecosystem. At some point an idea you develop may need funding, so knowing how to approach those conversations as they arise can benefit the change story you're writing.

Research and Pilots. When the organization or founder has enough funding to have developed a functional version of its product or program to share with others, they, like many, may seek opportunities to better understand how effective it is and what tweaks the product needs in order to make it more enticing for schools. Sometimes, this leverage point occurs before a product, program, or initiative is founded, such as if an academic institution or research group collaborates with a founder to develop a research-based product or program. Other times, this leverage point occurs after a product already exists and the organization wants to try it out in the field. Sometimes it is a combination of both. Whatever the case, this leverage point can be an empowering and valuable place within the system to create change.

Let's imagine that a district decides not to sign a longstanding contract with Reading Program ABC but agrees to participate in a pilot project with a small cohort of schools instead. A situation where only a few people once held the levers suddenly becomes a collaborative effort where many people have a voice—including researchers, the vendor, district and school leaders, educators, and students. These individuals have the opportunity to better understand the research underlying Reading Program ABC, learn from its implementation, and shift the product or process accordingly. Investigators, Creatives, and Inventors could especially thrive at this leverage point, but any of the archetypes could find a way to lead change here. My advice to educators who want to enter the story at this leverage point is to request transparency and agency of voice; doing so will give you more opportunities to lead real change, rather than only becoming a member of a focus group sitting behind a one-way mirror that doesn't really integrate your genius.

Products, Programs, and Purchases. Sometimes companies or organizations will skip the research or pilot phase altogether and begin to market their product or services, or the research has been done and the results are part of their marketing plan. Now we have a product, program, or service—essentially any tool, device, platform, content, or workshop that classroom educators will be expected to implement with students. Before I understood this macro perspective, I felt powerless at this leverage point. The textbooks have too often already been purchased, the software already downloaded, or the professional learning already underway before educators ever enter the scene, let alone have an opportunity to lead change.

Nevertheless, this is actually an incredibly powerful point of leverage for educators, even if it may not feel that way. What I know is that you, dear educator, are the crown jewel of any education product or program's success. If you find that your students hate the textbook, little by little, you will stop using it. If you find that the software is clunky and inefficient, you will go to great lengths to avoid it. If the professional learning workshop is a waste of your time, you'll walk out the door and keep doing you without it. Founders know this. Funders know this. Vendors, researchers, and leaders know this. While they may sign the dotted line without your input or insight, they know in their heart of hearts that they need you to love and buy into the product or program or you will stop using it. The contract will dry up and a new trendy product or program will beckon the dollars another way. Occasionally, an organization will have so much funding to support it that this is less of a problem than it is for other organizations, but more often than not, they cannot maintain the long game without you.

So if you absolutely love a product or program, you can advocate for it, and I have seen opportunities come to many educators as a result of this leverage point. I know educators who work for some of these companies to coach others or serve as ambassadors or contributors because they believe in the product or service and choose to lead the change they want to see. In the same vein, if you do not love a product or service and want to change the narrative around how it is used in your organization, there are ways to do that as well.

When I taught middle school, I was commanded from on high to use required textbooks purchased from a large publisher that were meant to "raise student reading scores" by simply reading from beginning to end and completing the accompanying scripted curriculum. Those were not the results I saw in my classroom from that particular product, so I chose not to use it. I started slowly by using other texts here and there. Then I started building lessons and projects around texts that engaged my students so much that my school leadership appreciated the results I was getting. Ultimately, I had to have a tête-à-tête with a district leader over my refusal to use the textbooks, which I did with as much professionalism as I could muster. She eventually decided to leave me alone because I was getting results my way, and I think she was tired of arguing with me. It wasn't easy, but I do believe that holding my ground about the efficacy of this product led to a better learning culture for myself, my colleagues who followed my lead, and most importantly, my students. The contract ran out with that particular vendor for that particular product, and the district did not renew it. This was a leverage point within a change story that I as a Creative whose zone of genius is rooted in student agency wanted to pull, which is why I had the stamina to see it through even at its most challenging.

Similarly, purchases are the commitment point at which these products, programs, or initiatives are acquired. Again, this may seem like a done deal by the time educators can enter the story, but it is another leverage point where educators can lead change if they decide to do so. In my own experience, quite a bit of purchasing actually happens at a more micro level than many founders and funders might imagine. The English department chair at a given school could have been the final decision-maker when Reading Program ABC was purchased, just as PLC leaders could have influence over the purchase of a professional learning program or data analysis software the entire faculty will be required to implement. When leaders in charge of budgets at the school or district level want to purchase a product or service, they often ask for input from educators. We will discuss leverage points from a micro perspective in a moment, but when and how money is spent can be a leverage point for educators who want to assert influence in this way.

Unfortunately, from my perspective, purchasing and funding at the macro level tend to be the spaces where fewer classroom educators have opportunities to influence change. Although I don't hope for it to stay that way. Education budgets are often set through legislation, then through high-level state and district leadership. There are plenty of educators who can and do involve themselves in the legislative process pertaining to educational budgets, but still more do not. However, where dollars are, opportunity looms. For those change archetypes with budgetary genius, choosing to pull the purchasing lever is certainly an opportunity to affect much-needed change in the education ecosystem.

Dissemination. Once the products and programs are purchased, the commitment is made, and thus begins the need to develop a plan for communication and buy-in. Diplomats, Storytellers, Sages, and Champions may especially thrive in this space if they have the energy to enter the story here, but many of the change archetypes can find this a worthy leverage point if they so choose. When the reading program has been purchased, the new approach to science instruction embraced, or the new civics curriculum adopted, a plan will need to be developed and executed as to how educators will put it to use. From my experience, this is not a quick process and requires time, energy, and leadership.

The dissemination phase is where I see many educators step into change leadership opportunities. In fact, I stepped into an opportunity to serve as an instructional coach when a new initiative had been adopted at the district level and schools were trying to figure out how to disseminate the concepts to educators in classrooms. The dissemination phase of any initiative often requires classroom educator experience because it is a bridge-building space. Ideally, classroom educators will have been part of any initiative from inception to implementation, but if you find yourself searching for a place to pull a lever, I would be willing to bet there are dissemination efforts within the system around you that need you right now. If you have an idea for a solution to a problem facing you, your colleagues, or your students, then aligning your idea with initiatives already in place that are in the process of being designed, planned, and messaged at your school, district, state, or even a national level, could provide a great opportunity to lead change.

Implementation. Once the wheels are in motion after a product, program, service, or initiative has been adopted and communicated to relevant stakeholders, implementation will inevitably land squarely on the shoulders of classroom educators. Implementation is the leverage point most accessible to educators in schools because it primarily takes place at the micro level. It is the phase at which every educator in the district has been trained and school leaders have been given guidance around expectations for rolling out the product or program. During implementation, Reading Program ABC will be scheduled into the school day, the software downloaded onto every computer, and the textbooks delivered to every classroom. Implementation is the nitty-gritty, hands-on space where educators influence the what, when, why, and how of any initiative.

It is also the space that can be the heaviest burden if the product or program has not been designed with educators and students in mind. This is unfortunately when educators may discover that students actually hate Reading Program ABC, which therefore causes them to shut down or disengage; or the data software that was supposed to create more efficiency actually does the opposite; or the textbooks are lacking and educators actually have to do more work to supplement them than originally imagined. If the product or program is helpful and supportive of educator efforts, then the implementation phase can be a great opportunity to shine.

At this leverage point, an educator's archetype can be more obvious than ever before. The district adopted a new project-based learning initiative? Diplomats will network for new ideas, Guardians will build coalitions of support, Champions will apply it to heartful causes that engage students more than ever, Investigators will analyze the impacts of its effectiveness in the classroom, Creatives will generate ideas that inspire their colleagues, Inventors will tweak the process, Storytellers will target the practicalities, and Sages will coach others who flail when challenges arise. The implementation lever is ready and waiting for every educator to pull at any given time within the education ecosystem and offers a micro lens we can break down even further for a closer look at other leverage points available to educators.

Change Story Case Study: NyRee, the Champion

"Hip-hop is just something that I always loved," says NyRee. "Listening to music and reading lyrics over and over is how I taught myself to read as a child when some of my teachers only saw me as a struggling Black girl. Once I led my own classroom, I vowed to teach toward the interests of my students. I wanted to apply my experiences and strengths as an engaging educator to let my students take the lead. Students would come into my classroom singing songs that I also listened to, and suddenly there was an instant connection with them.

"Because of my love of hip-hop, my principal asked me to teach a special area class on writing. Leaning into my love of hip-hop and knowing what I knew about what my students loved, too, I redesigned my classroom to look like a hip-hop video. I had a red carpet and graffiti on the walls. When they came into the classroom, we played with language and rhythm and explored the lyrics of songs we loved.

"When the school had a program about its namesake, we were tasked with writing and performing a rap about Phyllis Wheatley. At that point, one student said, 'I have a name for us: Young Prodigies.' Naming ourselves and creating our own hip-hop community was the catalyst for everything to come—performing in our community and continuing our writing during summer camps.

"The Young Prodigies have always been inspired by what's going on in the world. After a while, they started asking their own questions and exploring them as inspiration for their songs. For example, they would ask 'Why do we only learn about Black history during Black History Month?' or 'Why do we always start our history with slavery when our history didn't actually start with slavery?' They would add things like, 'Sometimes when the teachers start talking about slavery, the white kids in the classroom look at us, the Black students, and it's embarrassing.'

"I couldn't believe all these comments were coming from young people. What began as an approach to teaching in my own classroom has blossomed into a nonprofit my husband and I have cofounded called Hip-Hop into Learning. Over time, we have built this beautiful community together where the students explore and write about topics in response to their own questions about their lived experiences, their environment, and current events they care about.

"Not only do the Young Prodigies write about these issues, but they have collaborated with legislators to create policy, presented to leaders at state and national organizations, and performed their words on national stages. We have taken what could have been a ceiling limited to a single classroom and expanded it to an entire communitywide effort.

"My cause is to create experiences for students to lead change, and that is what we do in our programs. And I have learned through it all that I don't wait on the right situation to make me happy. I do the work of serving the students, and that ideal pulls me forward."

Leverage Points from the Micro Perspective

Leverage points at the micro level are those that change our immediate environment. Of course, much of the change that occurs locally ends up influencing the larger education ecosystem. An initiative created by a handful of educators in a single school can expand far beyond that school or district.

Any change archetype can enter any leverage point and find ways to align their strengths with worthy initiatives. Taking the time to consider the leverage points available at the micro level puts change leaders in a position to lead change stories on their own terms and with their own ideas and insights.

Strategy. Let's imagine that a new trend is sweeping the education world—Initiative XYZ. You know that your genius and archetypal fingerprint align well with Initiative XYZ, and you are excited to offer your energy to the effort.

Entering the leverage point of strategy may look like creating a committee that collaborates closely with other leaders to consider all the ins and outs of how Initiative XYZ might apply to your environment. If you think you might thrive at the strategic leverage point, consider how you might play a more strategic role in leading change around you. If you are a Guardian who is well respected and trusted among the staff, offer strategic insights about the feelings and behaviors of your colleagues to your leaders. If you are an Investigator who loves strategic planning with an evidence-based approach that you feel would benefit a change story you want to lead, offer your energy to a committee or leader who is beginning the planning process of an initiative you care about. Whatever your archetype, if you have a particular genius for understanding the big picture while also possessing strong tactical skills, the strategy leverage point of any effort could be a powerful place to lead the change you want to see.

Communication. This is one of the most critical leverage points, because messaging is everything when it comes to rallying support for a cause. We have all likely experienced a change effort that went south because it was misunderstood or there was a lack of transparency. When Initiative XYZ is adopted and the strategic planning is in motion, communication will be necessary to explain why the initiative matters and how the change will improve people's work.

At the school level, this often looks like conversations or announcements through faculty meetings, PLCs, team meetings, workshops, emails, and newsletters. However, there are more informal elements of communication that can also make or break any change effort: copyroom chit-chat, group happy hours and text threads, hallway small talk. For the innovative Diplomat, communication leverage points are golden opportunities to build communities that care about a specific change and want to see it through. The savvy Storyteller—who perceives early on how an initiative will be received before those in power do—can influence change by offering their communication genius to the cause.

Whether an initiative is trickling into classrooms from a broader trend or rising from more grassroots efforts, sharing the hopes and plans for achieving desired outcomes will fall on the shoulders of someone somewhere—and that someone will have quite a bit of power when it does.

Support. Let's say Initiative XYZ has a technical element that is difficult to understand or needs templates for applying the effort locally. People always require support when change is initiated, and those who offer it have leverage and influence. If you're a logical, far-sighted Inventor who loves to experiment first and plan later, sharing what you learn along the way provides you with an opportunity to influence how others apply change efforts to their contexts. If you're a loveable Champion who has amassed a following and cares deeply about the change at hand, you have invaluable leverage when you offer guidance to others.

Leaders who offer support to others during times of change serve as translators, guides, and stewards throughout the process, influencing how their colleagues perceive and apply the initiative to their contexts. Putting your strengths to use at the support point of any change effort will place you in the position of one on whom others rely—and to whom they listen.

Design. Whatever its originators may say, Initiative XYZ will never be a hand-me-down, out-of-the-box solution to whatever problem it hopes to solve. Schools and classrooms consist of human beings who are nuanced and messy and do not always abide by the rules set by founders or organizations who can misunderstand how people work. The initiative may still offer some value to educators and their students, but it may need a redesign that suits specific local needs—or maybe the initiative gives an energized Creative who wants to try something new a fresh idea.

The design point within any effort is a ripe opportunity to lead change, because inevitably what works in one context may not work in another. New ideas and approaches will always be needed not only at the beginning of a change story but also throughout it. Anyone with vision, imagination, and love for the blank page could thrive as a leader at this leverage point.

Culture. This leverage point requires leaders who care first and foremost about the people at the center of change. Guardians may naturally find themselves leveraging this point of any change story whether they sign up for the effort or not, but any archetype with a genius for listening and responding to the needs of others can find opportunities in this space.

Let's say educators find Initiative XYZ controversial or frustrating. Someone will need to step up at this point to empathize with those frustrations, offer perspective, or speak on behalf of those who are frustrated. I have seen change initiatives go south quickly when leaders start to command or lecture at this point rather than listen and adjust. Entering into any change initiative with a clear plan for navigating the cultural implications that arise is helpful for seeing it through to the impact it is meant to achieve. If you have a vision regarding this leverage point, you could be holding a highly influential golden ticket.

Facilitation. The word *facilitate* means "to make something easier." People who want to leverage the point of facilitation will be primarily focused on simplifying initiatives so others can better understand and execute them. If Initiative XYZ is complex, educators will need coaching from someone who both understands how to implement change and cares about them as people. Sages thrive in this space as natural mentors, but anyone with a genius for simplifying abstract concepts into concrete steps could create opportunities at the leverage point of facilitation.

Analysis. At some point, everyone will want to know if Initiative XYZ is working. Ideally, analyzing the impact of a change effort will be built into the process of implementing it, but unfortunately, this isn't always the case. However, those with a genius for analysis could find this leverage point an ideal place to lead change. Asking questions about the efficacy of any initiative is a worthy and powerful endeavor. Time, money, energy, and outcomes are all too often squandered toward efforts that do not actually get results. Being the person who can redirect the path based on reality rather than assumptions could save everyone a lot of heartache. Investigators make obvious candidates for leading change from this leverage point, but anyone with a knack for paying attention might win favor as an analyst.

✳ ✳ ✳

In Australia, bushfire policies and practices form an expansive ecosystem that includes politicians, researchers, emergency service providers, community leaders, educators, and so on. Nevertheless, Ken Strahan and John Gilbert have each found their leverage points within that system and have joined forces to create a new approach that is already leading to sweeping change. As educators who want to do the same within the education system, taking the time to consider the leverage points available to us at every level broadens the setting of our change stories and our perspective of our roles within it. There is a place for everyone to drive the plot and lead a change story. Before we approach the setting from the perspective of *influence,* pause here to consider what leverage points feel most approachable to you and what ideas you may have about leveraging them.

Change Story Case Study: Courtney, the Investigator

"Early in my career, I found myself as the sole teacher in my department, which was very isolating," says Courtney. "I realized that my students and I were struggling to find joy in art. I was incredibly burned out from having students depend so heavily on me to check over every single line they drew, every color they mixed. They were completely unable to work independently, and I discovered that I had set myself up to be way too important in my own classroom.

"I became curious about methods for shifting my approach to arts education, so I dove into research to learn new strategies for structuring my classroom. I allowed myself the freedom to try new things and be okay with failing. I completely revamped my approach to allow for more student-directed learning. Some of the things I did were major flops; freshmen couldn't seem to handle the amount of choice I gave them. But there were also some big successes.

"Because of the burnout I have experienced and witnessed among my colleagues, I have recently devoted a lot of time and energy to our school's culture and climate committee. I enjoy trying to investigate ways to recognize the good that is happening in our school community, and I try to lead by example in my own classroom. As with many others, the pandemic has caused me to question my career, my purpose, and what I want to give my energy to. I've found myself increasingly frustrated with some of the challenges unique to my own school as well as the general challenges that every educator is experiencing right now.

"Through this frustration came my inspiration to advocate for change and resolution. I began pouring myself into culture and climate work. Ultimately, I and one of the other committee members became the *de facto* culture and climate voices for the entire school. We focused on the staff experience first and are now pivoting to improving the student experience. Some of the issues I ran into were larger systemic problems—things that I couldn't do much about in the short term. For example, I couldn't change what time school starts in the morning, but I could allow my students to feel more engaged and collaborative by consistently asking for their input and advocating for their voice. At one point, I would tell my coworkers that my students were my PLC, and I was very intentional about using similar descriptions to the students directly. I'd say, 'I don't have a teacher team, so you guys are my team.'

"Together, we would get curious and creative to create change, and now I want to keep moving that change outward. I've found that I'm very personally fulfilled by listening, learning, and ultimately trying to provide creative solutions to the issue of low morale. This work has inspired me to seek out a job at the district level as a resource for culture and climate work at multiple schools."

Influence

Influence is often confused with power and authority. A principal, for example, is in a position of authority with certain direct powers over their staff. Hierarchical power places a person in a position to directly change a particular situation according to the level of their authority. Ideally, this power and authority has checks and balances: policies and practices that prevent tyranny. Too often, educators feel powerless because we have been trained to think of power in this way simply because of the structures in place within the system in which we work.

Influence is an altogether different kind of power. Influence is indirect and often invisible. A mentor does not have power over a mentee, but they do have influence. A colleague does not have power over a peer, but they may have influence. A student may not have power over their teacher, but they do have influence.

Having influence and *being influential* are also two very different things. You have influence across leverage points right now, but becoming intentionally influential within any of those spaces is another matter. Taking advantage of the leverage you have at both the macro and micro levels requires owning your influence and using it to lead the change you hope to see. It is a process that begins by recognizing your stakeholders and your sponsors for any change story you hope to write.

Stakeholders and Sponsors

Stakeholders are those who have something at stake when change occurs. Once an initiative is adopted, administrators, educators, students, families, and certain members of the community at large become stakeholders. When you decide to lead a change story—you want to start a new program, design a new approach, advocate for a specific cause, test a new idea, or whatever path to change you plan to take—you will be far more influential as a change leader if you build it from inception with your stakeholders in mind.

If a Champion who is passionate about equity and justice wants to develop a program that reinvigorates the civics curriculum in their district, their stakeholders would include the learners, educators, families, curriculum designers, community, administrators, and, very likely, policymakers. Pausing to understand how each of these groups might react to the change they want to lead within their environment suggests to the Champion what actions to take.

This does not mean pandering or trying to please everyone. That, as we all know, is impossible. Yet I have seen too many change efforts die before they even begin because the needs of certain stakeholders weren't properly considered. If students hate the reading program or their reading engagement sinks when forced to participate, the program won't last very long as is. If you have only consulted educators in your specific school, the statewide educator well-being project you want to implement may not resonate with educators in another region.

Stakeholder groups will also vary according to context. The community groups with a stake in school reading programs will differ from the community groups with a stake in civics curricula. Creating an action plan that considers all your stakeholders will help you be more influential and provide the foresight you'll need to find supporting characters for your change story.

By contrast, sponsors are people, sometimes in positions of authority, who will advocate for you and your ideas. In my experience, cultivating sponsors for any change effort is crucial to moving the work forward. Sponsors are those you trust and who trust you in return—those who can vouch for your strengths. They can also be people you don't know yet. The Champion who wants to reinvigorate the civics curricula may already have a sponsor in their school principal who believes in their idea, but the Champion can also look to other stakeholder groups for sponsors. If they want to take action at the district level, for example, they should find a sponsor in the relevant department who can help them develop and advocate for the change; if they want to take action at the community level, they should find community leaders whose work aligns to their vision and goals. Sponsors are partners who care about the same issues and have the same goals as you but who have some type of influence you may not have yet and can use it on your behalf.

You may feel nervous about cultivating relationships with stakeholders or sponsors, as doing so bucks the hierarchy or may seem transactional. However, there are ways to cultivate sponsors and build coalitions of stakeholders without feeling icky about it. The most important thing is to keep your purpose front and center. If you do this but others still find ways to criticize you when you push beyond the social norms of a hierarchical system that *needs* you to push on it, do your very best to silence those voices. Manage your energy, set boundaries, and keep moving.

Change Story Case Study: Jonathon, the Creative

"As the inaugural class of Hawai'i State Teacher Fellows," says Jonathon, "we were encouraged to reach out to our local education leaders to see if they would want us to share our work and learning with local area principals. I reached out to my local leader, and he asked me to present to him and all the principals on Kaua'i at one of their monthly meetings.

"Usually, these meetings are driven by the local leaders, but I was there to share some of what we had been learning through the fellowship, specifically through the disaggregation of data we had collected through teacher surveys and focus groups around the state. The hope was that local education leaders would use the data to drive local changes. As teacher fellows, we had no ability to demand any changes even if we had ideas spurred by what we had learned. We could just share our learning, our voices, and the voices of teachers across the state and hope that other leaders would find a way to use what we had shared.

"After this particular meeting, someone said how great it was to work with and learn from a teacher, which piqued my interest. My immediate follow-up question: 'How often do teachers join you here at these meetings?' The answer should not have shocked me, but it did: never. This was the first time that any of them could remember.

"I have rarely had a problem reaching out to or communicating with the traditional 'people in charge' as if I were their equal. I recognize the privilege in this attitude. My time in the fellowship helped me make even more direct connections to leaders across the state. These connections, and my confidence in my point of view as a lifelong community member and educator, gave me direct ways to share my ideas with people who might make changes. But standing in front of those principals at that meeting, their answer 'never' still echoing in my head, it occurred to me that all teachers should feel able to communicate and work with the leaders across the systems. Teachers, students, principals, and schools would all benefit if we more often worked with each other as equal partners while learning and educating.

"And so, after that principals meeting, when I was told I was the first teacher to join them, an idea occurred to me that seemed simple: teachers should be at these meetings regularly. I shared my idea with the director of the fellowship at the time, mostly to share with her my surprise that teachers were never part of these meetings. Her response was, 'What are you going to do about it?' My silence prompted her to tell me to write up a proposal with measurable goals and a detailed calendar. So I did. She then told me to share it with my local leader. I subsequently found myself creating a local fellowship of teachers to represent each school on the island, at all levels, to work with the local leaders.

"I ended up creating a yearlong program that blended professional learning for the selected teachers with partner work with the principals. We focused on developing our voices as experts and advocates. We focused on writing, on leading other teachers, and on how to include students in district-level education decisions. We also focused on learning how to work with other people effectively, knowing that many of the principals were not keen on having us around too much.

"The work bloomed from a one-year pilot project to a full-fledged fellowship, and suddenly I found myself learning how to lead the program while learning. I ran the fellowship for three years. The teachers who were involved all grew immensely. Some of them found the courage to make a move to complex or state-level leadership positions. Some found the confidence to write and publish their writing even beyond the requirements of the fellowship. Some convinced their principals to make permanent changes to their school-level leadership structures, such as by permanently including students at school-level leadership meetings.

"I'm proud of my work designing and leading the Kaua'i Teacher Fellowship, as we came to call it. I am also proud of the teachers who joined the work with me and how each of them grew and then positively impacted their colleagues and students at their own campuses. In building this program, we helped to normalize the inclusion of teachers and students in complex-level meetings. If that is the only lasting result, that is a win, but the work of designing and leading the fellowship has changed me. The way the principals meetings had been set up and run for decades was accepted as normal but really was a wall keeping voices out. I am now committed to removing as many unfair barriers as possible for students and for teachers."

Taking Action

Once you have taken the time to understand your stakeholders and cultivate a handful of sponsors who want to advocate for you, you can create an action plan. I have learned that the best approach to planning actions is to simultaneously plan immediate steps as well as the long-term vision—what I call *right-now* and *big-picture* actions.

Right-now actions are steps we can take today, tomorrow, next week, or within the next few weeks to move toward the change we want to see. These actions can serve as critical motivators, especially when the change we seek feels daunting. A Sage who wants to develop a collaborative mentoring program across the entire state can start *right now* by drafting a proposal. A Storyteller who wants to write an opinion piece for a national publication can start *right now* by outlining their ideas. Right-now actions get us moving toward our goal and lead us from today to the future we hope to create.

Big-picture actions are more complex and require support from others or an extensive time commitment. The Sage's statewide mentoring program will eventually require robust actions like establishing a community of committed educators to pilot the plan, buy-in from state leaders, and support systems for both mentors and mentees. The Storyteller will need to determine where they hope to publish and spend time learning about their audiences and editorial requirements, not to mention the time investment of writing and editing drafts.

Knowing what actions will be required of us down the line can help us take right-now actions that make big-picture actions easier to accomplish. Building from one end to the other can support your efforts to work toward your vision for change and provide you with your own custom action roadmap to plot the story from scene to scene. Use the following questions to guide you through some initial ideas for the actions you need to move your change story forward starting right now:

- What leverage points do you plan to address?
- What do you hope to contribute?
- What do you hope to gain?
- How will you influence this space?
- Who are your stakeholders?
- Who are your sponsors?
- What actions can you take right now to move change forward in this space?
- What actions can you plan for later to move change forward in this space?

Change Story Case Study: Reed, the Diplomat

"I entered the teaching profession after obtaining my MBA, joining the Peace Corps, and running my own business in Botswana," says Reed. "When I returned to the United States, I decided to become an educator. I wanted to do something impactful without chasing money. Honing my craft as a middle school English and social studies teacher was very challenging in the early days. I started to see success by combining skills I gained as an entrepreneur to organize engaging programs for my students.

"As I began to embrace my 'teacherpreneur' ethos, I realized my actual duties were far more than teaching students to read and write. My passion was driving an inquiry practice, fulfilling a hunger for learning new things, and creating opportunities for my students and the community at large. When my middle school was placed on the school district closure list, I became an accidental activist, fighting to save the middle school where I taught for 16 years. As a result of that effort, I became the founding humanities educator of a brand-new school called The U School.

"The U School is an innovative, open enrollment, competency-based school designed to change the college and career outcomes of Philadelphia youth. I have been teaching at the U School for seven years, leading our design thinking and project-based learning programs in order to advocate for and connect students with opportunities related to their own passions and interests.

"Recently, in response to the COVID-19 pandemic and the death by gun violence of one of my students, I incubated and designed the Bus 101 Side Hustle pipeline program. I said to myself, 'I need to lean more into the important economic and financial empowerment side of racial justice' as someone with previous business experience, an entrepreneurial ethos, and a wide network that crosses education, business, and startup spaces. So I got to work developing youth leadership programs to shift students toward an entrepreneurial mindset and prepare them to be responsible workers across industries.

"The program I am building inspires youth to start and sustain small businesses and develop entrepreneurial dispositions that will benefit employees, small-business owners, and youth alike. I provide leadership, Business 101, and side-hustle workshops that include synchronous and asynchronous training, one-on-one coaching, and mentoring. And I am using digital badging and credentialing for youth, leading to micro funds and startup support for individual passion projects and side hustles.

"The mantra that drives everything I do is 'I work alongside students to read, write, and make sense of the world, and I side hustle for social good the rest of the time.' As my experiences and network expand, I will continue to find opportunities for the young people I serve to expand their worlds, too."

10

PLOT TWISTS: NAVIGATING THE PEAKS AND VALLEYS OF YOUR STORY

We turn the Cube and it twists us.

—Erno Rubik (quoted in Scheffler, 2017)

Life and work come with plot twists. It's part of the deal. The "experienced evacuator" Ken Strahan interviewed didn't expect fire to come through his ceiling vent, but that's just how bushfire rolls sometimes. I guarantee much of what has happened in your own life in just the last few years also included unexpected twists and turns. We all know "*the best laid plans of mice and men often go awry*" (Burns, 2011), so we can save ourselves much heartache if we plan for these events as best we can. I also believe that many change efforts in education fail because we do not account for the inevitability of the unforeseen.

Keeping in mind the reality and possible repercussions of both the right-now and big-picture actions you plan to take can support you when the need for redirection inevitably arises. Use the following questions to extend your thinking of both the big-picture and right-now actions you plan to take:

- What results do you expect?
- What are some possible intended and unintended outcomes of these actions?

- What do you hope the impact of your actions will be?
- What obstacles could you potentially face?
- What might prevent the intended impact from occurring?
- How will you respond and shift accordingly?
- What will you do if unintended consequences or obstacles require you to change direction?

The Next Chapter: Amplification, Replication, and Translation

Whenever a change effort I've led has gained momentum, someone (often a sponsor) has inevitably asked, "How will you scale this?" With that question in mind, I would bust my hump trying to go bigger. It often went something like this: "Students loved that unit so much they are talking about it to their friends? Let's get the whole school to create units like this!" Or something like this: "We had 100 educators sign up in 20 minutes? Let's recruit 200!"

When something works, we tend to look for ways to make it work for more people. There is nothing wrong with that; this whole book is about inspiring educators to lead change that moves the entire system forward. Big, worthy goals are necessary and valuable to any change story, but scaling too quickly prevents us from truly reflecting on what made an initiative successful in the first place.

When a team of innovative educators designs a successful unit, for example, expecting everyone in the school to do the exact same thing in the exact same way is counterproductive because everyone has unique strengths and goals. When a side project that requires educator buy-in garners interest from a community of educators, pushing others to join can water down the engagement of the original interested parties who have a real passion for the cause. When a short, intensive program works, making it longer or more drawn-out risks derailing the magic it offers as is.

I have learned over time that sometimes we can get better and more authentic results by focusing on how to *amplify, replicate,* and *translate* initiatives rather than scale them (see Figure 10.1). These strategies require us to look closely at what works and expand in ways that elevate the strengths of our efforts.

Figure 10.1

Scaling Versus Amplification, Replication, and Translation

Change Story Background	What Scaling Conversations Look Like	What Amplifying Conversations Look Like	What Replicating Conversations Look Like	What Translating Conversations Look Like
You and a colleague took an innovative turn with a tired unit and collaborated to create a highly engaging and successful unit plan that students loved and learned from and even talked about with their friends. Everyone is talking about what a success it was.	"Let's get the whole school to create units like this!"	"Who might want to know about or learn from this success?"	"How could we apply this approach again?	"Where else might this approach work, and how might we share it with others in those contexts?"
You and a team of other change leaders decided to build a side project to address some specific pain points facing educators you know. You worked behind the scenes to design the vision. After after reaching out to educators within each of your networks, 100 educators responded positively and now want to be included.	"Let's recruit 200!"	"Who might want to know about this response from educators, and how might we call them to action?"	"What do we think we are doing here that is garnering such a strong response, and how could we do it again when we're ready?"	"Who else is doing what we are trying to do in a different way, and how might we learn from them and apply it to our plan?"
You and a team of other change leaders developed a program to address a specific issue that arose within your community. The program was successful and well received by stakeholders.	"Let's make it more complex and extend it!"	"Who should we share this success with, and how might we call them to action?"	"What did we learn from this success, and what plans should we make to do it again when and where it's needed?"	"Where else might a program like this be needed, and how might we share it with others in those contexts?"

Notice that by shifting our perspective from scale to these other lenses, we give ourselves the opportunity to pause and ask thoughtful questions about what's working and what's next. Ironically, in doing so, we actually begin the process of scaling our ideas. By amplifying, we seek new stakeholders and sponsors to move the work forward. By replicating, we extend our network and our impact. By translating, we spread our ideas and methods to other contexts and learn from them in return.

Sometimes these perspectives weave in and out of your own journey across a variety of change efforts. Even when a specific project has been unsuccessful, I have found that, years later, I still have opportunities to amplify it, replicate it, and translate it. Scaling can mean not only growing an initiative but also growing your genius and zone of excellence. When you gain skills and talents during a change story, you can write the next chapter (and sustain the change you seek) by thoughtfully stretching yourself and the work you hope to continue to lead.

Tried-and-True Steps for Starting Your Change Story Right Now

Use the chart in Figure 10.2 to outline the change story you want to write. Feel free to use this chart as a template any time you decide you want to lead a change effort. Additionally, the tried-and-true steps that follow offer a pathway that I have used often and shared with educators who have put it to use in phenomenal ways. Together, these serve as a mini change toolkit that could lead you to pleasantly surprising results.

Step 1: Learn as Much as You Can About Your Chosen Leverage Point

Once you know where to start your change story, acclimate yourself to that space as best you can. If you want to pitch a curriculum idea to your school leader, take the time to understand what goals they are trying to accomplish first. If your principal is highly focused on improving the school culture, learn about their vision and align what you want to what they want. If you want to propose a district program to support innovation, search the district website for their mission or vision and take the time to understand how the district views and hopes to expand innovation programs.

Figure 10.2
Plotting Your Change Story Planning Guide

How do you want to contribute? What do you hope to gain?	
Determine the leverage points you want to address. Where do you plan to intervene?	
Who are your sponsors and stakeholders in this space?	
What actions will you take now and later?	
What results do you expect?	
What impact are you seeking?	
How will you respond and redirect when obstacles arise?	
How will you amplify, replicate, or translate your efforts?	

When you illustrate that you understand the needs and goals of those operating within a particular leverage point, you have a stronger chance of securing the opportunity.

Step 2: Align Yourself with the Goals of the Leverage Point

Figure out how to connect what you want to what others at this leverage point want. For example, in the case of the principal focused on school culture, read up on the same research they're reading and connect the curriculum you want to create to what that research says. If the district has a strategic plan readily available on their website, pull key words and phrases from that plan that align to yours. You will almost guarantee a green light for your ideas when you approach leaders or organizations with an idea that solves a problem for them or addresses topics that matter for their work. Leaders want people to bring them solutions and will go to great lengths to clear the path for you to do so, but they have to know you are on the same team first.

Step 3: Create a Beautiful Proposal

When you understand your leverage and you have aligned your goals with those of the leader or organization you want to influence, draft a proposal connecting what you want to their mission or goals. Take the time to make sure the proposal is professional in content and attractive in appearance. Use tools like Canva or Google Workspace to guide you if you have never taken this step before. Your first interaction with someone who can help you lead a change effort should be an impressive one. Get people's attention by putting something in front of them that grabs their eye and sparks their interest. This may seem like an unnecessary step, but I have seen a beautiful pitch deck or well-developed concept paper move mountains. You will be illustrating that you can get things done and knocking everyone's socks off along the way.

Step 4: Include Clear, Efficient, and Relevant Content

Your proposal needs to demonstrate quickly and efficiently what you want to do, why you want to do it, what outcome you expect, what you are asking for, and how your idea will get something done the leader or organization really needs to get done. Make sure your beautiful document checks those boxes thoughtfully.

Step 5: Sponsors First, Stakeholders Second

Intuitively, you may be tempted to seek stakeholder input before you approach a potential sponsor for support. For example, you want to create that new curriculum for your school, so you ask 15 colleagues what they think about it before you approach your leader. I think this is a mistake. (Diplomats, hold onto your hats for a second here.) Although teamwork may make the dream work in the end, it's focus that gets us noticed in the beginning. If you really need thought partners at the early stage of an idea, by all means seek them out, but make sure you don't weigh down your fledgling idea with everyone else's opinions before it has the chance to take flight. When you feel good about your idea, find the sponsors you need before you take it to everyone else so your sponsors can clear a path for you first. Then bring on stakeholders who can clearly see the vision and path.

Step 6: Keep Your Archetype Central to Your Plan

Keep checking in with yourself as you move forward to make sure that who you are is central to the role you're playing in this change story. If you find at any point that you're drifting from your zone of genius, pause the plot long enough to either get back on track or renegotiate a new path.

Step 7: Balance Right-Now and Big-Picture Actions

Once you have a strong proposal and sponsors in place, make sure your action plan balances what is possible now and what you hope for later. I have seen change leaders get so focused on the minutiae that they lose the big picture (and vice versa). Keep both in perspective as you build your plan and as you communicate with others.

Step 8: Know the Path and Communicate It Thoughtfully

You know what change looks like for you, but moving forward can feel like walking through a tunnel. You can get so focused on what's at the end of it that you can't feel your way through the dark right now, or you're so focused on stepping through the darkness that you forget there is a light at the end. Balance both, but even more importantly, communicate what you see and how you are moving forward strategically with others. Not everyone is in the tunnel with you. In fact, most people, even your stakeholders, aren't. Find sponsors, a handful of stakeholders, and a great team of collaborators who understand your end goal, but don't waste your time trying to convince uninterested parties of the value of what you're doing. Just keep marching toward your goal with right-now actions that bring those who care along with you.

Change Story Case Study: Jessica, the Guardian

"For five years, I lived and worked abroad as a teacher and department head," says Jessica. "My partner and I decided to return to the United States after the 2019–20 school year. Hoping also to gain insight into what it looks and feels like to be a school leader in Chicago, I applied and was accepted to become a multiclassroom lead (MCL). MCLs' roles were created as part of a district initiative to distribute leadership. As an MCL, I taught half the day and coached teachers for the remainder of the school year.

"When the school year got underway, even though I loved being with students and working with teachers, I quickly became drained. My well-being took a huge hit and, as a result, I wasn't able to live up to my coaching vision or be the person I wanted for my friends, family, partner, and community. In late 2020, with this in mind, I began to look at other options. I had no idea where to start, so I began with the people I knew and trusted. I reached out to one of my best friends, who had recently gone through the job search process in a field tangential to education. Her recommendation was to talk to as many people as possible via informational interviews.

"Over the course of about five months, I spoke to 32 people. Some were educators in lines of work that were directly related to mine. Others worked for government institutions, public policy consultancy firms, nonprofits, and more. (I even spoke to people in UX design and design thinking!) While most of these conversations weren't formal interviews, they all left me with something new to think about. These conversations helped me to confirm that I wanted to stay in education, understand the opportunities that exist in the field beyond school-based roles, and parse out which most interested me.

"During one of these conversations, I was introduced to an education-focused public policy and advocacy fellowship program taking place over the summer. I reached out to a contact who worked for the organization running the fellowship and, when we talked, she explained to me the other program offerings, including a nine-month fellowship. I applied for, and was accepted to, both the summer and nine-month program. I was excited by the opportunity to continue working in education but at a different scale than in a school-based role.

"In one of my other conversations, a former educator who had shifted into policy work told me, 'There's a lot of strength and merit in coming from the classroom. There are a lot of folks who do this work who have never had classroom experience. I often walk into spaces where I'm the only one with classroom experience.' Her words were so empowering I wrote them down! They made me angry, to be honest. Teachers should be included in all policy decisions that impact their work and the learning of students. I realized my perspective as a classroom teacher would provide meaningful insight for policymaking. Soon, I transitioned into my nine-month fellowship role, where I currently work, in Chicago Public Schools at the district level through the Teacher Residency Program.

"Through this process, I've had the opportunity to explore ways of working, and I feel whole. I hope to continue that personal journey, while also finding ways to transform our schools, districts, and education system into a place where all teachers can have their humanity recognized and celebrated by themselves, by others, and by policies and institutions."

✳ ✳ ✳

When we compile all the pieces of our story's plot together, we have a change story to share. Sometimes those stories have happy endings, sometimes they have frustrating ones, but by writing one at all, we contribute to the forward movement of a stagnant system. We also stretch ourselves, which gives us courage and stamina for the next change effort. If we see problems around us that we know we have the capacity and energy to solve, there are steps we can take to solve them. We don't have to be bound by outdated belief systems about what is possible if we know exactly who we are and exactly what the world needs from us. Then we turn the page and keep moving the story along.

CONCLUSION

We only become what we are by the radical and deep-seated refusal of that which others have made of us.

—Jean-Paul Sartre (quoted in Fanon, 1961)

In 2015, an email changed my life. A fellow educator named Kip had sent the message to district colleagues letting us know about an opportunity he had come across called "The Redesign Challenge," a pilot project of The Bill and Melinda Gates Foundation focused on improving professional development for teachers. Someone holding a lever at that particular point in the system decided it was time to actually ask classroom educators what they thought, so dollars were allocated to recruit them.

I deleted the email.

I was busy at the time parenting two small children and teaching a loaded schedule of four preps. As an eternal Creative, I didn't make that situation any easier on myself either. I was constantly trying to teach old lessons in new ways. I went to great lengths to find interesting stories or topics anywhere I could. The same night I deleted Kip's email, I went to bed knowing I had just logged many hours of professional development that would not officially "count" in the eyes of the district. I had also just created a lot of beautiful lessons that many educators like me might have liked to see and could have possibly used themselves yet never

130

would because the system was not designed for that kind of widespread authentic collaboration among educators. This a-ha moment caused me to sit upright in bed, log back into my computer, and dig that email out of the trash. What if there *were* a more authentic professional learning platform that let educators be their most creative selves? I replied to Kip's email, and our friendship—as well as a journey I could have never imagined—began.

Redesign Challenge selected my proposal, and the Gates Foundation flew us to Washington, DC for an "Innovator's Weekend" where we collaborated with experts in technology, design, and media across a diverse collection of education organizations. I didn't know what to expect. People who had known me for years said, "You're going to DC to do *what?*" Because, although I had submitted the idea, I had little to no interest in or experience with technology at the time. I didn't even own a smartphone.

These experts asked questions, listened, and advised us as peers. It occurred to me that although I saw them as experts in technology, they recognized *me* as an expert in educational innovation. No one had ever recognized that before, nor had I ever thought of myself in that way. Suddenly, I realized that I belonged there, surrounded by creative, problem-solving, frustrated-yet-eternally-positive educators just like me. The educators who also followed their ideas didn't know how to make web platforms either; they didn't need to. There were experts and advisors for that. What we did have—in droves—were a creative spirit, a positive attitude, and classroom expertise.

Over the course of a couple of days, I learned a lot about myself, and I learned a lot about how to change. I learned that a person is not a set of defined boundaries and immovable traits but rather elastic. A curious, creative spirit who prefers a pen to a keyboard can create a virtual world that emulates the one inside their own head. I learned that true collaboration is not necessarily multiple people coming to the table and walking away with one product or idea; it can be many people, many ideas, and many iterations of those people and ideas. I learned that changing ourselves and creating new possibilities is messy—and we should embrace it. With that in mind, I kept pulling on the tiny thread my creativity had spun—a vision for a web platform that could connect curious, creative educators everywhere. I stayed in touch with the cohort of educators and experts I had met that weekend and decided to just keep following the trail and relying on their advice.

When I returned home, I found that my eyes had been opened to the education system writ large. I started looking around at the structures in place and the tacit codes that kept me and my colleagues feeling voiceless and helpless, in complete contrast to the experience I had just had. I felt I had reached a peak as a classroom educator, and yet a small part of me started to feel discontent in a way I never had before. A few months later, I discovered that I was a finalist for my state's Teacher of the Year award, and a little while after that, I learned that I had won.

As the Teacher of the Year, I was invited to work at the state department of education as its first "teacher in residence." I decided to take the leap after encouragement from my students and colleagues, but this opportunity came at a time when tensions were high. I found myself sitting in a closed-door meeting with the highest-level state department leaders, who were seeing a 90-page education reform bill for the first time. The room panicked as they started to read the bill, and I had absolutely no idea why. I took the not-yet-public draft bill home and read it cover to cover. I couldn't believe what I read. I was aghast that state legislators would propose such a sweeping reform in secret without any guidance from educators. That night, I called my friend Kip again, who called a handful of others, and suddenly we were all reading a secret draft education bill over the phone, rippling with outrage. But we also started churning out ideas.

As a Creative with a sudden window into the system, I took the role of creating a website that would share details of the bill with educators across the state, then collect their opinions to share back with legislators. Others on this savvy team stepped into their strengths, too. We all worked together using our talents, networks, and influence, and over time the legislators who created the bill recognized that educators were not happy with it as it was. Consequently, they changed it in collaboration with educators and other stakeholders until it became a piece of legislation that represented everyone, rather than a small few.

Meanwhile, I was also learning alongside some of the most talented change leaders I had ever met through the national Teacher of the Year network. I had a window through them and the work they were doing in their own states into how the issues I had always assumed were specific to me and my own school, district, and state were in fact ubiquitous. They inspired me with all the ways they were leading change in their own environments—revising curriculum, building programs, crafting legislation, leading protests, starting nonprofits, running for office, speaking, writing, presenting, and so on. Each of these educators refused to accept the status quo. I started to better understand how the educators in my own school and state were doing the same. The more my worldview expanded, the more I understood how the actions of change leaders could ripple far beyond their immediate surroundings. While I had always viewed myself as a bit of a creative rebel in the classroom, until that moment, I hadn't considered that I may have had much more influence than I'd ever imagined.

All the while, I kept pursuing the idea I had seeded in DC. I started to follow the breadcrumbs—little right-now actions that came to light. Sponsors here and there gave me insight into people, places, or opportunities I might pursue to move the idea forward. That breadcrumb trail eventually led me to a coffee meeting with a digital designer who suggested we go into business together and turn my idea into something real.

I took his advice. All of it. All the time. We got a little grant funding from the city and worked on building the platform. Because the founding and funding spaces were far beyond my acumen in those early days, I let the designer lead almost every facet of the business, assuming that my strengths lay elsewhere and I should stick to my own lane; I was *just a teacher with an idea*, after all.

After a year, I shifted from my classroom role to an instructional coaching role. The platform was still in the making, but I had learned a lot about business from proximity by then. I started to understand how to raise funds, manage finances, and some of the ins and outs of building a web platform. I still kept to my lane, even as new advisors and sponsors entered the scene and suggested I take more responsibility for the parts of the business I had mostly left to my partner to manage.

I didn't take action, but I listened. Over time, I started to recognize that maybe the designer and I had never been as aligned as I had thought. After another year, we got a few new funding opportunities that presented me with a real chance to fully step into the role of edtech founder, so I did. Again, my world expanded. I met people from every leverage point of the macro ecosystem of education, and I listened and learned. The voices around me kept saying I should take ownership of more aspects of the business, growing more urgent as my partner's actions increasingly seemed to contradict my own vision and plans. In hindsight, I see now that I kept ignoring the urgent calls from trusted advisors because I was afraid.

The truth is that even though my perspective on and understanding of power had expanded, they hadn't quite broken old beliefs I'd accumulated since first becoming a teacher—in particular, the belief that "I am just a teacher and there is only one lane for me."

I gave away 50 percent of a business built on my life's work as an educator because I did not believe I had the right to own it or the ability to run it myself. After a heartbreaking, soul-shattering legal battle to reclaim that 50 percent, I instead signed papers to give everything to him in full, while I chose to walk away. The email that changed my life in 2015 and inspired such a world-expanding journey had come to an abrupt end. The same day I signed those papers, I sent the following email to everyone who had supported me along the way:

> **Subject:** Farewell Curio
>
> #TeachLikeaRebel has been my motto since I began as a bright-eyed classroom teacher in 2005. It was my professional philosophy across four different schools over 14 years. It was my battle cry when I pushed back and pushed forward in and outside the classroom—when pushing meant bettering the lives of students. And it was an honor to build partners and collaborators over the last four years with Curio. Thank you for being a supporter, champion, advisor, believer, advocate, and friend all these years.
>
> I have chosen to leave Curio Learning, but my rebel philosophy will never change. And I am more passionate and committed to empowering educators than ever before.
>
> On to the next!
>
> Ashley

My palms were sweaty as I hit send on that email because I felt like a failure. I had taken a huge risk in leaving the school system to become a CEO, of all things. Over the course of that journey, I imagined that others looked at me and thought, "How dare she?" I often asked myself the same question. I had tried to step into another lane that felt foreign to me and learn my way through it, but it all came crashing down in one giant rubble heap of failure. Yet as people responded to my email, I realized that those beliefs were unfounded. I received hundreds of responses of goodwill and encouragement. Sure, somewhere out there in the world, some people may have been rolling their eyes at my audacity or even celebrating my perceived failure, but it turned out that a lot of people I respected thought otherwise.

One of those responses in particular has given me great guidance since. A mentor of mine said:

> Ashley, you are like the cherry tree. Its job is to bloom. Some of those blossoms blow away in the wind, some of them grow into cherries and feed the birds and squirrels that rely on the tree to create. It's not the cherry tree's job to worry how the wind blows. It's the cherry tree's job to keep blooming. That's you. Keep blooming, my dear.

When 2020 rolled around, I was reminded of my mentor's beautiful words as educators reached out to me for support, insight, and advice. Through the dark moments of my own change story, I had realized that any change I'd been part of was a result of my creative drive, so I started to offer the same kind of support to my colleagues. In their voices and fears and worries, I recognized my own. Rather than pushing each of them to create as I had, I instead prompted each of them to tell me all the ways they had facilitated change for themselves or others in the past. I tried to mirror their strengths back to them in a way that I should have done for myself.

Suddenly, the regret I felt about the losses I had experienced started to morph into anger on my colleagues' behalf. Friends who had accomplished so much in their careers shared their desires to leave the profession. Some of my most treasured collaborators felt they had no voice or ability to take action. My own children were being taught by human beings who felt helpless and told me so.

When a crisis came for the system, invaluable educators became collateral damage. Their influence seemed clouded in longstanding structures built to silence them. I was reminded of the moment I had given my own power away simply because I'd adopted a limited view of who I was and what I was capable of. By then, I understood that I was and have always been a Creative, and that identity is boundless.

My hope is that every educator who reads this book might learn from my mistakes and choose not to give away as much as I did before discovering their own boundless selves. I have learned through trial and error that when we view ourselves through a limited lens, we limit our potential and the potential for real change. Somewhere out there right now are thousands of educators—connection-driven Diplomats and Guardians with wide networks and deep relationships, advocacy-driven Champions and Investigators with passion and insight, generative Creatives and Inventors with fresh ideas and methods, and influential Storytellers and Sages with wise words and counsel—who sadly may not perceive themselves as the rightful leaders of a system built around their talents.

This is a tragedy. Until we create structures and opportunities within our systems to let these educators lead, we will continue to repeat the same mistakes of the past. Until these educators recognize what they are truly capable of and take the reins, we will all suffer from the invisible loss of the positive change that is within reach with their leadership but light years away without it.

Dear educator: I hope, for all our sakes, that you understand your worth and take ownership of every part of this system. If you see a problem you have the passion, purpose, and energy to solve, just start from wherever you are and see where it takes you. The voices within and without saying you've only got one lane are imprisoning all of us in a system that desperately needs your leadership. Those voices do not speak for everyone, and they should not speak for you. The rest of us wait with bated breath and hopeful hearts for the new narrative of education your change stories will write.

REFERENCES

A&E Networks Television. (2021, April 16). *Sitting Bull*. Biography.com. www .biography.com/political-figure/sitting-bull

Aliperti, J. R., Davis, B. E., Fangue, N. A., Todgham, A. E., & Van Vuren, D. H. (2021). Bridging animal personality with space use and resource use in a free-ranging population of an asocial ground squirrel. *Animal Behaviour*, *180*, 291–306.

Andrews, E. (2015, December 15). *10 things you may not know about Sitting Bull*. History.com. www.history.com/news/10-things-you-may-not-know-about -sitting-bull

Angelou, M. (1969). *I know why the caged bird sings*. Penguin.

Angelou, M. (2011). *Great food, all day long: Eat joyfully, eat healthy*. Virago Press.

Bellis, M. (2019, July 21). *Biography of Bette Nesmith Graham, inventor of liquid paper*. ThoughtCo. www.thoughtco.com/liquid-paper-bette-nesmith -graham-1992092

Beukes, L. (2020). *The shining girls*. Umuzi.

Bishop, E. (2011). *The fish*. Poets.org. https://poets.org/poem/fish-2

Burns, R. (2011). To a mouse. In D. Paterson (Ed.), *Robert Burns: Poems*. Faber and Faber.

Chow, A. R. (2018, July 11). Overlooked no more: Bette Nesmith Graham, who invented Liquid Paper. *New York Times*. www.nytimes.com/2018/07/11 /obituaries/bette-nesmith-graham-overlooked.html

Cleveland Clinic. (2020, October 21). *Why hugging is actually good for your health*. Cleveland Clinic. https://health.clevelandclinic.org/why-hugging-is -actually-good-for-your-health-video

Csikszentmihalyi, M. (2009). *Flow: The psychology of optimal experience.* Harper and Row.

Cuthbertson, A. (2016, May 20). Facebook finds just 3.5 degrees of separation between users. *Newsweek.* www.newsweek.com/facebook-finds-just-35 -degrees-separation-between-users-423991

Dickinson, E. (1890/2005). I dwell in Possibility. In R. W. Franklin (Ed.), *The poems of Emily Dickinson.* Belknap Press.

Doran, L., & Helm, Z. (2006). *Stranger than fiction.* Columbia Pictures.

Edelson, S. M. (n.d.). *Temple Grandin's "hug machine."* Synapse. www .autism-help.org/points-grandin-hug-machine.htm

Fanon, F. (1961). *Wretched of the Earth.* Grove.

Gillies, J. (1978). *Moneylove.* Warner Books.

Godin, S. (2018). *Linchpin: Are you indispensable?* Piatkus.

Godoy, M., & Douglis, S. (2021, December 28). Instead of New Year's resolutions, start and stick with "tiny habits." *NPR.* www.npr.org/2020/02/25 /809256398/tiny-habits-are-the-key-to-behavioral-change

Harbeck, J. (2013, December 12). Jimi Hendrix made his guitar sound like a human voice. [blog post]. Here's how. *Slate.* www.slate.com/blogs /lexicon_valley/2013/12/12/jimi_hendrix_rock_guitarists_make_their _insturment_sound_like_a_human_voice.html

Hardison, A. K. (2021). *Why Maya Angelou partnered with hallmark.* National Endowment for the Humanities. www.neh.gov/article/why-maya-angelou -partnered-hallmark

Hendricks, G. (2010). *The big leap: Conquer your hidden fear and take life to the next level.* HarperOne.

Holson, L. (2013, February 14). Steve Madden is back. *New York Times.* www .nytimes.com/2013/02/14/fashion/steve-madden-is-back.html

Itkowitz, C. (2021, October 27). The extraordinary story of the grandmother who committed her life to hugging soldiers. *Washington Post.* www .washingtonpost.com/news/inspired-life/wp/2015/11/14/the-extraordinary -story-of-the-grandmother-who-committed-her-life-to-hugging-soldiers

Jung, C. G. (1933/2001). *Modern man in search of a soul.* Routledge.

Jung, C. G. (2014). The *undiscovered self.* Routledge.

Lord Tennyson, A. (1850). *Ulysses.* Poetry Foundation. www.poetryfoundation .org/poems/45392/ulysses

Martin, W. P. (2004). *The best liberal quotes ever: Why the left is right.* Sourcebooks.

Matthews, K. (2003, January 24). A once-unthinkable collaboration. *CBS News.* www.cbsnews.com/news/a-once-unthinkable-collaboration

Mejia, Z. (2018, July 23). How inventing liquid paper got a secretary fired and then turned her into an exec worth $25 million. *CNBC.* www.cnbc.com /2018/07/19/inventing-liquid-paper-got-a-secretary-fired-and-then-made- her-rich.html

Metcalf, S. (2007, October 29). Town without pity. *The New York Times.* www .nytimes.com/2007/11/04/books/review/Metcalf2-t.html

Ouellette, J. (2012, June 28). It's a small world after all. [blog post]. *Scientific American.* https://blogs.scientificamerican.com/cocktail-party-physics/its-a-small-world-after-all

Parton, D. (2015, April 8). *Find out who you are and do it on purpose.* Twitter. https://twitter.com/DollyParton/status/585890099583397888?s=20&t=vftC-0qBuwCgoCkrnFsP1Sw

Rankin, J. (2019, April 16). Forget Brexit and focus on climate change, Greta Thunberg tells EU. *The Guardian.* www.theguardian.com /environment/2019/apr/16/greta-thunberg-urges-eu-leaders-wake-up -climate-change-school-strike-movement

Rossen, J. (2020, May 7). When Magic Eye Pictures ruled the world—and frustrated millions of people. *Mental Floss.* www.mentalfloss.com /article/622658/when-magic-eye-pictures-ruled-world

Scheffler, I. (2017). *Cracking the cube: Going slow to go fast and other unexpected turns in the world of competitive Rubik's Cube solving.* Touchstone.

Schultz, M. (2021, April 14). How to influence in sales. *Entrepreneur.* www .entrepreneur.com/article/368081

Schwartz, S. J., Luyckx, K., & Vignoles, V. L. (2012). In *Handbook of Identity Theory and Research* (pp. 99–115). Springer.

Stinson, L. (2019, April 17). *The hidden history of Magic Eye, the optical illusion that briefly took over the world.* Eye on Design. https://eyeondesign.aiga .org/the-hidden-history-of-magic-eye-the-optical-illusion-that-briefly-took -over-the-world

Strahan, K., Whittaker, J., & Handmer, J. (2018). Self-evacuation archetypes in Australian bushfire. *International Journal of Disaster Risk Reduction*, 27, 307–316.

Stump, S. (2015, December 25). *"Hug lady," 83, who gave out 500,000 hugs to soldiers, dies after battle with cancer.* Today.com. www.today.com/kindness /hug-lady-83-who-gave-out-500-000-hugs-soldiers-t63901

Weisman, A. (2014, May 28). Here's what Maya Angelou said to Tupac Shakur that made him cry. *Business Insider.* www.businessinsider.com/maya -angelou-made-tupac-cry-2014-5

Wenner, J. S., & Wolman, B. (1968, March 9). Jimi Hendrix on early influences, 'axis' and more. *Rolling Stone.* www.rollingstone.com/music/music-news /jimi-hendrix-on-early-influences-axis-and-more-203924

Whitman, W., & Reynolds, D. S. (1885/2005). Song of myself. *Leaves of grass.* Oxford University Press.

Yousafzai, M., Lamb, C., & Sudevi Thâc. (2015). *I am Malala.* Mindbooks.

INDEX

The letter *f* following a page locator denotes a figure.

ABOUT THE AUTHOR

 **Ashley Lamb-Sinclair** is an award-winning educator, author, speaker, and consummate coalition-builder whose passion is bringing people together around a cause. She is the 2016 Kentucky Teacher of the Year who served as the inaugural Educator-in-Residence with the state department of education where she supported and led efforts to amplify educator voice and agency to shape policy and practice. After 14+ years as a National Board Certified classroom educator, Ashley founded and spearheaded an edtech platform called Curio Learning to elevate creative idea development and authentic collaboration among educators. As founder and CEO, she received the Navitas Prize at the Milken-Penn Business Plan Competition and the Uber Girlboss Grand Prize. She also joined an extensive network of edtech leaders at the LearnLaunch Accelerator in Boston. Ashley has contributed to several publications, including *The Atlantic* and *The Washington Post*, and is an Oxford and Fulbright Scholar. She currently serves as a National Geographic Explorer stewarding the 2892 Miles to Go Geographic Walk for Justice alongside a collective of community storytellers and social justice leaders around the world. Ashley is a proud Creative who lives in Louisville, Kentucky, with her husband (a protective Guardian) and her two daughters (a wise Sage and a savvy Storyteller).

Related ASCD Resources: Change Management

At the time of publication, the following resources were available (ASCD stock numbers in parentheses).

Adventures in Teacher Leadership: Pathways, Strategies, and Inspiration for Every Teacher by Rebecca Mieliwocki and Joseph Fatheree (#118033)

CRAFT Conversations for Teacher Growth: How to Build Bridges and Cultivate Expertise by Sally J. Zepeda, Lakesha Robinson Goff, and Stefanie W. Steele (#120001)

Dream Team: A Practical Playbook to Help Innovative Educators Change Schools by Aaron Tait and Dave Faulkner (#119022)

Educator Bandwidth: How to Reclaim Your Energy, Passion, and Time by Jane Kise and Ann Holm (#122019)

Other Duties as Assigned: Tips, Tools, and Techniques for Expert Teacher Leadership by Jan Burgess and Donna Bates (#109075)

Reframing Teacher Leadership to Improve Your School by Douglas B. Reeves (#108012)

Stop Leading, Start Building: Turn Your School into a Success Story with the People and Resources You Already Have by Robyn R. Jackson (#121025)

For up-to-date information about ASCD resources, go to **www.ascd.org**. You can search the complete archives of *Educational Leadership* at **www.ascd.org/el.** To contact us, send an email to member@ascd.org or call 1-800-933-2723 or 703-578-9600.

WHOLE CHILD
TENETS

1 **HEALTHY**
Each student enters school healthy and learns about and practices a healthy lifestyle.

2 **SAFE**
Each student learns in an environment that is physically and emotionally safe for students and adults.

3 **ENGAGED**
Each student is actively engaged in learning and is connected to the school and broader community.

4 **SUPPORTED**
Each student has access to personalized learning and is supported by qualified, caring adults.

5 **CHALLENGED**
Each student is challenged academically and prepared for success in college or further study and for employment and participation in a global environment.

ascd whole child

The ASCD Whole Child approach is an effort to transition from a focus on narrowly defined academic achievement to one that promotes the long-term development and success of all children. Through this approach, ASCD supports educators, families, community members, and policymakers as they move from a vision about educating the whole child to sustainable, collaborative actions.

From Underestimated to Unstoppable relates to the **supported** and **challenged** tenets.

For more about the ASCD Whole Child approach, visit **www.ascd.org/wholechild.**

MOVING DATA

MOVING DATA

THE iPHONE AND THE FUTURE OF MEDIA

Edited by Pelle Snickars
& Patrick Vonderau

NEW YORK   COLUMBIA UNIVERSITY PRESS

COLUMBIA UNIVERSITY PRESS

Publishers Since 1893

New York   Chichester, West Sussex

cup.columbia.edu

Copyright © 2012 Columbia University Press

iPhone® is a registered trademark of Apple, Inc.

Library of Congress Cataloging-in-Publication Data

Moving data : the iphone and the future of media / edited by Pelle Snickars and Patrick Vonderau.

p. cm.

Includes bibliographical references and index.

ISBN 978-0-231-15738-4 (cloth : alk. paper)—ISBN 978-0-231-15739-1 (pbk. : alk. paper)—ISBN 978-0-231-50438-6 (e-book)   1. iphone (Smartphone)—Social aspects.

2. Application software—Social aspects.   3. Smartphones—Social aspects.

I. Snickars, Pelle.   II. Vonderau, Patrick.

QA76.8.164M68 2012

004.16'7—dc23

2011043733

Columbia University Press books are printed on permanent and durable acid-free paper.
This book is printed on paper with recycled content.

Printed in the United States of America

c 10 9 8 7 6 5 4 3 2 1
p 10 9 8 7 6 5 4 3 2 1

References to Internet Web sites (URLs) were accurate at the time of writing.
Neither the authors nor Columbia University Press is responsible for URLs that may
have expired or changed since the manuscript was prepared.

CONTENTS

MOVING DATA

Introduction

PELLE SNICKARS AND PATRICK VONDERAU

A LTHOUGH HE DID not wear his trademark black mock turtleneck, it was unmistakably Steve Jobs walking the red carpet at the Oscars in 2010, handsomely dressed in a tuxedo. Some bloggers spotted him; tweets were sent out; and excitement echoed across Twitter. Eventually, some pictures were taken, and even though Jobs might not have been a celebrated actor, Apple's CEO definitively proved to have star qualities. Apart from media mogul Rupert Murdoch, he was likely the richest person in the audience and, more importantly, at least for some, the most famous. Or as one blogger put it: "OMG it's Steve Jobs! I'm the only one yelling at him."[1]

Jobs's Hollywood "red-carpet moment" in many ways signaled a rupture in the prevalent understanding of media culture, a shift nobody would have expected only ten years earlier. Before then Apple was almost on the brink of ruin, and it is arguably when Jobs returned to the company in 1997—after being exiled for a decade—that Apple turned into a global icon of personal computing. Since then the company has cast something of a spell on both consumers and investors with its unique reputation in the consumer-electronics industry, and it has cultivated a devoted customer base—a group whom some would maliciously label the "Cult of Apple." The company's rise to worldwide fame has in many ways been epitomized by the iPhone, and since its launch, mobile telephony and home computing have moved to the center of today's globalized, branded entertainment industries.

Since its premiere in late June 2007, the iPhone has become not only the fastest-selling smartphone of all time but also a significant symbol of change in media engagement worldwide. Integrating communication and location services with motion pictures, sound, music, text—and more than 500,000 software apps to date—Apple's gadget has fulfilled the promise of an ever-expandable mobile media machine. It constantly invites its users to consume, produce, and share code; to connect and transmit; to talk and watch; to play and listen, to choose and buy; to search and organize; to measure and store—and by doing so, to translate all these practices into media experiences.

Cultures, Technologies, and Marketing Practices

The iPhone (and the iPad) indeed point to a convergence of technologies, cultures, and marketing practices that were previously deemed incommensurable. To begin with the last, Apple now rivals Hollywood in terms of average marketing expenditures: its advertising costs in 2010 rose to about $700 million dollars, and the Apple brand had product placements in at least ten out of the thirty-three number-one box office hits in the United States that year. Apple also constantly leaves promotional traces in print and pixel through a tight promotional symbiosis with news media in general and with tech blogs and technology sections in the press in particular. Apple products had about 2,500 unpaid appearances in U.S. television during September 2010, for instance, and the iPhone has been mentioned in almost 5,000 articles in the *New York Times* alone. It is with the appearance of its "Jesus phone," then, that the Apple brand seems to have become a phenomenon discussed globally in terms of its makers' infallibility, and some industry observers credit Apple with having overtaken Google as the world's most valuable brand in 2011.[2]

Apart from its advertising or branding practices, the iPhone is also symptomatic of the technologies that the entertainment industries have come to depend on for the computers, consoles, and software that constitute their infrastructural backbone. In a broader media-historical perspective, nothing seems to have shaken up established Hollywood distribution models as much as Apple's idea of marrying the iPod to iTunes. When the iPod was launched in 2001, it certainly was not the first MP3 player on the market, just as the iPhone was not the first—or best—smartphone around. But by synchronizing iTunes with the iPod (and later the iPhone and iPad), Apple integrated hard- and software in a way that would mark its shift into a global media company. Once advertised as turning "your Mac into a nifty digital jukebox," iTunes has over the years expanded to allegedly contain "everything you need to be entertained."[3]

Even though Apple's technologies have turned out to be highly functional for gaining control over music distribution through its iTunes store—which today holds a market share of 70 percent of global online music sales—Hollywood's media conglomerates are still ambivalent about letting Apple assume a similar role regarding film and television.[4] There is no doubt, however, that with its integration of hardware and software, Apple has become strategically involved in the media-distribution business to the point that Steve Jobs's appearance on the Oscar red carpet prompted bloggers to see him as sidestepping traditional Hollywood dealmakers, even claiming that the industry "had now officially been taken over by the geeks"—Jobs: "You make the content (or at least some of it), I'll deliver it."[5] If Hollywood (still mostly) deals in moving pictures, Apple is devoted to moving data.

Last but not least, if one considers the way the iPhone has affected culture or, more precisely, the production and consumption of cultural meaning, the circulating "texts" provided by the media industries, and the practices associated with their creation and experience, it might actually be design rather than content that one thinks of. Design, in fact, not only superficially but also substantially relates to the iPhone's capacity to innovate cultural and creative practices on a large, even global scale. Design establishes a correspondence between the technology and the market, thus allowing the coordination—within a single product like the iPhone—of different or even competing logics, ranging from questions about ways of using it (why buy it?), to actual usage (what to do with it in a particular situation), to the object itself (is it well made, functional, adaptive?).[6] The amazement so often associated with this device as a design object pertains to its capacity to fully answer these questions.

As part of this effort, the invention of "apps" has been particularly powerful in its combination of software design and price modeling. Today, apps fill Apple's phone with strings of code and equip it with functionalities not even imagined in the corporate headquarters at the product's 2007 launch, redistributing content produced elsewhere and adding genuinely new meanings to an object not originally conceived as a mobile platform for consumers to download data in a standardized format. In Apple's first iPhone TV commercials, for example, not a word was mentioned about "apps." The early advertisements, in fact, looked backward rather than forward, stating that "there has never been an iPod that can do this."[7] Hence, while Apple's understanding of the cultural logic of new forms of mobile computation was, at the time, as limited as anyone else's, after ten billion downloads from its App Store, accomplished in January 2011, the iPhone software platform has become "the most innovative in the history of computing."[8]

Still, since technology has increasingly turned into an integral part of both distributing and creating content, and since deals and partnerships that get that content onto different devices are crucial for companies operating in today's mediascape, Apple's rigorous regulation of access to content has prompted considerable objections. The criticism is not confined to the App Store's rigid terms of business but arguably pertains more to the company's latest corporate move to control and master cloud-based media solutions. Analogous to the long-promised celestial jukebox, cloud computing promises users free storage and automatic synchronization for all their media content. The possibility of accessing iCloud from any Internet-connected device certainly holds rich potential for digital multiplatform distribution, with the "app editions" of Warner Bros. films such as *Inception* (2010) and *The Dark Knight* (2008) forming a pertinent example of integrating feature film into online streaming services and social-networking sites. However, given Apple's competitive edge over companies such as Amazon and Google, which have introduced similar services, and given its ready consumer base of more than 200 million iTunes users, questions about its new market power still have to be explored.[9] How might iCloud services affect the production, distribution, and experience of media, and what challenges can we expect regarding media ownership, ecology, and, most importantly, the regulatory policies of the future? Moving slowly but steadily toward a media environment based on device control and a tightened hold on payment for and delivery of content, Apple has begun to be seen as something of a tech bully. This criticism can be expected to increase given that Apple shot past Microsoft in May 2010, as measured by the value of its stock, to become the world's most valuable technology company. As one blogger put it, "neither Hollywood nor the music industry wants a walled garden ecosystem that doesn't play well (or at all) with non-Apple devices."[10]

A History of Possibilities

In order to come to terms with Apple's iPhone, it is important to consider the dynamic intersection among these marketing, technological, and cultural forces. Despite the iPhone's economic success, elegance, and "revolutionary" newness, the question still remains how and why to engage in studying the iPhone as a media object in the first place. In their seminal book, *Digital Play: The Interaction of Technology, Culture, and Marketing*, Stephen Kline, Nick Dyer-Whiteford, and Greig de Peuter suggest investigating this interdependent dynamic of technology, culture, and marketing efforts as propelling the "circuit of capital" and growth in information capitalism. The political economy of media provides a critical but fairly general perspective on the iPhone as an "ideal-type commodity form," one that reflects the social organization of capitalism at its present moment.[11] Recent ventures into the field of media-industry analysis have testified to the productivity of this critical tradition.[12] Focusing solely on the iPhone "moment" in the media history of consumer capitalism, however, also introduces a number of fallacies that obscure—rather than clarify—what seems to be at stake. To favor the emergent and the immediate at the expense of the old and the contingent, or of failures and devaluation, often leads to a skewed picture of innovation processes and of media history generally, and potentially even to a fetishization of branded consumer products, which the iPhone epitomizes.

Archeological sensitivity is thus needed to unearth the wider network of technologies, discourses, and cultural practices within which the iPhone appeared, and also the detours, dead ends, and abandoned and discarded models that accompanied or preceded its rise to fame. Consider, for instance, how the American journalist Robert Thompson Sloss (1872–1920) in 1908 envisioned the future of mobile media in his contribution to the German book *Die Welt in hundert Jahren*. One century before the iPhone was launched, Sloss rightly predicted the advent of a "wireless century" marked by the availability of "pocket phones" that would allow instant and worldwide connections between individuals or even groups, for personal conversations from the North Pole as much as for conference calls to New York City; for transmitting sounds and music, moving images, and written documents; and even for making bank payments.[13] Although Sloss erred in stating that the mobile phone would drastically diminish criminality, he correctly identified its role as a medium of surveillance and news reporting in situations of crisis and political change. Somewhat unique in their precision, his observations still have to be seen as part of a much broader discourse of the imaginary, as one example of a sense of anticipation informing the history of ideas and technological try-outs on which our present understanding of "new media" is founded.[14] Following the development of photography (1810s), telegraphy (1830s), the telephone (1876), the phonograph (1877), moving pictures (1880s), and wireless telegraphy (1895), the "liveness" of simultaneity had become an experience and an object of experimentation by the late nineteenth century. Crystallizing around ideas of mobile televisuality, as exemplified in Sloss's 1908 vision of a pocket wireless, this cultural imagination took form in endless patents and variants before "smartphoning" developed as its current cultural practice. For evidence of the arbitrariness of the trajectories that led to the present, one might point to early plans for videophone systems such as the (never realized) telectroscope in 1877, for instance, or to the close inter-relation of transportation, music listening, and wireless (radio) communica-tion since the 1920s or to the attempts to develop portable electronic devices to increase workplace efficiency in the 1990s.[15] To stick to this last point, it was with the "Palm-Pilot," the first generation of handheld digital assistants, that the notion of "palms" entered the vernacular as a synonym for such de-vices. Research in Motion released its iPhone variant, the Blackberry, in 2002, and as one of the first convergent mobile gadgets it instantly became popular within the marketplace by concentrating on e-mail functionality for the busi-ness sector. As with other smartphones, the BlackBerry surfed the Web, yet its small screen size and lack of a multitouch display made it a weak competitor after the introduction of the iPhone.[16] Today, RIM and its BlackBerry still hold a fair share of worldwide smartphone sales, yet even with a constant line of new models, the company has not come close to matching the cultural impact of the iPhone. One key reason is that Apple has been aiming its smart-phone toward the individual user rather than enterprise sales—though this is not to say that Apple is *all* about "communicative capitalism," to invoke Jodi Dean's suggestive term.[17]

Situating the iPhone within this wider history of possibilities allows dis-tance from the spectacle of innovation and the "mise-en-scène of advertising" that characterize the current view on transient media.[18] Today, one may easily tap into the truism of convergence by declaring the iPhone to be the "uni-versal remote" for all sorts of available media content,[19] thus reducing media change to techno-teleologies and downplaying the wildly divergent mean-ings that the iPhone or any other medium might take on, depending on the contexts of its use. But even if one is sensitive to the political dimension of the iPhone's uses and to the ways "its presence activates and embodies a variety of heterogenous forces within and around a space,"[20] the question remains how to address or, rather, how to nail down this particular device analytically, given its slippery, hybrid, ever-changing nature. Is this about mobile commu-nication, smartphones, or the impact of a global brand on the entertainment sector? Or rather about innovative forms and formats and the platforms by which they are disseminated and made part of everyday practices? Or, again, about a medium and the way it regulates access to apps, music, games, videos, people, and media practices? And then, of course, there is not one single iPhone but rather four consecutive models so far, with a constantly modified operating system. So, what, indeed, are we talking about?

A Focus on Protocols

A frequently suggested solution to this problem, linked to the analysis of current media industries, consists in adopting the logic and terminology of industrial strategizing while maintaining an interest in, or possibly nostalgia for, the "cultural" and "social" aspects of media-commodification processes. Henry Jenkins famously introduced "transmedia" as a key term to label practices associated with media convergence, and the term has been readily taken up by industry professionals and academics alike because of its capacity to describe (and legitimize) industrial phenomena such as franchising, synergies, and product-line extensions, mainly by pointing out the relation to what storytelling, meaning making, and affective experiences seem to require. In a similar vein, Frank Rose's book *The Art of Immersion* argues that the Web is changing storytelling by addressing the way users *are* media—an approach that would be easily adaptable for the iPhone experience.[21] As productive as these and related accounts may be, replicating the logic of industrial planning and the rationalist agenda on which it is based often oversimplifies the contradictory and complex character of media change. While it is without any doubt vital to keep up with and study new industrial phenomena, it also seems key to adopt a different attitude to our particular object of study.

Grounded in the lived experience of our mediated everyday, this book investigates the iPhone as a media *dispositif* or apparatus: as emblematizing a radical shift in the relationships among the technological affordances, modes of address, and subject positions that once marked such "old media" as television or cinema.[22] Rather than retelling a story of unprecedented industrial innovation, this book sets out to critically scrutinize the iPhone as a media *dispositif* that is associated with specific technologies and with concrete protocols orienting its use. As Lisa Gitelman notes, the success of all media relies on our "inattention or 'blindness' to the media technologies themselves (and all of their supporting protocols) in favor of attention to the phenomena, 'the content', that they represent for users' edification and enjoyment. . . . When media are new, they offer a look into the different ways that their jobs get constructed as such."[23] One of the many aspects that make the iPhone such an interesting object of study is its capability to turn its "job" immediately into a blind spot, making us forget about Apple's intricate commercial and technological infrastructure by the way it offers play and recreation when we are just about to make—and pay for—a phone call. In fact, while traditional mobile-phone use has been one of the iPhone's weakest features, with dropped calls (and accidentally dropped phones) widely reported, Apple's smartphone offers a vast new potential for control technologies. On the one hand, this relates to "control" and "technology" in a narrow sense, as exemplified by the iPhone's hidden location tracker—discovered in spring 2011 by Alasdair Allan and Pete Warden—or by independently developed locative social-media apps for the iPhone such as Foursquare, BrightKite, Google Latitude, Whrrrl, or Loopt, which function as what Alice E. Marwick has described in terms of "prescriptive social software": "applications that encourage particular social behaviors and provide very clear rewards for behaving in the 'right' way."[24] On the other hand, "control" also pertains more broadly, and less negatively, to the study of media technology and protocols accompanying large societal transformations and the crises that occasionally follow. What the invention of photography, telegraphy, or the telephone meant for solving the crisis of control brought about by nineteenth-century advances in heavy industry, one might argue, the mobile Internet and the iPhone mean for today's advances in the media industries and for the "creative classes" on whose existence these industries' current growth relies.[25]

If there is a one common theoretical interest in the contributions collected in this book, it is in studying the various protocols associated with the iPhone's technological form. Gitelman's notion of "protocol" refers to the concrete arrangement of heterogeneous elements framing and expressing a variety of social, economic, and material relationships.[26] In the case of the iPhone, protocols include the aforementioned default conditions, normative rules, and control functionalities gathering around what specifies the iPhone technologically. The analysis of iPhone protocols also entails descriptions of its diverse forms of use (such as self-locating activities) and may even include billing cycles (famously illustrated by YouTube character iJustine of the viral video comedian Justine Erziak in her clip about the "300 page iPhone bill").[27] Studying protocols not least implies a closer look at the iPhone's technical protocols: the cellular, digital, and high-speed IP data networks without which today's mobile media would not be possible and the carriers operating those networks.

In fact, if the more than 180 million units sold since 2007 position the iPhone as the most central information technology of the last decade, its centrality also comes from its impact on mobile carriers. One crucial aspect of the device—that is, compared with other smartphones on the market—is the way it has altered the relation between phone manufacturers and carriers, at least in the United States. Without losing control over design, manufacturing, or marketing, Apple in early 2007 was able to negotiate a significant deal with AT&T. This was unusual since wireless carriers had traditionally treated phone manufacturers "like serfs," as *Wired* put it. The iPhone changed the balance of power: carriers were suddenly "learning that the right phone— even a pricey one—[could] win customers and bring in revenue."[28]

Hence, studying the iPhone means not only paying attention to its technological form and modes of use but also describing the ways this particular device hooks up to different networks, be they mobile or wifi. The iPhone has become the prototype of the constantly connected gadget, and together with the iPod Touch and the iPad it forms part of the ubiquitous computing continuum. In general, smartphone sales have grown five times faster than those of personal computers in recent years, although smartphone platforms account for less than 20 percent of all mobile handsets shipped globally. Industry observers predict that 2012 will be the year when the mobile becomes the new default for the tech industry. Carriers thus have a natural interest in getting a share of the increasing revenue, and they supposedly will because mobile data continue to grow at an exhilarating pace. According to some estimates, by 2015 there will be more than five billion smartphones and tablets connected to various mobile networks.[29]

At the same time, the liaison between Apple and AT&T has not been unproblematic. Thanks to this alliance, AT&T effectively has outperformed competitors such as T-Mobile USA, which lost 390,000 contract customers in 2010 because of its inability to sell the iPhone. AT&T's rise has occurred despite enduring network quality issues, failed preorders, and security leaks, which have contributed to its image as the "BP of cellphone carriers."[30] U.S. iPhone customers have long envied Europeans, who have been able to choose among many different carriers, and if the iPhone 4 has become Apple's most successful phone introduction so far, it was hardly because of AT&T's service. Consequently, in early 2011 Apple began to offer the iPhone 4 via Verizon Wireless, prompting what some would call a "U.S. iPhone war" between the two networks.[31]

In addition, for all of its success in the mobile smartphone business, the Apple iOS has lately been surpassed by other mobile operating systems. In 2011, Americans were buying more Android mobiles than iPhones—mainly because there are so many models using the latter operating system. The current and rapidly changing market positions of iOS, Android, and Windows

Mobile will likely give open standards an advantage in the future. Some blog-gers have even suggested that Apple's current leadership in the smartphone (and tablet) market may erode because the company no longer pays enough attention to the Mac. Apple might lose out on the smartphone market, es-pecially to Android, because it abandoned an open-source approach. Major components of the Mac OSX, including the UNIX core, are open source, which is not the case with the mobile iOS. And the open-source software community's immense pool of developers is, naturally, an advantage for all open mobile operating systems. The same goes for apps. Android's Market now has more than 400,000 apps and will soon numerically overtake the App Store because of the vast number of developers. Still, as a number of commentators have remarked, paid "quality apps" in Android's Market are scarce, and while the App Store is generating billions for developers, hardly anybody is getting rich in the Android Market.[32]

Disciplinary Frameworks

Whatever future economic developments may bring, the iPhone remains a cultural and technological prototype worthy of study in its own right. No other mobile phone has approached the iPhone's sociocultural impact or demonstrated the extent to which mobile technology shapes and alters media culture. Focusing on one specific mobile gadget such as the iPhone runs coun-ter to earlier mobile-technology studies, which in most cases adopt broader perspectives—with only a few exceptional case studies, notably on Nokia. For instance, Richard Ling's *The Mobile Connection* opens a vivid panorama on the cell phone's "impact on society."[33] However, studies of mobile technol-ogy have mostly been concerned with the general rather than the particular, speculating on the consequences of mobile communication for our everyday lives, teenage text messaging behavior, or new forms of coordinated com-munication and accessibility, to give just a few examples. In addition, before 2005 mobile studies did not pay much attention to the media dimension of cell phones. But as these devices started to become more sophisticated, inte-grating the features of an Internet-enabled personal digital assistant with that of a mobile phone, a camera, and a portable media player, scholarly interests naturally shifted toward issues of mediality. For instance, in his pioneering study *Cell Phone Culture* (2006), Gerard Goggin reflected about "the grow-ing cultural importance of mobile technologies" and the new status of cell phones as "mobile media." Goggin's book was published before the launch of the iPhone, yet many of his insights were spot on, stressing the centrality of cell phones "for media today and in the near future."[34] The present volume can, in fact, be seen as taking of where the Goggin's book ended. Then again, this book is less concerned with mobile technology studies. The essays in this collection take up not only the way moving pictures have turned into moving data, or the way data are moving with and via new mobile media, but also the various ways we are addressed, organized, and moved around by the concrete protocols launched with Apple's first phone a few years ago.

Despite its topical subject matter, the basic rationale of *Moving Data* is not the ambition to lay the grounds for yet another subdisciplinary label, an ambition whose productivity has been suggested by "mobile studies," "off-screen studies," or "transmedia studies," to name just three recent examples.[35] In turning from moving pictures to moving data, we do not need to reinvent our field of inquiry. Media studies offers a disciplinary framework for this collection of articles less in the sense that its contributions directly refer to notions of textuality, histories of production, and the televisual or cinematic experience—although some articles explicitly do so. Rather, the contributions to this book employ interests and issues brought up within the interdisciplinary media-studies tradition over the course of almost a hundred years, including institutions and practices, art and agency, and policies and politics. If we agree that media studies has never been a discipline in the strict sense of the word but rather has formed part of a transdisciplinary field of inquiry funneled by conceptual crossbreeding and constantly changing objects of study, then this book testifies to the ongoing vitality of this field.[36]

The studies of the media industry collected in this book extend more traditional analyses of film and television in three different ways. First, they put humanities-based research in dialogue with the social sciences, most notably sociology, anthropology, and economics. Second, the essays here go beyond traditional textual analysis or industrial history by engaging in a dialogue with practitioners working in the field and by attempting to explain industrial processes as they occur—that is, not only in retrospect. Third, analysis of Apple and the media industries more generally, as something worthwhile in itself, accommodates the interests of an increasingly media-savvy public while critically distinguishing itself from the promotional agenda and descriptive methods of journalism.[37] One might argue that these attempts to move beyond traditional media scholarship form a necessary response to key challenges within our field. Thus, the present book is also a follow-up to our previous jointly edited collection, *The YouTube Reader* (2009), which confronted similar challenges by focusing on Apple's archrival, Google.

About This Book

Returning to Steve Jobs's 2010 Oscar appearance, one indeed may wonder about the shifting alliances and the patterns of ownership and control linking and separating Apple, Google, and Hollywood. Having become Disney's largest individual shareholder, a member of Disney's board of directors, and a representative for Pixar, Steve Jobs arguably stood for an entirely different relationship with Hollywood than Google—and it has to be seen how this position will be maintained or be renegotiated following his untimely death on 5 October 2011. Both Apple and Google are essentially in the distribution business and have made the Internet a default option for their corporate strategies. YouTube, which Google owns, and the iPhone are net-based platforms to disseminate user-generated content of various kinds, with the former originally marketed as a "killer app" for the latter. But the responses of Hollywood and Madison Avenue to the two companies' endeavors have been almost antithetic. At the same time, as suggested earlier, Apple and Google have become fierce competitors on the smartphone market, with some bloggers predicting in 2011 that Google's freely distributed Android OS will erase the iPhone's once enormous lead. Whatever the outcome, the dynamics of this competition certainly are one reason that mobiles have become key to the future of media entertainment.

Yet what do today's embodied experiences of movement (and movies), the constant movement of data between multiple platforms, and the dynamic personalization of media actually imply? To what extent are the haptic pleasures of a gesture-based interface and a 3.5-inch display with touch controls challenging conventional notions of media usage and experience? How are ideas about user-led innovation, collaborative mapping, or creative empowerment to be understood and reconciled, if at all, with techniques of mobile surveillance, personal rights, and prescriptive social software? What about the economy of the App Store and the perceived "crisis of choice" in the digital era? Finally, in what ways might studying the iPhone contribute to the analysis of digital media, the history or philosophy of media technology, or a theoretical understanding of media as data? Addressing these and other questions, this book contains a mix of critical and conceptual articles exploring the iPhone as a technological prototype, a platform of media productivity, and as a part of media life.

The book has been organized into four main sections. "Data Archaeologies" follows Charles Acland's skeptical insight that all cultural analysis of media has to forgo a fetishization of "the conjectural at the expense of the organic" by opening media-archaeological perspectives on the iPhone.[38] De-essentializing the media object and situating it into a historical and comparative perspective, the articles in this section trace the "iPhone experience" across practices as diverse as visiting a cinema or an art exhibition. "Politics of Redistribution," in turn, focuses the iPhone as an "ideal-type commodity form" and, more specifically, on the various attempts and negotiations related to distributing audiovisual content over Apple's mobile gadgets. The third section, "The App Revolution," follows Barbara Flueckiger's interest in the "technobole"—a term borrowed from Frank Beau—that is, in analyses of technology that ultimately aims at understanding its position in culture and society. Hyped as revolutionary per se, Apple's apps require a particularly careful consideration of their practical, personal, and not the least political "applications." "Mobile Lives," finally, ventures into what Lane De Nicola in his contribution accurately calls "dark culture": the section investigates the omnipresent phenomena of our mediated everyday, otherwise mostly invisible to observation—from learning practices over the aesthetics of displays to the politics of end-user licensing agreements. The volume ends with a polemical piece of cultural criticism provided by sociologist Dalton Conley.

NOTES

1. Wayne Sutton, "OMG It's Steve Jobs!" 7 March 2010, http://waynesutton.net/omg-its-steve-jobs-im-the-only-one-yelling-at (15 June 2011).

2. Heidi A. Campbell and Antonio C. La Pastina, "How the iPhone Became Divine: New Media, Religion, and the Intertextual Circulation of Meaning," *New Media and Society* 12, no. 7 (2010): 1191–1207.

3. "iTunes Digital Music for your Mac," Apple.com (through the Internet Archive Wayback Machine), 18 January 2001, http://web.archive.org/web/20010124074700/www.apple.com/itunes/ (15 June 2011). For the current advertising, see http://www.apple.com/itunes/ (15 June 2011).

4. See Alisa Perren and Karen Petruska's chapter in this book.

5. Robert X. Cringely, "Apple's iPad Invasion. First Stop, Hollywood" *Infoworld*, 8 March 2010, http://www.infoworld.com/d/adventures-in-it/apples-ipad-invasion-first-stop-hollywood-972 (15 June 2011).

6. Antoine Hennion and Sophie Dubuisson, *Le design: L'object dans l'usage* (Paris: Les Presses de l'École des Mines, 1996), 111.

7. All Apple TV commercials can, naturally, be found on YouTube.

8. Steven Johnson, "Rethinking a Gospel of the Web," *New York Times*, 10 April 2010.

9. Ben Sisario and Miguel Helft, "Apple Is Called Poised to Offer 'Cloud' Music," *New York Times*, 20 May 2011. See also Sean Cubitt, Robert Hassan, and Ingrid Volkmer, "Does Cloud Computing Have a Silver Lining?" *Media, Culture, and Society* 33, no. 1 (2011): 149–58.

10. Barb Dybwad, "Apple Wants to Bring Hollywood Into the Cloud, Too," *Mashable*, 2 March 2010, http://mashable.com/2010/03/02/apple-itunes-hollywood-cloud/ (15 June 2011).

11. Stephen Kline, Nick Dyer-Witheford, and Greig de Peuter, *Digital Play: The Interaction of Technology, Culture, and Marketing* (Montreal: McGill-Queen's University Press, 2003), 50.

12. Jennifer Holt and Alisa Perren, eds., *Media Industries: History, Theory, and Method* (Oxford: Wiley-Blackwell, 2009). See also, for instance, Jon Agar, *Constant Touch: A Global History of the Mobile Phone* (Cambridge: Icon Books, 2004); Paul Levinson, *Cellphone: The Story of the World's Most Mobile Medium and How It Has Transformed Everything* (New York: Palgrave, 2004); Howard Rheingold, *Smart Mobs: The Next Social Revolution* (Cambridge: Basic Books, 2002); Rich Ling, *The Mobile Connection: The Cell Phone's Impact on Society* (San Francisco: Morgan Kaufman, 2004); and Gerard Goggin, *Cell Phone Culture: Mobile Technology in Everyday Life* (London: Routledge, 2006).

13. Robert Sloss, "Das drahtlose Jahrhundert," in *Die Welt in hundert Jahren*, ed. Arthur Brehmer (Berlin: Buntdruck, 1908), 27–50.

14. William Uricchio, *Media, Simultaneity, Convergence: Culture and Technology in an Age of Intermediality* (Utrecht: Universiteit Utrecht, 1997).

15. Cf. Glenn Jessop, "A Brief History of Mobile Telephony: The Story of Phones and Cars," *Southern Review* 38, no.3 (2006): 43–60. See also Clara Völker, *Mobile Medien. Zur Genealogie des Mobilfunks und zur Ideengeschichte von Virtualität* (Bielefeld: Transcript, 2010).

16. Brian Tufo, "BlackBerry Maker RIM Thought Apple Was Lying About iPhone in 2007?" *TiPb*, 28 December 2010, http://www.tipb.com/2010/12/28/rim-thought -iphone-2007/ (15 June 2011).

17. Jodi Dean, *Blog Theory: Feedback and Capture in the Circuits of Drive* (London: Polity Press, 2010).

18. Siegfried Zielinski, *Audiovisions: Cinema and Television as Entr'actes in History* (Amsterdam: Amsterdam University Press, 1999), 16.

19. Henry Jenkins, *Convergence Culture: Where Old and New Media Collide* (New York: New York University Press, 2006), 15.

20. Anna McCarthy, *Ambient Television: Visual Culture and Public Space* (Durham, N.C.: Duke University Press, 2001), 225.

21. Frank Rose, *The Art of Immersion: How the Digital Generation Is Remaking Hollywood, Madison Avenue, and the Way We Tell Stories* (New York: Norton, 2011).

22. Georgio Agamben, "What Is an Apparatus?" in *What Is an Apparatus? And Other Essays* (Stanford, Calif.: Stanford University Press, 2009), 1–24.

23. Lisa Gitelman, *Always Already New: Media, History, and the Data of Culture* (Cambridge, Mass.: MIT Press, 2008), 6.

24. The iPhone tracker for visualizing information saved in the iPhone's hidden location history file can be downloaded for free; see http://petewarden.github.com/iPhoneTracker/; Alice E. Marwick, "Foursquare, Locative Media, and Prescriptive Social Software," 22 April 2009, http://www.tiara.org/blog/?p=453 (15 June 2011).

25. Cf. James R. Beniger, *The Control Revolution: Technological and Economic Origins of the Information Society* (Cambridge, Mass.: Harvard University Press, 1986); and Richard Florida, *The Rise of the Creative Class: And How It's Transforming Work, Leisure, Community, and Everyday Life* (New York: Perseus, 2002).

26. Gitelman, *Always Already New*, 6. Cf. the contribution of Nanna Verhoeff and others to *Digital Material: Tracing New Media in Everyday Life and Technology*, ed. Marianne van den Boomen et al. (Amsterdam: Amsterdam University Press, 2009).

27. Justine Erziak, "iPhone Bill," www.youtube.com/watch?v=UdULhkh6yeA (15 June 2011).

28. Fred Vogelstein, "The Untold Story: How the iPhone Blew Up the Wireless Industry," *Wired*, 1 September 2008.

29. For a discussion, see, for example, Sarah Perez, "Mobile Data Explosion: Seventy-five Exabytes by 2015," *New York Times*, 1 February 2011.

30. David Pogue, "Ordering iPhone 4: What a Mess," *Pogue's Post: The Latest in Technology*, 15 June 2010, http://pogue.blogs.nytimes.com/2010/06/15/iphone-4-ordering-what-a-mess/ (15 June 2011).

31. Chris Smith, "US iPhone War Starts as Verizon Wireless iPhone 4 Launched," *Techradar.com*, 11 January 2011, http://www.techradar.com/news/phone-and-communications/mobile-phones/us-iphone-war-starts-as-verizon-wireless-iphone-4-launched-920922 (15 June 2011).

32. See, for example, Philip Elmer-DeWitt, "Why It's Harder to Make Money on Android Than on Apple's iOS," *CNNMoney*, 27 May 2011, http://tech.fortune.cnn.com/2011/05/27/why-its-harder-to-make-money-on-android-than-on-apples-ios/ (15 June 2011).

33. Richard Ling, *The Mobile Connection: The Cell Phone's Impact on Society* (San Francisco: Morgan Kaufmann, 2004).

34. Goggin, *Cell Phone Culture*, 13, 16.

35. See, for instance, Larissa Hjort and Gerard Goggin, *Mobile Technologies: From Telecommunications to Media* (New York: Routledge, 2009); Jonathan Gray, *Show Sold Separately: Promos, Spoilers, and other Media Paratexts* (New York: New York University Press, 2010); and universities offering courses in transmedia studies, such as Sint-Lukas Brussels University College of Art and Design (Belgium).

36. Cf. David N. Rodowick, "Dr. Strange Media, or How I Learned to Stop Worrying and Love Film Theory," in *Inventing Film Studies*, ed. Lee Grieveson and Haidee Wasson (Durham, N.C.: Duke University Press, 2008), 374–98.

37. Still, it certainly is a research challenge to keep track of the voluminous press coverage of Apple. Although speculations make up the bulk of company news and

information on the Internet is hard to verify, Apple's press releases and their reverberations in tech journalism are indicative of the company's much-criticized manner of keeping things under wrap, which has also led to a number of media controversies such as "iPhone-gate," for example.

38. Charles R. Acland, *Screen Traffic: Movies, Multiplexes, and Global Culture* (Durham, N.C.: Duke University Press, 2003), 17.

I
Data Archaeologies

CHAPTER I

With Eyes, With Hands

The Relocation of Cinema Into the iPhone

FRANCESCO CASETTI AND SARA SAMPIETRO

A S IS WELL known, the digital revolution has resulted in the overlapping and mingling of media. We now read the newspaper on our computers, listen to music on our telephones, and have been watching films on our televisions for a long time now. Yet, contrary to expectations, the landscape that is born of these phenomena is neither chaotic nor amorphous, for if it is true that media are no longer tied to an exclusive platform or technology, it is also true that they continue to possess their own identities. The newspaper, the radio, and the cinema retain their identities even as they assume new guises. On what does their ability to survive depend? What allows them to remain themselves regardless of their migration?

One commonly held opinion is that media enjoy a certain continuity because their new platforms are capable of "translating" or "absorbing" traditional apparatuses. The concepts of "recoding" and "remediation" advanced, respectively, by Lev Manovich and Jay Bolter and Richard Grusin,[1] lead in this direction. Ours is a different hypothesis and in some respects a more radical one: media survive because a type of *experience* that characterizes them survives.

The newspaper, the radio, and the cinema have refined certain ways of addressing the spectator and therefore of activating her senses, nourishing her knowledge, extracting her needs, and modeling her actions. The news narrates reality as a continuous event, thus appealing to our desire to be informed and our need to feel connected to things. Radio programs transform the environment into an aural flow and ask us to open our ears and trust in an unseen voice. The cinema restores to us the world as it exists, and it simultaneously constructs a new one. In doing so, it urges us to link the real to the possible. The media experience is the experience that media offer of themselves as well as the experience that, via themselves, they offer to the world. Wherever we follow the totality of events via words in the form of news, wherever there reaches us an aural flow guided by a voice and emitted by a speaker, wherever visual images in movement blend the real and the possible, fact and narration: it is there that we find, in some form, the newspaper, the radio, and the cinema. The particular technology that places us in this position is significant, but it is not decisive. Media have liberated themselves from their old devices, and they have acquired greater independence. What is important is that their particular ways of presenting content and presenting themselves—or, better yet, of giving life and of living—persist. In short, what assures their continuity are the ways in which they make us open our eyes, our ears, and our minds—ways that have been elaborated over time and by now have become distinctive characteristics for each medium. Each medium survives insofar as its way of involving us survives.

We will use the term "relocation" to denote the process through which a media experience reactivates itself and offers itself elsewhere with respect to where it originated, via different devices and in other environments.[2] Relocation involves repetition: at its foundation, in fact, there is something that returns, that multiplies itself, that makes itself more available to the point of stripping itself of its exclusivity, if not of its uniqueness. This follows the trajectory that Walter Benjamin described in detail in his analysis of the technical reproducibility of works of arts.[3] However, relocation does not entail the reproducibility of artworks or texts as much as it does the reproducibility of the experience: what is multiplied is the possibility of living a situation in contact with a medium outside of its traditional conditions.

Concurrently, relocation involves a transfer, and as a result of this shift, what seemed to pertain exclusively to one field implants itself elsewhere: it emigrates toward new territories, it conquers new spaces. We recognize here the logic of flows—of people, goods, money, ideas, and discourses—which Arjun Appadurai has recently characterized as one of the central characteristics of a globalized world.[4] However, relocation demonstrates that media are not merely "highways" that facilitate these flows: they are also ambits within which certain sensibilities are heightened and which, in turn, can be transferred into other contexts. Media are "worlds" that can be shifted elsewhere.

Therefore, we have a repetition and a transfer: a flourishing of copies and a settlement in a new territory. It is along these lines that relocation converses with those processes of convergence that signal the new media landscape— and the emerging media cultures.[5]

Filmic Vision in Movement: A Paradox and Two Conditions

Let us try to understand whether, and to what extent, the filmic experience is able to relocate to devices such as the iPhone. Seemingly, the individual and mobile mode of vision that characterize the iPhone is the exact opposite of the collective and immobile vision that cinema adopted from the time of its birth. The rise of cinema at the end of the nineteenth century created a clear-cut opposition between, on the one hand, spectacles based on fixed images and spectators free to move in space according to an individual route, as is the case with the panorama and the museum, and, on the other hand, spectacles based on mobile images (or at least almost mobile) and fixed spectators, gathered together in an audience in front of the screen, as in the theater or the magic lantern.[6] Cinema's inclusion in the latter group inevitably led to the characterization of the first group as noncinematic.

Nevertheless, in today's panorama of new media two conditions seem to emerge that render this opposition less radical. The first is the possibility of constructing "existential bubbles" that allow the subject to create an individual space even within collective environments. When using a medium in public situations, one often surrounds oneself with invisible barriers that offer refuge, even though one continues to feel open to the gazes of others. This situation is not dissimilar from that of the traditional movie theater, in which one slips from a collective encounter to individual attention to the film: in the first moment one confronts the surrounding public; in the second moment one enters into intimacy with what is represented on the screen.[7] The mobile cinematic spectator reactivates this situation. On the one hand, he is completely exposed to the surrounding environment; on the other hand, he suspends the reality that surrounds him when he turns his attention to the film offered to him by the device he has in hand and in so doing constructs a "bubble" in which he recuperates a direct relationship with the images on the screen. The reality surrounding such a spectator obliges him to engage in multitasking, but the institution of this "bubble" allows him to ideally replicate the spatial structure that characterizes the movie theater, even in open and practicable environments.

The second new condition is directly linked to the logic of convergence. The concentration of media on new devices may follow roundabout routes, employing other media as intermediate steps. This is the case, for instance, of the mobile spectator who watches a film: what she sees does not issue from the movie theater; rather, it is mediated by the television or the computer. This is evident at the level of provider; especially in Europe, and despite the ever-growing diffusion of applications such as Netflix and Hulu, the filmic material accessible on a mobile phone is usually taken from a television broadcast or from YouTube. This is also the case with regard to modes of consumption: a spectator may activate a style of vision that he learned by using the computer or watching television. Therefore, mobile media can host stationary media such as cinema because the latter is preadapted to the mobile situation, so to speak, thanks to a previous shift. A film "lands" on a mobile phone after a two-phase journey: it needs the intermediate stopover in order to arrive securely in its new media environment.

These two aspects, which we shall call the "bubble condition" and the "two-step condition," are crucial for understanding the relocation of the filmic experience on devices such as the mobile phone, the tablet, the laptop, and so on. They emerge clearly from an ethnographic study conducted in preparation for this essay, and they represent two partly original findings.[8] Now we shall examine them better within the framework of the experience of iPhone users.

The iPhone: Distinctive Characteristics

The first trait that emerged from our ethnographic study is the tendency of iPhone users to consider this media platform to be an advanced solution to the process of convergence. In particular, users perceived the iPhone, on a purely technological level, to be a device capable of guaranteeing a great range of uses: "You can use the internet on other cell phones, too, but you don't, because it's unwieldy in the end (m, 27)." But the iPhone is also perceived as a perfect meeting point between realities such as Google, Facebook, YouTube, Skype, Flickr, and so on: it allows one to bundle within a single instrument one's entire referential universe: "Everything that's hot now" (f, 25); "You have everything there. You really don't need anything else" (f, 33). Finally, various expressive forms cohabitate and intermingle within the iPhone.[9] So, for example, cinematic or television products become videogames, creating a path of consumption that is highly performative and involving.[10]

A second notion accompanies that of the ability to interpret media convergence: the idea that the iPhone possesses its own identity. This identity rises from its origin in the world of Apple: "As soon as someone who already knows Apple sees an iPhone, he knows that it is part of that family" (m, 27). Apple in particular has tried to do away with the appendices (the keyboard, buttons, stylus, etc.) in favor of their integration within the operating system: "What wins you over is the extreme cleanliness of the whole thing: the fact that it is all within one screen" (m, 29). The display therefore becomes the quasi-exclusive reference for interaction with the user, making explicit its double nature as screen and monitor. What we have here is both a visual device and an interactive interface,[11] a surface that mobilizes the eye as well as the hand: "At first it seems a little difficult, it confuses you . . . it's difficult to write or to page through photos; but then you realize that it's perfect, that it works" (f, 30); "The cell phone, the computer, the GPS, the agenda, it's all there . . . and that's not bad" (f, 25).

These first two aspects of the iPhone—its being a strong response to convergence and its being an identifiable device—shed light on how *two-step relocation* can get a footing. In fact, the iPhone has integrated within itself functionalities of other media, and, at the same time, it presents itself as the site of an intense and valuable experience: a true point of arrival with respect to the migration that cinema engaged in once it left its original environment: "It does things that others do—it incorporates lots of functions that are trendy right now—but once you have it in your hand, it seems like a completely different thing from all the others" (m, 35).

Alongside these two characteristics of the iPhone, others emerge with similar force. The first is the device's ability to place the user in the position of managing, in an autonomous and personalized manner, her own consumption practices, in terms of both content and function.[12] The user derives a sense of reassurance from this. The iPhone adapts to the contingent situations that characterize the day-to-day, and, at the same time, it offers solutions to individual choices: "If you, who manage everything, who decide what to do . . . you have many possibilities and you can choose one every time" (f, 33).

In addition to being a flexible device, the iPhone seems to also be "tidy" and "preorganized": it is not easy for the user to have the impression of being lost:

It's assuring to know that if any doubt arises I can always check the internet.

(f, 30)

And there's a ton of things that, at the beginning you say, "these are totally useless," which later you find yourself using . . . for example, I used the iPhone A-level app for the shelves I just put up at home.

(m, 35)

Even if you're not someone who is addicted to the iPhone, you're able to do everything no problem, and it's even tough to do any damage.

(m, 35)

This combination of flexibility and order is of fundamental importance when one considers that the iPhone is called upon to interact constantly with various environments—more or less dispersive and chaotic in nature—and then supply adequate responses. Within this framework the platform is asked to "tame the public sphere":[13] it becomes a "mobile home," a "home away from home" for the re-creation of a sense of intimacy, meditation, and familiarity within a strange and often hostile space.[14] The iPhone succeeds well enough at responding to these exigencies by helping the user isolate himself from the surrounding context through the sizable dimensions of its screen, the high graphic and acoustic quality of its playback, the considerable attractiveness of most of its applications, and the participation it requires of the user:

The visuals are beautiful and clear . . . it doesn't seem like a cell phone—you watch it gladly.

(m, 27)

Watching movies on the train is also a way of passing the time; if you don't, you end up staring out the window for hours, and you get bored.

(f, 30)

You can stick yourself in a corner of the train with your headphones on: this way you're a little protected.

(f, 25)

All of this allows us to consider the iPhone as a device that is particularly adept at constructing an "existential bubble" in which the spectator can find refuge while remaining exposed to the surrounding environment. It projects around itself an environment in which the distinctions tend to blur between work time and free time, between public time and private time, between public space and domestic space, between diversion-related consumption and work-related consumption.[15] However, it also allows its user to take control of all the aforementioned situations and gather them up in one single, personalized area—in a bubble.

Cinema and Video on the iPhone: The Mediation of YouTube

We have discussed the manner in which the iPhone opens itself up to a two-step relocation. But who filters the arrival of the video content? Through which intermediate steps does the content pass before arriving on the display screen? The iPhone allows for an array of access possibilities: podcasts, online streaming, files transferred from a PC, purchasing content from the iTunes store. However, what emerges above all is its connection with YouTube: it is thanks to YouTube that the iPhone can become a point toward which audiovisual and filmic experiences emigrate.

This connection between iPhone and YouTube rests primarily on the presence of a specific application.[16] The result is that the two realities seem to meld perfectly:

> [YouTube] seems to have been created just for the iPhone; you have all your videos there, and you click on the one you want to see.
>
> (m, 29)

> If I try to transfer a video onto my iPhone from my PC I go crazy; but, seeing as how you can get access directly to YouTube, it makes no sense to go crazy.
>
> (m, 27)

> Free, easy . . . I practically only watch videos [on my iPhone].
>
> (f, 30)

Furthermore, the access to audiovisual material via YouTube allows the user to avoid the constraints that characterize other channels. For the most part these constraints are technical (for example, the need to recode audiovisual content into the principle digital formats in order to make them usable on the iPhone, or the lack of Flash), distributional (the limited availability of cinematographic and serial content on the Italian iTunes store), and economic (the cost of content on the iTunes store). It is true that the in recent months the availability of new applications and services (e.g., Netflix) mitigates these obstacles, but YouTube continues to be a point of reference for the circulation of audiovisual content.[17] The effect is that YouTube becomes the cinematic archive par excellence. It is worth adding, however, that this two-stage relocation exacts a price from an experiential point of view. First of all, the content that YouTube supplies has by now absorbed many of its characteristics: texts are fragmented, reduced to pill-size doses, ready to be consumed with an often ludic and ironic approach. Here, cinema has, in part, un-*cinematized* itself.

YouTube also can be called upon both to recuperate content and to respond to environmental needs: consumption can be content oriented as well as context oriented. In the case of the former, the search originates from the desire to consume something specific—in our case, cinema—and in the case of the latter, one arrives at cinema from a different starting point—in particular, from elements linked to the circumstances of vision, such as the need to gather information, the pleasure of distraction, the desire to share specific content with others, and so on. Hence, a twofold effect: we have the creation of additional detours and mediations, but we also have the possibility of "finding" cinema even without necessarily having "searched" for it. This is precisely what happens when one uses the iPhone in order to furnish the environment, so to speak, resulting in a valorization of it nonetheless: "You see kids around—at the park, on the subway—who, in order to have fun and call attention to themselves, turn on videos and play them at high volume" (f, 25).

Practices of Appropriation

Let us analyze in depth the second condition that the iPhone seems to bring about: the construction of *existential bubbles*. YouTube proves useful at allowing subjects to create for themselves a dedicated and protected space in which to enjoy the filmic experience. In fact, it offers to the spectator a continuous flow of content, organized according to consequential associative chains. The passage from one video to another becomes immediate, stimulating, and in some ways "surprising" because it plays on the interpenetration between push-and-pull logic. On the one hand, the user is won over by the possibility of being able to autonomously access video material; on the other hand, she can abandon herself to the pleasure of various stimuli according to continuous associations, set off by her initial definition of relevance. This makes possible the creation of existential bubbles that have fragile walls that are easily perforated by the weight of external stimuli but are also easy to reconstruct.

The degree of closure and impermeability of the existential bubbles is strictly tied to the practices of appropriation of the audiovisual text. In particular, we may identify an *epidermal* experience, a *multifocalized* experience, and an *intimate* experience. The epidermal experience is associated with a "mobile and inattentive gaze, bored and fickle": essentially, this is a capricious manner of viewing.[18] The audiovisual becomes an object of distraction, which establishes a discontinuous and frivolous relationship with the spectator, who catches fragments of the texts, individual lines and images. In this case, the subject seems not to be particularly involved in the content, to the point of falling often into "bulimic" behavior patterns, resulting in quick and continuous jumps from one video to another: "One after another: you don't even watch them till the end" (f, 25). Accompanying this lack of involvement, however, is a high level of interaction with the device: the subject continues to act on the screen in search of pleasing content. This interaction with the apparatus seems to constitute one of the most attractive and fundamental aspects of this mode of utilization, often more relevant even than the appeal of the content itself: "You do it to play around a bit: I like playing with the screen" (m, 27).

The experience of multifocalized vision consists of "an attentive yet dispersive gaze, which does not concentrate on a single object, but devotes its attention impartially to various elements."[19] It is a mode of vision that dismantles hierarchies. Its center lies not with the audiovisual, or, better put, the audiovisual is not its only center. The act of vision is intertwined with a wide array of other activities (e.g., chatting with others nearby or monitoring the surrounding environment): "It drives my girlfriend crazy, but just because I'm watching a video doesn't mean I can't also be listening to her" (m, 29).

Finally, there is the intimate experience, "an experience centered on the screen, and characterized by an exclusive relationship with the text,"[20] or, in the case of YouTube, with the series of texts encountered and watched along the way. This experience of vision may develop into pure contemplation—an abandonment of oneself to the flow of video and stimuli proposed by the system—or into performance—a desire to act directly on the device in order to access the requested contents in line with one's own expectations: "I go in search of what interests me, period . . . not like those people who sit there for hours just wasting time" (f, 30); "I can also get fixated on YouTube, starting out by searching for my favorite singers' concerts, then from those to others' concerts, and I end up spending hours on it without realizing it" (m, 27). The contemplative and the performative nature of this vision refers back to a common matrix: the search for intimacy with the text and with the entire act of engagement with it, which can pass "through an abandoning of oneself to its suggestions . . . or through its appropriations and transformations."[21]

These three types of experience—epidermal, multifocalized, and intimate—create three types of experiential bubbles, endowed with different levels of resistance, duration, and strength. The epidermal bubble is created from the physical relationship with the device more so than from a relationship with the content: it is a bubble constructed around a certain "doing." The multifocalized bubble appears in all its ephemerality: it is constructed out of contingency. The intimate bubble presents itself as a strong reality: the spectator succeeds in effectively isolating herself from her context within it.

Bubbles also depend on the fact that they are either constructed around an individual vision or include various individuals. In the first case, the "quality" of the bubble is contingent upon the ability of the apparatus to respond to the user's requests and on the ability of the images to capture and hold the user's interest. In the case of collective vision, what is relevant is the possibility for the user to achieve a physical and affective proximity with somebody else: "If you want to, you can even watch something together with someone else. You just have to concentrate on the screen and stay close together. . . . I've watched tons of stuff together with my friends" (f, 25). From this follows, just as in the movie theater environment, the necessity of respecting behavioral norms and habits that not only facilitate the act of vision but also foster good relations with the other spectators: "You have to hold [the iPhone] at a little distance; and you also have to share the headphones" (f, 25). Furthermore, there follows the need to open oneself up to dynamics of negotiation, which call into play the choices of vision: "The you start: 'Let's watch this one. . . . No, that one . . ?' because one video makes you think of other ones, and you want to see something, but the other person has other tastes" (f, 25). Between the individual bubble and the collective bubble, a third case may be added: bubbles that can continually shatter as a result of intrusion by outside subjects or elements but that can easily and quickly reconstitute themselves, placing the subject back within an isolated context: "Your cell phone rings, the guy next to you asks you something, and so you get interrupted, but then you just start up again" (m, 29); "My girlfriend always does it: she asks me what it is, she glances at it, and then she leaves" (m, 35). The strength of the bubble depends on the fact that it can manifest itself, putting the subject in contact with the film "as if" he were in the traditional environment of the movie theater, even though he is acting in open spaces.

Conclusion

The analysis of the experience of mobile vision has allowed us to explore more deeply the process of the relocation of the filmic experience. If the latter can migrate toward situations that may appear distant from those of the movie theater, it is not only because of the introduction of new technologies but also a result of the intervention of certain conditions. Here we have pointed out two of them: the creation of existential bubbles in which the spectator may establish a personal relationship with film wherever she may find herself and the mediation of another medium through a two-step move, which allows for a smooth adaptation of cinema to the new device in which it inserts itself. In the case of the iPhone both these conditions seem to manifest themselves. This occurs principally through its marriage with YouTube. First of all, YouTube has figured out both how to incorporate past and present cinematic production within itself and how to adapt itself to apparatuses born not necessarily with the cinema in mind, such as the iPhone. In this way, YouTube acts as a bridge between the traditional filmic experience and the mobile filmic experience. The cost of this mediation is evident: the iPhone user experiences cinema in a fragmentary form and via the retakes and recuts that are typical of YouTube. Second, YouTube, in conjunction with the iPhone, helps users create specialized and protected spaces. It does this thanks to the quality of the image and sound offered by the iPhone and thanks to the ability of the YouTube system to involve the spectator in practices both performative and immersive.

The study of the migration of the audiovisual experience toward mobile devices, in addition to constituting a paradigmatic example of the relocation process, contains intriguing hints and questions with respect to the overall convergent media context. First of all, this study allows us to reaffirm the importance of reading the processes of convergence not as a simple combination of various media environments but as a continuous mingling of technologies, experience forms, and practices. The encounter between two platforms and between two modalities of use should always be framed within a larger and more complex phenomenon: there is never a direct route but rather an open and dialectic confrontation, and it never leads to a destination point but rather to momentary configurations, open to additional changes depending on innovative articulations of the sociotechnological landscape and the consumption practices inscribed within them. Second, from a phenomenological point of view, we have underlined the importance of carving out and of making sense of the fullness of the consumption experience—even in the contemporary media context, characterized by the multiplication and fragmentation of content and occasions of access. Via both contemplative dynamics and performative engagement, the activity of consumption is still capable of representing a strong moment—a moment that maintains its own definition and identity, notwithstanding the multiplicity of external references and interconnections.

NOTES

Translation by Daniel Leisawitz.

1. Lev Manovich, *The Language of New Media* (Cambridge, Mass.: MIT Press, 2001); Jay David Bolter and Richard Grusin, *Remediation: Understanding New Media* (Cambridge, Mass.: MIT Press, 1999).

2. For more on the relocation of the filmic experiences, see Francesco Casetti, "The Last Supper in Piazza della Scala," *Cinèma & Cie* 11 (Fall 2008): 7–14; Casetti, "Filmic Experience," *Screen* 50, no. 1 (Spring 2009): 56–66; and Casetti, "Back to the Motherland: The Film Theatre in the Postmedia Age," *Screen* 52, no. 1 (2011): 1–12.

3. Walter Benjamin, "The Work of Art in the Age of Mechanical Reproduction," third version, *Selected Writings*, vol. 4, ed. Marcus Bullock and Michael W. Jennings (Cambridge, Mass.: Belknap Press of Harvard University Press, 2003), 251–83. See also "The Work of Art in the Age of Its Technological Reproducibility," second version, in *The Work of Art in the Age of Its Technological Reproducibility, and Other Writings on Media*, ed. Michael W. Jennings, Brigid Doherty, and Thomas Y. Levin (Cambridge, Mass.: Belknap Press of Harvard University Press, 2008), 19–55.

4. Arjun Appadurai, *Modernity at Large: Cultural Dimensions of Globalization* (Minneapolis: University of Minnesota Press, 1996).

5. For a discussion of convergence and the cultural transformations attached to them, see Henry Jenkins, *Convergence Culture: Where Old and New Media Collide* (New York: New York University Press, 2006).

6. See Philippe-Alain Michaud, introduction to *Mouvement des images: The Movement of Images* (Paris: Centre Pompidou, 2006).

7. For a discussion of the two moments of the filmic experience, the observation of Erich Feldman remain quite valid: "Considérations sur la situation du spectateur au cinéma," *Revue Internationale de Filmologie* 26 (1956).

8. The ethnographic study was carried out in Italy during the first semester of 2010. It involved six subjects (three women and three men) between the ages of twenty-five and thirty-five, all of whom had been using an iPhone for at least six months before

the start of the study. The research was carried out in three phases. First, the subjects were interviewed individually in order to understand how they lived with the platform and its role in their daily lives. In particular the interview touched on the following elements: motivations for purchase; habitual practices of use, with particular regard to applications (calls, messages, photos, videos), places and times of use, and the aspects of the device (screen size, touch screen, the performative possibilities offered to the user, and so on); compatibility, the relationship between this device and other media systems (computer, mp4 player etc.), and the eventual articulation of cross-platform use; and the contents produced by and accessed through the iPhone (photos, video, etc.). Second, the subjects were asked to keep a consumption diary for one week, in which they described their daily use of the platform. In this way it was possible to photograph and map out the use made of the iPhone. Finally, a last telephone interview was carried out with the subjects in which they provided more details about the habits that emerged from their consumption diary. This ethnographic research was conducted by Sara Sampietro.

9. On this subject, see M. Rosi and F. Giordano, "Applicazione per iPhone: Tra film interattivo e gioco," in *Il film in tasca. Videofonino, cinema e televisione*, ed. M. Ambrosini, G. Maina, and E. Marcheschi (Ghezzano [PI]: Felici Editori, 2009).

10. One thinks, for example, of the game based on the quiz show *Who Wants to Be a Millionaire?* or of the games based on the TV series *Numb3rs*.

11. Maurizio Ambrosini, "Visioni digitabili. Il videofonino come schermo," in Rosi and Giordano, "Applicazione per iPhone," 18.

12. In the case of the iPhone, it is worth noting that the push toward personalization exists alongside an openness to socialization. Not only do the downloaded and continually updated applications take account of the user's tastes, needs, and personal interests, but they also constitute resources and objects of relational exchanges: "If you come to discover that a certain application is among the most downloaded ones, the desire to get it comes to you spontaneously" (m, 35); "Among friends who also have it, we are there every time discussing the novelties, applications that work better or worse, and then we exchange them . . . one time my girlfriend became angry, because my friend and I spent the entire evening doing only that" (m, 29).

13. Paul du Gay et al., *Doing Cultural Studies: The Story of the Sony Walkman* (London: Sage, 1997), 106.

14. M. Bull, "To Each Their Own Bubble: Mobile Spaces of Sound in the City," in *Media/Space: Place, Scale, and Culture in a Media Age*, ed. Nick Couldry and Anne McCarthy (London: Routledge, 2003), 285, 283. For more on the topic of this re-creation, see David Morley, "What's 'Home' Got to Do with It? Contradictory Dynamics in the Domestication of Technology and the Dislocation of Domesticity," *European Journal of Cultural Studies* 6, no. 4 (2003): 435–58; Barbara Scifo, *Culture Mobili. Ricerche sull'adozione giovanile della telefonia* (Milan: Vita e Pensiero, 2005); Giovanna Mascheroni, *Le comunità viaggianti. Società reticolare e mobile dei viaggiatori indipendenti* (Milan: FrancoAngeli, 2007).

15. For these reasons, Cooper defines nomadic media and their use as "indiscreet" in the sense that they break down consolidated distinctions (G. Cooper, "The Mutable Mobile: Social Theory in the Wireless World," in *Wireless World: Social, Cultural and*

International Issues in Mobile Communications and Computing, ed. B. Brown, N. Green, and R. Harper [London: Springer, 2002], 24). The following quotation from one of the subjects is apropos: "Even during some university classes and conferences, maybe you sit there and watch a video . . . you shouldn't do it, you should listen . . . but, you know" (f, 25).

16. YouTube is included in the basic applications packet that is implemented directly within the iPhone's operating system.

17. Particularly in Italy, in the time after our research was conducted, iTunes Italia has partially overcome earlier constraints with a film download and rental service, which is characterized by easier payment options and increased Italian-language content. Additionally, new software (Airplay, Air video) have been introduced in order to boost cross-platform integration and the streaming of audiovisual content. Concurrently, recent changes to YouTube have also been implemented that favor its continued widespread use, in particular, the new possibility of uploading videos that exceed fifteen minutes in length.

18. Mariagrazia Fanchi, *Spettatore* (Milan: Editore Il Castoro, 2005), 41.

19. Fanchi, *Spettatore*, 43.

20. Fanchi, *Spettatore*, 39.

21. Mariagrazia Fanchi, "Metamorfosi, divinazioni e presagi," in *Terre Incognite. Lo spettatore italiano e le nuove forme dell'esperienza del film*, ed. F. Casetti and M. Fanchi (Rome: Carocci, 2006), 110.

CHAPTER 2

Navigating Screenspace

Toward Performative Cartography

NANNA VERHOEFF

A WIDE RANGE OF innovative navigation software is being developed for the iPhone that makes new ways of navigating urban space possible. Interactive tours, augmented reality, locative media, and mobile navigation all contribute to an expanding and transforming field of cartographic screen practices that not only represent but also create space: a *screenspace*. This chapter explores how Apple's iPhone allows for a creative navigation that constructs such a hybrid space in which pervasive presence, embedded pasts, and evolving futures intersect.

With touch screen, camera, compass, GPS, network connectivity, and the diverse mapping applications that are currently being developed, the iPhone has effectively become a cartographic interface. The hybrid interface of this gadget allows its users to navigate not only the machine and its display but also the physical space surrounding it as it provides an interface for organizing bits, pixels, and spatial coordinates alike. In today's culture of ubiquitous digital mobility, the hybridity of the iPhone interface, as with competing smartphone models, thus impels us to investigate the complexity of navigation as a prominent cartographic and epistemological model, that is, a visual regime of navigation.

This navigational model, I will argue, brings about a shift in cartography as we have come to know it. Originating in the art of making maps but putting forward a new regime of understanding and representing space, mobile cartography has infused spatial representation with a distinct temporal and procedural dimension. The iPhone testifies to the advent of *performative cartography*. For it offers a dynamic map that emerges and changes during its user's journey. Both spatial categories of physical and information space are inextricably connected in a hybrid screenspace of this new form of mapping. Producing images while viewing them—a cartographic collapse of making-while-navigating interactive maps—the user-navigator engages physically with the iPhone in a temporally dynamic and spatially layered process. This process requires cooperation among the device's specifications (hardware), the applications' affordances (software), and the user's activity (interface) in a mutual undertaking of connectivity, participation, and mobility.

A Layered Interface

As a mobile, hybrid device, the iPhone has an interface that features a complex and layered structure of characteristics and affordances, which makes a broad range of interactive practices possible. Therefore, the iPhone may prompt questions about its specificity as a *hybrid object*.[1] Because it is a mobile device, questions concerning the iPhone's hybridity are intrinsically related to movement, touch, and the process of spatial transformation. In short, hybridity relates to iPhone *interfacing*, an entanglement of technologies, applications, and interactive practices. This interfacing takes place within what one might call a mobile screening arrangement, or *dispositif*.[2] In other words, the iPhone as a hybrid object is embedded within a mobile arrangement that encompasses both the perceptual positioning of the (mobile) user and the physical (interactive) interfacing with the screen. The screening arrangement in motion, taking place within public space and making connections with this space, establishes a *mobile sphere*: a space that is marked by mobility and connectivity and constructed within the (mobile) arrangement of user, location, and device.

This mobility in space is intricately bound to the mobility, or flexibility, of the on-screen space itself: the iPhone's interactive touch screen requires physical manipulation for its operation. Given the use of the iPhone for navigation, the mobility of the device makes it a visceral interface: the entire body of the user is incorporated in mobility and space making.

The iPhone has a cartographic interface for the simultaneous navigation of both on-screen and off-screen space. In a marked difference from historical screen uses such as televisual or cinematic viewing, the iPhone enables navigating both the machine itself and the physical space surrounding its user. The traditional distinction of making, transmitting, and receiving images is abandoned by virtue of the multitouch screen and the divergent practices of mobile "touch-screening." A further characteristic of the mobile screen is the way it positions the user within a mobile sphere, implying an ambulant locatedness and, consequently, flexible site-specificity. Such applications for the iPhone as Foursquare, where one can "check in" on specific locations, or TweepsAround, which uses augmented-reality software for (on-screen) visualizing the (off-screen) presence of Twitter connections in the area testifies to the popularity of these affordances of mobile location marking.

The iPhone's mobility and physicality, I argue, point toward the performative and embodied features of interactivity as being characteristic of navigation generally. From this point of view, navigation entails not only a spatial decoding of map information, orientation, and mobility but also a cultural trope that makes our sense of (spatial) presence, as well as (temporal) present, into hybrid and flexible categories. What I call screenspace is activated by the simultaneous construction of on-screen and off-screen spaces when traversing in fluid motion with navigation devices in our hands.[3]

As a device for navigation, the iPhone employs a layered interface. While intricately connected and, hence, difficult to isolate, conceptually there are three (nonhierarchical) levels that are all essential for navigation. First, navigation comprises the *internal interfacing* aspects of applications: the back-end operating system and software and, consequently, the *processing* of data. This includes so-called application-programming interfaces (API), making communication between applications possible, as well as the communication of the software with the graphical user interface that enables us to "read," to understand and use them. The Google Maps API is a good example; since it is open source, it has become a highly adaptable framework for all kinds of implementations. It is also suitable for mapping applications because it provides tools for mashups, or Web-application hybrids (i.e., the integration of data from different sources within, in this case, the mapping environment of Google Maps).

The second layer of the interface concerns the spatial positioning and connectivity of the apparatus in relation to physical as well as data space: the interface of the internal instruments of the iPhone that connect it to external space. This entails features such as the digital camera, GPS, Wifi/G3 connectivity, compass, and motion sensor or accelerometer, as much as calculating the position, orientation, and velocity and the screen. This level of the interface, in short, communicates between the hardware of the device and its surrounding "reality." It includes an *inertial* navigation system, which according to Oliver J. Woodman is "a self-contained navigation technique in which measurements provided by accelerometers and gyroscopes are used to track the position and orientation of an object relative to a known starting point, orientation and velocity."[4] This inertial positioning system is combined with the *absolute* positioning system of GPS that is based on a triangulation of geographical coordinates. Moreover, Internet connectivity also positions the device via wireless connection. The second layer of the interface, then, concerns *connecting* and *positioning* the interface, whether based on inertial, absolute, photographic, or wireless technologies.

Positioning is communicated to the user, who may see the on-screen image tilt or find a representation of her position and movement signified by an "arrow" in the on-screen maps and then may read this orientation accordingly and act or move. This is all taking place on a third level of the interface I call *user interaction*, enabling the communication between the user and the internal operation of the device (first level) as it is connected to the space surrounding it (second level). While the first level of the applications interface also includes the software operation of the graphical user interface, the way in which this data is visualized and made understandable operates at this third level of user interaction. This level contains user-feedback input options such as touch screen, buttons, "shake control" (making use of the inertial system), and also representational conventions of the user interface. In the case of navigation it entails the way spatial information is represented on the screen and interacted with by the user. For example, think of the way the road is represented on screen in navigation applications for the iPhone and how one can adjust, move, or zoom in or out by using swipes, taps, or pinching movements with fingers on the multitouch screen.

Significant for the touch screen of the iPhone is that at the level of user interaction it is an instrument for both input and output. This is the level of "access" to and the "experience" of data; the action literally takes place on the screen. The iPhone's display is a multitouch screen in a technological as well as practical sense: multitouch technology allows for many ways of touching: swiping, virtual scrolling or swirling, two-fingered pinch movements for enlarging or shrinking, and so on. The dynamic horizontal or vertical scrolling of screen content establishes a connection between the image on the screen and its off-screen spaces: the frame always is a detail from a larger whole, and the map is always larger than the part or detail that is displayed on screen. Objects can be moved outside and brought into frame by the swipe of a fingertip. Buttons, keys, sticks, or a mouse controller are made redundant as the screen can be tapped for commands, and finger pressure allows operation of the zoom of a virtual camera lens, for instance.

Seen within the layered constellation of its interface, as I have suggested, understanding the iPhone requires a triple perspective: it is a machine that processes and combines data, a sensor that connects and positions data, and a medium that produces perception. Within this constellation, its "products," experienced as visuals on screen by the user, can hardly be studied as fixed texts in either a temporal sense or in terms of authorship or agency. While walking and using the iPhone for an interactive tour, for example, the different layers of the interface operate together: location-based information is processed and communicated to the user via the screen. This complex layering of the interfacing process is not experienced as such because it is filtered by the user-interaction interface. However, the integration of these processes (data processing, spatial positioning and connectivity, and communication with the user) is the *condition of possibility* for creative navigation. That is, the mechanisms and affordances that underlie our actions are not experienced as discrete layers. As such, the hybridity of the iPhone interface provides the conditions for creative navigation of screenspace as performative cartography. In what follows, I will demonstrate how the iPhone's navigation constructs an urban space in which temporal and spatial layers intersect.

Tagging, Plotting, Stitching

Navigating with the iPhone by making use of digital maps shows us how both space and time unfold in practice. The basic principle of screen-based navigation is that we see how we move while how we move enables this vision. This mutually constitutive relationship between seeing and moving forms a new principle in real time, digital cartography. It is the movement that establishes the map. Reading space requires navigation, rather than the other way around because interactive digital maps build on the logic of tagging, plotting, and stitching.

Tagging essentially means labeling objects or locations with metadata. Tags are clusters of digital data and primarily operate on the interface level of internal applications. Usually we call these markers "tags" because of the way they appear: as textual or visual information or visuals on our screen. It is, however, important to distinguish the "tag" as data and the "tag" as symbol (visual or textual). The levels on which tagging works correspond to the levels of interfacing of the map: as metadata linked to objects, as on-screen inserts providing information in relation to specific objects or locations, or as a visual layering of hybrid screenspace. This warrants a precise terminology when analyzing how tagging functions as a central principle of digital (iPhone) cartography. Although tags primarily operate on the level of data processing, when they are visualized as clickables they activate the level of user interaction. On maps they often function as geotags: location-specific hyperlinks that make a connection between data/objects and location.

The specific practice of tagging objects in space, and inserting tagged objects in a map resembles a form of *plotting* space. Plotting entails marking locations and giving them a layered presence and added meaning. When these objects are "read" and used for navigation, a form of *tracing* occurs. And when objects are integrated into a navigable whole, this practice might be called *stitching*. While originally a term used for the montage of separate images into one panoramic image (a more horizontal, two-dimensional way of stitching), the term also applies to the more general practice of "sewing together" visual layers in digital cartography. In similar terms, the developers of the recently launched augmented-reality browser Junaio speak of the application's ability to identify objects and "glue" information to them, using the metaphor of sticky glue for the process of attaching information.[5]

Tagging, plotting, and stitching operate on multiple levels of the interface: tagging on the level of software communication (data connecting to data), plotting in terms of positioning (spatially connecting the objects), and stitching as becoming effective on the screen, where the user actually perceives the connections as navigable space.

On the iPhone, tags can activate different spatial and temporal layers. Dots on the map unfold, like spatiotemporal hyperlinks. The city becomes a navigable and clickable screenspace, a terrain of pop-ups that are triggered by real-life avatars in the physical world whose movements are traced on-screen by GPS. Two-dimensional maps are a flat and motionless representation of space within a fixed frame, based on a fixed scale, and a fixed, abstract perspective. The digital map is dynamic, layered, expandable, mutable, and flexible. In contrast, geotags bring together all levels of the hybrid interface of the iPhone. They combine data, they are locative and activated by positioning or connection, and they are perceived and activated on the screen.[6]

Geotagging photographs—the tagging of photographic images with GPS coordinates of the moment and time of photographing—underscores the geographical as well as temporal aspect of tagging. Geotagging permits mnemonic mobility as it allows the placement and tracing of digital footprints. We can understand this implication of memory as a reinstating of the "lost" indexicality of photography. Once upon a time, the story goes, the (analogue) photograph was a literal imprint of light, which allegedly proved spatiotemporal reality and thus provided the image with "authenticity." Digital photography "lost" this direct relationship from reality to image. Today, however, we can attach geographical coordinates as digital information by adding data about the exact location where the picture was taken. This location is not necessarily close to what is photographed, to the object of the image. But it does locate the object as well as the photographer in reality, with the geographical coordinates constituting the image's digital footprint.

The main use of geotagging is in applications that integrate geotagged objects or images in mash-ups or in navigation software. For instance, iPhone applications that use GPS maps allow downloads of points of interest uploaded by other users, marked by geotagged images. Online, a lot of "POI collections" are either hosted by developers of (mostly commercial) navigation systems such as TomTom, Navigon, or Garmin, or compiled by end users, and they are also used by other applications, such as geocaching games. Geotags make it possible to retrace these digital footprints. In their capacity to create locative and semiotic connections, tagging, plotting, and stitching entail a potential for participatory engagement. People can build their own archival collections, use them for exchange, or participate in creating collective archives. Tagged "mobile mementos" make collective image gathering or stitching possible, based on the collection, connection, or contribution of information derived from large social databases.

Microsoft's Photosynth is an example of a larger online database that hosts a collaborative image collection that can be used to stitch together multiple photographs of the same object, space, or event taken from slightly different points of view into a navigable, panoramic whole. The platform's slogan is, in fact, "use your photos to stitch the world." Images can be stitched together and users can navigate by scrolling through the interactive panoramic rendering of the image. The website offers prefab collections, showing buildings, animals, nature reserves, and interiors—anything that works in an interactive panoramic image and gives space to upload one's own synths to the database. An application like iSynth takes this navigational model and database logic of stitching to the iPhone. The iPhone screen interface, then, allows for a touch-controlled visual navigation in a composite and stitched image field.[7]

Stitching thus is a useful term to describe the activity of connecting individual elements to create a larger, cooperative collage. Larger databases serve the double purpose of, first, creating and sharing one's individual archive and, second, using the network as a larger repository. This makes longer-running events or games possible. Geocaching, for instance, is a treasure-hunt game that uses GPS coordinates tagged to "real" containers that hold objects. When they are found, these objects have to be replaced by new objects and the user thus becomes a participant in a continuing multiplayer game. This is a clear case of tagging and plotting, and the user's reading of the map as a form of tracing. Waymarking is a similar concept but does not use real-life containers for treasures; instead, it "offers" (virtual) POIs marked by other users.

These examples of locating the (physical) object of the image and subsequently repositioning, collecting, or sharing the image itself may have consequences for our understanding of time and space. The integration of photography in applications on hybrid devices contributes to a cut-and-paste worldview: a being in the world that consists of endless possibilities. Manipulation of digital images allows the user to frame pictures, to crop and make cut-outs, and to transpose, translate, transform, and paste these cuts into new contexts. As such, the world becomes a digital, clickable scrapbook consisting of different forms of data, overlapping information, connected dimensions, and multidirectional navigation.

(AR) Browsing

Another iPhone practice where tagging, plotting, and stitching converge is the browsing of augmented reality. Augmented reality is a container term for the use of data overlays on the real-time camera view of a location. Originating from developments in virtual reality, augmented reality is currently taking off in applications for mobile phones. At present it is a fast-developing field: from marker-based augmented reality to technologies of image recognition and experiments with haptic feedback that create a sensation of material depth of objects. The AR browsers Layar and Wikitude and, more recently, Junaio are rapidly expanding the possibilities of (consumer) AR browsing for smartphones that have a video camera, GPS, a compass, and an orientation sensor, thus entailing a new way of engaging with screenspace by effacing the map representation and using a direct camera feed with a superimposed layer of data.

AR browsers allow browsing data directly within "reality" as it is represented on screen. In short, the camera eye on the device registers physical objects and transmits these images in real time to the screen, where the image is combined with layers of data in different media. These layers have various scales and dimensions within one master frame. Information is thus superimposed on a real-time image on-screen.

The screen, however, is not transparent in fact but in effect: through real-time and simultaneous display. It looks like and functions like a transparent window, framed only by the edges of the screen. This framing is temporary and directly changeable by the user holding the screen. As such, in terms of screen-based representation, AR browsing provides a complex way of framing "reality." One might say that the screen itself frames the video image on-screen, even though the information is layered on the image—in a sense, frameless. The frame is the camera image that brackets off the contours of the world-as-image. With this new mode of "reality browsing" based on a camera feed, the scale of the map on screen equals our vision through the camera lens. And like that vision, it depends on the relative distance between us and the objects seen, and the perspective naturally changes according to our movements.

AR browsers like Layar, Wikitude, or Junaio provide platforms that employ layering for different purposes, ranging from commercial applications of location-based services (such as restaurant finders) to cultural interventions: virtual expositions, on-location galleries, and museum tours. This last is particularly interesting since augmented reality offers museums and other cultural institutions a new platform for exhibition in public space. The Stedelijk Museum in Amsterdam, for example, initiated the development of ARtours, an AR infrastructure for art tours, and held an AR exhibition of virtual art in 2010. Paradoxically, the location specificity resulting from augmented reality and the tagging and plotting of space can be transported to other locations without problems, as tags can be moved easily. Consequently, time- and space-specific events such as festivals may be used as a setting for temporary virtual exhibitions, as with ARtours. In augmented reality, exhibitions can travel, multiply, and coexist in space.

A first AR flash mob was organized in April 2010 in Amsterdam. Passersby could encounter all kinds of virtual statues while wielding their mobile phones simultaneously. Initiatives like this explore ways to bring AR applications into the public space for scheduled events.[8] A less time-based programming of AR tours that nonetheless deals with time is UAR, the urban augmented reality tour initiated by the Dutch Architecture Institute. The tour features large 3D buildings that were once present in a location, will be there in the future, or were designed but were never actually built. In the hybrid screenspace that the tour establishes, present, past, and past future coincide.

As these and similar cases demonstrate, augmentation indeed is "creative" in that it not only adds to space but also inherently modifies it, making space hybrid. I am interested here in creative activity as an activity where different levels of the interface "cooperate" with the user as navigating agent in a semiotic practice. In this sense, tagging, plotting, and stitching constitute a networked and temporally expanding cartography based on a cooperatively connected performativity. The constructive aspects of this creativity are also inherently participatory.

Performative cartography is a creative practice, but not creation ex nihilo. It is modeled on what Claude Lévi-Strauss and Gérard Genette once called "bricolage": a form of creation that works not from scratch but by recombining readymade bits and pieces. Yet this view, devised in the heydays of structuralism, was not meant in a critical way. Genette argued that literature is always by definition a bricolage since bits of language—words, syntax, and cultural clichés—always preexist any new formation.

From this point of view, bricolage is a structural property of all texts. As numerous scholars have pointed out, however, it also has an inherent subversive or critical potential, particularly when the text (in the broadest sense of the word) gets in the hands of the consumer, reader, or user. Marita Sturken and Lisa Cartwright describe bricolage as a cultural practice allowing us to create resistant meanings of commodities.[9] A similar, cultural-studies-inflected view on bricolage as resistance is to be found in the writings of Dick Hebdige, who sees bricolage as a subversive, highly personal remixing of commodity culture. Michel de Certeau's famous notion of textual poaching has enriched the idea of bricolage with a political slant, in accordance with his conception of tactics as the individual, possibly random negotiational or oppositional poaching of texts at the level of interpretation and production.[10] Henry Jenkins, finally, has appropriated the term textual poaching for fan culture and participatory culture from a perspective that highlights the fluidity between oppositional and hegemonic practices. According to Jenkins, this fluidity stems from a reading and interpretative positioning of media fans within popular culture. Jenkins's reading of dominant culture matches the new age of participatory culture and what he famously has termed convergence culture:

Patterns of media consumption have been profoundly altered by a succession of new media technologies which enable average citizens to participate in the archiving, annotation, appropriation, transformation, and recirculation of media content. Participatory culture refers to the new style of consumerism that emerges in this environment.[11]

Returning to forms of cutting and pasting in locative media practices, it seems useful to understand fluidity not only as a perspective *on* culture but also as a perspective *of* culture. In order to understand agency within dominant discourse and societal structures, it is important to pay respect to the critical and political potential of appropriation and bricolage in the creative process. Utopist views on digital media and interactivity notwithstanding, appropriation is not always critical, and even agency and creativity are not necessarily democratic, emancipating, or essentially political. It is therefore relevant to put these allegedly new forms of creativity and authorship into an historical perspective, for there is nothing new about this sense of creativity made of preused bits and pieces. However, appropriation and bricolage form part of cultural production, and in the case of locative media they even are vital to our conception of location and of our position in the world. What is new, and potentially problematic, is the conflation of this creative making as bricolage with a sense that the bits—because they emerge from geotagged locations—are anchoring us to the world. Instead of cutting up reality and thus transforming it into fiction, they appear to augment the former and obliterate the latter.

As a creative practice, augmentation implies transformation by virtue of adding and combining information. It also entails analytic and associative practices: cutting up and making links. Photoshop has taught us to deconstruct the image not only in flat (horizontal/vertical) sections or cut-outs but also in adding different 3D layers to a flat image. With sections and layers combined, tagging provides a *mash-up logic* to our understanding of the spaces surrounding us. It merges layers of information that create a hybrid space, and paradoxically it also tears this space apart. It makes visible the exchangeability and hence the design of information layers.

This mash-up logic that we may recognize in the navigation of a layered reality also entails temporal and experiential aspects of mobility. Mashing up engages us with the objects in their specific place while adding temporal layers, a form of mnemonic spacing. Its logic requires some sort of spatial stability because objects need to be in place for some time in order to function as markers for tags. As such, mash-up logic relies on archival information attached to a spatial presence. AR layers are built on databases (archives) of metadata attached to geospatial information. This is a temporal act. Moreover, the mash-up logic provides means to experience a "different" city, hence, constructing a city of difference.

Engagements

Creative practices that make use of the (layered) interface of the iPhone as navigation device involve different interactive engagements with an array of cartographic applications. It is possible to discern at least three different ways in which the broad concept of interactivity becomes specific for navigation: first, as the point where interface and agency meet (and where performativity is actualized); second, where navigation is understood as a constructive (and participatory) form of interactivity; and third, as yielding a haptic engagement with screenspace.

The interface affords possibilities for making space: it is an instrument in this process for navigation as *constructive interactivity*. The examples I mention entail not only browsing or constructing pathways but also actively making connections and adding to or modifying the structure, building new constellations within the (changing) collection of data. This includes practices of uploading, tagging, and putting objects on the map. Navigation understood as *participatory interactivity* would focus on, for example, cutting and pasting, adding and modding. Understood as the agency of participation, this means the active intervention of an individual user in the content or structure of maps or collections. Constructive forms of interactivity in the use of applications that allow for adding content, tagging locations, and connecting content are participatory acts embedded in networked constellations. The contribution the individual can make in collective networks is specifically relevant for agency in social media.

These two aspects of interactivity, or means for agency, contribute to another aspect of navigation with the iPhone: the successive rendering of changing positioning in physical space that is, in turn, used for reading and traversing space. I propose to consider this the *haptic* aspect of engagement. Engagement brings together aspects of agency: doing and experience, seeing and feeling. It is haptic engagement, understood as form of interactivity and as experience, that is significant for mobile screen gadgets.

One might explore how a conceptualization of the haptic precisely addresses the intersection of touch and physical interaction with the experience of the device, on the one hand, and the agency in and experience of spatial unfolding on the other. It is in haptic engagement that the creative meets the cartographic, so to speak. "Haptic" derives from the Greek verb *aptó*, which means to touch; the term is currently widely used in three fields of study—art, cinema, and interface, in order to qualify a certain way of looking, a specific gaze. In that sense it is opposed to another kind of gaze, namely, the optical one. Aloïs Riegl introduced the term in 1901 to differentiate between haptic and optic art. Differentiated from the optical gaze, which is limited to the eye that sees at a distance, haptic "looking" means that the look can graze the object, caress it with the touch, and, by extension, all the senses, entailing close proximity.[12]

Regarding the interactive practices and haptic engagements of navigation that my argument has been focusing upon, my concern is not so much with the experience of touching the interface but with the experiential aspect of the procedural, unfolding creation of space in navigation of the body-and-machine in motion. Here, the notions of the haptic and performative are useful distinctions in opposition to representational regimes of space. In mobile navigation a dynamic notion of cartography is being unfolded. Cartography is not a precondition for but a creative *product of* navigation, and, as such, cartography is more than a systematic representation of space. It is a performance of screenspace that entails the collapse of reading, making, and expressing of space in the collaboration of the device and its user, activating all layers of the mobile device in a mobile sphere.

Conclusion: Toward Performative Cartography

Representation as characteristic of traditional cartography entails *fixed* outcomes of the creative production processes: results such as images, statements, models, and materials can be distributed, transmitted, stored, or tagged. However, I consider the view of cartography as representation insufficient, especially for mobile navigation but even for traditional cartography. Our contemporary mapping interfaces foreground precisely these processes of flux, simulation, remediation, and mobility. Instead of foregrounding the "re-" of repetition, we need to conceptualize the "pre" of representation, that is, not only the "pre-" of making present (presentation) but also in the temporal dimension of the processes *before* representation or, better yet, the process in which representation comes into being.

The experience of navigation unfolds in space at the moment of its occurrence. Hence, it is procedural, in the sense that movement through space and interaction with on-screen layers of digital information and off-screen geographical and material presence unfolds in time. But not only does it take time—it *becomes* over time. A conception of time that includes the productive or literally creative aspect of time is relevant here; it includes change *in* time. To conceptualize a shift from *representational* cartography to navigation as a *performative* cartographic practice, this new cartography taps into non-Newtonian thinking, breaking with a Euclidian model of space. According to the Newtonian paradigm, time and space are absolute and measurable phenomena that work along the lines of a predetermined mechanical, progressive logic. An Euclidian model of space can constitute a basis for thinking in terms of multiple dimensions. Yet this model assumes an immobile grid in which all objects take place within a fixed system of (Cartesian) coordinates.

Instead of the traditional divide between space and time, performative cartography implies a reconceptualization of relative and positional dimensionality as more fluid than a fixating spatiotemporal positioning because it is a procedural experience. Time and space unfold in practices and so do not work along predetermined lines. The concept of performativity, then, signifies change and difference. Perhaps mobile technology operates within Euclidian space, but the experience of it does not.

Representation entails more or less fixed outcomes of creative production processes. The results, such as images, statements, models, and materials can be transmitted or stored. This would be an insufficient understanding for some contemporary media practices and approaches to these practices that foreground process, mutability, flux, simulation, remediation, notions of becoming, and mobility. These characterize the process in which representation comes into being in its performativity. Christian Jacob, in his seminal study on the semiotics of maps throughout history, addresses precisely the question of the conceptual status of the map as representation, medium, and interface:

> An effective map is transparent because it is a signified without a signifier. It vanishes in the visual and intellectual operation that unfolds its content. The map spreads out the entire world before the eyes of those who know how to read it. The eye does not see; it constructs, it imagines space. The map is not an object but a function. Like a microscope, a telescope, or a scanner, it is a technical prosthesis that extends and refines the field of sensorial perception, or, rather, a place where ocular vision and the "mind's eye" coincide. As a mediation, an interface, it remains hidden.

This double-sidedness of the map as object and function brings about a paradoxical status, if not a "conceptual vacuum," as Jacob calls it. Yet "what defines the map is the mediation of representation, a mediation that is a sig-nifier with its own codes and conventions (symbolization, schematization, miniaturization, colors, nomenclature, vertical overview, etc.)."[13] We can thus discern the materiality and interfacing operation of the map and the content it is supposed to mediate while being transparent. Because representational maps work according to a Cartesian dualistic logic, a certain phenomenon *is being mapped*.

The common practice of geographical mapmaking can be seen as example of a representational map. Land is mapped along the lines of and x- and y-axes, and subsequent maps represent the changes through time. A dualism is thus to be found in the relation between the phenomenon and the map, but also between the spatial element and the element of time. Yet coupling time and space and inserting duration into matter encourage a qualitative shift away from this dualism.[14] What does a map look like when it is in movement, in flux, and when we talk about practices of mapping and navigating instead of the map as an object? Then the map is a spatial and temporal *event*. It is spatial because it does not map preexisting height, breadth, and depth, and temporal because it does not map a spatiality *in* time. Focusing on the map as a navigational tool and on navigating as a practice that occurs in time as well as space invites us to rethink the dualist frame of the representational map. As a consequence, the cartographical experience of iPhone navigation needs to be conceptualized anew. Since space and time unfold *in* practice, experiences do not happen in space and time but are themselves events. This is why these experiences constitute an immanent spatiotemporality. I have suggested that we can productively investigate the hybridity of the iPhone as an interface for navigation—a perspective on both object and practice that opens up a view on navigation as a truly hybrid practice and on its cartography as a way from representation and towards performativity. This is where pervasive presence, embedded pasts, and evolving futures can intersect in screenspace.

Notes

1. Elsewhere, I have proposed speaking of mobile gadgets as theoretical consoles rather than theoretical objects: Nanna Verhoeff, "Theoretical Consoles: Concepts for Gadget Analysis," *Journal of Visual Culture* 3 (2009): 279–98.

2. The term "*dispositif*" is derived from early French film theory, developed by Jean-Louis Baudry to provide a theoretical construct of what is often called in English the "cinematic apparatus," and it helps us to analyze the material and spatial specificity of the "set-up" within which screens operate. See Jean-Louis Baudry, "Ideological Effects

of the Basic Cinematographic Apparatus" and "The Apparatus: Metapsychological Approaches to the Impression of Reality in the Cinema," in *Narrative, Apparatus, Ideology*, ed. Philip Rosen (New York: Columbia University Press, 1986), 286–98, 299–318.

3. Nanna Verhoeff, "Screens of Navigation: From Taking a Ride to Making the Ride," *Refractory* 12 (2008), http://refractory.unimelb.edu.au/2008/03/06/screens-of -navigation-from-taking-a-ride-to-making-the-ride/ (15 June 2011).

4. Oliver J. Woodman, "An Introduction to Inertial Navigation," in *Technical Report UCAM-CL-TR-696* (London: University of Cambridge Computer Laboratory, 2007).

5. "Junaio has extended its capabilities beyond the usual location based internet services. Not only may the user obtain information on nearby POIs such as shops, restaurants or train stations, but the camera's eye is now able to identify objects and 'glue' object specific real-time, dynamic, social and 3D information onto the object itself. Enrich your packaging, books, posters, flyers, magazines or whatever you can think of with junaio glue." See http://www.junaio.com/glue (15 February 2011).

6. Marc Tuters and Kazyz Varnellis, "Beyond Locative Media," *Leonardo* 4 (2006), speaks of two kinds of cartography in the broader genre of locative media: annotative cartography, based on tagging, and phenomenological cartography, based on the tracing of movement. This is close to my terminology here, although I wish to analyze the merging of these two forms in performative cartography as it is made possible by the hybridity of the iPhone's interface.

7. Relying on outsiders' making use of the assembled database is called crowd mining, a business model with a more top-down connotation and different from the cooperative rhetoric of the advertising. But the use of multiple amateur image feeds can also create a new cooperative "YouTube" aesthetic. For example, in 2010 the rock band Radiohead supported a fan initiative to make and distribute online a movie of their 2009 concert in Prague filmed by about fifty cell-phone cameras.

8. For information about the exhibition, see http://ikophetmuseumplein.nl/, and for the flash mob, see http://sndrv.nl/ARflashmob/ (15 February 2011).

9. Marita Sturken and Lisa Cartwright, *Practices of Looking: An Introduction to Visual Culture* (New York: Oxford University Press, 2001), 350.

10. Dick Hebdige, *Subculture: The Meaning of Style* (London: Methuen, 1979); Michel de Certeau, *The Practice of Everyday Life* (Berkeley: University of California Press, 1984).

11. Henry Jenkins, *Convergence Culture: Where Old and New Media Collide* (New York: New York University Press, 2006), 554.

12. Aloïs Riegl, "Late Roman Art Industry" (1901), in *Art History and Its Methods: A Critical Anthology*, ed. Eric Fernie (London: Phaidon, 1995), 116–26; Mark Patterson, *The Senses of Touch: Haptics, Affects, and Technologies* (Oxford: Berg, 2007).

13. Christian Jacob and Edward H. Dahl, eds., *The Sovereign Map: Theoretical Approaches in Cartography Throughout History* (Chicago: University of Chicago Press, 2006), 11–12.

14. For a Bergsonian understanding of time, duration, and materiality, see Elisabeth Grozs, *Time Travels: Feminism, Nature, Power* (Durham, N.C.: Duke University Press, 2005). I am indebted to Iris van der Tuin, who pointed out Grozs's phrasing to me in relation to nondualist thinking.

CHAPTER 3

The iPhone as an Object of Knowledge

ALEXANDRA SCHNEIDER

I N THE 1990S the mobile phone, rather than the digital image, emerged as "the economic-technological basis for a vast industrial and infrastructural expansion."[1] Now, the (moving) digital image has become an integral part of mobile telephony. With an object like the iPhone, film history, the history of telecommunication, and the emergence of the digital intersect in complex ways that traditional film historiography never anticipated. Over the last ten years, concepts such as "media convergence" or "remediation" have proven to be useful starting points to account for the multilayered dynamics of the digital image in the age of mobile telephony. In exploring the iPhone as technological object and media platform, I follow Nanna Verhoeff's approach to what might be called "gadget analysis," an approach that permits one to "articulate the intertwinement of historical and theoretical thought, allowing us to turn from the one to the other."[2] Speaking of the Nintendo DS console, Verhoeff underlines the hybridity of the object, its materiality and "interface utility." My interest follows hers in discussing the iPhone as a theoretical object within a cinema studies framework. Much like the Nintendo console, the iPhone "hovers between three things": it is "a device we hold in our hands," "a screen we look at as well as through, and it is a screen we touch," and, finally, the iPhone is "at once an invisible and visible platform—a machine for haptic output of the applications one can play on it."[3] Like Verhoeff I take my cue from Hubert Damisch and propose to study the iPhone as a "theoretical object." In particular, I am interested in what the iPhone as a theoretical object tells us about an emerging new order of visual and sensory perception, not the least in relation to established modes of verbal and visual communication.

Phone Home

A quick Google search for images of the iPhone yields up an intriguing image of unknown origin that shows E.T. the Extra-Terrestrial from Steven Spielberg's eponymous 1982 film holding an iPhone in his (her?) hand. The image could be read as saying "Why didn't I think of this?" or "Finally those humans are getting it!" Either way, the pictures seems to suggest that if E.T. had had an iPhone rather than the improvised device he assembled from bits and pieces found in a shed he would have been able to go home sooner. E.T., ever the carrier of multilayered messages, shows up in this picture not by coincidence but as a paradigm, a figure of transition (an epistemic *Kippfigur*) in the iPhone's genealogy as an hybrid object at the threshold between cinema and telecommunication. With his glowing finger and his unshakable belief in the virtues of telephony, E.T. can be read as an imaginative anticipation of recent advances in media technology and aesthetics.

Putting E.T. and the iPhone together in the same picture makes sense because the iPhone is a telecommunication device but also a video device capable of showing moving pictures. Furthermore, the iPhone is a device operated by a touch screen. While the Extra-Terrestrial had the gift of a glowing finger to get in touch with people in a literal sense, the iPhone enables us to communicate, and particularly to phone home, at the touch of our fingertips—that is, to communicate like E.T. In that sense, the image of E.T. with the iPhone points to a realignment of telephony and film but also, and more fundamentally, to a realignment of the senses of sight, hearing, and touch.

Some people would argue that such an alignment, to the extent that it is happening, is driven by technology: The iPhone, like so many technologies before it, not only offers new ways of organizing our lives but also, in the process, fundamentally alters the structures of our experience. However, the curious temporality of the picture of E.T. with the iPhone suggests a different understanding of the role of technology. The copresence of E.T. and the iPhone is an image of a "*rendez-vous raté*," a meeting that, sadly, never took place. The iPhone came too late to solve E.T.'s problems in the film, and only with the iPhone are humans finally catching up with their extraterrestrial visitor. While an emblem of techno-euphoria on the surface, the image has a melancholy and melodramatic undertone of "if only . . . !" Yet at the same time the image posits the iPhone as the realization of something that had been thought of long before, not necessarily by humans but by a higher intelligence, perhaps nature herself, whose superior design has been waiting for an opportunity to reveal itself and now has finally done so to in the form of a new technology.

Change was certainly in the air when *E.T.* first appeared in 1982. Steven Spielberg's film was released one year before the first commercial mobile phone, the Motorola DynaTAC 8000x, appeared on the market. The Motorola sold for the price of a small car—nearly $4,000. Given its high price and exclusive appeal, the DynaTAC was bound to become associated with 1980s conspicuous consumer culture. Gordon Gekko owns one in *Wall Street* (USA 1987, Oliver Stone), as does Patrick Bateman, the psychopathic killer of *American Psycho,* Brett Easton Ellis's 1991 novel that was turned into a film by Mary Harron, released in 2000. *E.T.* slightly predated the mobile phone but appeared at the dawn of a new era of telecommunications technology and media experience. The Spielberg film was rereleased twice, in 1985 and in 1991, but it was, perhaps symptomatically, a telecommunications operator, the British Telecommunication Company BT, that secured an afterlife for *E.T.* on theater screens outside of repeat screenings of the film itself.[4] In 1999, BT launched an ad campaign entitled "Stay in touch." In the teaser for that campaign, which advertised e-mail and high-speed Internet access, scenes from the original Spielberg movie were used to promote BT's services. Toward the end of the teaser, the voiceover explained: "BT has E.T. The extra technology you need to stay in touch, like e-mail and high-speed Internet access. . . . So you can do much more than just phone home."

But what more can you do than just phone home? For E.T., to stay in touch meant to be reconnected to his fellow extraterrestrials. Spielberg's film, however, is not just about telephony and the possibility of reconnecting with lost relatives. As has been noted repeatedly, E.T.'s glowing finger, prominently displayed on the film's famous poster, refers to one of the most famous paintings of the renaissance, Michelangelo's ceiling of the Sistine Chapel in Rome, which shows God giving the spark of life to Adam through a touch of his finger.[5] In the film's poster, E.T.'s finger provides the spark of life, supposedly to his human friend Greg. It is an image that reanimates the mythical act of creation in the age of the movie blockbuster, pointing to a spiritual dimension of the narrative of the lost space traveler. The recurrence of this image in British Telecommunication's 1999 campaign for high-speed online access presages one of the key promises of the iPhone: access to the world at the touch of your finger—access from the vantage point not only of a passive recipient of news and information but also of an active creator of worlds, a curator of media environments. The return of E.T. the Extra-Terrestrial as E.T. the extra technology supposedly puts the client of BT in a position where she, too, experiences the magic touch of the golden finger giving life to everything through an act of communication, simply by "getting in touch."

Some people may remember that Nokia, the Finnish pioneer of the mobile phone age, used the Michelangelo image in the mid-1990s not in advertising but as an element in the operation of their phones. Whenever a Nokia phone was switched on, Michelangelo's finger of God providing the spark of life to Adam would flash onto the screen. Some years later this animation was replaced by two shaking hands, an image that remained true to the original meaning in the sense that the tactile continued to serve as the paradigm for communication. The Michelangelo animation was introduced after Nokia adopted its new brand slogan, "connecting people," in 1992. To "stay in touch," the verb used in the BT slogan, usually means "to stay connected," to be in contact. The verb "to touch," of course, resonates with different meanings: as a transitive verb it refers to physical contact, to a perception through the tactile. The association of digital communication with the sense of touch in the 1990s may or may not be a coincidence. But in both Nokia devices and the BT campaign, mobile telephony and digital telecommunications are insistently and, as if in a wordplay on the Latin root of the term "digit," quite literally aligned with the finger and the sense of touch. As information and communication become increasingly immaterial, one is tempted to speculate, the devices and practices of communication tend increasingly toward the material and the haptic.

At the same time, one can be touched: affected by a sentiment, just like E.T., whose heart glows in bright red and orange whenever the creature gets emotionally agitated. More than just a provider of the spark of communication and, therefore, life, E.T. is also a hypersensitive recipient of touching messages, an exemplary figuration of the new possibilities of mobile telephony through his highly conspicuous capacities for both staying in touch and being touched. But there is more to E.T., the figurative melodramatic paradigm of post-1990 digital telecommunications. In McLuhan's famous phrase, media are "extensions of man," that is prosthetic devices that enlarge and enhance the communicative reach of human beings. In the film, E.T. produces a prosthetic device that is decidedly on the low-tech end of the scale:

an improvised assemblage of spare parts and toys. Through this precarious piece of technology E.T. deploys a gift of communication that is vastly in excess of the boundaries of human communication to begin with. However, the assemblage of the spare parts and toys is not so much an extension of E.T.'s body as the means of transforming the entire set of elements, including the body, into a new device of communication. Rather than a McLuhanian device for anthropological enhancement that compensates for the limitations of the human (or, for that matter, extraterrestrial) condition, it is a Deleuzian machine in which the individual device matters less than the connection and articulation of elements and that transforms the body into an element of a new set of connections that redefines, or "repurposes," the individual elements. In that sense, E.T. marks, if you will, a postanthropological stage in media theory. With E.T.—who, in a sense, represents a figuration of the posthuman body as much as does the Cyborg—the body, in an assemblage with toy-style elements of technology, becomes the medium, or rather the machine that enhances and transcends the limitations of human communication. As we know from a moment in the film eternalized on the film's second famous poster, E.T. manages to transcend the limits not only of language but also of gravity. He can make a child's bike fly, going vastly beyond, by virtue of his innate capacities, the enhancement of the human body provided by the bike itself. What BT's campaign calls "extra technology," then, is a technology that endows the common user with an E.T.-like gift of communication, a quasi body or machine of communication that always already transcends the boundaries of "normal" human means of communication. In the media culture addressed by and epitomized by the BT ad, E.T. and the gadgets with which he is associated come to stand for an enhanced state of communicativeness, one in which the gift of E.T.'s hypercommunicative body is available to anyone who uses the right gadget.

To Pinch or Not to Pinch

When Apple launched the iPhone in April 2007, it was first and foremost a telecommunication device, providing mobile phone connections and Internet access. Two years after the iPhone's first appearance on the market, with the 3GS version released in 2009, Apple added video-recording features. The initial lack of a video camera did not impede the new device's impact. The iPhone was successfully marketed as "the revolutionary mobile phone," which proved to be true on two accounts. While consumers reacted enthusiastically, competing manufacturers of mobile communication devices apparently reacted with fear. At the point of the iPhone's initial release, executives at RIM, the manufacturer of the Blackberry device, were in a state of denial and refused to believe Steve Jobs's claim that Apple was able to provide sufficient battery power to light a screen the size of the iPhone's on a mobile device.[6]

Perhaps the most revolutionary aspect of the iPhone, however, was the substitution of traditional phone dials and the Blackberry miniature keyboard with a touch screen. Touch screens had been developed and used in various devices such as subway and railway ticket-vending machines for years, and it seems clear in retrospect that before the iPhone the potential of the touch-screen technology for mobile telephony had not been realized. What makes the iPhone touch screen distinctive and marks a significant advance over ticket-machine varieties of the touch screen is that the surface is completely touch sensitive, i.e., the touch-sensitive areas are not limited to certain proscribed icons. Depending on the application, the iPhone surface can be touched, rubbed, and even caressed. It is a surface that asks for an entire repertoire of tactile gestures rather than merely a functional handling.

When he first introduced the iPhone and its touch screen at one of Apple's now legendary product-launch ceremonies, Jobs strategically, and cleverly, introduced a specific verb to describe the kind of touch that the screen of the iPhone required: "to pinch." "To pinch" means to squeeze between the finger and thumb or between the jaws of an instrument. "Pinching" may be associated with a modest form of pain. The idea of being "pinched" does not necessarily evoke the sense of a tender touch, and the etymology of the corresponding French verb *pincer* (from which the English word derives) confirms this intuition. In the seventeenth century, when the verb first appeared, a "*pincer*" was also a *saisir d'amour*, a state of being touched (or moved) by a feeling of love. Rather than a piece of glass that supplants a series of buttons, icons, or a keyboard, the introduction of the verb "to pinch" suggests the touch screen surface of the iPhone is rather like a skin, a touch-sensitive surface that registers my every touch in its specific degree, direction, and expressiveness.

Whether Steve Jobs's proposition will become established as a figure of everyday speech remains to be seen. At the moment it appears that most people refer to the pinching mode (enlarging and scaling down of images) more in terms of zoom in and zoom out rather than in terms of "pinching" the visual object. It seems clear, however, that Jobs's choice of words intended to mark a shift from a merely visual approach to a haptic approach to visual objects. The semantics of "zooming in" and "zooming out" and the camera metaphor are no longer entirely adequate to this type of object and process. Again, the digital calls for the digit, the finger.

Yet at the same time the iPhone is now, in its third and fourth generations, also a camera and a portable cinema, complete with a "Cinemascope" application for film viewing. In this context, it is interesting to note that if the iPhone marks a shift from the knob to the switch to the screen as a semantically loaded technical skin, the etymology of the word "screen" reaches back to its earliest uses as a shield for warriors made of animal skin. Not only was the screen originally a protective skin, but in a media-historical genealogy, the current becoming-skin of the screen may be traced back to the nineteenth century and to early optical toys such as the flip book, where the physical contact and manipulation was a prerequisite of the visual experience. What the "pinchable" iPhone screen points us to, then, is a realignment of sight and touch around the sensitive surface of the screen. As I would argue, this realignment amounts to a specific kind of the return of the culturally repressed. The "pinchable" touch screen marks the reintroduction to the field of visual media of a tactile dimension of vision that was part and parcel of what we have come to call "pre-cinema" but had no place in the cinema when it became the culturally formative medium of the early twentieth century. Film theorists have been thinking about the tactile dimensions of the film experience for more than a decade now (i.e., for as long as telecommunications corporations have associated the digital with the digit and touch). In many ways the emergence of the iPhone and its touch screen valorizes the intuitions of such theorists as Vivian Sobchack and Laura U. Marks.[7] At the same time, the iPhone as a theoretical object forces us to rethink the configuration of moving image and embodied experience along the lines of how, through new technologies, touch and the tactile have once again become a key aspect of the visual experience.

Touch and Visual Perception

A visit to an art exhibition in a traditional museum space in the company of small kids will teach you not only about art but also about culture more generally. The most striking, and probably also most obvious lesson, concerns the issue of looking as opposed to touching. As a parent in an exhibition with small kids who are not yet quite able to read, you find yourself repeating one basic rule: "Look, don't touch" (or, as the Swiss German version goes, "Nur mit dae Augae luagae, noed mit de Fingaer"—"Look with your eyes, not with your fingers"). Communicating this rule becomes necessary for two reasons: first, art exhibitions usually feature objects that we are not supposed to touch, as even grownups find out when they get too close to a painting and are reprimanded for it by a museum guard, and, second, small children explore the world through the tactile and olfactory senses as much as through the sense of vision, by putting objects in their mouth and touching them rather than by merely looking at them.

Conventional exhibitions of paintings usually do not feature signs instructing the visitors that they are not supposed to touch the exhibited material. This rule is implicit in the practice of exhibiting artworks. But in some contemporary art exhibitions you are either explicitly invited to touch the exhibited art work or reminded not to touch it. The basic ethos is still the same: hands off! The invitation to touch the artwork has to be made explicit because it is commonly understood that we are not supposed to do that. Interestingly enough, this has not always been the case. As Constance Classen has shown, the traditional hands-off ethos of the museum came into practice only in the mid-nineteenth century. Early museums, she writes, "were not exclusively hands-off affairs."[8]

"Touch had an advantage over sight in that it was understood to be the sense of certainty, an association symbolically grounded in the biblical tale of Thomas, who needed to touch the risen Christ to believe in his reality."[9] Until the eighteenth century, at least, touch remained one of the master senses. It verified perception and gave solidity to other, less reliable impressions. According to Classen, the end of the nineteenth century marked the end "of the use of the proximity senses of smell, taste and touch," and they were relegated to the realm of the nursery and the "savage." Civilized adults were deemed to comprehend the world primarily through sight, and secondarily through hearing.[10]

The shift from the tactile to the visual coincided with the emergence of a new regime of scientific knowledge and, in particular, an ideal of "objectivity" evolving around the figure of the scientist as a detached observer. In short, during modernity close contact between visitors and exhibits was no longer allowed, as looking had become a central human feature—a fact that naturally can be linked to the emergence of moving images. In a broader cultural perspective on cinema history it can, thus, be argued that cinema was both complicit in, and a driving force of, the shift away from the tactile dimension of knowledge acquisition. In a related argument, film scholar Wanda Strauven has claimed that "the institutionalization of the cinema gradually got rid of all the features that determined the (potentially) interactive *dispositif* of early cinema, such as hand-cranked projectors." Strauven describes early rube films, for example, *Uncle Josh at the Moving Picture Show* (1902), as "a turning point in this institutionalization process that inevitably suppressed the more active conditions of the nineteenth-century observer and turned the viewer mode into the dominant mode of moviegoing. Porter's rube film confronts the 1902 audience, in this sense, with a form of spectatorship in extinction".[11]

In line with Strauven's point, one can argue that from the moment of its emergence cinema helped to enforce a regime of visual and nontactile knowledge, which today is undergoing a process of reconfiguration. In fact, if the argument that cinema played a role in the establishment of a new discipline of the body and the senses at the dawn of the twentieth century has any merit, then the emergence of a popular gadget that reintroduces and relegitimizes the once-common link of vision and touch must be seen as a shift in terms not only of media technology but also of epistemology. In order to illustrate and explain this shift, another Spielberg example can be referred to: *Minority Report* (2002), based on a story by Philip K. Dick written in 1956. Produced five years before the release of the iPhone, the film features Tom Cruise as Chief John Anderton, a criminal investigator with prophetic capabilities working for a "pre-crime" prevention unit in Washington, D.C. Anderton's primary work tool is a command post with a set of fluid, immaterial touch screens. In a dynamic and almost feverish choreography of body and hand movements relating to these screens Anderton can draw up images of past, current, and even future events, alongside other information, texts, statistics, mathematical formulae, and so on. Like an iPhone user Anderton "pinches" images and information displays. He basically dances with the images that appear at the touch of his hands and disappear according to his movements. Anderton's office, or work station, is, if you will, a nonportable version of the iPhone.

How does Anderton's office tool relate to the current epistemological shift in media culture? The immateriality of the images and the information, as well as the screen itself, can be read, I would argue, as presaging and explaining the epistemological shift epitomized by the iPhone. As a handler, a "pincher," of immaterial images and immaterial surfaces and interfaces, Anderton turns out to be two steps remote from Uncle Josh. Uncle Josh wants to touch the object but finds out that there is no object, only a screen. Anderton never actually touches the screen—because the screen he uses is not a material surface—yet he reliably obtains the object (or information) he wants. It is therefore perhaps somewhere in between the fictional characters of Anderton and Uncle Josh that one comes close to the figure of the iPhone user: she is part Uncle Josh, part John Anderton. Like Uncle Josh, she actually touches the screen, since the touch screen is a material object, but like Anderton, she can make any object of knowledge appear on the screen at the touch of her finger.

Three Regimes of Touch, Vision, and Knowledge

In view of a historical epistemology of media, the settings and figures presented above, from E.T. to Anderton, can be seen as emblematic for specific regimes or alignments of vision, touch, and knowledge that have emerged and succeeded one another over the last two hundred years. One can, in fact, distinguish between three major regimes: At first, there is an alignment of material object, touch, vision, and knowledge. It is culturally permissible and technically viable to gain knowledge of an object by both looking at and touching the material object. The emblematic figure of this regime is Uncle Josh, the rube, before he ever gets to the cinema. Second, one might see the emergence of a regime with which both the art museum and the cinema are thoroughly complicit, where vision and touch become separated and knowledge becomes scientific, objective knowledge of both material and immaterial objects based on distant observation and measurement. The emblematic figure of this regime is the educated, well-behaved spectator who has learned that she is supposed to look and not touch. She represents the norm that Uncle Josh, once he enters the cinema, fails to obey, or the ideal toward which Uncle Josh should educate himself. Third, today we witness the emergence of an alignment of touch, vision, and immaterial objects of knowledge, which become accessible by way of a screen, a nonspecific material object. *Minority Report*'s Anderton is the emblematic figure of this new regime, in which we mere mortals participate thanks to touch-screen devices like the iPhone.

The difference between Anderton and the iPhone user is that the latter still touches and operates a material device. However, the touch screen is a hybrid object. The screen itself may be a material object, but the objects to which it provides access are immaterial and devoid of physical consistency. The iPhone invites an analysis similar to that proposed by Nana Verhoeff in her discussion of the Nintendo playstation: "The console is best understood as a thing, instrument and interface at the same time. It is in this multiplicity that it is perhaps less a medium than a carrier of mediality." Moreover, Verhoeff continues, unlike other mobile "media players, a console is, in part, an empty interface. The software application determines part of the interface, in dialogue with the hardware elements. The complex of characteristics of the portable console as a versatile object, a thing/medium, demands a theoretical grasp on the phenomenon."[12]

Similarly, the iPhone as an object and the objects that the iPhone produces call into question our very definitions of medium and mediality. For a long time, and quite successfully, media studies have operated based on technological definitions of the medium. German media studies, *Medienwissenschaft*, for example, evolved from a focus on hardware, on the history of technology as media technology, and proceeded to analyze power relations and aesthetic phenomena as mere aftereffects of the technological base. Less stringently, but quite as cogently, film and television studies have based their epistemologies on quasi-technological definitions of their object of study: the cinematic *dispositif*, the television set, and so forth. Yet the scholarly challenge of the iPhone is not its effect on media convergence nor its multifunctionality and multiple formatting. Rather, the iPhone calls into question a number of basic distinctions, particularly the distinction between materiality and immateriality and that between (material) object and (social) action. Thinking about the iPhone thus forces us to acknowledge the hybrid nature of the devices and the practices that the device enables along the lines of the theoretical framework of actor network theory. It also forces us to acknowledge a fundamental instability and fluidity of the (im)material object—or medium—itself. In the new regime of vision, touch, and knowledge we have indeed become parts of a Deleuzian machine, elements in an assemblage, a set of couplings and connections that can, and do, redefine the sense and purpose of the individual element.

Let me illustrate this point by relating a final anecdote. In Switzerland, Apple has failed in their attempt to register iPhone as a trademark. The court argued that unlike the brand name iPod, which is a new verbal coinage without precedent in any natural language, iPhone is a homophone of an English language sentence that, in a colloquial abbreviation, describes the activity of using a telephone in the first-person singular. This sentence, the court argued, belongs in the public domain and cannot become the property of a person or other legal entity. As far as I know, the court's decision has so far not been detrimental to Apple's business interests. No competitor has dumped low-priced smartphones named iPhone on the relatively small market of Switzerland as yet. One could, of course, argue that it was never Apple's intention to own a part of a natural language or the practice thereof. But I would claim that the court's intuition was basically correct. In a way, an ownership stake in what the buyer does with the device is precisely what the iPhone (and other smartphones) are all about. Smartphones in general, and the iPhone in particular, are operated through apps that allow for specific activities and come in many varieties—but also at a price. As a customer, you pay for the license to do what you want with the device you already own. In a way, this is not much different from the introduction of pay TV at the end of the 1970s. But then again, the app is something fundamentally new. It expands the market for media beyond devices and programs and extends into the realm of social behavior. Apple sells gadgets and software, but, perhaps more importantly, it also sells patterns of activity and behavior. The iPhone calls into question the distinctions among medium, format/program, and user. We are now free to look and touch, but we pay a price for access to that new regime of knowledge.

NOTES

1. Thomas Elsaesser, "Early Film History and Multi-Media: An Archaeology of Possible Futures?" in *New Media, Old Media: A History and Theory Reader*, ed. Wendy Hui Kyong Chun and Thomas Keenan (New York: Routledge, 2005), 15.

2. Nanna Verhoeff, "Theoretical Consoles: Concepts for Gadget Analysis," *Journal of Visual Culture* 3 (2009): 290.

3. Ibid., 280, 296.

4. http://news.bbc.co.uk/2/hi/entertainment/314327.stm retrieved 10.02.2011.

5. In critical literature, on of the earliest instances to highlight this connection was probably an article by Andrew Gordon, "E.T. as Fairy Tale," *Science Fiction Studies* 10, no. 3 (1983): 293–305.

6. http://www.tagesanzeiger.ch/digital/internet/iPhone-Stunde-Null/story/10695895 (10 February 2011).

7. Vivian Sobchack, *The Address of the Eye: A Phenomenology of Film Experience* (Princeton, N.J.: Princeton University Press, 1992); Sobchack, *Carnal Thoughts: Embodiment and Moving Image Culture* (Berkeley: University of California Press, 2004); Laura Marks, *The Skin of Film: Intercultural Cinema, Embodiment, and the Senses* (Durham, N.C.: Duke University Press, 2000); Marks, *Touch: Sensuous Theory and Multisensory Media* (Minneapolis: University of Minnesota Press, 2002).

8. Constance Classen, "Museum Manners: The Sensory Life of the Early Museums," *Journal of Social History* 4 (2007): 896.

9. Ibid., 900.

10. Ibid., 896, 907.

11. Wanda Strauven, "The Observer's Dilemma: To Touch or Not to Touch," in *Media Archaeology: Approaches, Applications, Implications*, ed. Erkki Huhtamo and Jussi Parikka (Berkeley: University of California Press, 2011), 177.

12. Verhoeff, "Theoretical Consoles," 295–96.

CHAPTER 4

Media Archaeology, Installation Art, and the iPhone Experience

JENNIFER STEETSKAMP

A PPLICATIONS FOR THE iPhone and for smartphones in general come in many shapes, ranging from practical tools to funny toys. Thus, it is hardly surprising that media artists, like others who have a hand in digital technologies, use the Apple App Store to distribute their work. The App Store is used not only for new work but also for the emulation, migration, and reinterpretation of older media artworks, some of which were originally designed for desktop computers and the World Wide Web but find new functionalities, such as the possibility of touch, in smartphone apps. In practical terms, this appears to be a logical choice. As the artist and researcher Jonah Brucker-Cohen suggests on rhizome.org, the App Store paradigm seems to solve some of the main problems of distribution that artists were still confronting during the 1990s desktop era.[1] Now, media art blends almost seamlessly with other apps, and it is sometimes hard to distinguish it from more "commercial" creative inventions.

The issue of discriminating between art and nonart, however, will not be the main focus of this essay, nor will the problem of media art distribution and preservation, or the iPhone as the epitomization of some original promise. Instead, I will take the fact that artists use the iPhone to revisit and revivify their own media technological past as an anecdotic point of departure for my own reflections on the iPhone experience, media archaeology, and moving-image installation art. Concerning the media-archaeological emphasis of this article, Erkki Huhtamo's early art-related approach provides a rather helpful model of thinking. Huhtamo has pointed out the tendency of early 1990s media art to become a framework for revisiting the media-technological past. Within this context, he describes the artists' "archaeological" approach as not necessarily excluding newer technologies but using them to construct links and connections with media history, pointing to possible blanks and forgotten paths.[2]

While Huhtamo mainly refers to artists' strategically putting new technologies into dialogue with older ones (some of which are already obsolete), to conceive artworks as tools for analyzing relations between present and past could be considered productive in a much wider sense, as could the idea of new technologies that allow for retracing one's steps as a media historiographer. As I would like to claim, even in works of art that do not explicitly address media change, experiential aspects of predominant technologies and media formations—such as GPS-based smartphone applications and cinematic modes of perception—can be detected and related to one another.

This is where I come to what I call the "iPhone experience": a contemporary way of relating to our surroundings for which mobility, embodiment, and positioning are essential. While the iPhone is still relatively new, it questions many common assumptions about media-technological pasts in ways that reintegrate mobile technologies with various other histories, from cinema and television to "low-tech" and "no-tech" experiences in diverse environments. My analysis will revolve around a set of notions related to the iPhone experience: "layering," "positioning," and "location awareness," terms that are derived from the mobile-tech contexts of digital imaging, augmented reality, and GPS-based data generation and retrieval. To test my findings, I have chosen what might at first sight seem a rather unlikely case study, a monitor-based installation work: Kutluğ Ataman's *Küba* (2005), which is contemporary and timely in a thematic sense but technologically more old-fashioned, not least in that it predates the launch of the iPhone in 2007. Ultimately, the aim of this essay is to show that the iPhone experience, in fact, extends and exceeds the realm of the iPhone or smartphone itself, and can, thus, function as a vantage point for media archaeological comparison.

The iPhone experience

This type of experience draws heavily on the possibility of changing and taking positions in space, and it presupposes embodied human perception.

Many smartphone applications make these features rather explicit. For instance, iPhone and Android apps such as the Layar Reality Browser enable a different experience of urban territory as they provide a virtual expansion of the concrete physical reality the user encounters. The Netherlands Architecture Institute has used this software to develop its own app, called UAR (Urban Augmented Reality), which promises an expanded experience of the city by offering information about particular architectural constellations the user encounters and three-dimensional models of future scenarios concerning specific sites. In that respect, one could talk about a double projection of past and future onto one temporarily fixed and always augmented "present," which the mobile device is pointed at.

But there are obviously many other examples of applications that "augment" reality, many of which use GPS data to localize the position of the user.[3] What is generally relevant in the case of these augmentation strategies, which are broadly associated with the field of augmented reality, is the fact that the information is *embedded* in existing physical environments. In contrast to virtual reality, which tries to overcome the gap between "here and now" and a "there and then" of a second, simulated space that ought to replace physical reality, AR acknowledges the impossibility of a perfect, multisensory illusion and, thus, of absolute approximation. The small screen of the handheld mobile device is therefore not at all at odds with the app-driven attempt to enhance local and time-specific experiences, as the screen space does not serve as a substitute for the real thing: it rather helps us understand our surroundings by offering extra layers and additional information.

Yet in an even less literal and probably more flexible sense, AR can also be associated with general enrichment of urban territory as Lev Manovich has indicated with his broad notion of "augmented space," which includes all kinds of information-saturated physical environments and goes beyond a strict technology-specific understanding of what "augmentation" could entail.[4] Even though Manovich suggests that the resulting experiences are something new—based on the inseparability of physical space and informational layers— the very notion of inseparability and the non-techno-determinist angle that enable comparisons with more human-centered, hermeneutic approaches to urban encounters also point toward a predigital and proto-electronic past. In fact, if "information" and "data" are thought of as not strictly derived from the *computational* context of information processing but in relation to human cognition, the notion of augmented space might offer valuable insights on how to conceptualize site-related experiences in a more general way, that is, from the perspective of various "interfaces" for which site-related iPhone use is merely the most obvious example.

Layering

Beyond the confines of techno-determinist literalism, this understanding of urban layering and the fundamentally expansive dimensions and enhancing qualities of the iPhone experience allows for addressing similar qualities in quite different, less "high-tech" contexts, such as the aforementioned forty-channel installation *Küba* by the Turkish artist and filmmaker Kutluğ Ataman. In *Küba*, old television sets are combined with secondhand furniture in the exhibition space, and each of them shows one of forty interviews with the inhabitants of an Istanbul shanty town of the same name, an urban conglomeration that cannot be found on any map. The stories that are told reflect the precarious state of the neighborhood, which serves as a shelter for dissidents of all kinds, people who often have problems with the Turkish state apparatus for ethnic, political, or religious reasons.[5] The thread of these narrations seems to be the attempt to somehow locate and relocate oneself in the hope of eventually making a place "one's own" (which is, essentially, a quest for selfhood, a recurring theme in Ataman's work).

Before traveling to various other venues (including mobile spaces), the work was shown at an abandoned mail-sorting office at the heart of London.[6] Subsequently, the TV sets were dispersed through the city, to be installed individually at various public and semipublic venues, from charitable organizations and service companies to educational and cultural institutions, where they established a new type of dialogue with the existing environment. In fact, one could conceive of Ataman's artistic strategy as an attempt to add additional "layers" to a present situation: adding Istanbul to London; cinema, television, and the home to the art space; the inhabitants' accounts to spaces where rather different stories unfold. However, this "layering" should not be taken too literally; it has to be considered mainly in terms of conceptual complexity, the layers referring to the different interpretive dimensions of a singular situation tied to a particular site. Hence, they are at once concrete and imaginary, tangible and projective. In this sense, they are not only of a spatial or site-related but also temporal and historical.

Interestingly, this methodic layering closely resembles a more "hermeneutic," that is, human-centered, understanding of site-related information retrieval, as Irit Rogoff has recently described in terms of a practice of "regional imagining," a notion she develops in regard to another, related work by Ataman (*Mesopotamian Dramaturgies* [2009]). This practice is foremost defined as "a relationship to place and space that projects upon it a series of possible expansions not perhaps materially available but that have deep roots within what we perceive as the realm of the possible." Correcting herself slightly, she subsequently makes clear that "it is a projection that has nothing to do with expansion but rather relates to the effort to think oneself into another relation to the world." And, as she states further on, this "regional imagining" manifests itself as a "cultural, topographic layering of numerous coexisting narratives and time-scales," which are, however, interwoven to such a degree that they no longer constitute separate archaeological strata, not unlike the strata of Manovich's augmented space.

Indirectly referring back to the urban theme of *Küba*, this idea is directly derived from the experience of Istanbul. Rogoff describes how she and the artist Stefan Roemer, while researching for an Ataman exhibition, were guided through the city by local culture workers, who explained to them which people—such as Armenians, Jews, Greeks, and so on—lived at various locations in earlier phases of history. Rogoff speaks in this context of a "larger past self." Thus, "regional imagining" is also about positioning oneself; it is a method of "(self) regioning." It implies a possibility "to activate and to actualize notions of location away from being located by an authority of knowledge or a political authority."[7] Yet even if this is initially about human memory and imagination, it still has a lot in common with other types of urban layering, for instance, the "layers" of digital images on handheld devices, in which real-time recordings of actual sites are combined with site-specific data. A fitting example for this is (alternative) sightseeing apps that allow city visitors to access historical information about particular sites.[8]

Positioning

A second important characteristic of the iPhone experience is the double sense of positioning oneself and of positioning technologies, that is, tracking technologies (as in GPS). Positioning is impossible without a fundamentally mobile user or spectator, which, at the same time, is also one of the key characteristics of installation art, and of *Küba* in particular. However, in this case, considering the nature of the work, the mobility of the spectator might rather be associated with "zapping behavior" than with making use of apps to retrieve location-based data. Hence, the main media-technological framework that is referenced in the case of *Küba* seems to be television rather than mobile technologies, especially considering the homelike feel of the presentation, which is evoked by the secondhand furniture and TV sets.[9]

Interestingly, the emphasis is not on the *live* qualities of television broadcasting here (as it is with many TV-related artworks from previous decades) but on the specificities of watching television, that is, of the reception situation. It seems to point to the living-room experience as a "default position," an assumption that is immediately undermined by the fact that, in the London version, the monitors subsequently traveled to other locations. Yet their reinstallment at various other sites in the city did not make their placement appear "unnatural"; it almost seemed as if they had always been there. At this point, TV is apparently linked to a broader urban screen culture, similar to what Anna McCarthy suggests with her observation that television is not a placeless medium but inhabits all kinds of sites (including public space). In that respect, it is always already augmenting reality, at times even closer to urban screen culture than to the living room.[10] From this viewpoint, television and mobile technologies are much more closely related than one would initially assume.[11]

It is rather striking, then, that most of the *Küba* interviews are conducted in interior spaces (only a few are seemingly located in private gardens), a fact that is mirrored by the homely arrangement of the initial exhibition space. Nowhere do the viewers get any street views, aerial shots, or impressions of the neighborhood that would allow them to locate and identify a place. The ambiguity of the subjects' positioning, which is also present in the unmapped status of the neighborhood, becomes visible. Paradoxically, this does not happen through a total denial of location and an acknowledgment of placelessness (as is often performed by Web- and desktop-related media theories), but through a simultaneous recognition of both site-relatedness and embededdness, on the one hand, and the possibility of repositioning, on the other. One's position is never fixed, yet it is context-specific. The "there" and "then" still have to be determined and therefore remain temporarily unstable. As deictic markers, they are so-called *shifters*, a kind of discursive placeholder, a linguistic notion that Thomas Elsaesser has linked to the screening event of cinema.[12] In addressing the apparent indeterminacy of the "there," *Küba* exposes the relative ambiguity of positioning as one of the key principles of site-related imagination techniques, of which mobile technologies are probably the most paradigmatic.

But one could even go further at this point: translated to the "here and now" of the installation, there is an interesting parallel between the indeterminacy of the "there" and the mobility of the exhibition visitors ("here"), who move around between the screens without ever been assigned a final place. The various positions they can inhabit in the space are initially not occupied but are simultaneously articulated as potential places of (re-)positioning. They are shifters, too—in both a discursive and spatial sense—as they enable the visitors to construct the "text" of the artwork through spatial movement but also refer to their literal mobility, to their ability to *shift*, to change their position in space. This tendency is complemented by the fact that, because of the installation's continuous relocation, the screens are, in fact, *mobile*, even if their movement is rather slower than that of mobile devices. Thus, the spatial arrangement is based on a fundamental flexibility—or ambiguity—concerning the positions it enables—"here" or "there." Yet the "content" remains related to the place one positions oneself in, where a screen or device is temporarily located. In that, *Küba* resembles so-called locative media practices. I would suggest that the installation does not simply stage a television audience, but it also evokes the "we" of mobile technologies.

The necessity of spatial positioning and continuous relocation for accessing new information suggests that moving-image installations overlay the museum (or comparable art spaces) with cinema- or television-related "data" and that the museum itself—as much as television or cinema, for that matter—includes properties that are connected to the field of mobile technologies, such as the mobility of the audience members or the (relative) mobility of the frame. In this regard, the installation is as much a model of museum experience as an interface among various media-technological *dispositifs*. As a consequence, it also allows for comparisons between the museum and the individual media constellations. This is not to say that there are no differences between the museum and the "mobile" experience. Obviously, my argument functions only if human imaginative experience remains the main focus of attention rather than technological specificities. And even then, there may be important points where the different frameworks do not converge. Yet from the perspective of the notions explored in this essay—layering, positioning, location awareness—there seem to be striking parallels, shedding light on media-historical relationships beyond the confines of media-technological determination. In that respect, the iPhone merely suggests a higher degree of flexibility on certain levels (for instance, in regard to the mobility of the screen), while being more restrictive than older media on others (for example, tracking or the controlling aspects of data management). In the end, however, this appears more as a question of degree (or radicalization) than categorical distinction—at least from the viewpoint of the users and their relationship to what is accessible in terms of information, in other words, what can be experienced.

Installation art, as famously suggested by Douglas Gordon's *24 Hour Psycho* (1993), is often about the asymmetry between the seemingly limitless amount of archived material, including the infinite possibilities of recombination, and the spatiotemporal restrictions of its experience.[13] This, however, is also a feature of mobile technology applications that make use of GPS and database information: site-related access resembles human embodied experience in that it excludes access to the totality of data "out there." The "here and now" is overlaid by just a small section of the "there and then"—elsewhere and in the past/future, or even in relation to the actual site. Positioning, in this sense, is also a method of selection and framing—just like pointing your iPhone at a particular site in order to retrieve relevant information.

Location Awareness

But where does this leave us? What about the way installation art oscillates between the two poles of devices and human memory and imagination? Doesn't it gloss over important differences between the media configurations it incorporates and invokes? Isn't the associative use of AR-related notions such as "layering" and "positioning" too problematic?

In this section I will examine the potential conceptual discrepancies between *Küba* and the iPhone experience, centered around the notion of "location awareness." Thomas Elsaesser's 2003 text "'Where Were You When . . . ?'; or, 'I Phone, Therefore I Am,'"[14] begins with a small anecdote about a homeless man walking and talking to himself. Elsaesser used to encounter this man frequently in a particular part of Amsterdam, and one day saw someone else who seemed to exhibit the same kind of behavior—a mobile phone user. No longer unacceptable social behavior, public self-involvement was suddenly everywhere. Yet, according to Elsaesser, there is a fundamental difference between the two individuals: while the homeless person has fallen through the social net, the guy who was talking on the phone was not only in contact with somebody else, he was also technologically tracked, reassuring him of his very existence. As Elsaesser phrases it: "I am the pinpointed set of coordinates in a global positioning system. I phone, therefore I am."[15]

As much as this quote points to the fundamental unavoidability of positioning and the way our experience is dependent on it, it also exposes the location-aware technological features of tracking and data collection that go along with the use of GPS-based applications but are clearly not part of more old-fashioned moving-image installations such as *Küba*. According to the media artists and theorists Marc Tuters and Kazyz Varnelis, spatial positioning, in the context of mobile technologies, is connected to two different strategies of data generation: "Broadly speaking, locative media projects can be categorized under one of two types of mapping, either annotative—virtually tagging the world—or phenomenological—tracing the action of the subject in the world."[16] While Tuters and Varnelis mainly discuss artistic interventions that employ these technological strategies to create extensions of reality or increase the user's awareness of a location, it stills seems a valuable distinction concerning the different dimensions of AR applications in general. One might even divide the second characteristic of locative media—tracing the action of the subject—into two subcategories: the supra-systemic perspective of data mining, for which the users are interesting only because their behavior generates economically relevant data; and the singular perspective of accessing local data, which is linked to an individual's experience of a particular site. Both occur in relation to the first type of—annotative—mapping, but the way the configuration of subject-device-site is conceptually framed differs vastly. The first is about *sensed data*, the second about the human sensorium—two types of location awareness, so to speak.[17]

From the supra-systemic (economic, technological, posthumanist) angle, there might be a huge difference between the residents of *Küba* and the "we" of mobile technologies. While the inhabitants of the neighborhood derive their identity from the fact that they (want or have to) remain untraceable and uncontrollable, iPhone users actually take pleasure in the fact that they are constantly reminded of their localizability (whether this happens in the context of activist artistic projects or in regard to commercial applications). In that respect, the distinction between the two groups of people is not unlike the differentiation between Elsaesser's homeless guy and the mobile phone user: untraced and marginalized (with both its positive and negative connotations) vs. traced and instrumentalized but seemingly participating. And, in many respects, the problem is obviously even more complex than that.

Making a Place One's Own

Nonetheless, a radical differentiation can only occur at the supra-systemic level because the experiential dimension suggests a shared common ground based on continuous dislocation or repositioning, attempts to (re-)locate oneself, that is to say, *to make a place one's own*, similar to Rogoff's notion of "(self) regioning." This is all about relating in a particular way to a specific environment, which is also reflected by Julian Bleecker and Jeff Knowlton's more experience-based definition of "locative media":

> The locative media that is of most immediate concerns is that made by those who create experiences that take into account the geographic locale of interest, typically by elevating that geographic locale beyond its instrumentalized status as a "latitude longitude coordinated point on earth" to the level of existential, inhabited, experienced and lived place. These locative media experiences may delve "into" the historical surface of a space to reveal past events or stories (whether fictional, confessional or standing on consensus as factual). Locative media experiences may also cross space, connecting experiences across short or long geographic, experiential, or temporal distances. At its core, locative media is about creating a kind of geospatial experience whose aesthetics can be said to rely upon a range of characteristics ranging from the quotidian to the weighty semantics of lived experience, all latent within the ground upon which we traverse.[18]

Even though Bleecker and Knowlton still consider GPS technologies a "boundary marker" for the category, this reading nevertheless indicates a view *from the inside* that raises questions radically different from what I have called the supra-systemic vision and creates opportunities for tracing links and connections between different sets of media practices, now and in the past.

The shift to embedded experience is also what eventually motivates Rogoff's project—and Ataman's, as he makes clear that the people he is interested in "are not on the periphery of society but in the very center of their own lives."[19] The perspective is always that of multiple selves distributed in space, *taking place at the same time*. One could also argue that beyond any literal data sensing by the apparatus, the installation could also be conceptualized as "location aware" since it establishes a relationship between what it gives access to—that is, Küba, the place—and the "here and now" of *Küba*, the installation, which is located in an equally abandoned space. In this way, the installation functions as a context in which parallels among different media-technological *dispositifs* and sociocultural contexts can be detected.

Hence, media history is not a history only of particular technologies and devices or even spatiotemporal arrangements. It can also take the form of an archaeology of embodied human experience, constructed along the lines of different groupings of a "here and now" vis-à-vis a "there and then," related to particular sites, with the possibilities of positioning within the configuration as a focal point. The necessity for positioning induced by the era of mobile technologies opens our view to the fact that even television and cinema ask the viewer-users to position themselves in a particular space. As the (human) iPhone experience points to experience per se as an overarching principle and connecting factor, it serves as an important reminder of its irreducibility. Employed in a conceptual way, it becomes the main ground on which to explore the various feedback loops between cultural tropes and technological developments, without taking one as the mere supplement or result of the other. In effect, the iPhone experience points to the fact that all (human) experience is essentially layered, positioned, and location aware.

Let me finish by returning to the tendency, mentioned in the beginning of my essay, of media artists re-creating their 1990s desktop work as an iPhone app. While giving the initial impression of conceiving of the "iPhone" as an eschatological endpoint of technological development, finally allowing the artworks to behave properly, "like they were supposed to," I would argue for the reverse: the fact that it was possible to "iPhonize" them maybe suggests that the iPhone (or any similar device), despite its new technological possibilities and applications, heavily draws on existing conceptual principles and experiential parameters, explicating and enhancing their realities.

Notes

1. Jonah Brucker-Cohen, "Art in Your Pocket: iPhone and iPod Touch App Art," *Rhizome.org*, 7 July 2009, http://rhizome.org/editorial/2009/jul/7/art-in-your-pocket (6 January 2011); Jonah Brucker-Cohen, "Art in Your Pocket 2: Media Art for the iPhone, iPod Touch, and iPad Graduates to the Next Level," *Rhizome.org*, 26 May 2010, http://rhizome.org/editorial/2010/may/26/art-in-your-pocket-2 (6 January 2011).

2. Erkki Huhtamo, "Time Traveling in the Gallery: An Archaeological Approach to Media Art," in *Immersed in Technology: Art and Virtual Environments*, ed. Mary Ann Moser (Cambridge, Mass.: MIT Press, 1996), 233–70 (see in particular 243–44).

3. See local applications such as AMS 3.0 Tours and Best Scene in Town, both developed by De Waag Society, Amsterdam, or Google Maps adaptations that function on a more global (yet also local) scale, such as historypin. See also artistic precursors, such as *34 North 118 West* (2004), by Jeffrey Knowlton, Naomi Spellman, and Jeremy Hight, which is based on the use of tablet PCs with GPS navigation software.

4. For a discussion, see Lev Manovich, "The Poetics of Augmented Space," *Visual Communication* 5, no. 2 (2006): 219–40.

5. The artist had an agreement with the inhabitants of Küba that the work would not be shown in Turkey, which was undermined by the fact that the Turkish tabloids started to write about it in connection with the London show.

6. The London presentation was, in fact, the second time the installation was exhibited, as it was first shown at the Carnegie Museum in Pittsburgh. The installation traveled extensively in the following years. It was shown in railway carriages in Germany, on a boat traveling up the Danube River, and at a magistrates' court in the south of England. On many occasions, the places of exhibition were somehow connected to issues addressed by the work, such as migration, identity, and survival.

7. Irit Rogoff, "Regional Imaginings," in *Unleashed: Contemporary Art from Turkey*, ed. Hossein Amirsadeghi (London: TransGlobe, 2010), 48, 49–50, 48–49.

8. For examples, see note 3.

9. For a more detailed discussion, see Hito Steyerl, *Die Farbe der Wahrheit. Dokumentarismen im Kunstfeld* (Vienna: Turia+Kant, 2008), 78–80.

10. Anna McCarthy, "From Screen to Site: Television's Material Culture and Its Place," *October*, no. 98 (Fall 2001): 93–111.

11. At this point, I have to thank Nanna Verhoeff for providing part of this argument in a lecture she gave in Amsterdam on November 13, 2007.

12. Thomas Elsaesser, "New Film History as Media Archaeology," *Cinémas* 14, no. 2–3 (2003): 75–117.

13. Steyerl, *Die Farbe der Wahrheit*, 83.

14. The first time I saw the now rather curious title, I misread it as "IPhone, therefore I am," instead of "I phone, therefore I am." This happened despite the fact the "i" in "iPhone" is not necessarily referring to the "I" of the first-person singular (a deictic marker indicating a particular discursive position); it is nevertheless widely interpreted in this manner. For a further discussion, see Thomas Elsaesser, "'Where Were You When . . . ?'; or, 'I Phone, Therefore I Am,'" *PMLA* 118, no.1 (2003): 120–22.

15. Elsaesser, "'Where Were You When . . . ?'" 122.

16. Marc Tuters and Kazys Varnelis, "Beyond Locative Media: Giving Shape to the Internet of Things," *Leonardo* 39, no. 4 (2006): 357–63 (see in particular 359).

17. Anthony Townsend, "Locative-Media Artists in the Contested-Aware City," *Leonardo* 39, no. 4 (2006): 345–47 (see in particular 345).

18. Julian Bleeker and Jeff Knowlton, "Locative Media: A Brief Bibliography and Taxonomy of GPS-Enabled Locative Media," *Leonardo Electronic Almanac* 14, no. 3 (2006): http://www.leoalmanac.org/journal/vol_14/lea_v14_no3–04/jbleecker.html (6 January 2011).

19. Maria Hlavajova and Kutluğ Ataman, "Kutluğ Ataman: Küba/Paradise: Everyone Is a Mother's Child," e-mail conversation, July 2007, http://www.bak-utrecht.nl/?click[newsletter] (6 October 2010).

CHAPTER 5

Hard Candy

KRISTOPHER L. CANNON AND JENNIFER M. BARKER

Hold your breath. Make a wish.
Count to three. Come with me,
And you'll be in a world of pure imagination.
—*Willy Wonka and the Chocolate Factory*, 1971

"No touching, no meddling, and no tasting!
Is that agreed?"
—ROALD DAHL, *Charlie and the Chocolate Factory*, 1964

F ROM ITS FIRST appearance, the iPhone offered what no other phone or music player or computer did: a uniquely hand-held device that, while satisfying the soberest of adult telecommunication needs, also appealed to the inner child. Its makers marketed the iPhone not just as a phone in the ordinary sense of the word but as a magic tablet of a kind, capable of the most amazing transformations right before our very eyes. It's a phone, an MP3 player, a movie player, a camera, a noisemaker, a flashlight, a gaming device, a GPS, a Web browser, a carpenter's level, and so on and so on.

Apple's most recent interfaces and ad campaigns have cultivated an attitude of childlike wonder on the part of its consumer base, in part by shrewdly maintaining an atmosphere of mystery and magic surrounding the product and its inner workings. Indeed, part of the joy and pleasure in using the iPhone lies in the way it seems to work "as if by magic."[1] In this sense, Steve Jobs and the Apple designers recall Willy Wonka who, when asked how his glass elevator manages to move in any direction whatsoever and stay aloft without the use of cables or any visible support system, answers, "'Candy power! One million candy power!'"[2]

The parallel between Steve Jobs and Willy Wonka is instructive on many levels. Both are visionary CEOs faced with the difficult task of naming a successor to a company that has come to represent, more than a product, a school of thought and a devoted fan base. Though a biographical and industrial comparison is tempting, we will entertain instead the idea that the phenomenon of the iPhone is itself like candy in that—like candy—it demands, provokes, and enables a kind of experience that is fundamentally contradictory, in ways that are variously productive and problematic.[3] The iPhone encourages playful behavior wherein users are allowed to ignore the boundary between function and fun, as Steve Jobs affirms when he tells Stanford University graduates to "stay hungry, stay foolish."[4] In short, Apple invites its adult consumers to play with their iPhones in the way children play with their food.

Moreover, the iPhone designers and marketers share Willy Wonka's profoundly ambivalent attitude toward the nature of childhood itself. For Apple, as for Wonka, childlike play is idealized and feared at the same time, something to be celebrated—indeed, recruited—but it is also to be tamed. We will argue that the iPhone—as both machine and marketing campaign—trains us to be a particular kind of consumer, one who relishes the pleasure the iPhone has to offer with childlike amazement but who learns to enjoy in moderation and, ultimately, to keep one's hands to oneself.

Play with Your Food *and* Your Phone

We are told, as children, to not play with our food, but, as Steven Connor notes, sweets are designed to be playthings.[5] They are "things that we do things to," handling them before placing them in our mouths "where we play with them anew. . . . Sweets are meant to go in and out . . . the only kind of food that we are allowed to see the results of eating." As such, "they give us access to an otherwise most secret and invisible process, [that] of rendering something part of the outside world part of us." This notion of "rendering" is key not only to the experience of candy but also to the experience of childhood, both of which, Connor tells us, "let nothing persist as it merely, drearily is."[6] In the imaginative world of childhood, where "children are shown as having a knack for metaphorical substitution,"[7] things can transform magically and materially into other things: a cardboard box is both a container and a castle, a wooden spoon both a kitchen utensil and a magic wand. Candy is similarly metamorphic. It constantly takes the shape of something else; think of gummi bears, chocolate bunnies, ring pops, marshmallow Peeps, candy necklaces, and even (on the darker side of things) candy cigarettes or licorice whips.

The metamorphic pleasures of candy are also multisensory pleasures, for, as Connor writes, "sweetness is always more than taste." This is not only because taste is inextricably bound up with smell, sight, and touch but also because sweetness derives from the interactive "essence of eating" rather than from the ingredients themselves.[8] Though people young and old experience any given phenomenon through multiple senses simultaneously, children are especially unbound by schematic, Aristotelian divisions of the senses into five discrete modalities. Roald Dahl emphasizes this characteristic of his book's hero early on:

> Every day, little Charlie Bucket, trudging through the snow on his way to school, would have to pass Mr. Willy Wonka's giant chocolate factory. And every day, as he came near to it, he would lift his small pointed nose high in the air and sniff the wonderful sweet smell of melting chocolate. Sometimes, he would stand motionless outside the gates for several minutes on end, taking deep swallowing breaths as though he were trying to *eat* the smell itself.
>
> (*Charlie and the Chocolate Factory*, 38)

In other words, Connor explains, "sweet things really do not taste of themselves; they taste of our own pleasure in them."[9] The pleasure of the iPhone, like its siblings, is not what *it does*, but what it invites *us to do to it*, and how it invites all of our senses to the table. Apple imagines, designs and markets every product, including the iPhone, in a similar way: as technologies that go beyond function, as art objects and playthings designed to appeal to multiple senses and to provoke an interactive engagement with them, right down to their curvaceous contours, smooth textures, and colorful surfaces.[10] Apple's aesthetic yields products that, like the fruit that inspires the company name and logo, are pretty, playful, even "lickable," "candy-colored," and "delicious."[11]

Styled in distinctive Apple fashion (and a far cry from the stale, bargain-bin phones with which consumers and industry leaders were familiar), the iPhone immediately sparked enthusiasm. Before the iPhone was announced to consumers, Steve Jobs met with AT&T in 2006 to show the prototype to Stan Sigman, who was regarded as a conservative, engineering-oriented executive in the mobile telephone industry. *Wired* rumored that after seeing the iPhone, Sigman became "uncharacteristically effusive, calling the iPhone 'the best device I have ever seen.'" Sigman reacted with amazement. His reaction draws attention to a shift in the mobile phone handset market, where industry leaders had come to think of handsets as "cheap, disposable lures . . . to snare subscribers."[12]

Upon the iPhone's first unveiling and subsequent public preview at Mac-World in 2007, references to Apple gestured toward not only the awe-inspiring magic of its products but also the central role played by its leader. By one account, 2007 became a "magically significant year" for Apple, whose "secret weapon" was Steve Jobs, who seemed to many to be "Willy Wonka and Harry Potter rolled up into one."[13] If Jobs bears a resemblance to Wonka because of his penchant for control over and personal involvement with successful design aesthetics, the iPhone also recalls some of the candyman's confections.

Indeed, in its first form, the iPhone was said to look "like an expensive bar of chocolate wrapped in aluminum and stainless steel."[14] Like the bar of chocolate Charlie unwraps in hopes of finding a Golden Ticket, the iPhone is a multisensory feast. While iPhones build on functions at work in the iPod, the iPhone does much more than continue or reference the older hardware. The iPhone is no skeuomorph, merely referencing (and reducible to) traces of previous technological interfaces.[15] The iPhone's multisensory modalities involve transformation and incorporation in the way child's play and children's candy do. It is an *additive* technology (in addition to being addictive, for some): it does this and this and . . . and so on. In the process, the iPhone reconfigures our senses by *becoming multisensory*.

Listen: Its function as MP3 player is as popular and pronounced as its conventional phone functions, of course, and its sound is not only clear but also intimate. The iPhone begs to be plugged into users' ears but is, simultaneously, willing to listen to us (speak on the phone, speak commands through voice control, or speak to ourselves while we record voice memos), which collapses the distance between inside (the machine) and outside (our bodies).

Touch: The iPhone was among the first devices to omit the conventional keypad, and it introduced an entirely different kind of tactile interaction. As Wonka's lickable wallpaper invited users to taste décor in rather unconventional ways, an early advertising slogan for the iPhone was "Touching Is Believing," which tells us how to believe in *magical, seemingly impossible* transformations, *not* everyday correspondences.[16] From the moment we turn it on we are invited to touch—the ironic "click" of the keys in fact conjures up a sense of pressure and compression that isn't *really* there—as well as to tap, slide, swipe, turn, flip, shake, pinch, and more.

Orient: While there is still no way to "smell" the iPhone (one imagines there'll be "an app for that" soon enough), it involves the "sixth sense," or proprioception, in a way no other phone does: its accelerometer gives it the preternatural ability to match the image's orientation—portrait or landscape—to its user's physical orientation in space—upright or horizontal. This function is amazing but also somewhat dizzying, prompting Apple to include an orientation-locking feature in iOS 4.0 for the iPhone, but, dizzying or orientated, we still want to feel and see it.

Look: Its most notable feature, perhaps, offers both tactile and visual pleasure—the slick, shiny touch screen beckons the user's fingertips to its sentient surface. Indeed, Apple proclaims that their retina display in the iPhone 4 is the "sharpest, most vibrant, highest-resolution phone screen ever," which is merely an extension of other rave reviews for its eye-catching colors and astonishing definition.[17] Apple's second TV advertisement for the iPhone called itself a "How To,"[18] but a generation raised on conventional push-button phones might have been thinking "How on earth?" Here, we see the iPhone being held by a human hand, in close-up, as a voiceover offers simple explanations: "This is how you turn it on. This is your music. This is your e-mail. This is the Web. And this is a call—on your iPhone." The iPhone's deceptively simple form entices us to watch carefully as it morphs, like an Everlasting Gobstopper, from one thing to the next.

Like the Gobstopper, the iPhone requires our rapt attention, and unlike the stale hard candies found at the bottom of Grandma's purse or stuck between the cushions of the living-room sofa, the iPhone offers up endless play and transformation. It's "eye candy" in the most playful and profound sense, but when it comes to making sense of the iPhone, it seems that WYS is anything but WYG.[19] As Willy Wonka and Alice in Wonderland knew, Steven Connor explains, the "meaning [of sweets] is pure metamorphosis. . . . Sweets are magical objects, because their shape is there to be transformed, to transform themselves under our touch. They are subtle, paradoxical, alchemical, polymorphous substances."[20]

(Some) Children Are the Future

As meticulous as they are about their products, Jobs and Wonka are even more selective when it comes to their fans and followers. Both visionary CEOs have a distinct, and contradictory, image of the ideal consumer for their product. If, as Connor says, sweet things taste of our pleasure in them, Jobs and Wonka exact precise control over that particular ingredient as well. We must be trained to be "good users" who take pleasure in just the right way. In Roald Dahl's novel, both filmed versions, and telecom industry accounts of the iPhone, certain characters arise who model "good" and "bad" behaviors.

Tim Richardson addresses the competitive nature of the confectionary industry, which structures secrecy as a "necessity for originality and innovation."[21] This is why, of course, the worst kinds of "consumers" are thieves and spies. Wonka makes his long-standing animosities plain as he and his troupe of children visit the Inventing Room: "'Old Fickelgruber would give his front teeth to be allowed inside just for three minutes! So would Prodnose and Slugworth and all the other rotten chocolate makers!'" (87). It's much the same in the mobile media world, where even inadvertent mistakes can lead to a corporate crisis.

March 19, 2010, would have come and gone like any other day on Apple's Cupertino campus had Gray Powell not left his phone—an iPhone prototype—at the bar where he had celebrated his birthday the night before. This phone, deceptively encased to look like an iPhone 3GS, was uncased to reveal the much-anticipated iPhone 4. Gizmodo obtained this phone weeks later (in exchange for $5,000 in cash) and gave the public a first look. Technology blogs like Gizmodo are adept at reporting rumors about Apple products they assume or hope are approaching release, but Gizmodo's iPhone 4 acquisition twisted this typical rumor-mill model. The focus on product releases by technology blogs, followed by frenzied comments and speculations, affirms consumer desires to know about or see Apple products before their release,[22] which became an obvious motivation for Steve Jobs to drive demand by securing Apple's Cupertino campus against employees who might share product information or prototypes.

Unlike Wonka, Jobs could not simply close down production and shut the factory gates, nor can (or ought) he import a reliable, indentured team of Oompa-Loompas from far-flung lands to take over production. Apple's security, steeped in paranoia about product information leaks or theft, is no different than the security devised for candy and confection companies like Wonka's. Until Gizmodo acquired Powell's iPhone 4, Apple's "legendary security" had worked perfectly. Product information remained private until release—aside from "a blurry factory photo here, or some last-minute information strategically whispered to some friendly media there." Most products are protected "behind armored doors, with security locks with codes that change every few minutes," and prototypes, like the iPhone 4, are "bolted to desks" and remain under the watchful eye of "Apple secret police."[23]

One might wonder if the iPhone 4 "leak" was no more than a calculated marketing strategy, but it seems unlikely. Not only does Apple announce or reveal products strategically—most of their new hardware is announced during planned events or through "quiet," unexpected updates on their Web-based storefront—but Apple also took legal action against Gizmodo (and its owner Gawker Media) to collect their lost property.[24] As much as Apple seeks control over its employees, the blogosphere, and news outlets, it seeks even more eagerly to control its users and fans, whom the company trains to be patient users. Apple issues unspoken instructions: be patient consumers, keep your appetites for more in check by waiting until it is your turn to consume, to play.

"There are five children in this book," Roald Dahl writes on the opening page of *Charlie and the Chocolate Factory*, and all five serve as models (good and bad) of consumer behavior. Only one will earn Wonka's respect and the invitation to carry on his legacy: Dahl introduces him simply as "Charlie Bucket, the hero." That Wonka chooses Charlie to run the factory says a great deal about his paradoxical notions of childhood. What makes Charlie heroic, in the eyes of Wonka at least, is that he's childlike in all the right ways and none of the wrong ones.

Childlike wonder is the first and foremost among Wonka's requirements, and it seemed to be close to Jobs's heart as well. Apple's logo, products, and marketing reflect a similar value placed on amazement and belief in magic and the impossible. It's "the Internet in your pocket," said an iPhone ad. "People have been dreaming about video calling for decades," another might say. "The iPhone makes it a reality, and makes reality magical." However, as Connor points out, "sweetness is so important to us, that it generates rituals and protocols. Sweets are surrounded by complex rules and prescriptions, the infallible signs of the presence of magic." If there is something imaginative about taking pleasure in the smell, shape, and texture of candy, there's also something potentially rude about "playing" with one's food in this way.

The iDon'ts: Or, Be Clean, Be Tidy, and Keep Your Hands to Yourself

Indeed, as imaginative and playful as Wonka is, it is important to note that he is also very rule-bound and quite bossy, issuing repeated warnings and prohibitions. "Don't touch!" he shouts to his guests in the Inventing Room. "And don't knock anything over!" (88). If Charlie is a good candidate for factory owner, it's because he is first a good consumer: he doesn't ask too many questions, doesn't push past his awe to figure out just how the magical things work, and dares not challenge Wonka's account of things like gravity and television. The iPhone, too, has distinct "role models" of behavior and consumption. The iPhone trains us to use it in the "right" way, to be the "right" kind of user. We should be childlike in all the "right" ways—joyous and imaginative and playful—but avoid any behavior that might be construed as destructive, demanding, or dismissive by the laws of property and propriety. We must enjoy but only in ways deemed appropriate by Apple. Paradoxically, Apple's desire for control will also incite and foreshadow how consumers respond to the darker, addictive side of sweets (after all, "candy" is also slang for cocaine).[25]

Rule 1: Keep your screen clean. "Are there any more elaborately erotic coverings than the wrappers of sweets, waxy, crackling, filmy-wrinkled?"[26] The iPhone's "elaborately erotic" touch screen is smooth as glass, inviting to the sense of touch. Of course, each finger tap, swipe, or caress of the cheek while taking a call results in a visible trace of our touch, and the pleasure a user experiences from the iPhone registers tactilely and visually as a smudge on the face of the phone. Likewise, if one touches the iPhone when it's already smudged, one feels the smudge (of whatever, whoever touched it last) being transferred to one's fingers. No matter which way we type, touch, press, or play, there is one guarantee: the iPhone will show signs of *its taste* for our touch.[27] These touches stick as traces of the iPhone's response to a user; the iPhone's screen shows signs of its taste, appreciation, and even love for our touch. These are signs of our experiences with sweetness, traces of our enthusiastic consumption of the iPhone's graphical user interface (GUI), which ocassionaly becomes a bit gooey.

However, the iPhone is *ambivalent* about the proximity between bodies and objects, both attracted to and repulsed by human skin. The smooth, glassy screen has become increasingly oleophobic with the release of each new generation. Indeed, Apple provides a microfiber cloth for just this reason, suggesting, like Wonka, that there is something vile about dirtying hard-candy surfaces with human skin and that a proper user will remove those sweet, sticky traces. Because of these oleophobic screens, an entire (microfiber) cloth industry has emerged, creating iPhone- and iPad-specific products with brand names like "Cloth Addiction."[28] These cottage industries are not only becoming commonplace but also gesture at screen-cleaning expectations that give way to appropriately clean addictions.

Rule 2: Tidy up! Applications are one of the most obvious ways to play (rudely) with an iPhone. The applications we personally select and download add a layer of richness and individuality to the iPhone user experience. Apple's iPhone App Store offers millions of applications for users to download, each addition transforming the phone from its default, factory form. We can "tweet," bank, draw, or browse. We can look at our screen through the camera, where our world becomes virtually—almost magically—augmented with information and graphics from elsewhere. We can confront rather sinister, egg-stealing pigs and, with the flick of a finger, send Angry Birds in flight to bring about their demise. While many applications are free to download, the ability to purchase apps so easily makes the App Store an ideal environment for a greedy or gluttonous consumer who must own everything in sight, like the spoiled rich girl in Dahl's book. Veruca Salt would be the epitome and the envy of all iPhone app downloaders because she would doubtlessley sweeten her iPhone experience by obtaining every application she desires. She could push the iPhone experience by squirreling away countless applications. Well, almost countless. The iPhone was restricted to nine pages of applications with sixteen apps on each page (that's 144 slots Veruca could fill) until the release of iOS 4.0, which incorporated "folders" as another "layer" for iPhone interaction.

Don't just tap an app, tap a folder to be hypo-linked,[29] splitting the screen to reveal a deeper layer of the iPhone interface. Folders remind us how candy—like Gobstoppers or Advent calendars—becomes sweeter with additional layered or compartmentalized surprises. We may become guilty of excessive downloads, but our touches and taps on hypo-linked folders will take us to apps we've long forgotten—apps we hadn't tried or savored. Folders function as organizational tools, but they easily become "tiny prisons for truculent apps," as Ian Bogost humorously quipped.[30] Each folder allows us to hoard more apps on a page or file away the apps we don't use or like, but folders can also be used as hiding places. Embarrassed by your Farmville addiction? File your app at the bottom of a folder where no one can see. Do your coworkers think you read too many gossip columns? Place your blog reader in a folder for "travel" to hide the trail to your reading habits. But, remember: Apple wants us to learn to be tidy app users, to properly categorize and organize the messiness of numerous app pages. This is why folders are given a preliminary title if we place two similar apps together, but when these apps don't serve the same function, the iPhone will remind us of Apple's organizational expectations. Place a game app in a folder with the Clock app and the iPhone automatically generates a folder label: "Games." This automated process suggests one of two things: either one app is a misfit (the Clock app is usually a "utility") or that a user enjoys playful, personalized organization (in this case, a personal take on time).

Rule 3. Keep your hands to yourself. If Wonka so closely associates himself with play and pleasure, why does he warn his guests against greed or excessiveness? For that matter, why doesn't he offer them candy cigarettes? Surely a man so bent on the addictive properties of his products could capitalize on candy cigarettes, but Wonka knows best: children mustn't meddle and must learn restraint to prevent bad behaviors.

Perhaps the most obnoxious and dangerous addict, in Wonka's estimation, is young Mike Teavee who, upon visiting the Television Room, insists on being *part* of the process, even if he must accelerate things. Despite Wonka's urgent warnings of imminent physical danger, Mike chooses to send himself "over the air" as the first person on Wonka-Vision. His blatant disregard for rules, as well as his destructive enthusiasm, resembles those iOS jailbreakers who disregard Apple's recommendations for appropriate operating-system use. In many cases, iOS jailbreakers may merely want to have a taste of new software or programs, to have more than they are offered in the App Store, just as Mike *must* appear on Wonka-Vision first and as Violet Beauregarde cannot resist the temptation to chew the three-course stick of gum before anyone else in the world. Wonka makes it clear that this product is in its nascent stages and not yet ready for consumption. Violet disregards the warnings and rudely inserts herself into the production process by claiming for herself the role of product tester.

Ordinarily, Connor writes: "We seek to detain sweetness. That is why so many sweets are designed to be held in the mouth—or, in a perverse reversal of the perversity of the sweet, to melt, yearningly and disappointingly on the tongue. Sweetness is identified with the excess of taste over aliment, with prolonging itself. In learning how to make sweetness last, children learn on their tongues the lesson of deferment upon which all cultural life is based," a lesson Mike, Violet, and Augustus fail miserably.[31] Oddly, Willy Wonka recoils at Augustus's and Violet's disgusting habits, yet some of his products invite this kind of play with the boundaries between inside and outside and between our bodies and the world. Wonka beams with pride at his invention of lickable wallpaper and eatable marshmallow pillows, for example, and he proclaims the Everlasting Gobstopper to be remarkable in part because it changes color once a week, but he doesn't explain how would one know that, unless one is rude enough to take the sticky, wet candy out of one's mouth to inspect it. Jailbreakers, who likely relish the criminal allusions of the nickname they've been given, do so in part out of an ornery love for the object. In that sense, we can draw a direct parallel between "jailbreakers" and "jawbreakers," those consumers who love the Gobstopper or the Tootsie Pop, for example, but who cannot resist the temptation to break it apart and see how it works, to see the striated rainbow or the gummy chocolate layer that produces, respectively, its changing colors or its surprisingly chewy interior.

Jailbreakers may appear to be hungry for more but Apple deems them *too* hungry and, Steve Jobs might have added, *too* foolish. Apple tries to control their jailbreaking-prone consumers as if they were Wonka's children, with insatiable and thus inappropriate appetites. You want to jailbreak your iPhone? Apple will void your warranty.[32] You want to alter its innards? Apple will childproof each phone with proprietary screws you can't remove.[33] These consumers enact the childlike wonder that Wonka and Jobs encourage in their fan base and, in fact, take that wonder to its extreme. "Jailbreakers," who want more from their iPhones than Apple offers, support Kathryn Bond Stockton's description of candy as "the quintessential instance of create-in-order-to-destroy: the dream of manufacturing what you will profusely and on the spot consume, not as a necessity but strictly as luxury."[34] When we swallow, we destroy. Jobs, like Wonka, understood that these are the same kids who stake out a spot behind the Christmas tree to catch Santa in the act, or tie their loose tooth to their finger in order to catch the Tooth Fairy. They cannot help but want to learn the secret of that which entrances them, even if they destroy the object: the destruction *is* the pleasure.

We get a sense of this perverse pleasure, this ornery love for their object, with a phone that's been Pwned. One of the common jailbreak tools, Pwnage allows consumers to unlock their iPhones and access the file systems restricted by the iOS software. The tool's default setting is to replace the familiar Apple logo with a pineapple during the jailbreaking process. While there is an advanced option to remove this custom Pwnage logo, the pineapple logo replacement is a standard software setting, perhaps a bittersweet touch. Jailbreakers who use tools like Pwnage to "open up" their iPhones can push the limits of the technology they are given. Are you under a mobile-phone service contract? Do you want your laptop to use your iPhone's data connection? Jailbreakers discovered how to answer these questions before Apple offered official solutions. The paradox is, of course, that the candy and the iPhone themselves encourage and invite such "bad behavior" because they appear to work as if by magic and, indeed, are marketed that way. Wonka doesn't offer the children candy cigarettes or cigars because he seems to understand how childlike curiosity and consumption can go awry. Apple shouldn't be surprised by the destructive activity of jailbreakers: by designing products that work "as if by magic," they facilitate the desire to see inside or beyond the surface. Jailbreakers and jawbreakers reveal that the pleasure of cracking code or candy is intrinsic to the iPhone experience, even though the magic and mystery disappear in the process.

A World of Imagination

In contrast to the abundance of bad role models Roald Dahl gives us, we get one Charlie Bucket to show us the way to proper behavior. Charlie—"the hero" and the good boy, by any measure—is *impossibly* good, too good to be true. In Dahl's original story, there's really not much *to* Charlie, who gets very little dialogue beyond his expressions of wonderment and awe. He inherits the factory because he is Wonka's ideal fan and follower: imaginative, open-minded, good-hearted, but not one to ask too many questions or push boundaries of any kind.

Wonka reveals his ambivalent attitude toward childhood when he divulges his reasons for putting on this Golden Ticket lottery and factory tour in the first place: "Mind you, there are thousands of clever men who would give anything for the chance to come and take over." Wonka doesn't want a grown man to run his factory, though, because "a grownup won't listen to [him]; he won't learn. He will try to do things his own way and not mine. So I have to have a child. I want a good sensible loving child, one to whom I can tell all my most precious candy-making secrets" (151). Wonka wants it both ways: smart candy consumers who are full of imagination but who are enthralled with spectacles he creates. He encourages imagination but wants it kept with the confines of his own factory and his own rules: "No touching, no meddling, and no tasting! Is that agreed?" (87). One wonders if this wasn't the same dilemma facing Jobs and Apple executives as they contemplated the future of the iPhone and their company. Steve Jobs took medical leave on three occasions in the years preceding his retirement, prompting concerns about the future of the company. It is as if Jobs functioned as an irreplaceable father and sole authority, and responses to his absences at Apple—fluctuations in stock value, for example—echoed this sentiment.[35]

Jobs understood why Apple is called "crazy" when it alters and changes its products based on anticipated technological trends or revolutions, but he imagined that these choices do not affect the consumer. Perhaps this suggests that his notion of the consumer was narrow, decidedly passive, and even patriarchal.[36] The irony is, of course, that this ambivalence toward the consumer is at odds with the image Apple marketers have always maintained of their products. The now-famous "Mac vs. PC" ads depict the typical Apple fan as a free-thinking, independent, and imaginative hipster in contrast to the dronelike PC user, constantly at the mercy of the impersonal PC operating system. Ads for the Mac, the iPod, the iPhone, and now the iPad have repeatedly struck hard the notes of creativity, imagination, and play: MacBooks have "vroom with a view" (2007); "life is random" with iPods (2005): iPads are "magical," "revolutionary," and "delicious" (2010–2011): and the iPhone continues to "change everything" (2010). At the heart of the iPhone and, perhaps, of Apple, however, is an unnerving ambivalence toward these very values. Like candy and Wonka himself, the iPhone invites and provokes childlike, curious, playful, and "rude" behaviors even as it mitigates against them in extreme forms. In the design, licensing, and marketing of the phone, we see an elaborate attempt to negotiate these elements—on the one hand, taste, touch, smell, pleasure, indulgent consumption, rule-breaking curiosity and, on the other hand, sight, hearing, moderation, respect for rules, laws of ownership, trademark—in a way that maintains a deliciously untenable, unstable balance between our senses, between childlike and adult attitudes (or play and pragmatism), and between the object and its consumer. The iPhone encourages and desires sticky, intersensorial childlike, imaginative play . . . but maintains a harder, steadfast form to keep products in hand and users in check as not to get out of hand.

Notes

1. Although we discuss the iPhone, Apple (and Steve Jobs) refers to the iPad as "magical." It is interesting and important to note that the iPad was made available to the public after the iPhone even though it was the prototype with "magical" qualities that structured the iPhone design and interface aesthetic. See Peter Kafka, "Apple CEO Steve Jobs at D8: The Full, Uncut Interview," *All Things Digital*, 7 June 2010, http://d8.allthingsd.com/20100607/steve-jobs-at-d8-the-full-uncut-interview/ (20 June 2011).

2. Roald Dahl, *Charlie and the Chocolate Factory* (1964; New York: Penguin, 1998), 147; all further citations appear within the text.

3. Comparing Jobs with Wonka and the iPhone with candy seems to be emerging within other contexts as well. After we began writing this article we came across an animation from CollegeHumor.com that portrays Jobs in the role of Willy Wonka while the Wonka Factory is re-created as an Apple product factory. See Nick Bachman, "Charlie and the Apple Factory," CollegeHumor.com, 2 March 2011, http://www .collegehumor.com/video/6440954/charlie-and-the-apple-factory (20 June 2011).

4. Steve Jobs, "How to Live Before You Die," Stanford University Commencement Address, 12 June 2005, http://itunes.apple.com/us/itunes-u/steve-jobs-2005 -commencement/id384463719?i=85145537 (4 October 2011).

5. Recent work by McKenzie Wark and Michiel de Lange confirms that the increasingly thin line between work and play is a key component to the understanding of mobile media. See Michiel de Lange, *Moving Circles: Mobile Media and Playful Identities* (Rotterdam: Erasmus University Rotterdam, 2010); McKenzie Wark, *Gamer Theory* (Cambridge, Mass.: Harvard University Press, 2007).

6. Steven Connor, "Sweets," from BBC Radio 4, *Rough Magic*, 30 January 2000, transcript available at http://www.bbk.ac.uk/english/skc/magic/sweets.htm (20 June 2011).

7. Kathryn Bond Stockton, *The Queer Child, or Growing Sideways in the Twentieth Century* (Durham, N.C.: Duke University Press, 2009), 15.

8. Connor explains how "the shape and texture of a sweet, its characteristics as an object, are vital supplements to its taste." See Connor, "Sweets." Further, the more ethereal qualities of candy—the smell of chocolate and the sound of Pop Rocks, for example—play up what Connor calls elsewhere the "intersensoriality" of perceptual experience: Steven Connor, "Intersensoriality," lecture at The Senses conference, 6 February 2004, http://www.bbk.ac.uk/english/skc/intersensoriality/ (June 20, 2011).

9. Connor, "Sweets."

10. Jonathan Ive, Apple's senior vice president for industrial design, is frequently cited as the driving force behind Apple's visual aesthetic, which began when he redesigned Apple's iMac lines to be more curvaceous and colorful and continues to the present. For more discussion about the Apple design and aesthetic, see Jason D. O'Grady, *Apple Inc.* (London: Greenwood Press, 2009).

11. O'Grady, *Apple Inc.*, 13, 99; "Delicious" iPad advertisement (Apple, Inc., 2009).

12. Fred Vogelstein, "The Untold Story: How the iPhone Blew Up the Wireless Industry," *Wired*, 1 September 2008.

13. Tony Avelar, "The Apple of Your Ear," *Time*, 12 January 2007, http://www.time.com/time/magazine/article/0,9171,1576854-5,00.html (4 October 2011).

14. Ibid.

15. N. Katherine Hayles defines the skeuomorph as a design feature that has no function beyond its reference to a technological feature from a previous time. The example she offers is the artificial stitching on the dashboard of a car, which does not function beyond citing an historical moment when materials were stitched to fit car dashboards. See N. Katherine Hayles, *How We Became Posthuman: Virtual Bodies in Cybernetics, Literature, and Informatics* (Chicago: University of Chicago Press, 1999), 17.

16. Apple's advertisement was originally published in *Details* magazine (August 2007); also discussed on *MacDailyNews*, "Apple Debuts New iPhone 'God Phone' Print Ad (with image)," 12 July 2007, http://macdailynews.com/2007/07/12/apple_debuts_new_iphone_print_ad_with_image/ (20 June 2011).

17. See "Apple—iPhone 4—Learn About the High-Resolution Retina Display," Apple, Inc., 2010, http://www.apple.com/iphone/features/retina-display.html (20 June 2011). For examples of the reviews, see Daniel Eran Dilger, "Apple's iPhone 4 Retina Display Places First in Lab Tests," *Apple Insider*, 1 July 2010, http://www.appleinsider.com/articles/10/07/01/lab_tests_compare_apples_iphone_4_retina_display_to_rival_phones.html (20 June 2011).

18. See http://www.youtube.com/watch?v=kL4ZBEOexsk (20 June 2011).

19. The iPhone rejects the "what you see is what you get" interface model, opting instead for perpetual change and surprise.

20. Connor, "Sweets."

21. Tim Richardson, *Sweets: A History of Temptation* (London: Bantam, 2003), 24.

22. Consider one fan-based parody, where unseen but anticipated products are discussed as if they will magically appear at any moment. See "Mac vs. PC: iPad," 2010, http://www.youtube.com/watch?v=kTsQAFqRbo8 (20 June 2011)

23. Jesus Diaz, "How Apple Lost the Next iPhone," *Gizmodo*, 19 April 2010, http:// gizmodo.com/5520438/how-apple-lost-the-next-iphone (20 June 2011).

24. References to these updates are frequently posted on technology blogs under titles like "Apple Quietly Updates . . ." Apple's concerns about security are also illustrated by its decision to hire a "Global Director of Security," who previously specialized in naval warfare information. See Arik Hesseldahl, "Exclusive: Apple Taps Former Navy Information Warrior for Global Director of Security," *All Things Digital*, 22 January 2011, http://newenterprise.allthingsd.com/20110122/apple-taps-former -navy-information-warrior-as-global-director-of-security/ (20 June 2011).

25. The connection between mobile devices and addiction is not new. Consider the long-standing "Crackberry" nickname for Blackberry devices. See, for example, Gary Mazo, Martin Trautschold, and Kevin Michaluk, *Crackberry: True Tales of Blackberry Use and Abuse* (New York: APress, 2010).

26. Connor, "Sweets."

27. See, for example, the smudged signs for different applications used on the iPad: Brian Barrett, "Decoding your iPad's Smudges," *Gizmodo*, 11 February 2011, http:// gizmodo.com/5758143/what-your-ipads-smudges-say-about-how-you-use-it (20 June 2011).

28. See http://www.powerthreads.com/clothaddiction/ (20 June 2011).

29. The tap moves below or "under" the surface, rather than hyperlinking "over" to another page.

30. Ian Bogost, "I like to think of iOS4's app folders not as organizing tools, but as tiny prisons for truculent apps," ibogost, Twitter for iPhone, 23 June 2010, 1:05 p.m., http://www.twitter.com.

31. Connor, "Sweets."

32. Leander Kahney, "Apple's Official Response to DMCA Jailbreak Exemption: It Voids Your Warranty," *Cult of Mac*, 26 July 2010, http://www.cultofmac.com/apples -official-response-to-dmca-jailbreak-exemption-it-voids-your-warranty/52463 (20 June 2011).

33. Kyle VanHemert, "Apple's Making It Impossible to Open Up Your iPhone by Secretly Swapping Its Screws," *Gizmodo*, 20 January 2011, http://gizmodo.com/5738887/ apples-new-screws-make-it-impossible-to-open-up-your-iphone (20 June 2011).

34. Stockton, *Queer Child*, 238.

35. For references to discussions about Jobs's medical leaves and retirement, see Yukari Iwatani Kane, "Apple's Jobs Takes Medical Leave," *Wall Street Journal*, 15 January 2009, http://online.wsj.com/article/SB123196896969848882901.html (20 June 2011); and Yukari Iwantani Kane and Joann S. Lublin, "Apple Chief to Take Leave," *Wall*

Street Journal, 18 January 2011, http://online.wsj.com/article/SB1000142405274870339 6604576087690312543086.html (20 June 2011). It is not surprising that, in discussions about Tim Cook's promotion to CEO at Apple, commentators expressed hope that Cook could bring to the position the enthusiastic and inspirational qualities for which Jobs was known. Indeed, Engadget's live blog during the release of the iPhone 4S describes Cook as looking "cool, comfortable. Genuinely happy and excited," though they noted his style to be "a bit more subtle than Steve's, a bit more understated." See Tim Stevens, "Apple's 'Let's Talk iPhone' Keynote Liveblog!" *Engadget*, 4 October 2011, http://www.engadget.com/2011/10/04/apples-lets-talk-iphone-keynote-liveblog/ (4 October 2011).

36. Kafka, "Apple CEO."

II
Politics of Redistribution

CHAPTER 6

Personal Media in the Digital Economy

GÖRAN BOLIN

THE MOBILE PHONE has become the media technology that by far the most people in the world have access to. At the time of this writing, the International Telecommunications Union reports that around 90 percent of the world's population has access to mobile networks, and that out of the 5.3 billion mobile subscriptions around the world, 940 million are for 3G services. These figures should be compared with statistics for Internet users in the same report, where it is estimated that there will be 2 billion Internet users by the end of 2010 but that penetration is substantially higher in Europe, the Americas, and the CIS countries.[1]

One explanation for this enormous spread of the mobile medium is that it is a truly personal medium that you bring with you as you go. If landline phones, radio and television, and books and newspapers are collective media, shared among members of a household, the mobile phone is tightly connected to an individual. This means that households (except single-person households) that previously shared one landline subscription today have acquired individual subscriptions for all family members. No wonder, then, that since 2003 there are far more subscriptions for mobile phones than there are for landline telephones in the world.[2]

The mobile phone or smartphone—if these are indeed the correct labels for a multifunctional microcomputer—is a technology undergoing rapid transformation. In the 1970s, engineers dreamed about developing "personal dynamic media" that would overcome some of the limitations of contemporary mass media, making them more dynamic and versatile. The efforts to develop these media, however, concentrated on the personal computer, making possible alterations of typefaces, drawing, and other human-machine interaction.[3] Today, the mobile has become this personal dynamic medium, adding mobility as its most dynamic feature. With 3G technology, and moving fast into the fourth generation of mobile devices, the mobile has fewer and fewer features that make it different from a laptop. This 3G technology has also contributed to the popularity of the smartphone, and notably the iPhone.

The success of the iPhone among mobile phone users has almost made the brand synonymous with smartphones, just as other successful brand names in history have become umbrella terms also for their competitors on the market, such as Jeep and Xerox. Many have also attributed the success of the iPhone to its design and to smart PR work, including having hired enthusiasts first in line at its launch to hype the iPhone as a major innovation. The combination of high investment in design and PR is, of course, not new, but it might be argued that Apple has been especially successful in integrating these two market strategies. The iPhone is but one in a row of highly visible products ranging from the iPod to the most recent iPad. And as the example above indicates, the success stories around Apple's products are to a certain extent part of the PR campaigns, thus making these into self-fulfilling endeavors.

Several authors have pointed to the fact that the iPhone "pushes the mobile much more towards the computers and the Internet."[4] Although the iPhone was not the first smartphone—Nokia launched its 9000 Communicator in 1996—the popularity of the iPhone has revived and created the market for the technology. Today, with the iPhone being the market driver ("the phone that has changed phones forever," as the hype goes),[5] many of its competitors have sought to mimic its success, developing their own similar models with touch-screen technology, most notably Sony Ericson, Nokia, Siemens, and HTC. Sales of smartphones have also increased dramatically. In the first three months of 2010, sales of smartphones in Sweden increased by 244 percent, and around 50 percent of all phone units sold are smartphones.[6]

Most of the studies on smartphones such as the iPhone have focused on the new adaptations and the new functions that they bring to their users. A less discussed consequence of this approximation of the computer is that the mobile phones have truly entered into the digital economy. If the revenue streams from mobile telephony previously have been based on made calls and sent text messages, with smartphones a range of new possibilities arise because it radically alters the medium as technology—from a tool for primarily interpersonal communication to a multimedium that includes all the possibilities of the computer: e-mailing, surfing the Web, using search engines and apps, watching streamed video, listening to music, engaging in e-commerce, checking the weather, booking tickets, and so on. With widespread access to mobile and 3G technology, and with the increased possible uses of the new smartphones, many have set their hopes on the mobile for the further commodification of the digital landscape. But as Rowan Wilken and John Sinclair have found, mobile advertising has been slow in its start, and is still "waiting for the kiss of life."[7]

That mobile advertising has not taken off does not mean, however, that no one hopes for new business models to arise from the agenda of the telecommunications business. The implications of what a wireless digital economy will mean are yet to be analyzed. This article aims to contribute to such an analysis by exploring how industry perceptions of mobile phone users are shifting: from users of an interpersonal medium to a mass audience. I will explore this new audience in terms of how an "audience commodity" was constructed in previous mass media settings, centering on radio, television, and the press. I will examine the relationship between interpersonal and mass media, such as how technological developments connected to digitization have altered the market for media commodities and contributed to the development of new business models. I will also discuss the profound consequences of this shift for our ontological understanding of what it means to use a mobile phone.

Mass Media—Personal Media

In the 1950s the nature and character of the mass media, the mass communication process, and, hence, the mass audience began to be discussed and analyzed. Charles Wright made a lasting impact on the field of media and communication studies with his *Mass Communication*, published 1959. Wright defined three featured characteristics of mass communication: the audience should be "large, heterogeneous, and anonymous"; the communication experience should be "public, rapid, and transient"; and the communicator should "be, or operate within, a complex organization that may involve great expense."[8] Although Wright never made an exhaustive list of the media technologies he had in mind, it is quite obvious that his definition excluded some that others might argue are mass media. Books, hardly fulfill the criterion of being a transient medium. Music records do not have this quality either, so Wright's definition privileged electronic media, radio and television, as well as the press.

Thus, the preoccupation with the press, radio, and television has come to define the field of media and communications research, although the terminology has changed. In John Thompson's highly influential *The Media and Modernity*, he distinguishes among face-to-face, mediated, and mediated quasi interaction, describing the last in terms similar to those Wright used thirty-five years earlier, for example, "monological" and "oriented towards an indefinite range of potential recipients."[9] With increasing digitization, many have called for the abandoning of the concept of "mass" in favor of concepts such as "personal" media. These media are described by Marika Lüders as "the tools for interpersonal communication and personalized expression, for example, mobile phones, email, Instant Messenger, homepages, private weblogs (blogs), online profiles and photo-sharing sites." On these sites, "individuals create personal media content in non-institutionalized settings." In addition, "the most distinguishable feature of personal media, barring a few exceptions, is the required type of activity of all parts involved as actors in more or less symmetrical communication processes."[10]

Seemingly, then, the rise of mobile media, such as the mobile phone, with its distinctly individual character—you literally carry it with you like an extension of your own body—fulfilled Marshall McLuhan's idea of media as extensions of man.[11] It is hard to put the prefix "mass" in front of such media, and so technology has given the kiss of death to mass media, mass communication, and the mass audience. Few media scholars would use these concepts any longer, and the ideas that followed in their footsteps of aggregated viewer, listener, or reader behavior have died with them. However, the concept of a mass audience began to be criticized in the 1950s with Raymond Williams's famous dictum that "there are in fact no masses, there are only ways of seeing people as masses."[12] With the rise of qualitative research into media users, this quotation became a guiding light, and with the further development of media use in reception theory and media ethnography, there seemed to be no turning back to regard media users as masses in the way they were regarded by early mass communication research and cultural critique. Raymond Williams probably did not realize at the time the enormous impact this single sentence from the last chapter of *Culture and Society* would have on research of media users.

The abandonment of the concept of mass media in favor of personal media seems logical. However, there is a fair amount of ideological baggage attached to the concepts of personal media, and an overemphasis on the possibilities of the individual media user—just as much as the mass concept of earlier debates was rife with ideology. If we consider various characterizations of personal media, it is, of course, true that when we speak with our friends on a mobile phone or chat on Facebook or Twitter, the communication we engage in is symmetric. However, it can hardly be considered as taking place in a noninstitutionalized setting. On the contrary, this setting is heavily institutionalized, not to say commercialized, as our behavior on the platform and the data we provide make us the target of tailored commercial messages. And the ways in which we are addressed by those messages are far from symmetric. Communicative space thus equals commodified space. I shall return to this discussion in a while, but I wish to ground it with a more general account of digitization and its effect on the media commodity.

Digitization and the Media Commodity

The digitization of media is actually not one but two processes. On the one hand, we have seen the rise of new digital media based on the computer. The Internet and the World Wide Web, if we are to consider them media in their own right, and, naturally, mobile phones are such media—at least if we think about the mobile after it was culturally domesticated in an everyday media environment. On the other hand, older media have also turned from analogue to digital: movies are to a lesser and lesser extent made on celluloid film, and if one is, postproduction is often digital, as are distribution and screening. Newspapers are not made from manuscripts over print types to paper sheets but directly on the computer, with digital editing and printing. Most book publishing is produced the same way. Music recordings are not made on tape anymore but with the help of digital software, which opens new possibilities of manipulation. And with services such as the Swedish platforms Spotify (for music) and Voddler (for filmed entertainment), distribution and consumption are entirely digitized, making it necessary for the consumer to invest heavily in means of consumption in order to decode the digits into accessible form. I have discussed these processes at length elsewhere,[13] but it is sufficient in this context to point to the fact that the more digital equipment we surround ourselves with, the deeper the commercial penetration of our life worlds (which naturally does not contradict the fact that these same technologies are appreciated and valued by their users for the increased possibilities of communication and creativity that they bring).

The mobile phone was, however, not a digital medium from the start, and neither were its first forms personal. It developed out of radio technology and in the early 1900s was used for marine communication on passenger ships and freighters rather than for private purposes, with the exception of radio amateurs who used it to connect with like-minded people.[14] In the early 1980s, the Nordic Mobile Telephone system in the Scandinavian countries developed the first standards that made it possible to communicate over a network that crossed national borders. After this, the dissemination of mobile telephony on a large scale took off. And when the digitally based GSM developed soon after as a European standard, the dissemination of phones grew even wider. Digitization is, hence, at the heart of the business models that today are in their infancy, models that are likely to dominate the mobile environment in the near future.

There are three principal kinds of media business models, centered on three distinct commodities: the text, the audience, and the service. The most foundational business model is based on commodified text, resulting from the possibilities of mass production of the written word after the invention of the printing press. The basic principle is that the producer of the text, whether it is in the form of a book, a magazine, or a newspaper, sells this commodity and gets money in return. Thus, a market for texts arose, and, with it, organizational principles developed. The second business model arose when producers of commodities other than texts wanted to send out information about their products through advertising. The daily newspaper was an appropriate forum for such information, and gradually newspapers incorporated advertising on their pages. From around the mid-1850s, advertising became a natural ingredient in most newspapers, which meant that newspapers mixed the text-based with the audience-based model: some of its revenues came from sold copies, and some from selling the buyers of copies to advertisers. Finally, a third business model developed not out of the mass media but rather from the postal system. This model is not based on a commodity; it does not sell content nor seek to attract an audience for advertisers. It is a service offered to potential communicators. Through the postal system, interpersonal communication can occur through the provision of a communications structure. The service sold is the opportunity to use this communications system. This service model is also the basis for the telephone system. Neither of these systems produces texts; rather, they are entirely dependent on user-generated content—in fact, they are both designed to encourage interpersonal communication at a distance.

The service model, however, is not used only for interpersonal communication. We all know that there are ways of using the postal system for the distribution of mass-marketing messages as well as personally addressed advertising. We get junk mail in our mailboxes, and we get personally targeted mails trying to convince us to buy this or that commodity, to take advantage of services, or to engage in ideal associations or in community service. Basically, this is also what we receive in our electronic mailboxes. While the text-based and the audience-based models were centered on mass mediated texts, either as commodities in themselves or as means to reach an audience, the service-based model can be considered an early form of personal media (where communication between senders and recipients were symmetric but hardly took place in noninstitutionalized settings).

Thus, it is not difficult to see the analogies among the postal system, the telephone system, and digital mobile media when it comes to the way in which customers are addressed. There are, however, some notable differences. When you are addressed as a target of commercial messages through the postal or the (landline) telephone system, you are addressed as a social subject structured by income, gender, age, geographical belonging, education, and so on. When you are addressed as a digital customer it is not your social self that is addressed but your digital IP address. The difference is at times not significant—but at times it is.

Impersonal Media

Historically, revenues from the mobile phone business were based on the "traffic commodity," as Elizabeth van Couvering, has put it.[15] Initially, this meant voice calls and text communication. It was in the interest of mobile-phone operators to increase voice calls and text messages as much as possible. This was accomplished in several ways: through favorable pricing structures, cheaper calls and text messages within the same service provider, and so on. For horizontally integrated companies, the different parts of the company could be used. Modern Times Group in Sweden, for example, encouraged their hosts at the radio channel Rix FM to come up with ideas for radio shows built around audience call-ins. The company owned not only Rix FM but also the major mobile-phone-service provider Tele 2.[16]

The traffic commodity, however, has extended beyond talking and texting to include the forms of communication made possible by smartphones,

for example, Internet search, e-mail, GPS services, communication on social networking sites, and, increasingly, new geosocial applications such as
Foursquare or Gowalla. In a study by the Pew Internet Research Center on
mobile and social networking, the use of geosocial communication by U.S.
citizens has spread to 4 percent of the online population.[17] With this increase
in communicative opportunities, traffic also increases dramatically. In Sweden, the number of mobile phone users that read news, watch television or
video clips, send and receive e-mails, use GPS, and engage in social networking did not increase dramatically between 2009 and 2010: from 19 percent of
all mobile users to 22 percent. However, users of these services have increased
their consumption of online mobile news by 50 percent, use of e-mail from
20 to 51 percent, and video viewing from 7 to 32 percent.[18] The amount of
traffic has expanded dramatically, no doubt because of the extended possibilities that come with new and improved applications for iPhone and other
smartphones. An obvious example of this is the use of YouTube, particularly
since this platform has a default app on the iPhone. Traditional mass media,
such as the main Swedish broadsheet *Dagens Nyheter* and the main television
channels—public service broadcaster SVT as well as commercial TV4—also
developed user-friendly apps for the iPhone soon after its introduction.

Mobile media such as the smartphone also have a specific traffic-enhancing
feature in international roaming. All smartphone users who have made the mistake of not disconnecting the data-roaming function when going abroad have
learned the hard way about the high costs of transnational communication.
International roaming traffic is expensive, and the mobile-communication
service providers are the ones to benefit from this. Nokia's slogan, "Connecting People," might ring true in a national setting, but when it comes to
transnational communication there are still obstacles to on-the-move global
connection. And as this traffic commodity is based on transferred megabytes,
spam takes on a new function, becoming beneficial to mobile service providers as it contributes to increased traffic. Cloud computing is also fitting in
well with the digital economy as it encourages increased online presence and
increased Internet traffic.

Pure traffic is thus the basic commodity for mobile digital media. The
more bytes that flow through cables and over airwaves, the larger the commodity or, rather, the more the commodity multiplies. However large or
multiplied this data commodity is, it is not the only commodity. Information
on traffic and on user behavior can also be refined and sold in the same way as
information on television audiences and audience behavior can be packaged
for circulation on a market. This could be called the traffic commodity 2.0.

When the iPhone and other smartphones contributed to the increase of traffic through expanding apps, it meant not only that the volume of transferred terabytes increased but also that these enormous amounts of data can be processed and differentiated in a way that was not meaningful when talk and texting was made on one machine and Google searches, Facebook updates, and Twitter messages were conducted on another machine, with another IP address. With all these functions merged into one machine, with one IP number, it has become possible to monetize digital behavior through contextual and predictive-behavioral targeting.

Several agencies specialize in contextual and behavioral targeting, such as nugg.ad in Germany, Phorm in the United Kingdom, and Adaptlogic in Sweden, whose slogan is, "We deliver more valuable clicks." In the words of Joseph Turow, contextual targeting occurs when the "search engine firms make agreements with websites that allow their software to read the pages of the sites and places ads at the side of their Web pages when they find words their advertising clients have chosen."[19] This is, for example, what happens when you buy a book from Amazon and then get an offer about buying another title, all based on the fact that people who have bought the same book have purchased certain other titles.

A variant of contextual targeting is behavioral targeting, which adds a historic dimension to search-engine marketing. This technique gathers information about users' movements on the Web, for example, when someone uses a search engine to try to figure out where to go on holidays, and uses previous search patterns to inform the user about hotels, travel agencies, and so on. In order to target behavior, the agencies engaged in this activity connect internet service providers (e.g., Telia, Telenor, BT) with search engines (e.g., Google, Yahoo), advertisers, and publishers to the presumable benefit for all. The British agency Phorm has developed a service they call Open Internet Exchange, which they claim will revolutionize the online advertising industry. Its "innovative platform and key partnerships—with advertisers, agencies, publishers and ad networks and ISPs—create value and opportunity throughout the digital advertising ecosystem. The OIX is powered by Phorm's proprietary ad serving technology, which uses anonymised ISP data to serve the right ad to the right user at the right time—the right number of times."[20]

Contextual and behavioral targeting are not specifically bound to smartphones. Web-navigation habits can be taken advantage of by advertisers via nonmobile platforms such as stationary computers. A third possibility, which is specifically tied to the smartphone and its GPS technology and cannot be used with nonmobile platforms, is location-based marketing. In the introduction to his book *iSpy: Surveillance and Power in the Interactive Era*, Mark Andrejevic describes an idea presented by Google to make the city of San Francisco into a free-to-use wireless area.[21] Location-based marketing techniques provide the incentive, that is, using the GPS function of mobile phones to target specific commercial information to mobile users—the right user not only at the right time and the right number of times but also in the right place. Presumably, this would bring relevant information to consumers from the shops that he or she passes by.

When Andrejevic's book came out in 2007, location-based technology was in its infancy, and it was just a dream for Google, ISPs, and publishers or advertisers to be able to use targeted, place-based advertising to customers. After the wide dissemination of iPhones and other smartphones, a few years later this is increasingly becoming the area in which those with interests in the business of search and digital mobile media are engaged. Indeed, Eric Schmidt, the CEO of Google, was quoted in August 2010 as saying: "If I look at enough of your messaging and your location, and use artificial intelligence, we can predict where you are going to go."[22] So what was something of a fantasy a couple of years ago is quite real today. For example, shopping malls offer a service to consumers whereby they receive notices and advertisements made possible by the cooperation of mobile service providers and local businesses. Shoppers visiting the shopping mall Skrapan in the inner city of Stockholm are offered membership in the Skrapan customer club, with the promise to receive "exclusive offerings, benefits and invitations via SMS directly into your mobile," on the condition that you agree to the club being allowed to "localize my mobile's position in order to send out special offers and invitations on the right time, at the right place."

For the interested parties in this emerging market for "database marketing," as Turow terms it, endless opportunities arise. Whether this type of marketing will become "prescriptive" in changing social behavior, as Alice Warwick speculates on her research blog (tiara.org), is still an open question, although the potential is not hard to imagine. However, there are also reasons for the advertising industry to be nervous. First, over the years a number of ad-blocking consumer technologies have appeared, starting with the television remote control in the 1970s, the time-shifting VCR a few years later, the TiVo (in the United States), and other technologies that allowed consumers to avoid commercials. There are also indications that young people develop "ad-skipping" strategies while surfing the Web.[23] This has provoked descriptions of consumers as powerful, nearly almighty. Advertisers now speak about audiences "hav[ing] the same power as elite media organizations."[24] Paradoxically, this idea is also found among some media researchers who emphasize the power of media users and the personal media. However, with contextual, behavioral, and location-based targeting, the mobile-communications industry must negotiate the thin boundary between the benefits of total intelligence and the privacy concerns of mobile users. And they struggle to convince mobile users how beneficial these techniques are—how they will reduce spam and other irrelevant advertising—they talk equally about the "online ad revolution" and the "privacy revolution" supposedly brought on by their services. It is easy to see that it is in the interest of the mobile-communications industries to foster the discourse of consumer power.

Conclusion: From the Social to the Digital Commodity

It might be argued that many views of the mobile-communications industry are still partially informed by the traditional mass-media discourse, long since abandoned by media researchers. However, digital media concern a new kind of mass, a personalized aggregate (but still an aggregate) refined from vast amounts of information about user behavior and geographical position. In the words of the marketing agency Alterian, the business has moved "from mass marketing to mass personalization," which nicely captures this development of mass thinking.[25] The iPhone might be considered personal media, but as a generator of the traffic commodity or as part of cloud capitalism, it matters less who a user is in terms of sociological variables such as age, gender, education, or marital status, and more *where* the digital presence is and whether it is mobile enough to be accessible to location-based advertising and traffic. User traffic and behavior are the new commodity: not the social mobile user but rather the user's activities on the Web. What counts is presence and movement in digital space rather than status in social space.

Turow's concept of "mass customization" better captures this process than the concept of mass personalization because even if consumers think that they are addressed as individual subjects, they are not. It is the digital self, constructed from the digital traces of the individual's communications equipment, that is targeted by advertisers and their associates. This has less to do with the individual qualities of the subject than with idealized—and aggregated—user profiles. So while smartphones are becoming more and more popular, and more liberating for mobile users, the uses of the smartphone are also becoming more and more commodified and of greater interest to market(ing) interests. It might not feel that way if you are a user, but it certainly has a bearing on the political economy of mobile communication.

As I have pointed out in this essay, the meaning of being a mobile phone user has shifted dramatically with the introduction of smartphones in general and the iPhone in particular. As the increasing number of applications for the iPhone has made it possible to surf the Web, engage social-networking sites, and take advantage geosocial information, all of which are undeniably to the advantage of smartphone owners, this has simultaneously opened up a new market for mobile-service providers, ISPs, and the whole telecommunications sector. Whether we value this positively, as a win-win situation, or find it to be only a new form of exploitation will depend on our ontological position more generally, but it is a technological, social, and economic fact that needs to be acknowledged—and researched further in the near future.

NOTES

1. International Telecommunications Union, "The World in 2010" (2010), http://www.itu.int/ITU-D/ict/material/FactsFigures2010.pdf (15 February 2011).

2. Rich Ling, *The Mobile Connection: The Cell Phone's Impact on Society* (San Francisco: Morgan Kaufman, 2004), 13.

3. Alan Kay and Adele Goldberg, "Personal Dynamic Media," *Computer*, no. 10 (1977): 31–41.

4. Gerard Goggin, "Adapting the Mobile Phone: The iPhone and Its Consumption," *Continuum*, no. 23 (2009): 231–44.

5. Lev Grossman, "Invention of the Year: The iPhone" *Time*, 1 November 2007.

6. Mattias Inghe, "Jättetest och guide—32 smarta mobiler," *PC för alla*, 16 October 2010.

7. Rowan Wilken and John Sinclair, "'Waiting for the Kiss of Life': Mobile Media and Advertising," *Convergence* 15 (2010): 1–19.

8. Charles Wright, *Mass Communication: A Sociological Perspective* (New York: Random House, 1959), 13.

9. John B. Thompson, *The Media and Modernity* (Cambridge: Polity, 1995), 85.

10. Marika Lüders, "Conceptualizing Personal Media" *New Media and Society* 10 (2008): 683–702.

11. Marshall McLuhan, *Understanding Media: The Extensions of Man* (New York: McGraw-Hill, 1964).

12. Raymond Williams, *Culture and Society, 1780–1950* (Harmondsworth: Penguin, 1958), 300.

13. See, for example, the discussion in Göran Bolin, "Notes from Inside the Factory: The Production and Consumption of Signs and Sign Value in Media Industries,"

Social Semiotics 15 (2005): 289–306; and Bolin, "Symbolic Production and Value in Media Industries," *Journal of Cultural Economy* 2, no. 3 (2009): 345–61; and, especially, Bolin, *Value and the Media: Cultural Production and Consumption in Digital Markets* (Farnham: Ashgate, 2011), esp. chap. 4.

14. Ling, *The Mobile Connection*, 6.

15. Elizabeth van Couvering, "The History of the Internet Search Engine: Navigational Media and the Traffic Commodity," in *Web Search: Multidisciplinary Perspectives*, ed. Amanda Spink and Michael Zimmer (Berlin: Springer, 2007), 177–208.

16. For a vivid description, see Fredrik Stiernstedt, "Maximising the Power of Entertainment: The Audience Commodity in Contemporary Radio," *The Radio Journal* 6 (2008): 113–27.

17. Kathryn Zickuhr and Aaron Smith, "Four Percent of Online Americans Use Location-Based Services," Pew Internet and American Life Project, http://www .pewinternet.org/Reports/2010/Location-based-services.aspx (15 February 2011).

18. Olle Findahl, "Svenskarna och Internet 2010," http://www.iis.se/ (15 February 2011).

19. Joseph Turow, *Niche Envy: Marketing Discrimination in the Digital Age* (Cambridge, Mass.: MIT Press, 2006), 90.

20. For further information, see http://www.phorm.com/.

21. Mark Andrejevic, *iSpy: Surveillance and Power in the Interactive Era* (Lawrence: University of Kansas Press, 2007), 1.

22. "No Anonymity on Future Web Says Google CEO," Thinq.co.uk, 5 August 2010, http://www.thinq.co.uk/2010/8/5/no-anonymity-future-web-says-google-ceo/ (15 February 2011).

23. A Swedish study using eye-tracking methodology found that fifteen-year-olds surfing freely on the Web only perceived 10 percent of banners and other commercial messages. See Louise Ekström and Helena Sandberg, "Reklam funkar inte på mig," *Unga, marknadsföring och Internet* (Copenhagen: Nordiska Ministerrådet, 2010).

24. The statement was made by the communications consultant Ian Leslie at the Changing Advertising Summit 2008 in London (13 October 2008), where the advertising industry met with ISPs, search engines, web optimizers, and other stakeholders.

25. For a discussion, see http://webcontent.alterian.com/.

CHAPTER 7

Big Hollywood, Small Screens

ALISA PERREN AND KAREN PETRUSKA

I N NOVEMBER 2010, the president of distribution for Walt Disney Studios, Bob Chapek, spoke to the press about his company's failed efforts to come to terms with the other major Hollywood studios regarding an ambitious digital-rights-management proposal. The studios had been unable to agree upon a common technology and infrastructure through which consumers could, at their leisure, access content "in the cloud." Of this unsuccessful endeavor, he observed, "When you go into the industry groups, it's like a bill in Congress. . . . Everyone tries to attach something to it and it becomes something it's not intended to be."[1] After negotiations led nowhere, Disney chose to forge ahead with its own "Disney All-Studio Access" initiative instead of partnering with many of the other major Hollywood studios and device manufacturers in their "UltraViolet" digital-content-management initiative. These ventures, along with Time Warner's TV Everywhere, ultimately served a similar objective: namely, to develop software that enabled consumers to view media that they purchased or rented across a host of devices, including smartphones, tablets, personal computers, and television sets. Though a relatively simple goal, executives at each company struggled to develop corporate policies and technological standards that determined when and where consumers accessed their content. Despite the efforts of the "industry groups" noted by Chapek, the major Hollywood studios could not form a consensus about how digital content might be distributed and retrieved. It seemed that the only thing that united these different parties was that they did not want to cede too much control to Apple.

Chapek's observation was made in reference to a specific industry initiative. Yet his statement might also be read far more expansively, in effect summing up the wide-ranging struggles between Hollywood and Silicon Valley over digital-distribution practices. Among such diverse stakeholders as the major media conglomerates, consumer-electronics companies, and online retailers, everything from business models to technical specifications was the subject of ongoing negotiation and debate. In general, Silicon Valley businesses, including Apple, sought to provide the widest range of films and television programming from such companies as CBS, Comcast/NBCUniversal, Disney-ABC, News Corp/Fox, Time Warner, and Viacom/Paramount in order to lure and retain consumers as well as sell devices. Nonetheless, Hollywood's major media conglomerates frequently pushed back, determined not to follow the same fate as the music industry in the early 2000s, which they believed had let Apple have too much control in dictating the ways that digital music was made available to consumers via its iTunes software.[2]

Apple's Media Ecosystem

The legacy of the music industry's decline persisted as a prominent narrative for the film and television industries. A widely held belief among executives in these industries was that Apple's iTunes upended the business model for music, effectively destroying the CD market.[3] The oft-repeated tale held that the music labels allowed Apple too much authority over everything from marketing to pricing. This narrative appeared regularly in industry trade publications and haunted Hollywood executives who depended upon tight control over the windows through which consumers accessed their content. As but one example, when asked why the studios rejected Apple's proposed $.99 television-episode rental plan, *Hollywood Reporter* quoted an unnamed executive who confirmed precedent influencing policy: "If we head down this path, we're starting down the same slippery slope where the music business went."[4] Anxious that working too closely with Apple would adversely affect their business models, many studios approached Apple's overtures with extreme caution.

Beginning with the video iPod in 2005, and continuing with the iPhone and iPod Touch in 2007 and, soon after, the iPad in 2010, Apple engaged in a particularly contentious tug-of-war with most of the major studios over how and when film and television content traveled to assorted devices. Apple was not the only technology company that attempted to offer media content to consumers on various screens from 2005 to 2010. In fact, a number of other industry monoliths (Google, Amazon) along with several small-scale start-ups (Boxee, Roku) competed to license Hollywood entertainment for display on a variety of devices. However, because of a range of factors, including the precedent it had set with the music industry, its dominant market power, and its powerful brand identity, Apple's overtures were met with especially strong apprehension by Hollywood. Not only did each conglomerate seek to extract wildly different terms from Apple, but different *divisions* of these conglomerates often interacted with CEO Steve Jobs's company in vastly different ways.

As a means of underscoring the complicated status of the contemporary rights landscape, this article provides case studies of how prominent divisions within two particular conglomerates, Time Warner and Disney, responded to Apple's ambitious efforts to build a consumer electronics "ecosystem."[5] The article focuses on Apple devices broadly, rather than strictly the iPhone, because from the perspective of Apple, the iPhone figured as but one component in its expanding media ecosystem. At the center of this ecosystem was iTunes. In most instances, for the Hollywood conglomerates, a decision to make content available for sale or rental through iTunes demanded they make a larger commitment to the wider Apple economy. Yet the closer one examines the interactions between Apple and the major media conglomerates, the more complex, contradictory, and at times flat-out irrational the contemporary landscape for licensing Hollywood content appears. Though no single factor explains the deviations in behavior from company to company, division to division, the focus here upon U.S.-based prime-time fictional television content attempts to narrow the focus enough to identify key commonalities and divergences in Time Warner's and Disney's interactions with the Apple ecosystem.

Approaching the topic of digital distribution from a case-study perspective differentiates this article from most that have come before.[6] Of the limited number of scholarly studies of Hollywood's digital-distribution strategies thus far, most have tended to focus predominantly on the *continuities* in business strategies and corporate practices across conglomerates.[7] Though there is much value to be had in looking for these types of similarities, such approaches can have the unintended side effect of downplaying the widespread sense of chaos and confusion in the media industries from the mid-2000s to the early 2010s.[8] By looking at the ways these key divisions of two Hollywood conglomerates dealt with Apple, it is easier to understand the often tense dynamic between those that owned the content and those, such as Apple and its competitors, that sought to disseminate it to new platforms and devices.

Apple may have envisioned an orderly and coherent world where a seemingly infinite amount of Hollywood entertainment could be purchased "on demand" through its iTunes store and consumable on any iDevice.[9] However, the major media conglomerates—including the one with which it had the closest ties, Disney—frequently had different visions for how and when consumers would access their content. During the early 2000s, content producers generally opted for a conservative approach, limiting content availability and avoiding experimentation with Web-based distribution. However, as broadband diffusion increased and piracy through peer-to-peer networks became viable for a growing number of people, the incentive to act grew. The collapse of the DVD market and the weakening of the syndication market by the mid-2000s further encouraged companies to pursue new revenue streams.[10] During this experimental phase, the studios' commitments with Apple and others were short-term; contracts remained limited in scope.

As Amanda Lotz notes, 2005 marked a turning point for the television industry in terms of its digital distribution strategies. The year began with the launch of YouTube and concluded with the introduction of the video iPod.[11] During the course of the year, television networks shifted from a largely defensive stance toward new digital platforms to being far more active in when and where they made their content available. These producing companies were not indiscriminate in licensing their content, however. Rather, an array of factors fed into which companies they chose to strike deals with and what content they opted to make available. How a producing company acted depended in part on its distinctive organizational structure, in part on the flexibility of its business models and the viability of its existing revenue streams, and in part on the specific visions and objectives of its lead executives. In the case of Disney, in particular, a notable transformation began in the company's structure, strategies, and leadership that led it to cultivate an especially close relationship with Apple. To survey the evolution of Disney's digital distribution strategy, then, is to survey the establishment and expansion of Apple's video-based ecosystem.

Disney and ABC: A Cautious Camaraderie

Disney, like the other major media conglomerates, initially treaded carefully into online distribution. In the early 2000s, the company released only a limited number of titles to outlets such as the on-demand download service Movielink and the subscription-based streaming site CinemaNow. As their names suggest, these companies were primarily focused on motion pictures. A number of factors hindered their growth, including limited broadband diffusion; only 53 percent of American households had access to high-speed Internet as of May 2005 according to a Pew Internet Study.[12] Such ventures were also attacked for their "puny selection, poor quality and overly rigid copyright protection."[13] Unsurprisingly, neither these nor other pre-2005 on-line video efforts took off.[14]

Disney's CEO, Michael Eisner, was particularly notorious for the tight control he exercised over his company's intellectual property. As James B. Stewart chronicles at length in *DisneyWar*, this is far from the only reason that Eisner was notorious at this time.[15] In fact, the Disney CEO had come under fire from the press and industry for a variety of reasons, including his micromanagement, his failure to renegotiate a distribution contract with Pixar, his inability to develop new hits with the ABC broadcast network, and his struggles to fight off an unwanted takeover bid from Comcast. While Eisner had been praised for his effective management skills through much of the 1980s and 1990s, in the new millennium, he was attacked by several prominent figures, including Walt Disney's nephew Roy E. Disney and the head of Pixar/Apple, Steve Jobs.[16] The pressure from these various parties led Eisner to step down in September 2005; his second-in-command, Robert Iger, replaced him in October as CEO and rushed to appease shareholders, Comcast, and Jobs.

Iger had a far different vision for Disney, and he moved swiftly to implement it. This vision placed Apple—and Steve Jobs—front and center. Immediately upon taking office, Iger sought to "repair relations" with Jobs and purchase Pixar outright.[17] Disney had maintained a lucrative distribution deal with Pixar beginning with *Toy Story* (1995) and running through its most recent release, *The Incredibles* (2004).[18] However, Jobs's acrimonious relationship with Eisner led him to seek other distribution partners. Such a move threatened to cost Disney billions of dollars. Iger therefore began his effort at mending fences by striking a deal to sell ABC and Disney Channel shows on iTunes. Making Disney content available for consumption through Apple devices promised to increase the value of the devices. Hardware, after all, had little value without content, or software. And Disney content was certainly highly desirable content for many consumers. It is notable that this landmark moment in the digital distribution of television content occurred as part of an executive's efforts to rebuild institutional and interpersonal relationships.

The announcement of this arrangement took place in October 2005, in tandem with Jobs's introduction of the new video iPod to the press and public.[19] For a price of $1.99 per episode, viewers could now download such ABC hits as *Lost* (2004–2010) and *Desperate Housewives* (2004–2012), as well as Disney Channel shows *That's So Raven* (2003–2007) and *The Suite Life of Zack and Cody* (2005–2007), and view them on their computers or transfer them from iTunes to video iPods.

Iger achieved his primary objective, ownership of Pixar, the next year when Disney purchased Pixar outright for $7.4 billion.[20] This deal gave Jobs a 7 percent stake in Disney, making him the company's largest shareholder. Subsequently, Jobs's input would be sought by Disney for everything from "store design and videogaming to China."[21] The Disney-Apple relationship proved to be mutually beneficial: Jobs offered Disney his advice, and Disney offered Apple its content. In 2006, Disney became the first company to sell movies through iTunes.[22] This announcement came at the same time that Apple introduced its first effort to marry the Web and the television with its "iTV" device—later renamed Apple TV. In 2010, Disney's ABC video player figured prominently in the introduction of the iPad.[23] That same year, Disney, along with Fox, became the first to agree to rent television shows for 99 cents per episode through the next-generation Apple TV.[24]

Though ABC and Disney Channel programs typically were among the first available for download on each new Apple device, the 2005 deal to sell ABC and Disney Channel shows on iTunes was the most significant, for it was this move that best signaled the stunning shift in Disney's practices and the arrival of the post-network era.[25] As *Broadcasting and Cable*'s J. Max Robins notes, this initial deal between Disney and Apple marked "a 180-degree turn from the control-freak way the House of Mouse used to approach distribution of its product. Under former chairman Michael Eisner, it is unlikely Disney would have entered into such an arrangement, where it ceded this much control of the distribution of its precious brands."[26] Robins went on to observe that this agreement signaled that Iger had "emerged as a paragon of innovation." Indeed, later moves made by Iger and his team of executives reveal a company aggressively rethinking its practices and challenging long-standing business models.

By making content available on Apple devices, Disney placed decades-long relationships with cable operators, broadcast affiliates, and the creative community at risk. Such relationships were further upset as Disney expanded its digital-distribution efforts beyond Apple to other technology companies. In 2006, Disney, along with most of the other major studios, made its programs available for download on Amazon's new on-demand service.[27] Also that year, Disney supplemented the download-to-own model it had explored with Apple with free advertiser-supported streaming sites.[28] Disney aired select shows on Disneychannel.com and ABC.com at no charge to viewers. The following year, Disney struck a deal to make its branded video player available through AOL Video.[29] Iger quickly emerged as one of the most outspoken executives, emphasizing the studios' need to experiment with new technologies and windowing practices.

Jobs's close ties to Disney and Apple's strong dependence on Disney programs by no means guaranteed an exclusive relationship between the two companies. In 2007, the download-to-own and advertiser-supported models that Disney favored for computers and video iPods were joined by a subscription-based experiment on mobile phones. Disney made such shows as *Grey's Anatomy* (2005–), *Ugly Betty* (2006–2010), and *Lost* available on video-equipped Sprint phones. For twenty dollars a month, viewers could watch the four most recent episodes of these ABC programs.[30] This deal is particularly notable because it occurred shortly after the iPhone had been introduced. However, no similar arrangement was struck between Disney and the iPhone's exclusive carrier, AT&T. Disney executives had their own set of objectives—objectives that continued to evolve based on a range of economic, technological, industrial, creative, and organizational factors. Solidifying relationships with Jobs/Pixar proved to be an overarching goal for Disney, but it remained just one part of a complex set of calculations that Iger and his executives made regarding what content to license and where and when to license it.

Another central objective for Iger, and by extension, his staff, involved strengthening the Disney brand.[31] Executives operated under the assumption that if Disney properties had clear brand identities, then viewers would follow them from one platform to the next. This logic is apparent in a telling statement made by Disney-ABC Television Group president Anne Sweeney at the time the company began to move beyond its exclusive relationship with Apple:

> This is a different phase of distributing our content. First was download to own. Second was watch for free with advertising, and this next phase is really making sure that the player . . . was a really great experience for people and really helped us build out this multiplatform ecosystem we'd developed for Disney's content. We're in different forms in different places.[32]

Sweeney's statement here might seem to echo the "anytime, anywhere" rhetoric that grew increasingly prominent with the arrival of the post-network era. However, though Disney certainly became more willing to experiment with business models and test new digital-distribution opportunities, by no means should the company be seen as freely or recklessly offering its content for consumption on computers and mobile devices. Rather, Disney opted for outlets where it could foreground its brand and retain strong copyright protections.[33] Further, Disney only offered certain types of programs from certain types of channels. With just a few exceptions, the ABC programs that Disney made available were those in which it served as both financier-studio and distributor.[34] Programs that Disney licensed for initial broadcast but in which it had no financial stake in (for example, the Warner Bros.–produced *The Middle* [2009–]) typically remained unavailable for download or streaming. ABC's limited investment in broadcast stations proved to be another structural factor that enabled it to offer more content on new platforms than its broadcast competitors. As one investor told *Variety*, "They don't have many stations . . . [and so] they have less to protect than other conglomerates."[35]

Significantly, ABC content proved to be particularly conducive for digital distribution because so much of it was serialized. In most cases, serialized programs held less long-term syndication value.[36] Thus there was an incentive for ABC to capitalize on this programming more immediately through alternative distribution methods. Further, serialized shows such as *Lost* or *Brothers and Sisters* (2006–2011) demanded more consistent viewership than episodic shows such as NBC's *Law & Order* or CBS's *CSI* franchises. By making such serialized shows available for viewing on various online and mobile devices, viewers might more easily catch up and, ideally, return to watch these shows during their initial broadcast time. Meanwhile, newer programs served a promotional function, potentially attracting new (and often younger) viewers than might be attained through linear television consumption.

Offering cable programming on iTunes proved to be a far trickier proposition. In general, content from cable program services—including channels in which Disney had an investment, such as ESPN and Lifetime—has had a more limited presence on digital platforms. This is because cable program services make a large portion of their income from subscription fees paid by multiple system operators such as Comcast. MSOs are less likely to pay big fees to cable program services if the content is readily available elsewhere. Despite this fact, Disney raised eyebrows of cable and satellite operators by offering select Disney Channel shows through iTunes and on Disneychannel .com. In making current episodes of certain shows available as they aired on the Disney Channel, the company took a lead role in disintermediating content.[37] Disney made this choice in the interest of exploiting programs such as the *High School Musical* series (2006, 2007, 2008) that had a relatively short shelf life. Disney Channel shows often burst onto the scene and became pop-culture phenomena only to quickly fade in popularity as their youthful audience matured. Presuming that the Disney brand was potent enough to keep cable operators paying subscription fees, Disney took a risk and licensed particular programs to digital outlets. Other companies, including, most notably, Time Warner, proved far less willing to make such moves.

Time Warner and HBO: Corporate Policy and Control

The case study of Disney demonstrates one company's willingness to partner with Apple and experiment with alternative distribution methods. In contrast, the case of Time Warner reveals a company committed to sustaining more traditional distribution models. In striking contrast to Disney, Time Warner generally resisted or denied the destabilizing influence of new technologies upon long-standing business structures, modes of production, programming practices, and consumer-producer relationships. This case study of Time Warner echoes many of the themes provided in the Disney example, including the impact that a company's leader, in this case Time Warner chair Jeffrey L. Bewkes, can have upon a company's approach to digital distribution. Yet it also shows how differences in the philosophies of lead executives, variations in corporate structure, differences in business models, and distinctions among the types of content produced can lead to dramatic differences in how major media companies behave in the digital space. It is true that Disney and Time Warner shared a desire to control how consumers accessed television programming created by the various producing entities under their corporate umbrella. Time Warner's approach, however, diverged from Disney's in significant ways that highlight the confusing terrain of content licensing.

Time Warner chair Jeff Bewkes has worked with the company since 1991, but he did not play a leading role in its transformation until after he became CEO in 2008. The following year, under his supervision, Time Warner spun off both Time Warner Cable and AOL. Jeff Bewkes attributed the sale of both companies to part of the "reshaping of Time Warner . . . enabling us to focus to an even greater degree on our core content business." The sale of these divisions marked Time Warner's move away from distribution technologies and toward a greater emphasis on the production and licensing of content.

The new, streamlined Time Warner was primarily a content company; in fact, in 2010, *Deadline*'s Tim Adler reported that 80 percent of the company's revenue came from television programming.[38]

During this period of restructuring, Jeff Bewkes introduced an ambitious initiative called "TV Everywhere," a concept since adopted by Comcast Corporation, Dish Network, and others.[39] In simplest terms, the concept speaks for itself—television content should be available on demand to viewers on any screen through whatever type of broadband access they have at their disposal. According to the *Los Angeles Times*, TV Everywhere may be interpreted as a conscious reaction against Apple. As Dawn Chmielewski and Meg James observed in an article about Time Warner's leadership in developing TV Everywhere, "The cable industry and the studios are working to hold Apple at bay, racing to come up with an alternative that will keep their business intact. . . . One solution: TV Everywhere." In an editorial written by Bewkes for the *Wall Street Journal*, he clearly positioned TV Everywhere and Time Warner in relation to companies like Apple.[40] He perceived the debate about new media devices such as the iPhone as part of an epic battle between TV industry incumbents like Time Warner and new entrants to the television business like Apple.[41]

When describing these "new entrants," Bewkes specifically identified several companies: "Because TV Everywhere is an idea and not an object, it may lack some of the glitz factor of new devices and services recently announced by Amazon, Apple, Google, Sony and others." Expanding on his ideas about these companies, Bewkes contended, "Let's be clear about what these new entrants are not: They are neither programmers nor distributors." To state that Apple and Amazon, companies that deliver content through iTunes and Amazon Video On Demand, are not distributors may seem odd, but in this case, Bewkes seemed to be defining the term "distribution" according to business practices established by incumbents—namely a dual revenue stream (i.e., subscriptions and advertising) and well-developed windowing strategies.[42] For Bewkes, technology should not disrupt but rather be "harnessed" to support and advance the current business model of television distribution. From his perspective, new entrants "must also support or improve the industry economics that have led directly to the cultural and commercial renaissance that television is now experiencing."[43] Bewkes's approach, therefore, invites companies like Apple to find a place *within* the established business models of television.[44]

What seems most significant in Bewkes's statements in this editorial is his denial that he seeks to protect "outdated paradigms," instead championing an industry that is "emerging as the dominant medium of the digital age."[45] Nevertheless, Time Warner had clearly developed their own means of online distribution designed to protect current relationships and existing income streams. Whereas Disney took steps toward disintermediating content from conduit in releasing ABC and Disney Channel shows to iTunes, Time Warner moved to redefine and solidify established relationships in the most conservative ways possible.

Time Warner's actions in the digital space with HBO illustrate how one of its subsidiaries worked with Apple even as it began to establish an infrastructure that operated independently of Apple's ecosystem.[46] Three words best summarized HBO's approach to digital distribution: access, retention, and control. According to *Variety*'s Susan Young, HBO had long fostered a reputation as a technological innovator in order to provide access to its subscribers. In 1991, HBO was the first premium channel to offer multiplexing (multiple channel streams under one brand, as with HBO Signature). It then launched HBO.com in 1995 and created HBO On Demand for cable subscribers in 2001. According to HBO copresident Eric Kessler, providing access for subscribers who pay extra to enjoy HBO-produced series was crucial because it demonstrated that their programming was worth the extra cost: "The greater the access viewers have to the content, the more they will use it and the longer they will hold on to the service."[47] In other words, access led to retention. Apple devices that are enabled with HBO applications have therefore served as one means to provide access. A desire to control their content, however, led HBO to demand particular terms in its relations with Apple.

Though HBO demonstrated a willingness to partner with Apple's iTunes, it stipulated unique terms in the licensing of its content. Apple's insistence that all TV programming be similarly priced proved to be endlessly frustrating to content providers. Because of these conditions, several companies either halted negotiations with Apple or refused to renew their initial distribution arrangements. For example, NBC Universal removed its content from the iTunes Store in 2007 after Apple refused to cede to its demands during a pricing dispute. Commenting upon NBC's decision to cut ties with iTunes, Brooks Barnes of the *New York Times* explained that the iPhone sparked anxiety that Apple's entrance into the mobile video market would disrupt the value and structure of the television industry as it had the music industry. Though Apple didn't give ground to NBC, HBO did successfully negotiate an increase in the price for individual television episode downloads.[48] In 2008, Apple allowed HBO to charge anywhere from $1.99 to $2.99 for episodes of select series such as *The Sopranos*. Moreover, Apple agreed not to release individual episodes of currently airing HBO series for purchase on iTunes until the DVD release, thereby enabling Time Warner to sustain existing distribution windows.[49]

At the same time that HBO content appeared on iTunes, the pay-cable program service also made several other distinctive moves into mobile distribution. This included partnering with other mobile-device manufacturers, developing a unique infrastructure to distribute HBO content to subscribers, and erecting certain barriers to selected platforms developed by Apple and Netflix. For instance, the Internet portal HBO Go—in development since 2008—promised to provide four times the content of HBO On Demand.[50] In order to offer this service, cable providers made individual deals with HBO. A 2010 deal with telecommunication operator Verizon provided its FiOS subscribers with access to HBO Go, but at the time of the deal, the Flash-enabled HBO Go remained incompatible with Apple's operating system and therefore with devices like the iPhone. Later that year, HBO announced HBO GO would become available to Apple device users by early 2011. Meanwhile, HBO continued to refuse to allow streaming access to its content on Netflix, even though its main competitor, Showtime, had done so. Explaining a decision not to partner with Netflix, Kessler contended, "there is value in exclusivity."[51] The examples provided here of HBO's behavior demonstrate that despite Time Warner's rhetoric supporting a TV Everywhere strategy that provides consumers with access to content across all platforms, its subsidiary's licensing strategies depended upon a complicated set of negotiations with each potential distributor. Indeed, mobile devices may have offered television content, but this did not guarantee that big media companies such as Time Warner would let that content move freely.

TV Everywhere served as a means by which Time Warner provided "added value" to cable program services such as HBO, TBS and TNT—added value that helped these program services sustain high per-subscriber fees from MSOs. Nevertheless, though its strategy was designed to protect Time Warner's existing business models, the company—as well as the cable industry more generally—faced a number of challenges. Most notable was the threat of "cord cutting." Though the subject of much debate, early evidence suggested that an increasing number of cable subscribers were canceling their subscriptions because of the rising cost of cable subscriptions as well as the enhanced programming options available through digital over-the-air television, DVDs, and online streaming sites such as iTunes, Netflix, and Hulu (or Hulu Plus). The accessibility of content through illegal means such as torrents also proved an attraction to many viewers. Although Bewkes repeatedly rejected that cord cutting was occurring at the dire rates suggested by some, several reports confirmed that HBO's subscriber base was in decline. Moreover, the number of cable subscribers in the United States dropped for two quarters in a row in 2010 in an industry that had experienced unprecedented and continuous growth for decades.[52]

This decline in cable subscriptions, perhaps attributable to the weak economy in 2010 or to premium program offerings perceived as being less attractive than in earlier years, nevertheless invited questions about the future of the cable business. As a result, companies like Time Warner seemed willing to consider radical possibilities. As news of cable's declining subscription numbers hit the press in November 2010, Bewkes issued a cryptic statement implying his company would consider providing cable programming to nonsubscribers in the future. In other words, he indicated the possibility that viewers might one day be able to bypass companies like Time Warner Cable and subscribe to HBO à la carte: "[On] the question you raised about HBO going direct, we do have the ability to do that. And it's not something that we have decided to do today because . . . we have a very good relationship . . . [with] all the different distributors. . . . If that doesn't work well, or speedily enough, then we have the option of adding a direct sale of HBO."[53] The power of Disney's brand might enable it to take similar steps. While this action represents a nuclear option for program services—exploding long-standing business models, windowing practices, and corporate relationships—it is no longer inconceivable in the post-network era. Importantly, Bewkes's statement reinforces that technology is not the primary factor limiting the exploitation of new revenue streams. Instead, relationships dependent upon a particular, historical business model often determine the application of technology. Bewkes could have delivered HBO programming to nonsubscribers for a transaction fee, but he had not done so because of his established partnerships with incumbent distributors. Corporate policy, it seems, trumps technology.

Conclusion: TV Everywhere Remains Elusive

The relative mobility of video content may be a popular topic among scholars, journalists, and technology bloggers. Still, the practice of accessing content on mobile devices may not be a true trend with consumers—at least, not yet.[54] Two studies in 2010, one by a mobile-traffic management firm and one by Nielsen, reported that 10 percent of the owners of mobile devices were responsible for 90 percent of traffic.[55] Thus, we are mainly discussing early adopters, who often have particular habits that differ substantively from the broader media audience. As Max Dawson argues in his examination of the digital television transition, industry and scholarly attention to early adopters, those who most quickly embrace new media technologies, has not only created a distorted sense of a digital divide but also contributed to a research deficit.[56] It is important to recognize that companies like Disney and Time Warner seem to be acting more in anticipation—or fear—of the future than in response to contemporary consumption practices. To wit, "Today is the beginning of 'the end of TV as we know it' and the future will only favor those who prepare now," reads a report prepared by IBM Business Consulting Services in 2006 for senior business executives in the media industries.[57] Content producers are being active in a way that the music industry was not in the interest of having greater control over their destiny. Despite conglomerate efforts to control the distribution of mobile content, the future remains uncertain: people may not adopt these devices, adoption may be very slow, or change may happen in unanticipated ways. What is certain, however, is that the current landscape of digital media distribution is one of confusion and chaos—some shows are available on multiple digital platforms, while others cannot be found anywhere. This chaos and confusion can also be felt at the level of consumption, particularly for those who are not technologically savvy.

News reports in early 2011 suggested that consumers may have less difficulty finding programs in the digital space in the future. In mid-2011, for example, the Digital Entertainment Content Ecosystem, a consortium of sixty media companies including Comcast, LG and Nokia, IBM and Cisco, Netflix, and Best Buy, planned to launch their aforementioned "UltraViolet" system, an online storage system that allows users to access their stored video media content on up to twelve different devices.[58] Notably, the DECE had not yet entered into a deal with Apple. This means that the content stored through UltraViolet may not be accessible through the iPhone, iPad, or other Apple devices.[59] Also, UltraViolet will store only purchased, not rented, content despite the popularity of a rental model. As tech blogger Ryan Lawler pointed out, studies showed a decline in the rate of online media purchases but an increase in the rate for digital rentals in 2010.[60]

Apple has its own initiative that competes with UltraViolet and is designed to provide access to content across platforms. This initiative is called Airplay and consists of proprietary software for Apple's operating system.[61] Airplay allows users to wirelessly transmit any video content compatible with the iOS across devices. For instance, a user may start watching the most recent episode of ABC's *Cougar Town* (2009–) on her iPhone and then view the rest of that episode on her Apple TV. As the DECE and Apple's own efforts demonstrate, the trend toward cloud-based storage systems is growing. The functionality of individual systems nevertheless remains a work in progress.

As the examples of the competing DECE and Airplay digital storage systems indicates, the truly "device-agnostic" application has not yet been developed—nor does it look likely to be developed any time soon.[62] Thus, in spite of the talk of television "anywhere, anytime" espoused by ventures such as DECE and by companies such as Time Warner and Disney, actual corporate practices reveal aggressive efforts to lock down the circulation of content in ways that best serve companies' economic interests. Similarly, despite the rhetoric of access espoused by Apple marketing, Airplay has failed to deliver on its promises. Released with an iOS update in November 2010, the software was tested by tech bloggers at *GigaOM*, who discovered that a number of applications available on the iPhone did not support Airplay. Even the Apple-produced (but Google-owned) YouTube application performed poorly.[63] While it may seem technology has not yet caught up to the imagination,[64] it may be truer to say that Apple is building towards a larger goal. Such a goal, though far from clear at present, seems to involve all Apple devices and lead to a yet-to-be-defined objective central to its evolving product ecosystem.[65]

A challenge for research about Apple and its devices is the flurry of reporting that arrives with each large-scale Apple announcement. Over the last decade, the mainstream press has sustained a love affair with Apple. Whereas major announcements by other technology companies such as Amazon and Microsoft are often buried in the technology pages of newspapers—if they are covered at all—every move that Apple makes generates thousands of words in print and pixels. This voluminous coverage certainly makes it easier for researchers to track Apple's every move and follow its shifting relationships with the Hollywood conglomerates. However, at the same time, such coverage makes it even more difficult for researchers to make conclusive statements about digital-distribution practices and challenges.[66]

Throughout all of this reporting, however, one point does remain consistent: the ability to sell devices depends on the availability of media content. By extension, a device without enough content will not revolutionize any consumer's television habits or the industry's fundamental operations. When Apple launched the second incarnation of Apple TV—a lighter, cheaper, and more versatile streaming-only system—sales remained low. Many media analysts surmised this was caused in part by the lack of available Hollywood content.[67] As Holman W. Jenkins Jr. contended in the *Wall Street Journal*, "What we want is to watch anything we want whenever we want, for a single monthly price." This desire, though understandable, fails to account for the decades-old infrastructure, business models, corporate practices, and cultural attitudes that support and sustain the television industry. As just one notable example, syndication dollars continue to provide much of the revenue that offsets the cost of producing multi-million-dollar-an-episode programs. Companies are reticent to push online distribution efforts too far for fear of jeopardizing the income generated through this revenue stream. The future of television remains unclear, to be sure. Nonetheless, by understanding the issues that underlie conglomerate decision making, scholars, consumers, and activists are better able to demand not only more diverse content but also, perhaps, even more open platforms.

NOTES

1. Andrew Wallenstein, "Disney Rethinks Role of Keychest in Film Distribution," *paidContent.org*, 12 November 2010.

2. Article after article mentions how the Hollywood studios did not want to end up following the same path as the music industry. For example, see Saul Hansell, "Forget the Bootleg, Just Download the Movie Illegally," *New York Times*, 4 July 2005; David Carr, "Steve Jobs Stakes Out the TV Den," *New York Times*, 5 May 2008; Jennifer Netherby, "Digital Cloud's Dark Lining," *Variety*, 2 November 2009.

3. David Goldman, "Music's Lost Decade: Sales Cut in Half," *CNNmoney.com*, 3 February 2010.

4. Andrew Wallenstein, "Why Apple Rental Plan Alienated Most Studios," *Hollywood Reporter*, 2 September 2010.

5. Netherby, "Digital Cloud's Dark Lining."

6. Wolter Lemstra et al., "Just Another Distribution Channel," Mobilware Conference Berlin, Germany, April 2009, offers a macroview of the impact of the smartphone upon the business model of the media industries, but this generalized approach overlooks particularities and idiosyncrasies that operate at the conglomerate and division levels.

7. This may be partly attributable to delay in terms of academic publishing but also an overemphasis on production over distribution. See also Amanda Lotz, *The Television Will Be Revolutionized* (New York: New York University Press, 2007); Jennifer Holt, "Which Way to the Mothership? New Directions for Television Distribution," unpublished manuscript, 2011. In a previous essay, Alisa Perren addressed continuities in digital distribution strategies across the conglomerates. This chapter provides a counterpoint to that study, illustrating the differences. See Perren, "Business as Unusual: Conglomerate-Sized Challenges in the Digital Arena," *Journal of Popular Film and Television* 38, no. 2 (2010): 72–78.

8. The lag time from writing to publication certainly contributes to the paucity of scholarly work. Significantly, there is no shortage of trade and journalistic discourse — the challenge for researchers involves sorting through and making sense of the massive amount of material that has been generated about digital distribution.

9. As Ed Bott points out, the concept of "ownership" shifts when you move from physical to digital copies. In fact, viewers don't actually "own" digital programs. See "Who Owns Your Digital Downloads? (Hint: It's Not You)," *ZDNet*, 3 January 2011.

10. Journalists began to note a decline in the DVD market beginning in 2006. See Ben Grossman, "The New Deal: How TV Executives Will Find Digital Dollars in the Coming Year," *Broadcasting and Cable*, 2 January 2006, 16; Jonathan Bing, "Auds: A Many-Splintered Thing," *Variety*, 2 January 2006, 1.

11. The year 2005 also marked the breakthrough of web 2.0 phenomena and social media. Lotz, *Television*, introduction.

12. John B. Horrigan, "Broadband Adoption in the United States: Growing but Slowing," Pew Internet and American Life Project, http://www.pewinternet.org/Reports/2005/Broadband-Adoption-in-the-United-States-Growing-but-Slowing.aspx (15 January 2011).

13. David Pogue, "Film Rentals Via the Web: A Studio Cut," *New York Times*, 15 May 2003.

14. By mid-2004, Movielink reported that it rented approximately 75,000 titles per month, amounting to less than $5 million per year in revenue. Ben Fritz, "Justice Department Ends Probe in Movielink," *Variety*, 4 June 2004, 8.

15. James B. Stewart, *DisneyWar* (London: Simon & Schuster, 2008).

16. Jobs's relationship with Hollywood had tightened as Pixar produced more feature films and as the company was incorporated into Disney.

17. This goal became particularly important for Disney because its own animation division continued to struggle to develop hits internally. See Richard Siklos, "Cool, a Video iPod: Want to Watch 'Lost'?" *New York Times*, 16 October 2005.

18. If Disney did not strike a new agreement with Pixar, *Cars* (2006) was to be the last film released through the partnership. See Laura M. Holson, "A Demure Pixar Takes No Notice of Eager Suitors," *New York Times*, 24 May 2004.

19. John Markoff and Laura M. Holson, "With New iPod, Apple Aims to be a Video Star," *New York Times*, 13 October 2005.

20. Ben Fritz, "Friend or Foe?" *Variety*, 19 June 2006, A2.

21. Richard Siklos, "Bob Iger Rocks Disney," *Fortune*, 19 January 2009, 80–86.

22. John Markoff and Laura M. Holson, "Apple Plans to Inhabit Living Room," *New York Times*, 13 September 2006.

23. Marc Graser, "Biz Mad for iPad Apps," *Variety*, 5 April 2010, 1.

24. Marc Graser, "99-Cent Store; Apple TV Revamp Dives Into Rentals," *Variety*, 2 September 2010, 1.

25. Lotz outlines the contours of the post-network era in *The Television Will be Revolutionized*.

26. Max Robins, "The Iger-Pod," *Broadcasting and Cable*, 17 October 2005, 5.

27. Other companies proved more willing to work with Amazon than Apple in part because Amazon let them set their own price. Amazon was also attractive because it

threatened the potential monopoly that Apple exercised over the video-on-demand market.

28. Anne Becker, "ABC's Appealing Deal: The Spark That Ignited Multiplatforms," *Broadcasting and Cable*, 19 June 2006, A2.

29. Anne Becker, "ABC's Sweeney on Digital Plans," *Broadcasting and Cable*, 24 September 2007, 3.

30. Gary Levin and Edward C. Baig, "Sprint, ABC Dial in to Television on the Go," *USA Today*, 15 May 2007.

31. Siklos, "Bob Iger Rocks Disney."

32. Becker, "ABC's Sweeney on Digital."

33. Markoff and Holson, "With New iPod."

34. The struggles over licensing *Scrubs* for digital platforms underscore why vertical integration proved increasingly desirable as companies sought to exploit the digital space. During most of its time on the air, *Scrubs* was produced by Disney-ABC but aired on NBC. Complicated rights negotiations ensued to make it available on iTunes. In fact, at that time *Scrubs* was the one of the few programs available on iTunes to be financed by one company and broadcast by another. See Jacque Steinberg, "Digital Media Brings Profits (And Tensions) to TV Studios," *New York Times*, 14 May 2006.

35. Jill Goldsmith, "Thanks to Pix, Wall St. Bullish on Mouse," *Variety*, 1 May 2006, 50.

36. Ibid.

37. Graser, "99-Cent Store."

38. Cynthia Littleton, "Ten Years of Tumult." *Variety*, 21 December 2009, 1; Aaron Smith, "Time Warner to Split Off AOL," *CNN Money*, 28 May 2009; Jessica E. Vascellaro, "Time Warner Sees Ally in Web," *Wall Street Journal*, 6 October 2010; Tim Adler, "Jeff Bewkes: 'Network TV Has Whip-Hand Over YouTube and iTunes,'" *Deadline.com*, 28 September 2010.

39. Comcast has branded its TV Everywhere initiative as Xfinity; Verizon has FiOS; and Dish Network has its own version of TV Everywhere as well.

40. Jeff Bewkes, "Opinion: The Coming Golden Age of Television," *Wall Street Journal*, 6 October 2010.

41. There are technological challenges with TV Everywhere, including the necessity to verify cable subscribers' account status, in addition to the challenge of establishing licensing deals with content providers. This case study, however, focuses on the theory of TV Everywhere in its relation to Apple more than its implementation.

42. As noted in the earlier case study, Disney does not see itself as a traditional television-distribution company because it does not have extensive investments in affiliate stations.

43. Bewkes, "Opinion."

44. Time Warner's decision to partner with Google TV confirms that Bewkes is not opposed to partnering with "new entrants." See also Dawn C. Chmielewski, Jessica Guynn, and Meg James, "Networks Block Google TV to Protect Themselves," *Los Angeles Times*, 21 October 2010.

45. Chmielewski, Guynn, and James, "Networks Block Google TV."

46. Bewkes's company is much more heavily invested in cable and less involved with broadcast. Time Warner owns the premium channel HBO and also the basic cable channels under Turner Broadcasting, including TNT, TBS, CNN, and others. The subsidiary Warner Bros. owns a 50 percent stake in the CW Network, but there is not space here to delve into the CW's digital-distribution strategy, worthy of its own case study.

47. Susan Young, "Digital Push Important Part of HBO's Growth," *Variety*, 8 November 2010.

48. NBC and Apple announced a new deal with more flexible pricing in September 2008. See Alex Weprin, "NBC, iTunes Strike New Deal," *Broadcasting and Cable*, 9 September 2008.

49. "Apple Introduces HBO Programming on iTunes," *Telecomworldwire*, 14 May 2008; Brian Stelter, "HBO Shows May Sell on iTunes for $1.99+," *New York Times*, 13 May 2008, 3.

50. In January 2011, HBO Go was available to subscribers through Verizon's FiOS, AT&T's U-verse, and was in beta testing with Cox Cable. It was not yet available to HBO subscribers with other cable companies, like Comcast.

51. Gary Levin, "It's not TV, It's HBO—On Your Computer; Network Adds Broadband Option," *USA Today*, 21 January 2008; Shawn Oliver, "HBO Go Is The Pay-Model Hulu Has Been Searching For," *Reuters*, 19 February 2010; Ronald Grover, "Netflix Lust for 'True Blood' Is Unrequited as HBO Blocks Path," *Bloomberg.com*, 17 August 2010.

52. Chmielewski, "Company Town"; Andrew Wallenstein, "Exclusive: HBO Subscribers Dwindling," Associated Press, 13 September 2010; Brian Stelter, "Cord Cutting? Cable Subscriptions Drop Again," *New York Times*, 17 November 2010.

53. Ryan Lawler, "Could HBO 'Go' Direct to Consumers?" *Gigaom.com*, 3 November 2010.

54. See, for example, Jessi Hempel, "What the Hell is Going On with TV?" *Fortune*, 3 January 2011; Jon Healey, "The Boxee Box: Not Ready to Replace a Cable Box (Yet)," *Los Angeles Times*, 28 December 2010; Kevin Purdy, "Ditching Cable for the Web: How Much Can You Save Buying, Renting, or Streaming TV?" *Lifehacker.com*, 19 October 2010; Nick Bilton, "HBO Go, the Best Online Video Service I Cannot Use," *New York Times Bits* blog, 17 February 2010.

55. Marc Graser, "Mobile Video Use Overestimated, Report Says," *Variety*, 20 January 2011.

56. Max Dawson, "Television Between Analog and Digital," *Journal of Popular Film and Television* 38, no. 2 (April 2010): 95–100.

57. IBM Institute for Business Value, "The End of Television as We Know It: A Future Industry Perspective," IBM Corporation, 2006.

58. Marc Graser, "Hollywood Clicks with UltraViolet Digital Locker," *Variety*, 5 January 2011.

59. Dan Nosowitz, "DECE's Plans for Digital Movie Purchases May Confuse and Anger You," *Gizmodo*, 4 January 2010.

60. Ryan Lawler, "UltraViolet's Real Challenge: People Don't Buy Movies Online," *Gigaom.com*, 11 January 2011.

61. Kyle Van Hemert, "How Apple's Airplay Is About to Change Your Life," *Gizmodo*, 22 November 2010.

62. Kyle Van Hemert, "Use Airflick to Send Non-iTunes Video from Your Mac to AppleTV," *Gizmodo*, 20 December 2010.

63. Janko Roettgers, "Video: Apple's AirPlay is Kind of Pointless," *Gigaom.com*, 22 November 2010.

64. Technological limitations do exist. The FCC chairman Julius Genachowski's efforts to convince broadcasters to auction a share of their spectrum space to wireless companies underlies the fact that the infrastructure needs to be expanded to meet rapidly increasing demand for streaming video content.

65. Jonny Evans, "Google TV? Apple's Five Secret Weapons," *Computer World*, 5 October 2010.

66. This might contribute to the reticence of media studies scholars to publish on this topic.

67. Matthew Moskovciak, "Apple TV Review: Outstanding Design, but Light on TV Content," *CNET*, 30 September 2010.

CHAPTER 8

Pushing the (Red) Envelope

*Portable Video, Platform Mobility, and
Pay-Per-View Culture*

CHUCK TRYON

W HATEVER ELSE THE iPhone might be, it is also a machine for promoting and cultivating highly personalized media and communication experiences. The iPhone, with its seemingly unlimited array of
applications and customizations, allows users to reshape the cell phone so
that it is an expression of personal interests. Although Apple has relentlessly
promoted these interactive aspects of the iPhone, discussion of the iPhone
also emphasizes its entertainment uses. This emphasis was promoted in one
of the earliest Apple ads, "Calamari," from 2007, in which an iPhone user,
while watching *Pirates of the Caribbean*, develops a sudden craving for sea-
food. He then stops the movie, effortlessly opens a search engine, locates a
nearby restaurant, and taps a button on the interface to dial the restaurant for
a reservation.

In Apple's ad, the viewer, transformed into a user through the power
of interactive media, remains unseen except for his hands, which navigate
the phone with the fluidity and gestures of a magician's, taking the everyday activities of movie watching and eating out and transforming them into
something verging on the miraculous. As Isabel Pedersen observes in her
astute reading of Apple's rhetoric, "the ad subtly depicts the subject's transformation toward good consumerism; actions seem to end in some sort of

purchase."[1] While Pedersen emphasizes the advertisement's promotion of the practices of consumption—and the iPhone's ability to make one a better consumer—Apple's advertising discourse offers an equally explicit positioning of a *mobile* consuming subject, one who has a mastery not merely over the iPhone technology itself but also over the urban environments in which the iPhone would quickly become commonplace after its 2007 launch.[2] Apple also implies that the iPhone user can afford to pursue these activities, both financially and in terms of leisure time.

Several years after the iPhone had been firmly established as a popular portable communication device, the movie-rental service Netflix announced the launch of an official application that would allow Netflix customers to access their video queue and to watch movies over streaming video, using either a 3G or Wi-Fi connection on an iPhone or iPod Touch (the iPad already had a Netflix app). The Netflix app joined Hulu Plus in allowing users to watch recently broadcast TV shows or feature-length movies on the iPhone. In addition to promising a high-quality video image, the press releases announcing the launch of both services also placed emphasis on the ability of consumers to access entertainment content whenever and wherever they wished. Both announcements also touted the fact that users could start watching a movie on one device and finish it on another, picking up exactly where they left off, creating what amounts to *platform mobility*, a concept I will use in this article to encompass the ongoing shift toward ubiquitous, mobile access to a wide range of entertainment content.[3] Platform mobility entails more than the diverse screens and platforms through which we access entertainment. It also includes the ability to deliver a vast menu of entertainment choices to the viewer, wherever he or she may happen to be.

In addition to providing new modes of access to streaming video, platform mobility also reshapes the definition of film and television as media. Enthusiastic reviews, such as a breathless blog entry on *Wired* by Eliot Van Buskirk, picked up on the promise of media and platform mobility, describing the Netflix app as offering "DVD anywhere," the ability to watch movies and television shows anytime and anywhere. This access, Van Buskirk argues, provides iPhone users with the ability to "re-evaluate" how they would consume TV shows and movies in the future, presumably providing them with an agency over their media content unavailable to other audiences, an underlying assumption that informs the technology blogs and consumer guides that often report on the introduction of new delivery systems and technological platforms.[4] Thus, Netflix and Hulu, in announcing their iPhone apps, built upon the discourses of media mobility and consumer empowerment in order to promote the pleasures of seemingly ubiquitous access to video entertainment.

This chapter uses the publicity surrounding the launch of the Netflix and Hulu Plus apps for the iPhone to reconsider the discourses of media mobility. It starts by tracing the role of platform mobility in reshaping the media of film and television. In this context, I am drawing from Lisa Gitelman's argument that media are defined not merely through technological aspects but also through social, legal, and economic protocols.[5] Both mobile phones and mobile video have challenged many of these social norms, especially when it comes to complaints about individuals conducting ostensibly private conversations in public places while similar complaints about watching movies in public places have also been registered. In some ways, many of the changes associated with portable media reinforce existing aspects of what Raymond Williams once described as "mobile privatization," in that media reception becomes personalized, directed toward fragmented, atomized audiences.[6] In addition, portable media threaten to unsettle existing perceptions of the TV show or movie as a definable media object, challenging traditional expectations regarding how we watch TV and movies. While DVDs, especially box sets of TV series, worked to "package" shows into a coherent object, streaming and mobile video potentially transform those texts yet again into ephemeral objects, available for purchase or rental in the cloud, changing how viewers engage with video entertainment. Finally, digital distribution also shapes the ways in which studios work to redefine the consumption habits of movie audiences. Rather than focusing on a DVD market, built primarily around sales, that has been declining for several years, the media industries now turn to a digital distribution strategy that emphasizes a pay-per-view model, in which consumers are provided (often temporary) access to a film or TV episode.

In order to engage with these promises of personal liberation through portable media, this article will unpack three major components of media consumption that are ostensibly transformed by digital distribution: the mobility of the consumer, the diversity of entertainment choices (in terms of both content and platforms), and the distribution practices of the media industries. One of the challenges of thinking about these shifts has been the difficulty of settling on a single term to describe the object that is being watched or consumed by iPhone users. Although Netflix is predominantly associated with movies and Hulu Plus with TV, their catalogues do not focus on a single medium. In fact, Netflix might be roughly compared to a cable channel like HBO that delivers movies, TV shows, and, in very limited cases, such as the series *House of Cards*, original content. Thus, in some cases, I have opted to use the word "video" to describe the content distributed via streaming platforms, even though the word typically is used to refer to short-form content found on sites such as YouTube and Vimeo. Although "video" is a somewhat more ambiguous term, it also highlights the degree to which the distribution protocols associated with movies and television have begun to overlap, even while audiences continue to identify distinctions between the two media, often privileging one medium over the other, usually with movie enthusiasts arguing for the aesthetic superiority of film, an argument that becomes difficult to support when both texts are viewed on a three-inch screen.

In addition to the challenge of defining the "object" of digital distribution, I have also found myself wavering between a variety of terms to describe the actual people who consume, watch, view, use, and (in some cases) share entertainment with, on, and among their portable media players. For this reason, I have avoided settling on a single term, such as "spectator," to describe people engaged with or immersed in platform mobility. Instead, platform mobility seems to demand that people shift between a variety of roles and protocols that shape their engagement with video content, whether that entails watching a movie, rearranging a Netflix queue, or providing a distraction for bored children during a long wait at the doctor's office. Although these changes seem to promise a radical transformation of entertainment culture, they are also, as we will see in our discussions of the media industry, likely to become a means of restabilizing industry control over media content, in much the same way that studios eventually asserted control over video and cable distribution. This effort to control the consumption of media content is part of what Siva Vaidhyanathan calls a "pay-per-view universe," which "involves the efforts of the content industries to create a 'leak-proof' sales and delivery system."[7]

These changes are reflected in the distribution models associated with both Netflix and Hulu Plus. Netflix began as a DVD-by-mail service in 1997, but with the increase in broadband access (and postage costs), the company began focusing on distribution via streaming video, eventually creating a "streaming-only" plan that allowed customers to watch as many movies as they wanted for $7.99 per month, in addition to their DVD-by-mail services. (This model would have been complicated even further by the splitting of the streaming and DVD-by-mail services into two separate companies, as Netflix announced it would do in 2011. Only a few weeks later, it changed its mind and returned to the status quo.) Once viewers have logged into the Netflix app on their iPhone, iPad, or iPod Touch, they can see their "top picks," films that the Netflix recommendation algorithm has determined to be of interest to the user. In some cases, these recommendations may be placed in improvised genres such as "quirky satires" (which lumps together such disparate films as the Joaquin Phoenix mockumentary *I'm Still Here* and the Tim Burton film *Mars Attacks*) or "Visually-Striking [*sic*] Cerebral Dramas," such as *The Thin Red Line*. The bottom of the screen includes links to a list of genres, to the user's instant queue, and to a search box, while the top of the screen includes a list of streaming videos that the user began but has not yet finished watching, allowing her to move seamlessly from one platform to another. Pressing the title then allows the user to choose to add the video to her queue or to play it immediately. Select the latter option opens the streaming screen, allowing the movie to play. Users can pause the movie and can fast-forward or rewind using a scroll bar that appears when the screen is touched, making it possible to move purposefully to specific scenes. The screen itself offers a relatively crisp, if small, image, although a streaming video is likely to consume both quite a bit of data and a significant amount of battery power, posing two of the biggest challenges for users who wish to consume videos on the go.

Similarly, Hulu began as a "free," advertising-supported distributor, providing access to recent episodes of selected TV shows, as well as a small selection of movies. Although users were provided with only a few "trailing" episodes of recently broadcast TV shows, they were typically enough to allow fans to catch up on shows that they had missed. Thus, fans of the TV series *The Office* could watch on Hulu an episode they missed during the normal broadcast schedule in order to ensure that they were able to participate in "water-cooler" conversations about the show at work. Hulu Plus offers a significant expansion of content, however, by allowing subscribers to access the full current season of a wide range of ABC, Fox, and NBC TV shows, including *Glee, Modern Family, The Office,* and *30 Rock*. Viewers also have access to full series runs of several current and past shows, including *The Office, Buffy the Vampire Slayer,* and *Desperate Housewives,* offerings that were eventually curtailed when Fox announced that it would require Hulu users to wait eight days to see new episodes of its shows. Although subscribers are now expected to pay for this deeper access, the shows are still interrupted by short advertisements, suggesting that digital delivery may continue to be subsidized by an assemblage of payment models. No matter what, platform mobility feeds into an on-demand culture defined by flexibility in when and where people consume media.

Mobility

Mobile video has become a widely discussed part of the entertainment industry. In a discussion of the 2011 Consumer Electronics Show, Will Richmond remarked that, "mobility is video's next frontier, one that could transform our media consumption experiences, liberating individual consumers from watching in a fixed location."[8] Research into media consumption habits seemed to confirm that mobile access was increasing. According to the Pew Internet and American Life Project, the percentage of U.S. mobile-phone users accessing the Internet from their mobile devices increased from 25 in 2009 to 38 in 2010.[9] Similarly, Nielsen reported that there was a 43 percent increase in the number of people using mobile video between 2009 and 2010, suggesting a dramatic increase in mobile access. Nielsen also estimated that each mobile video user watched about 3.5 hours worth of video per month, a tiny percentage of overall TV consumption. However, given that mobile phones are often not the first option for watching video, these numbers suggest a gradual adoption of mobile platforms, especially when the habits of younger viewers are taken into consideration.[10]

Promises of platform mobility are explicitly tied to discourses of personal television and the promises of individual choice, in terms of when, where, and what people watch. As Lisa Parks observes, "personal television," especially in its mobile incarnation, extends the logic of what Williams refers to as "mobile privatization," in that these tools contribute to increasingly atomized and isolated subjects. For Parks, these tools reinforce "middle-class fantasies of transport, personal freedom, and citizenship."[11] Writing before the advent of the iPhone, Parks anticipates that these new delivery systems will both expand the number of locations where people watch TV and alter the practices of watching, leading to changes such as the decreased authority of television channels and a decline in centralized media experiences that can feed into a larger sense of media citizenship when users are no longer required to tune their televisions to a specific station at a specific time. Amanda D. Lotz adds that platform mobility has "led the television audience not only to fracture among different channels and devices, but also to splinter temporally."[12] In this sense, platform mobility seems to be fragmenting audiences along two separate trajectories: first, in terms of the television schedule that determines *when* people watch and, second, in terms of the vast entertainment menu that opens up wider choices of *what* people watch.

Despite fears that platform mobility would lead to increasing audience fragmentation, the potential for freedom from the constraints of a specific programming schedule continues to entice digital-media enthusiasts. These fantasies about platform mobility are powerfully encapsulated in a blog post announcing the launch of Hulu Plus. Hulu's CEO, Jason Kilar, positions himself as a TV fan—rather than an aggregator or middleman—while also emphasizing the social role of television as a means of unifying a larger public, commenting about Hulu that "we are proud to say that we love TV shows. TV shows entertain billions of people across the globe and are among the most durable, high quality forms of storytelling in our society. TV shows play a significant role in billions of people's daily routines."[13] Although the iPhone may actually increase fragmentation and atomization, Kilar invokes the image of a large collective audience drawn in by their shared enjoyment of TV. Kilar also underscores the platform's ability to allow mobile viewing by narrating a hypothetical viewing experience in which a viewer begins watching an episode of a television show in her living room on her TV before migrating to another room in the house to watch on an iPhone where no TV is available. Later, he imagines the same person finishing that episode the next morning while standing in line at a "local café," reinforcing the perception that platform mobility can serve as a means either for alleviating boredom or for making periods of enforced waiting more productive.

Although Kilar eventually highlights the ability to watch Hulu Plus on the go, it's worth emphasizing that his narrative initially emphasizes mobility within the home, allowing users to move between devices within the home, a practice that appears to be relatively common as users can take their iPhone to bed with them, settling down to watch a favorite show (rather than, or in addition to, reading in bed) before falling asleep. It's also worth noting that this platform mobility should not be equated with what a number of film critics have described as "platform agnosticism," the belief that media audiences, especially younger viewers, regard all screens as essentially equal. In fact, it seems unlikely that watching on portable screens will ever fully supplant other screens. If anything, audiences have become more acutely aware of the varying implications of screen choice. In fact, this "heightened platform consciousness," to use Charles Acland's phrase, remains an integral part of the process through which users negotiate their relationship to screen culture. This is a variation of what Henry Jenkins refers to as the "black box fallacy." As Jenkins writes, "there will be no single black box that controls the flow of media into our homes. Thanks to the proliferation of channels and the portability of new computing and telecommunications technologies, we are entering an era when media will be everywhere."[14] In fact, platform mobility, which encourages users to move between devices, illustrates that consumers are unlikely to receive content through a single platform.

Cord Cutting

These attempts to develop a commonsense understanding of how media-industry systems operate have also led to increased attention on the changing value of media texts. Although the promises of personal media mobility are enticing, they typically ignore the degree to which Netflix and Hulu Plus are caught up in a larger pay-per-view culture in which media companies seek to shape (and often limit) access to movies and TV shows, with complex implications for media consumers and producers. This pay-per-view society, in which consumers pay for temporary access to a movie or TV show, shapes not only how media industries package and distribute TV shows and movies but also how consumers perceive their relationship to media institutions. By describing the entertainment industry in terms of a pay-per-view society, I am not suggesting that consumers will necessarily pay every time they decide to watch a movie or television show. Both Hulu Plus and Netflix offer monthly subscription plans rather than rentals of individual shows or movies. Instead, we are increasingly moving toward distribution models that require consumers to pay for temporary, often fleeting, access to a given text, a shift that is powerfully reflected in the e-book industry, as discussed by Ted Striphas. As Striphas notes, publishers have instituted such technological controls as "time-limit licenses," usage caps, and encryption systems, as well as legal mechanisms such as the Digital Millennium Copyright Act, to develop tighter control over how e-books are disseminated, a challenge similar to the one faced by the TV and movie industries as they seek to define how users will access, own, and store digital content.[15]

The Netflix and Hulu Plus apps were released amidst a turbulent moment in the history of movie and television distribution. The changes included a significant decline in DVD sales, numbers that were not significantly affected by the introduction of the HD format, Blu-Ray. According to the *Los Angeles Times*, DVD sales revenue declined by 7 percent in 2010, continuing a streak of several years in which DVD sales decreased.[16] In addition, there was a slight but noteworthy decline in pay TV subscriptions, a practice that became known in industry discourse as "cord cutting." Although nearly 90 percent of all households continued to subscribe to some form of pay TV, whether satellite or cable, there were a number of anecdotal reports that tracked consumers choosing to shift away from costly cable subscriptions in order to consume media on an assemblage of platforms and devices, such as Netflix, Hulu, and YouTube instead.[17] The concept of cord cutting implies, of course, breaking a consumer's dependence upon cable TV as a provider of entertainment and information. Although the embedded metaphor of the mother-child relationship is rarely explored in industry discourse, it is instructive to consider the ways in which it frames the relationship between consumers and the media industry. Despite our potential separation anxieties regarding the safety, comfort, and familiarity associated with cable or satellite TV, we no longer need to be "fed" access to television through (expensive) subscription services. In addition, cord cutting also places emphasis on the potential for mobility, on the ability to consume content wherever we want. Technology blogs, such as *New Tee Vee*, actively promoted cord cutting as a viable alternative to cable and satellite subscriptions, implying that Netflix and Hulu could cover most users' entertainment interests. However, in a video entitled "Cord Cutters' Confessions," the *New Tee Vee* editors acknowledged some limits to cord cutting, including the lack of access to live TV, especially when it came to sporting events, as well as a sense of isolation caused by the fact that cord cutters would be unable to watch TV shows or movies that are not available online. Thus, although cord cutting offered many of the benefits of à la carte programming—consumers ostensibly don't have to pay for programming they don't want to watch—platform mobility also brings with it the transformation of TV from a mass medium designed to address an entire nation to an individualized, atomized one that focuses on smaller segments of fans and niche audiences.

To some extent, this pay-per-view culture opens up new access points to movies and TV shows, with the result that media texts in any individual format may now be regarded as disposable. Thus platform mobility potentially decreases the value of any specific iteration of text. At the same time, this ability to access a movie, an episode of a TV series, or even an entire set of episodes (say, an entire season of *Lost*), allows us to direct more concentrated attention toward these texts. If we are provided with relatively permanent and ubiquitous access to a "copy" of a TV show or movie, the overall value of any single copy diminishes, even while our engagement with selected texts increases. These contradictions have been shaped by earlier models of digital distribution, in which movies and TV shows are seen as files we can access independently of any schedule, whether through the popularization of digital video recorders or DVD box sets that anthologize entire seasons of TV series, allowing fans to watch episodes at their convenience. As Jason Mittell argues in his discussion of DVRs, these media tools are "part of an ever-changing menu of programming to be accessed at our convenience."[18] Mittell's arguments illustrate the ways in which DVRs actively derail the effects of the "flow" produced by television networks seeking to keep audiences consistently engaged and tuned in. Similarly, as Derek Kompare argues (about DVD box sets of TV shows in particular), digital distribution has led to "a regime premised on individual choice, marked by highly diversified content, atomized reception, and malleable technologies."[19] Netflix and the iPhone extend this logic even while complicating some of the original assumptions discussed by Kompare and Mittell. Although this menu-driven approach to storing and accessing TV shows persists, the role of the DVD as a "tangible media object" (to use Kompare's phrase) has been destabilized by the mobility of streaming video.

This ubiquitous access complicates traditional models of film and television distribution. Despite the promises of individual choice and freedom, pay-per-view culture actually depends upon limiting access to content, at least at selected times in the life of a film or TV show or by restricting where users can access a video or how they can share it. As Jeff Ulin argues, movie studios are "financing and distribution machines" focused on maximizing profit.[20] This entails maintaining control over various intellectual properties and dividing up those rights as carefully as possible as a movie circulates through a variety of media channels. This desire to control access to content was illustrated in the conflicts between the movie studios and the DVD rental companies Redbox and Netflix. Because studios believed that the cheap rentals offered by Netflix and Redbox were cutting into DVD sales, they sought to create a "retail window" that would allow studios to sell DVDs at retail prices for several weeks before they would be available for rental through Netflix and Redbox. Both companies agreed to a twenty-eight-day window, with Netflix accepting the terms in order to gain access to the rights for more streaming content that could be disseminated on platforms ranging from laptop computers to iPhones and via set-top boxes to users' TV sets.[21] Thus, rather than offering ubiquitous access to an unlimited range of film content, Netflix is embedded in a larger system of "controlled consumption."

Broken Windows

Discussions of streaming video—especially when they are caught up in the hype over platform mobility—almost invariably emphasize the idea of unlimited choice, a concept that Chris Anderson famously characterized as the "long tail." He argued that online retailers such as Amazon, Apple's iTunes store, and Netflix were better positioned to profit in a digital economy because they were able to expand their catalogues through the use of digital storage.[22] Similarly, David Denby, in an article lamenting the "platform agnosticism" of youthful media consumers, worried that the movies available for download on the video iPod were "the first trickles of a flood" that would ultimately displace the theatrical experience. In fact, digital distribution, like other modes of media distribution, depends on studios' retaining some forms of scarcity. The former Lucasfilm, Paramount, and Universal executive Jeff Ulin bluntly argues that "distribution is all about maximizing discrete periods of exclusivity."[23] Instead of providing unlimited access to film and TV series, mobile platforms often offer only a narrow selection of choices.

Despite this ability to access mobile entertainment, the industrial implications of Netflix on the iPhone are less than clear. Given the rapidly changing media environment and the emphasis on platform mobility, it is tempting to view Netflix as changing industry practices. However, as David Poland points out, Netflix's decision to focus on streaming video rather than its DVD-by-mail service has actually pushed its "window" further away from the theatrical release date, leaving Netflix to claim rights to stream movies typically found in DVD "remainder bins," well after studios have exhausted other revenue streams. For Poland, "streaming . . . is the third and nearly final window."[24] Poland goes on to point out that in November 2010 only one of the previous twenty Oscar winners for Best Picture and two of the top-twenty highest-grossing films of all time were available through Netflix's streaming service, suggesting that the promises of "DVD anywhere" don't refer to all DVDs, at least not in the current distribution system. In addition, many cable television channels that pay for syndication rights to first-run TV shows have begun to see Netflix and other streaming services as competitors; the chairman and CEO of Turner Broadcasting, Phil Kent, warned TV show suppliers that selling to subscription video-on-demand services such as Netflix will "have a significant impact on what we'll be willing to pay for programming or even bid at all."[25]

Portable-media consumers also faced geographical barriers when it came to accessing movies and TV shows. Although Netflix expanded its streaming service into Canada early in 2010 and Latin America in summer 2011, the service did not have the rights to stream a number of films there, a restriction that Tama Leaver has referred to as "the tyranny of digital distance."[26] Even though Netflix established a version of their streaming video service in Canada, they could only offer a "fraction" of the movies available in the United States. Furthermore, restrictions on bandwidth use have made it difficult for Canadian users to take full advantage of the streaming service. According to *CTV News*, just days after Netflix announced its Canadian launch, "Rogers

Communications Inc. changed the data limits on its 'Lite' Internet service from 25 gigabytes per month to 15."[27] As a result, most Canadian users were limited to about half an hour of video content per day unless they were willing to pay significantly more for their Internet service. Likewise, both Hulu and Netflix are unavailable in much of Europe, a situation that complicates conversations about popular films and TV shows for international scholars and fans. Although non-U.S. consumers may be familiar with movies and TV shows from reading about them online or seeing promotional clips and trailers, their access to watching those videos legally through online or streaming channels may be constrained.

A similar example is the music service Spotify, which allows users to listen to and share any song by any artist for free. The service, which is paid for through advertising and monthly premium subscription packages, allows users to store music on their tablets, iPods, and mobile phones and is available throughout much of Europe. This access has led observers to compare the service to a public "utility," readily available to provide music on tap. However, because of more complicated rights systems, the service was unavailable in the United States until 2011. In most European countries, Spotify's founder, Daniel Ek, was able to negotiate with centralized national organizations of artists, while in the United States, he had to negotiate with individual labels.[28] Thus, as is the case for the movie industry, "digital distance" often proves to be a major barrier to full mobile access to entertainment.

Finally, the promotional discourse framing platform mobility sometimes obscures the materiality of delivery systems and devices. As Charles Acland reminds us, "screens are things: they are the products of industry and labor; they take up space; they are made of solid substance; they change people's bodily orientation."[29] On the one hand, Acland's comments remind us that iPhones, whether used for making phone calls or watching a movie, are material artifacts that can get lost or tossed into a junkyard. In other circumstances iPhones require users to navigate their bodily orientation toward the phone's screen if they choose to watch a movie or TV show.[30] Further, although the delivery of movies and TV shows to our iPhones may seem almost magical, the material aspects of these technologies shape their use. The Netflix app, in particular, required such a large amount of bandwidth that technology journalists speculated that Apple and Netflix waited until AT&T, the company that provides wireless service for iPhones, ended their unlimited 3G wireless data plans before releasing the app.[31] In addition, streaming video, at least for now, tends to consume battery power quickly, making it difficult to view an entire film without having to plug the phone into an electrical outlet. Thus, although the discussions of platform mobility seem to imagine an audiovisual culture in which screens are ubiquitous, spectators are mobile, and entertainment selections are infinite, that platform mobility is, in fact, constrained by a variety of technological, legal, and social factors.

Conclusion

Many of the questions about platform mobility reemerged in early 2011, just as I was completing this chapter, when six major studios—Lionsgate, Paramount, Sony, Fox, Universal, and Warner Bros.—announced the creation of UltraViolet, a digital-distribution initiative that would allow consumers to access movies and TV shows stored in the cloud. Households would be able to create accounts with up to six members who could view content via up to twelve devices. The device would allow consumers to purchase a movie once, on DVD, and then upload that content to a "digital locker," which they could access whenever or wherever, using a designated code from any of the twelve devices associated with the account.[32] In this sense, UltraViolet seemed to offer a solution to the problems associated with platform mobility. Rather than being required to purchase the same content multiple times, consumers were assured that the digital format—unlike VHS and, presumably, DVD—would never become obsolete. Although the planned service offers "lifetime content ownership rights," it remains unclear whether consumers, who are now accustomed to subscription video services such as Netflix, will be willing to pay to "own" digital content.[33] In fact, many technology observers concluded that consumers have become accustomed to the logic of platform mobility, in which they access content through various pay-per-view or subscription services.[34] Although it is difficult to predict whether users will buy in to Ultra-Violet, many users seem content to rely upon transient access to media texts. But much like the Netflix and Hulu Plus apps for the iPhone, UltraViolet is submerged in the challenges introduced by platform mobility.

Ultimately, these delivery systems point to unsettled questions in media studies today: How are viewers or users negotiating screen culture in the era of platform mobility, and how do these media-consumption practices reflect a new common sense regarding media use? Media-consumption habits involve a complex assemblage of technological artifacts, legal arrangements, and corporate negotiations, but they are also shaped by advertising, as well as the discourses of technology experts. Thus, the debates about cord cutting, in particular, reflect the development of a practical knowledge about the media ecosystem as users navigate their relationship to the platforms and delivery systems through which they consume media. Rather than viewing platform mobility as merely reinforcing a segmented, atomized media culture, we should instead engage with ways in which users adapt these tools. Understanding this complex intersection between technological form and social protocols can provide us with a clearer account of everyday screen culture in the era of media mobility.

NOTES

1. Isabel Pedersen, "'No Apple iPhone? You Must Be Canadian': Mobile Technologies, Participatory Culture, and Rhetorical Transformation," *Canadian Journal of Communication* 3 (2008): 375.

2. For a discussion of the iPhone and discourses of mobility, see Chuck Tryon, *Reinventing Cinema: Movies in the Age of Media Convergence* (New Brunswick, N.J.: Rutgers University Press, 2009).

3. "Netflix App Now Available for iPhone and iPod Touch," Netflix.com, 26 August 2010, http://netflix.mediaroom.com/index.php?s=43&item=366; Jason Kilar, "Introducing Hulu Plus: More Wherever. More Whenever. Than Ever," *Hulu Blog*, 29 June 2010, http://blog.hulu.com (15 February 2011).

4. Eliot Van Buskirk, "DVD Anywhere: Netflix Arrives on iPhone, and Doesn't Disappoint," *Wired*, 26 August 2010.

5. Lisa Gitelman, *Always Already New: Media, History, and the Data of Culture* (Cambridge, Mass.: MIT Press, 2008), 7. See also Amanda D. Lotz, *The Television Will Be Revolutionized* (New York: New York University Press, 2007), 29.

6. Raymond Williams, *Television: Technology as Cultural Form* (New York: Schocken, 1974).

7. Siva Vaidhyanathan, *Copyrights and Copywrongs: The Rise of Intellectual Property and How It Threatens Creativity* (New York: New York University Press, 2001), 181.

8. Will Richmond, "CES Takeaway #3: Mobility Is Video's Next Frontier," *Video Nuze*, 12 January 2011, http://videonuze.com/ (15 February 2011).

9. Aaron Smith, "Mobile Access 2010," Pew Internet and American Life Project, 7 July 2010, http://www.pewinternet.org/Reports/2010/Mobile-Access-2010.aspx (15 February 2011).

10. "More Americans Watching Mobile Video," *NielsenWire*, 8 December 2010, http://blog.nielsen.com/ (15 February 2011).

11. Williams, *Television*; Lisa Parks, "Flexible Microcasting: Gender, Generation, and Television-Internet Convergence," in *Television After TV: Essays on a Medium in Transition*, ed. Lynn Spigel and Jan Olsson (Durham, N.C.: Duke University Press, 2004), 137.

12. Parks, "Flexible Microcasting," 135–37; Lotz, *The Television*, 35.

13. Kilar, "Introducing Hulu Plus."

14. Charles Acland, "Curtains, Carts, and the Mobile Screen," *Screen* 50, no. 1 (Spring 2009): 148–66; Henry Jenkins, *Convergence Culture: Where Old and New Media Collide* (New York: New York University Press, 2006).

15. Ted Striphas, *The Late Age of Print: Everyday Book Culture from Consumerism to Control* (New York: Columbia University Press, 2009), 42–43.

16. Ben Fritz, "Six Studios Seek to Lift Barriers to Online Sales of Films and TV Shows," *Los Angeles Times*, 7 January 2011.

17. Ryan Lawler, "Now It's a Trend: 119K More Cords Cut in Q3," *New Tee Vee*, 17 November 2010, http://gigaom.com/video/cord-cutting-q3/; see also Ryan Lawler, "When All Content Is Personalized, Who Needs Networks," *New Tee Vee*, 17 December 2010, http://gigaom.com/video/personalization-vs-tv-networks/ (15 February 2011).

18. Jason Mittell, "TiVoing Childhood: Time-Shifting a Generation's Concept of Television," in *Flow TV: Television in the Age of Media Convergence*, ed. Michael Kackman et al. (New York: Routledge, 2011), 49.

19. Derek Kompare, "Publishing Flow: DVD Box Sets and the Reconception of Television," *Television and New Media* 4 (2006).

20. Jeff Ulin, *The Business of Media Distribution: Monetizing Film, TV, and Video Content* (New York: Focal Press, 2010), 4.

21. Chuck Tryon, "Redbox vs. Red Envelope, Or, What Happens When the Infinite Aisle Swings Through the Grocery Store," *Canadian Journal of Film Studies* 20, no. 2 (fall 2011).

22. Chris Anderson, *The Long Tail: Why the Future of Business Is Selling Less of More* (New York: Hyperion, 2006). It's worth noting that Anderson's arguments applied more to content aggregators than to content producers. Although storage costs were comparatively small, independent producers of film, video, and music often found themselves competing in an increasingly crowded marketplace.

23. David Denby, "Big Pictures: Hollywood Looks for a Future," *The New Yorker*, 8 January 2007; Ulin, *The Business of Media Distribution*, 31.

24. David Poland, "The Evolution of Netflix," *Movie City News*, 26 November 2010, http://moviecitynews.com/2010/11/the-evolution-of-netflix/ (15 February 2011).

25. Andrew Wallenstein, "Turner Chief Explains How TV Industry Will Neutralize Netflix," *PaidContent.org*, 5 January 2011, http://paidcontent.org/ (15 February 2011).

26. Tama Leaver, "Watching *Battlestar Galactica* in Australia and the Tyranny of Digital Distance," *Media International Australia* (February 2008).

27. Susan Krashinsky, "Netflix Confronting Canadian Challenges," *CTV News*, 15 August 2010, http://www.ctv.ca/generic/generated/static/business/article1866312.html (15 February 2010).

28. Neal Pollack, "Spotify Is the Coolest Music Service You Can't Use," *Wired*, 27 December 2010.

29. Acland, "Curtains, Carts, and the Mobile Screen," 149.

30. Denby complains about trying to get comfortable while attempting to watch a feature-length film on his video iPod.

31. Eliot Van Buskirk, "Netflix for iPhone Is Coming, Subject to AT&T's Data Caps," *Wired*, 7 June 2010.

32. Carolyn Giardina, "Consortium of Studios, Manufacturers Throws Weight Behind UltraViolet Management System," *Hollywood Reporter*, 6 January 2011, http://www.hollywoodreporter.com/ (15 February 2011).

33. James Niccolai, "UltraViolet Could Mean You'll Really Own that Movie," *PC World*, 7 January 2011, http://www.pcworld.com/ (15 February 2011).

34. Ryan Lawler, "UltraViolet's Real Challenge: People Don't Buy Movies Online," *New Tee Vee*, 11 January 2011, http://gigaom.com/video/ultraviolet-rental-vs-purchase/ (15 February 2011).

CHAPTER 9

Platforms, Pipelines, and Politics

The iPhone and Regulatory Hangover

JENNIFER HOLT

A T THE MACWORLD Expo in January 2007, CEO Steve Jobs announced that Apple was reinventing the phone and giving the world a "break-through Internet communications device."[1] It would do the work of a video iPod, a mobile phone, and an Internet-enabled computer all in one. It would also have patented touch-screen controls, visual voicemail, Internet browsing, video capability, and apps that could provide everything from stock market updates to surf reports. One thing it would not have: a regulatory framework to accommodate all of those services found on one device. As Jobs proclaimed, the convergence of telecommunications, media, and computing represented by the iPhone has indeed been a dream come true for consumers. For policy makers, however, it has created a nightmare.

By the time of the iPhone's launch, contemporary media and telecommunications industries had taken on new dimensions and functions that had rendered many fundamental tenets of their regulation inadequate and irrelevant. Thanks to technological advances and the ripple effect of shifting business models in the digital era, there are different industries regulated by disparate policy regimes now housed together on one device or platform. Add the dramatic pace of innovation and rapidly blurring boundaries between media and telecommunications into the mix, and the result is that the standards of regulation have grown out of touch with reality. Essentially, policy has been outpaced by technological and industrial advances, as regulators are struggling to accommodate a digital and convergent media landscape. Legal analysts agree that the pace of digitization and convergence, which has united previously separate applications and protocols in one communications platform, has also created major problems for regulators. As one legal scholar argues, "To harness the full potential of this convergence, a wholesale, bottom-up revision of basic communications law is necessary."[2] Content and carriers no longer conform to their originally designed borders or boundaries—computers now deliver phone calls, privately owned cable wires deliver "free" broadcast programming, phones now deliver information and entertainment—and that has created a regulatory crisis.

This crisis has left regulatory policy unable to address the needs of consumers, the requirements for a competitive marketplace, or the responsibilities to the public interest (which have yet to be substantively conceptualized or reimagined for a digital media environment). Instead, there are converging markets for entertainment, information, and communications being regulated by policies designed by, in, and for another era. In fact, the Federal Communications Commission (FCC) is partially regulating the iPhone and similar devices with policy fundamentals first written in the era of the telegraph.

Convergence is certainly not a new phenomenon or idea. While it has been a prominent feature of academic and popular discussion since the early 2000s, the term has a much longer history than is usually acknowledged. In fact, convergence is a concept that has been active in regulatory discourse since the 1960s. In what would become known as the *"Computer I* Inquiry," the FCC began to investigate the best way to treat and regulate computer networks that were already beginning to pose some tough questions for regulators. The agency was concerned with the growing interfaces between computers and communications and labeled this dynamic "convergence" in 1966. In the inquiry, which one attorney for the FCC labeled "a necessary precondition for the success of the Internet,"[3] it was noted that this convergence had already "given rise to a number of regulatory and policy questions within the purview of the Communications Act," and thus the FCC began grappling with some of these fundamental issues of classification and regulatory design.[4]

Forty-five years later, these regulatory and policy questions have yet to be resolved. The arrival of the Internet and subsequent accelerated convergence of distribution technologies has created a much larger "regulatory hangover"—the inability of policy to keep pace with technological developments. This disconnect has become particularly pronounced in the language and concerns of media policy, where technology has transformed communications industries and, in turn, wreaked havoc on the foundational rationales for many regulatory paradigms.

This chaos presents pressing economic, technological, and cultural dilemmas about regulation in an era of convergence. Among them: How should regulators treat a device that contains as many platforms, paradigms, and services as the iPhone? How will the battles over the Internet's regulatory classification affect the future of the iPhone and similar devices? How do contemporary regulatory politics determine the ways in which services on the iPhone will be classified and regulated in the future? This chapter will address these dynamics by examining the historical trajectory of regulating broadband networks and the role that the iPhone has played in reconceptualizing the importance of platforms and devices to the pipelines that service them.

A Ticking Timeline

In many ways, the current regulatory crisis—and hangover—is fundamentally about distribution. When the functions and purposes of distribution "pipelines" are no longer singular, which function and attendant regulatory standard should take precedence? Which rationale drives policy? The iPhone receives and transmits voice, video, and data, either through wireless telecommunications networks or wireless broadband networks. The similar ability (and regulatory permission) for wireline providers to carry numerous different types of media through one cable or wire has led to the current crisis in media and communications policy. In short, the government needs a new framework that somehow accommodates multiplatform voice and data applications and networks. This is extremely complicated, as it is often impossible to distinguish where one service ends and the other begins, such as with Internet telephony or the transmission of entertainment or data over telephone wires. As the telecommunications policy expert Rob Frieden has written, "the FCC cannot make bright line, either/or distinctions between services, and because vastly different regulatory burdens apply based on which classification the Commission picks, marketplace competition can become distorted."[5] There is also the attendant imperfect science of making content distinctions—if and where one type of content "ends" (e.g., voice) and the other "begins" (e.g., data)—when looking at convergent media services.

Additionally, there is the critical difference between *intramodal* competition (among service providers using the same technology, such as numerous wireline long-distance carriers competing with one another for phone customers) and *intermodal* competition (between different technologies providing the same service, e.g., wireless companies competing with wireline long-distance carriers). It is largely because of intermodal competition—such as video that can be provided over phone wires and telecommunications that can be provided via cable—that separate regulatory regimes are now competing with one another. Even though these providers are offering the same service to consumers, they are subject to different regulations because of their technological infrastructure.

One particularly vexing host of problems in this arena has been the regulation of Internet service providers (ISPs) and the classification of broadband services. This history of broadband regulation is one of the more contentious and contested policy histories and represents the hangover engendered by the growing disconnect between the capabilities and practices of new digital technologies and the policies designed to police them. Thus, the iPhone's simple switch that allows the user to choose between using Wi-Fi networks and AT&T's 3G network (in the United States) for an Internet connection also links the user to a host of not-so-simple regulatory battles that have been playing out for years—battles to determine how we classify and regulate content that is delivered over mobile technologies like the iPhone and how the technological infrastructure of smartphones will be treated by regulators and experienced by consumers.

Currently, in the United States there are separate laws and provisions for regulating what are known as "information services" and "telecommunications services." As of this writing, broadband service is being regulated as an "information service" under Title I of the Communications Act of 1934, as amended by the Telecommunications Act of 1996. The Telecommunications Act created the category of information services, which are defined as "the offering of a capability for generating, acquiring, storing, transforming, processing, retrieving, utilizing, or making available information via telecommunications, and includes electronic publishing, but does not include any use of any such capability for the management, control, or operation of a telecommunications system or the management of a telecommunications service."[6] In other words, they can make information available via telecommunications but they can't own or operate that system. Information services are distinguished from (and regulated less stringently than) telecommunications services, which appear under Title II of the Communications Act and have the important distinction of being *common carriers*.

The common carrier status is a crucial element of the battle over broadband classification.[7] Congress first enacted common common carrier legislation in 1910 for the telegraph and telephone.[8] "At the heart of common carriage," Tim Wu explains, "lies the idea that certain businesses are either so intimately connected, even essential, to the public good, or so inherently powerful—imagine the water or electric utilities—that they must be compelled to conduct their affairs in a nondiscriminatory way." These businesses are subject to stricter regulations as they are viewed as essential infrastructure for the national economy and public welfare and must be available to the general public without prejudice. In general, Wu notes that telecommunications, banking, energy, and transportation are identified as common carriers.[9] Broadcasters are not considered common carriers. At this point, neither are Internet service providers (even if they are telecommunications companies), and that distinction has been the focal point of contention in much of broadband's regulatory history.

Although Internet service in the United States is not currently viewed as warranting common carrier status under the law, it has historically enjoyed such privileges in the American media landscape. Indeed, the classification of broadband access as a telecommunications service is essential to preserving "net neutrality," or what are essentially common carriage principles for the Internet. The importance of maintaining these common carriage requirements are paramount for a host of cultural, economic, and industrial concerns, including the cultivation of a free and open Internet, with the flow of information not subject to influence or control by conglomerate gatekeepers, political forces, or censors of any kind; the stimulation of investment in developing platforms and technologies; and maintenance of a competitive marketplace that encourages and supports continued innovation. One only has to look at how Internet access has been manipulated by governments in China, Iran, North Korea, Cuba, and, most recently, during the January 2011 uprising in Egypt (among others) for examples of what can happen when these principles are not enshrined in new media policy.[10]

In the United States, cable has been regulated separately from both telecommunications and broadcasting, but their regulatory histories have been intertwined for many decades. One moment of this convergence can even be found in the Cable Communications Policy Act of 1984, the first federal policy specifically designed to guide the FCC's regulation of cable television. It represented a shift in the FCC's approach from restricting cable's growth to a new era of promoting its expansion. This act also had implications for the telecommunications industry (and, ultimately, the future regulation of Internet service providers) largely because it codified cross-ownership restrictions to prevent telephone companies and cable companies—sworn enemies already by that point—from owning one another. This 1984 provision basically restated the cross-ownership ban that was enacted by the FCC in 1970 and ensured that cable and telecommunications would be regulated separately.[11] Thus, cable was allowed to continue its expansion without the threat of competition from the telecommunications companies, and telephone companies were prevented from offering cable services to their local subscribers. A fierce rivalry raged on between the two, despite regulations and laws preventing the baby bells from encroaching on cable's territory, and telecommunications was forcibly kept out of the entertainment industry—and the video delivery business—until the ban was repealed in 1996.[12]

In a separate but related matter, the baby bells began lobbying for legal relief from the AT&T consent decrees in 1984 in order to get a foothold in the video market; with the Telecommunications Act of 1996, they finally got their wish. Once it was signed into law, the phone companies were allowed to operate as information providers and were no longer restricted to offering only phone services. Now, the door for was opened for telecommunications companies to begin providing cable and Internet services as well.

Still, the FCC required the phone companies to provide some measure of protection for consumers, and they were treated as common carriers when providing high-speed DSL service over their wires. Marvin Ammori, Susan Crawford, and Tim Wu harked back to this time in a widely circulated letter to FCC chairman Julius Genachowski in 2010. When urging Genachowski to protect and preserve the open Internet, they argued that given the early requirements for phone companies providing high-speed Internet service, "it is accurate to say that before 2002 Internet access was protected from discrimination."[13] Nevertheless, the cable industry did not want to be subject to the same restrictions as DSL service providers and consequently asked for an exemption from the requirements that phone companies faced. This is when the current classification debacle picked up speed.

Cable modems had historically been treated the same way as Internet service provided by phone companies—i.e., as a "telecommunications service"—but in 2000, the Ninth Circuit court ruled that cable broadband operators actually provided a combination of "telecommunications" and "information" services, offering a decision that only created greater confusion for regulators.[14] Shortly thereafter, the Bush FCC put forth its 2002 Cable Modem

Order, which defined cable Internet service providers as an information service.[15] This basically exempted ISPs from common carriage regulations by
separating them from the more heavily regulated Title II telecommunications
services. Activists have been demanding the return of the telecommunications classification for ISPs ever since, in order to preserve common carriage
principles for the Internet and regulators' ability to enforce those principles
and maintain an "open Internet."

The (re)classification drama continued, as the U.S. Ninth Circuit District
Court reversed the FCC's cable modem order in 2003 and went back to the
characterization of ISPs as telecommunications services/common carriers.
Two years later, in what became known as the "*Brand X* case," the United
States Supreme Court upheld the FCC's 2002 policy in their 2005 ruling on
National Cable and Telecommunications Association v. Brand X Internet Services.
This decision reversed the Ninth Circuit and took cable modem services back
to being classified as Title I information services. The Supreme Court's decision in the *Brand X* case reaffirmed the FCC's 2002 cable modem order and
released Internet service providers from common carriage requirements.[16]
This meant that Internet service providers were reclassified four times in five
years by federal agencies and the courts, ultimately arriving at the Supreme
Court's decision in 2005 that cable modem services are Title I information
services and, therefore, not common carriers.

One of the most interesting aspects of the *Brand X* decision was the scath-
ing dissent (moment of clarity?) from Justice Antonin Scalia. Scalia disagreed
with the court's reasoning that since cable modem service did not offer high-
speed Internet access separately and by itself—it needed the help of other services, applications, and functions—then it did not actually "offer" high-speed
access to the Internet. Scalia argued that this was analogous to a pizzeria
saying that it did not offer pizza delivery, even though it bakes pizzas and
bring them directly to your house. "The pet store may have a policy of selling
puppies only with leashes," he continued, "but any customer will say that it
does offer puppies—because a leashed puppy is still a puppy, even though
it is not offered on a 'stand-alone' basis." So just as pet stores bundle puppies with leashes and pizzerias bundle baking with delivery, Scalia saw that
cable modem bundled cable and telecommunications services and refused to
deny the existence of either one. He concluded by saying that "after all is said
and done, after all the regulatory cant has been translated, and the smoke of
agency expertise blown away, it remains perfectly clear that someone who
sells cable-modem service is 'offering' telecommunications." As for the court's

decision, Scalia finished his dissent by simply stating: "It is a sadness that the Court should go so far out of its way to make bad law."[17]

Nevertheless, the court had spoken. The FCC then based its own Internet Policy Statement (adopted in August 2005, less than two months after the *Brand X* decision) on the Telecommunications Act, which holds separate regulatory regimes for carriers providing telephony and those providing information services.[18] The Supreme Court decision and the resulting regulatory approach by the FCC has drawn the agency into an "existential crisis" according to media reform group Free Press, "leaving the agency unable to protect consumers in the broadband marketplace, and unable to implement the National Broadband Plan."[19] This crisis was evident when the FCC later censured Comcast for "throttling bandwidth hogs"[20] or limiting the services of customers who were on BitTorrent and using more than their fair share of Comcast's bandwidth. The FCC said that what is known as throttling Internet traffic (restricting it) was illegal and in violation of the FCCs rules to "preserve and promote the vibrant and open character of the Internet."[21] Although the company was not fined and no rules had been set up, Comcast still turned around and sued the FCC over its order—and won. The FCC's sanction was struck down by the D.C. Circuit Court of Appeals in April 2010 because the court ruled that the FCC did not have authority under Title I of the Communication Act to regulate the Internet or tell Comcast what it could or could not do. Therefore, in somewhat of a catch-22, the decision to regulate ISPs as information services also, according to this court, removed the agency's authority over Internet regulation.

The consumer advocacy group Public Knowledge argued that the FCC's decision not to call ISPs common carriers was based, in part, on the unrealized expectation that competition in the broadband sector would flourish.[22] There are rarely, if ever, more than two ISPs to choose from in any given market in America. This situation is completely different in other parts of the world; in some European countries, for instance, there is often a choice of more than twenty different Internet service providers. Furthermore, the U.S. providers that have emerged have hardly shown themselves to be worthy stewards of consumer rights or concerned with customer service. Comcast has been particularly egregious in this regard, blocking BitTorrent and other peer-to-peer sites back in 2007 and threatening in 2010 to block Netflix unless the service paid a fee for the bandwidth it requires.[23] The current state of indecision leaves consumers (and content providers) vulnerable, leaves pipelines in control, and leaves devices like the iPhone at the mercy of ISPs who have the power to deliver value (and valuable content) to these platforms—and the power to take it away.

The Politics of Technology

As a result of the D.C. Circuit Court's decision in April 2010, the FCC found itself with no legal authority to preserve any type of "net neutrality" without ISPs being classified as common carriers. This sent the FCC's legal argument for enforcing an "open Internet" into chaos: it was based on their 2005 Internet Policy Statement, but according to the courts, the agency lacked the legislative mandate necessary to continue. The Telecommunications Act did not specifically say the FCC could regulate ISPs or the Internet. Therefore, Congress would have to pass a law giving the FCC the authority to do so.

At the time of this writing, that is not looking likely—especially if the March 2010 congressional hearings on the National Broadband Plan are any indication. Most discussions of net neutrality met with great hostility, particularly from Republican members of the House who are the current majority. Representative Mike Rogers (R-MI) confronted FCC chairman Julius Genachowski on his proposals, arguing that the agency should not stand in the way of free-market competition. "We ought to get out of their way and let competition reign the day," Rogers said. "Netscape . . . [and] Facebook . . . didn't happen b/c of this social justice notion, 'we're going to have this exchange of information, and we're going to be in the backyard and have Kumbaya and play drums.' It happened because somebody was going to make some money."[24] Rhetoric like this is emblematic of how undeniably powerful and enduring the mythological construct of the "free market" remains. Remarkably, it still endures in the wake of the 2008 economic crash and its attendant critical lessons on the dangers of deregulating crucial sectors of the economy, and despite the fact that ISPs have already proven that the competition and consumer benefits that were supposed to arise out of the FCC's 2003 cable modem order never came to pass.

In the midst of this regulatory limbo, in August 2010, Google and Verizon offered up their own "legislative framework" for the FCC to consider when crafting the nation's Internet access policies.[25] These companies were strange bedfellows indeed. Google had been a longtime supporter of net neutrality and had been rather active in urging the public to join the fight to preserve an open Internet.[26] After all, its business model depends on billions of consumers being able to access its properties (YouTube, Google, Gmail) quickly and without having to pay extra for speedy service. Verizon, on the other hand, has fought against the open Internet as the company has much to gain financially from a "tiered" system that could charge content providers more depending on the speed of transmission. The proposal included arguments for transparency, limiting the FCC's jurisdiction, and assorted loopholes for managing networks and eliminating "net neutrality" requirements for wireless services.

The arrogance of two major stakeholders purporting to help the FCC establish policy to regulate themselves might have been funny if it did not have such a serious effect on shaping the terms of debate for the press, lawmakers, and the FCC. In fact, just four months after Google and Verizon proffered their immodest proposal, the FCC passed new net-neutrality rules that looked strikingly similar. In December 2010, hoping everyone might be on vacation and away from their computers, the FCC came out with new net-neutrality rules that didn't make anyone happy, leading many to label them "fake net neutrality." These rules echoed many of the principles put forth by the companies they would be regulating, most notably in their support of nondiscrimination practices—except for all wireless networks. The three-to-two vote along party lines did protect content providers and consumers from "throttling" and said the ISPs cannot adjust providers' connection speeds on wired Internet service. Nevertheless, it left wireless wide open for discriminatory practices at a time when Internet traffic is moving steadily away from wired devices and relying more and more on wireless networks.

The community of policy scholars, journalists, and activists following this issue were largely disdainful of the FCC's rules as they were crafted. Rob Frieden encapsulated most complaints quite succinctly when he wrote, "The rationale for exempting wireless does not pass the smell test. . . . The technical and operational aspects of wireless strongly necessitate the non-discrimination requirement."[27] As Lawrence Lessig observed, "Policymakers, using an economics framework set in the 1980s, convinced of its truth and too arrogant to even recognize its ignorance, will allow the owners of the 'tubes' to continue to unmake the Internet—precisely the effect of Google and Verizon's policy framework."[28] A cofounder of *Wired* magazine, John Battelle, weighed in on the partnership as well: "Imagine if, back in 1997, we had ceded the early Web economy to Comcast and AT&T so they could create 'choke points' that 'gave us what we wanted.' Where would we be now?"[29]

Almost immediately after the FCC's announcement, Verizon had one of its own: in January 2011, the company asked a federal appeals court to toss out the net-neutrality rules just put forth by the FCC. This was despite the watered-down rules' being almost exactly what Verizon proposed with Google just a month before, particularly in areas such as consumer protection, nondiscrimination, transparency, "reasonable network management," and treatment of wireless.[30] Verizon's attorney in the proceedings had led Comcast's 2008 lawsuit against the FCC (and won), getting the courts to say that the FCC did not have the authority over the broadband Internet-access service at issue in that case. Verizon claimed that the rules were illegal and asked for the whole net-neutrality order to be vacated by the court. Despite the similarities to its own plan, despite the fact that the rules were clearly written with overriding concern for Verizon's interests, Verizon was unhappy enough about the threat of FCC regulation in any form that it went to the courts. "We are deeply concerned by the FCC's assertion of broad authority for sweeping new regulation of broadband networks and the Internet itself," Verizon senior vice president and deputy general counsel Michael Glover said. "We believe this assertion of authority goes well beyond any authority provided by Congress, and creates uncertainty for the communications industry, innovators, investors and consumers."[31]

Essentially, Verizon did not want the FCC to exercise any authority over broadband networks or the Internet, and the company would rather take the odds that Congress—a body much slower to act and full of members who take millions of dollars from the telecommunications industry—might be more sympathetic to its needs than President Obama's FCC. This strategy of appealing to Congress is more in line with Verizon's larger goals, anyhow—much like legal analysts and consumer-advocacy groups (although for different reasons), the company has been quite vocal about the need for major renovations to the current legislative framework and the growing disconnect between current industry conditions and those in place at the time that key regulations were conceived. Verizon vice president Thomas Tauke has said the proposed use of Title II (labeling broadband as a common carrier telecommunications service) highlights "the danger of attempting to apply statutory provisions intended for the telephone industry of the 1900s to the communications and Internet world of the 21st Century. . . . Now is the time to focus on updating the law affecting the Internet."[32] Verizon's public positions are representative of most telecommunications companies, which have held inconsistent and contradictory positions on regulation—demanding it one minute, condemning it the next.

Even the iPhone has been caught up in the politicking, with the industry consultant Bret Swanson testifying before the FCC that it might not have been developed if net neutrality was in place. "The Apple iPhone may never have emerged if we had blocked or discouraged the type of 'exclusive,' 'discriminatory' deals like the one Apple (a new entrant to the mobile market) struck with AT&T," he claimed. "Apple's entry was a move fraught with uncertainty, and the partnership with AT&T allowed both sides to make the investments of time and money necessary to execute a monumental project. The iPhone unleashed wave after wave of innovation in the mobile arena—like 'app stores'—thus pushing all competitors at many layers of the wireless value chain towards more dynamism and openness than ever before."[33] Such testimony and public posturing of various players like Apple has helped to define the ways in which the technologies at issue are discussed, debated, and framed for lawmakers. This particular example of using the iPhone's success as a platform to make an argument for the care and feeding of pipelines is quite shrewd but ultimately supports the interest of ISPs, as opposed to the iPhones or any other platforms that they service.

Dumb Pipes, Smartphones

In the end, these infrastructure politics are also helping to redefine the power dynamics between platforms and pipelines, with Apple and the iPhone playing a significant role in this shift. Indeed, Apple basically changed the wireless business model, creating a phone that had value in and of itself. Some have argued that the iPhone has actually transformed the U.S. mobile-phone industry, like *Wired* editor Fred Vogelstein. "For decades," he writes, "wireless carriers have treated manufacturers like serfs, using access to their networks as leverage to dictate what phones will get made, how much they will cost, and what features will be available on them. Handsets were viewed largely as cheap, disposable lures, massively subsidized to snare subscribers and lock them into using the carriers' proprietary services. But the iPhone upsets that balance of power."[34] As a result, emphasis in the marketplace is increasingly focused on the device itself (platform) instead of the service (pipeline)—the United States is full of iPhone owners who will tell you that they actually buy and keep their phone for reasons that have nothing to do with AT&T's service and that the service, in fact, is the worst part about owning the phone.

This has not hurt AT&T's competitive position—yet. AT&T and Verizon currently enjoy 60 percent of the wireless market share of revenue and subscribers in the United States and continue to increase these numbers thanks to the iPhone. But it may hurt Apple's credibility with consumers, particularly if the pipelines don't improve, because the competition on all platforms is growing stronger. By originally partnering with AT&T, the country's largest telecommunications company, Tim Wu notes, "Apple was aligning itself with the nemesis of everything Google, the Internet, and once even Apple itself stood for."[35] Interestingly, it was (former) Google CEO Eric Schmidt who was actually on stage with Jobs at the original iPhone launch in 2007. However, within just a few years, Schmidt was no longer anywhere to be seen around Jobs after several business disputes and intensifying competition between Apple and Google drove a wedge between the companies and Schmidt resigned from Apple's board of directors in 2009.

Nevertheless, this power shift from delivery systems to devices in the eyes of consumers (and marketers) has changed the way that carriers and manufacturers are conducting business in the $150 billion wireless industry. Part of this can be ascribed to the role of Steve Jobs and his management of the relationship between Apple and AT&T. Still, Vogelstein has argued that by giving so much control to Jobs, AT&T "risked turning its vaunted—and expensive—network into a 'dumb pipe,' a mere conduit for content rather than the source of that content."[36] Whether this newly ascribed agency to consumers, manufacturers, and developers has turned wireless networks into dumb pipes—carriers without agency—has yet to be determined, particularly by regulators. In fact, that is precisely what is at stake: how conscious, how active, how controlling can these pipelines actually be when delivering content to smartphones? A dumb pipe is traditionally an open pipe, so as far as net-neutrality advocates are concerned—the dumber the better. In all likelihood, however, regulators, lobbyists, consumers, lawyers, judges, and politicians will continue to spar over this until regulatory language is rewritten for a convergent, digital, intermodal, multiplatform era.

NOTES

1. The video of Jobs's keynote at the MacWorld Expo in January 2007 (with transcript) can be found at http://dotsub.com/view/d924d37a-caad-449a-a898-af8cb68f790b (15 February 2011).

2. John T. Nakahata, "Regulating Information Platforms: The Challenge of Rewriting Communications Regulation from the Bottom Up," *Telecommunications and High Technology Law* 1 (2002): 98–99.

3. Robert Cannon, "The Legacy of the Federal Communications Commission's Computer Inquiries," *Federal Communications Law Journal* 55 (2003): 167–206.

4. Federal Communications Commission, "Regulatory and Policy Problems Presented by the Interdependence of Computer and Communication Services and Facilities," Notice of Inquiry, 7 FCC 2d 11, 8 Rad. Reg. 2d (P&F) 1567 (1966).

5. Rob Frieden, "What Do Pizza Delivery and Information Services Have in Common? Lessons from Recent Judicial and Regulatory Struggles with Convergence," *Rutgers Computer and Technology Law Journal* 2 (2006): 247.

6. From Communications Act of 1934, 47 U.S.C. § 153, sec. 3, 20 stat. (1934)

7. The Communications Act of 1934 declares that it is "unlawful for any common carrier to make any unjust or unreasonable discrimination in charges, practices, classifications, regulations, facilities, or services for or in connection with like communication service, directly or indirectly, by any means or device, or to make or give any undue or unreasonable preference or advantage to any particular person, class of persons, or locality, or to subject any particular person, class of persons, or locality to any undue or unreasonable prejudice or disadvantage."

8. See Mann-Elkins Act, Pub. L. No. 61-218, 36 Stat 539 (1910).

9. Tim Wu, *The Master Switch: The Rise and Fall of Information Empires* (New York: Knopf, 2010), 58.

10. See Lucie Morillon and Jean-François Julliard, "Web 2.0 Versus Control 2.0," Reporters Without Borders report, March 18, 2010, http://en.rsf.org/web-2-0-versus -control-2-0-18-03-2010,36697. Also see Cristina Venegas, *Digital Dilemmas: The State, the Individual, and Digital Media in Cuba* (New Brunswick, N.J.: Rutgers University Press, 2010), for an in-depth look at the complexities of Internet censorship in Cuba.

11. The cross-ownership ban would last until 1996 when it was removed by the Telecommunications Act.

12. See Jennifer Holt, *Empires of Entertainment* (New Brunswick, N.J.: Rutgers University Press, 2011), 145–47.

13. Letter from Marvin Ammori, Susan Crawford, Tim Wu to Julius Genachowski, 30 April 2010, http://www.freepress.net/files/Crawford_Ammori_Wu_Letter.pdf (15 February 2011).

14. See AT&T Co. v. City of Portland, 216 F.3d 871, 876-80 (9th Cir. 2000).

15. "FCC Classifies Cable Modem Service as 'Information Service,'" FCC news release, 14 March 2002, http://www.fcc.gov/Bureaus/Cable/News_Releases/2002/ nrcb0201.html (15 February 2011).

16. National Cable and Telecommunications Association v. Brand X Internet Services, 545 U.S. 967 (2005).

17. Justice Scalia, "Dissent in National Cable & Telecommunicaitons Assn. V. Brand X Internet Services," 545 US 976 (2005), part 1, http://www.law.cornell.edu/ supct/html/04-277.ZD.html (15 February 2011).

18. Federal Communications Commission, "FCC Policy Statement, 05-151," 5 August 2005, http://hraunfoss.fcc.gov/edocs_public/attachmatch/DOC-260433A1.pdf (15 February 2011).

19. Matthew Lasar, "Comcast 1, FCC 0: What to Look for in the Inevitable Rematch," *Ars Technica*, April 2010, http://arstechnica.com/telecom/news/2010/04/ comcast-1-fcc-0-what-to-look-for-in-the-inevitable-rematch.ars (15 February 2011).

20. Andy Kessler, "The iPhone, Net Neutrality, and the FCC," *Wall Street Journal*, 10 June 2010.

21. FCC, "Policy Statement, 05-151."

22. Matthew Lasar, "New Regulatory Battle Brewing Over ISP Classification," *Ars Technica*, February 2010, http://arstechnica.com/telecom/news/2010/02/are-isps-common-carriers-let-the-debate-begin.ars (15 February 2011).

23. See Brian Stelter, "Netflix Partner Says Comcast 'Toll' Threatens Online Video Delivery," *New York Times*, 29 November 2010.

24. Mike Rogers is quoted from Hearings on National Broadband Plan, 25 March 2010, House Committee on Energy and Commerce (Subcommitttee on Communications, Technology, and the Internet). Transcripts and video available at http://www.c-spanvideo.org/program/BroadbandPlan.

25. See "Verizon-Google Legislative Framework Proposal," http://docs.google.com/viewer?url=http://www.google.com/googleblogs/pdfs/verizon_google_legislative_framework_proposal_081010.pdf&pli=1.

26. See "A Note to Google Users on Net Neutrality," http://www.google.com/help/netneutrality_letter.html (15 February 2011).

27. "The Good, the Bad, and the Ugly in the Google-Verizon Legislative Framework," *TeleFrieden* blog, 9 August 2010, http://telefrieden.blogspot.com/2010/08/google-and-verizon-have-developed.html (15 February 2011).

28. Lawrence Lessig, "Another Deregulation Debacle," *New York Times*, 10 August 2010.

29. Chris Anderson, "The Web is Dead? A Debate," *Wired*, 17 August 2010.

30. See Nate Anderson, "Why Is Verizon Suing Over Net Neutrality Rules It Once Supported?" *Ars Technica*, January 2011, http://arstechnica.com/tech-policy/news/2011/01/verizon-sues-over-net-neutrality-rules-it-once-supported.ars (15 February 2011).

31. "Verizon in Challenge to FCC on 'Net Neutrality,'" unsigned, *Ottowa Citizen*, 20 January 2011, http://www.ottawacitizen.com/news/Verizon+challenge+neutrality/4141460/story.html (15 February 2011).

32. Matthew Lasar, "Verizon: FCC Is a Haunted House and Can't Regulate the 'Net," *Ars Technica*, March 2010, http://arstechnica.com/telecom/news/2010/03/verizon-fcc-is-a-haunted-house-that-cant-regulate-the-net.ars (15 February 2011).

33. Bret T. Swanson's comments before the FCC in the matter of Preserving the Open Internet, Broadband Industry Practices, http://fjallfoss.fcc.gov/ecfs/document/view?id=7020441342 (15 February 2011).

34. Fred Vogelstein, "The Untold Story: How the iPhone Blew Up the Wireless Industry," *Wired*, 9 January 2008.

35. Wu, *The Master Switch*, 271.

36. Vogelstein, "The Untold Story."

CHAPTER 10

A Walled Garden Turned Into a Rain Forest

PELLE SNICKARS

M ORE THAN TEN months after the iPhone was introduced, Lev Grossman in *Time* magazine reflected upon the most valuable invention of 2007. At first he could not make up his mind. Admittedly there had been a lot written about the iPhone, he argued—if truth be told, a massive number of articles, with extensive media coverage, hype, "and a lot of guff too." Grossman hesitated. He confessed that he could not type on the iPhone; it was too slow, too expensive, and even too big. "It doesn't support my work e-mail. It's locked to AT&T. Steve Jobs secretly hates puppies. And—all together now—we're sick of hearing about it!"

Yet when Grossman had finished with his litany of complaints, the iPhone was nevertheless in his opinion, "the best thing invented this year." He gave five reasons. First of all, the iPhone had made design important for smartphones. At a time when most tech companies did not treat form seriously, Apple had made style a trademark of their seminal product. Of course, Apple had always known that nice, smart design was as important as good technology, and the iPhone was therefore no exception. Still, it was something of a stylistic epitome—and to Grossman even "pretty." Another of his reasons had to do with touch. Apple didn't invent the touch screen, but according to Grossman the company engineers had finally understood what to do with it. In short, Apple's engineers used the touch screen to innovate past the graphic user interface, which Apple once pioneered with the Mac, to create "a whole new kind of interface, a tactile one that gives users the illusion of actually physically manipulating data with their hands."

Another reason, in Grossman's view, that the iPhone was the most valuable invention of 2007, was its benefit to the mobile market in general. On the one hand, the iPhone was built to evolve, and in years to come (as we now know) he expected numerous upgraded versions. On the other hand, the device would all likely push competing smartphone companies to invent new products that would work even better, not the least in regards to service providers. Mobile phones are lame because "cell-phone-service providers hobble developers with lame rules about what they can and can't do."

The main reason, however, that Lev Grossman decided to name the iPhone the tech invention of 2007 was as simple as it was technologically complex. In his view, the iPhone was not a phone—but rather a mobile computing platform. When Apple came up with the idea and produced the iPhone, "it didn't throw together some cheap-o-bare-bones firmware," Grossman praised. It took OS X and "squished it down to fit inside the iPhone's elegant glass-and-stainless-steel case." In his opinion this made the iPhone into more than just a tech gadget; rather, it seemed to him the first genuine walk-around computer. Thus, as a potent hardware it could potentially be filled with numerous wonderful programs and applications. In fact, one of the trends of 2007, as Grossman finally put it, was the idea that computing belonged not only in cyberspace but more so in the real world. The iPhone simply got "applications like Google Maps out onto the street, where we really need them."[1]

The iPhone as Platform

The notion of "platform" is frequently associated with the Web 2.0 phenomena. As is well known, after 2005, social media and user-driven content rapidly became ubiquitous on the net; Facebook and YouTube began their rise to fame, and the Web changed in a cumulative rather than technological way. Targeting the iPhone as a mobile computation platform fits nicely into this new digital pattern, and, as stated in the introduction to this book, there is more than one resemblance between the iPhone and YouTube. Indeed, already in 2007 the iPhone promised an endless array of differentiated usage, which gradually became a fact. Today, the iPhone is not only a great e-mailing device and game console; it can transform itself into a flute, a blood-pressure machine, or even an 8 mm vintage camera. In short, perceived—and increasingly promoted by Apple—as a software platform, the iPhone has become a universal device with a seemingly endless array of possibilities.

Such a teleological way of looking at technological devices, however, remains a poor way of understanding computer history. On the contrary, it needs to be stressed that at the time of Lev Grossman's writing there was no tech-determinational factor regulating or even dictating a development in this direction. In Apple's initial iPhone TV commercials, for example, nothing is mentioned about "apps"—let alone a mobile computing platform. When launched the iPhone was perceived and marketed as a smart *phone* to surf, e-mail, and call with. Nothing else. Apple, in fact, argued it had reinvented the phone, which in a sense was missing the point because calling with the new device soon became a peripheral activity. Still, Apple decided to call the device an *iPhone*: interpersonal communication was central and the practice of calling was, hence, upgraded with the iPhone's innovative design and multitouch display. An iPod could play music—which also became possible on the iPhone—and in many ways Apple saw the iPhone as an upgraded continuation of the earlier device. However, it was still hardware that Apple had manufactured and hence obtained absolute control over, making it no different from other company products.

Nonetheless, 2007 saw quite a lot of debate and discussion as to whether Apple would allow other, external developers to write code for the iPhone. Initially, the company would only accept what were then called "Web applications," which ran through the browser Safari. It seems, however, that Apple (and notably Jobs) gradually altered its opinion regarding these third-party applications, in spite of company tradition. Given what was to come, this became an utterly important change of mind. In mid-October 2007, some weeks before Grossman's article, Jobs uploaded a short blog post on Apple's Hot News—simply signed "Steve"—where he promised to release a software development kit for the iPhone's iOS:

> Let me just say it: We want native third party applications on the iPhone, and we plan to have an SDK in developers' hands in February [2008]. We are excited about creating a vibrant third party developer community around the iPhone and enabling hundreds of new applications for our users. With our revolutionary multi-touch interface, powerful hardware and advanced software architecture, we believe we have created the best mobile platform ever for developers. . . . It will take until February to release

an SDK because we're trying to do two diametrically opposed things at once—provide an advanced and open platform to developers while at the same time protect iPhone users from viruses, malware, privacy attacks, etc.[2]

Lev Grossman's vision of the iPhone as a mobile platform was a direct consequence of Jobs's post—and maybe the core reason that it was a significant invention for him. Nevertheless, Grossman made the ironic comment, that "after a lot of throat-clearing"—not to mention the claimed Apple "protection" from "attacks"—Jobs finally decided to open up the iPhone. Furthermore, Jobs hoped to create a vibrant "community" around the device, a term (like the notion of platform) often used in relation to Web 2.0. In effect, as Grossman stated, this meant that "you" and people other than Apple employees "will be able to develop software for it too. Ever notice all that black blank space on the iPhone's desktop? It's about to fill up with lots of tiny, pretty, useful icons."[3]

And fill up it did. If Jobs envisioned "hundreds of new applications" in his blog post, today there are more than 500,000 apps available in the App Store. Apple has certainly created a lively community around the iPhone, which is as vibrant as it is profitable: "There's almost no limit to what your iPhone can do."[4] Indeed, perceiving the iPhone as an "open platform" in many ways makes it resemble sites such as YouTube, at least in an economic sense. Like YouTube, Apple's App Store is a hybrid economy where free programs and apps intermingle with ad-funded and purchasable apps, but every transaction (be it in terms of money or data) is controlled by Apple. The Apple SDK kit is essentially open to any developer—even if the resulting code always needs to be approved by Apple. The core difference, however, between many Web 2.0 enterprises and the App Store is that Apple remains in total control—and makes more money. Google, for example, does not supervise the uploading process on YouTube, which after all is the reason for the site's popularity and dominance. It does loosely monitor it afterward, but Apple's App Store works the other way around—on its "open platform" all apps are strictly controlled before use. Nonetheless, this kind of policing of content has resulted in a similar dominant market position.

In spite of this peculiar and extraordinary market situation, Apple has managed to develop its App Store into that "vibrant third party developer community" that Jobs once envisioned. When this universal, old-fashioned general store of code was launched during the summer of 2008—a few months after the initial SDK was released—there were approximately 500 apps available. As few tech-interested persons have missed, the number grew at an exhilarating pace. In March 2009 Apple's mobile computing platform had already attracted "new software and new functions in droves," according to Walt Mossberg. He bluntly stated that owing an iPhone was one thing, but "the App Store is what makes your device worth its price. It's the software, not the hardware, that makes these gadgets compelling."[5] In November 2009 Apple boasted more than 100,000 available apps, and the rest is already computer history. In late January 2011 the App Store reached 10 billion downloads. As a consequence, it has been argued that the iPhone software platform might be the most innovative in the history of computing, and the very notion of the "app" has led to major changes in how the Internet works. The Web might not (yet) be as dead as some proclaim, but the app phenomena has definitely transformed the digital domain and altered the basic structures of URLs and links. Today, the app seems, in fact, to be on its way to replacing traditional computer programs; as the name suggests, you can't find any programs in Apple's App Store—only apps, which, of course, function as programs.

Nonetheless, if Apple received criticism for the closedness of the iPhone in 2007, before the SDK release, it still does. Apple continues to manufacture closed devices and monitor code and software like no other tech company, the argument goes. Complaints have become even more frequent as Apple has tightened its grip. In February 2011, for example, the company announced it would now require that all content experiences that can be paid for in an app must be purchasable *inside* the app—from which Apple naturally collects a 30 percent fee. As the app universe closes in, and apps no longer can direct users to an open Web browser for transactions, bitter and harsh condemnations on the net have become ubiquitous. There are innumerous websites, blog posts, and articles discussing Apple's openness or closedness—not the least regarding the iPhone's iOS and its relation to Google's "open" and free Android mobile operating system.[6]

One of the major topics intensely debated in the digital domain at present revolves around this issue of Apple's "app universe" versus Google's "open Web," in general, and which mobile OS will end up victorious, in particular. Hence, it comes as no surprise that Google's (recent) CEO, Eric Schmidt, proclaimed in autumn 2010 that "closedness" is Apple's core strategy. As a former Apple board member, Schmidt should know. "You have to use their development tools, their platform, their software, their hardware," he complained. And even when you submit an app, "they have to approve it. You have to use their distribution. That's not open. . . . The inverse would be open."[7]

Departing from Schmidt's quote, as well as the unquestionable fact that the App Store recently reached 10 billion downloads—despite being a strictly controlled market—the purpose of this chapter is to dialectically reflect on the critique of Apple's business strategy. By using the iPhone as a particular case, as well as to discuss "open" versus "closed" in relation to innovative technology in general, I will argue that a restricted and controlled digital domain seems to have its advantages. If open platforms have been seen as promoting innovation more effectively than proprietary ones, then the App Store proves the opposite. Criticism delivered by a commercial opponent (Google) is naturally biased, but the sheer number of app developers working for Apple testifies that even though Eric Schmidt might be right, he is also wrong. Apple is not about being open; on the contrary, control and restraint are and have been key to its success. But I seek to problematize the commonly held belief that openness is *always* preferable in digital development, a claim fundamental to the open-source philosophy.

On Tethered and Generative Technologies

During recent years a number of media-savvy critics have expressed a kind of love-hate-relationship with Apple. Their arguments are basically the same as Eric Schmidt's: Apple's products are as excellent as they are closed. John Batelle, for example, admitted that in the 1980s he had two sentiments regarding Apple: he both liked the company and detested it. In a March 2010 blog post, he wrote, "Apple has created an extraordinary new environment for developers and entrepreneurs [the App Store], and once again, it has fostered pretty much the same two sentiments."[8]

From a more academic perspective, the critique of Apple has often included a dash of net social activism and hacker idealism. Jonathan Zittrain, for example, has been one of the most fervent critics of closed devices like the iPhone, Xbox, or TiVo. From the advent of the Arpanet in the 1960s, the subsequent Internet was perceived as an open communication platform. Tim Berners-Lee certainly saw the World Wide Web as a collaborative medium, which his notion of the Read/Write Web testifies to. Yet according to critics of Apple, this kind of general openness, which has been the underlying tech philosophy of the net and the code and machines used for constructing it, has gradually been undermined by a new wave of personal technologies that cannot be modified by users, be they specific developers or general consumers.

Because of the success of Apple's iPhone, Zittrain has focused his critical skills on this device, maliciously nicknaming it the iBrick. "The iPhone . . . is sterile. Rather than a platform that invites innovation, the iPhone comes pre-programmed," is one of many harsh judgments in his book *The Future of the Internet—and How to Stop It* (2008). According to Zittrain, the iPhone's functionality is locked to users, and Apple can even change it via remote updates. And to those "who managed to tinker with the code to enable the iPhone to support more or different applications," Zittrain writes, "Apple threatened (and then delivered on the threat) to transform the iPhone into an iBrick."

As a consequence, Zittrain has argued that the iPhone cannot be generative—basically meaning innovative—"beyond the innovations that Apple (and its exclusive carrier, AT&T) wanted."[9] According to him, this is a shift in Apple's product policy, an alteration he terms the "arc of Apple." In the late 1970s, Apple—rather, Steve Wozniak—constructed the reprogrammable Apple II, a machine that was "totally generative," as Zittrain put it in an interview in *Newsweek*. When Wozniak stepped down at Apple, it was Steve Jobs who then "came out with the Mac that made it so much easier to use while retaining the generative quality and allowing everyone to write code for it." And now, Jobs is "bringing us the iPhone, which in version one is completely locked down." So whereas we could all once innovate for the Apple II, Zittrain concludes, only Apple is going to innovate for the iPhone.[10]

This *Newsweek* interview was published in May 2008, and Zittrain's seminal book was likely finished in late 2007 since in it he mentions that the announced SDK kit may allow "others to program the iPhone with Apple's permission."[11] In other words, the App Store was not even launched when Zittrain's remarks and comments were made. One might suspect that after 10 billion downloads he would have changed his mind, but his book-related blog reveals that he has hardly altered his opinion. A number of later postings are as critical of Apple and the iPhone as ever.[12] In fact, already in the *Newsweek* interview, Zittrain jokingly quoted an announcement from Jobs, saying: "OK, we're going to allow third-party apps, but you can't just hand an app to someone, you have to put it through the iPhone store, and we reserve the right to take a cut for every app. And if we don't like the app, we can kill it."[13]

Zittrain's remarks are interesting as a general symptom of an Apple critique that lately has gotten momentum from the company's dominance and its success in dictating the rules for both soft- and hardware for personal electronic devices. Certainly, he deserves credit for articulating early doubts regarding the control mechanism of the App Store and the subsequent debate that has followed around Apple censorship. When it comes to policing the App Store and the company's seemingly arbitrary rules for determining whether an app contains objectionable content, this type of early critique is spot on. Yet the bigger picture remains obscure—not the least if compared to opinions expressed by third-party developers working with the iOS platform for their businesses. In a number of interviews that I conducted with Swedish app developers in late 2010, for instance, none of the company representatives expressed any critique of Apple and the App Store.[14] On the contrary, all enterprises—from smaller start-ups to major IT players in the national arena—praised the App Store as a semiopen platform for the creative sector. Indeed, some even pointed to the fact that Apple had created a marketplace where code could finally be exchanged (and not pirated) for real money.

Of course, as a gatekeeper Apple controls this particular market, but the developers I interviewed did not see this as a negative. Rather, from a developer's perspective, this means that all available apps will work properly on any given Apple device. Some firms hinted at problems that could occur given Apple's control, notably regarding censored content, but these were marginal statements. In general, all the enterprises praised Apple for creating the App Store and opening it for third-party developers—vividly expressed through the fact that none had any hesitations in letting Apple collect 30 percent of app revenue.

Thus, even though some people within the tech industry see the iOS as innovative, critics of Apple (notably hackers and open-source proponents) insist that the iPhone cannot by default be a generative technology since it is not essentially open. The central thesis of Zittrain's book claims such "generative technologies" as the most important for the development of the digital domain. On a personal computer, for example, anyone can write code and distribute it to anyone else. A PC is, hence, generative since it has "the capacity to produce unprompted, user-driven change," to use Zittrain's own phraseology. In his opinion, the problem is that consumers "are increasingly moving away from generative technologies like the PC and towards tethered ones like the iPhone." In contrast to generative technologies, a tethered device restricts usage—or rather, it can only be used in the manner that the manufacturer has envisioned. Hence, it does not inherently have the capacity to create user-driven change. "Tethered technologies are not adaptable, nor are they accessible, nor, in some cases, are they particularly easy to master," Zittrain has stated on his blog—quite a remarkable statement in relation to the iPhone.[15]

To be fair, Jonathan Zittrain in no way detests Apple's smartphone. On the contrary, he has stated that he thinks "it's really cool. I just don't want it to be the center of the ecosystem along with the Web 2.0 apps." Instead of tethered devices like the iPhone, he has made a general call for "a more grass-roots dot-org effort to help secure generative systems."[16] His concern is far greater than a critique of a single product: a broader fear that the wide-ranging capacity for innovation and creativity might decline as tethered tech becomes more popular—and maybe sets a new default value for personal gadgets. Of course, one might turn the issue around and ask whether PCs will continue to be the dominant generative computer technology. Steve Jobs, for one, has stated that he believes personal computers will become a kind of basic workstations in years to come and that other digital devices (smartphones, tablets, etc.) will be used for general consumption. "When we were an agrarian nation, all cars were trucks. But as people moved more towards urban centers, people started to get into cars. I think PCs are going to be like trucks," as he put it in a talk at the D8 conference during the summer of 2010.[17]

Since there are more than 500,000 apps in the App Store—most of them made by third-party developers—claiming that these products are not generative is utterly strange. The broader question, however, is whether Apple, with its tight control, can continue to be successful in a competitive mobile market where rivals are openly licensing their software to other companies. "There is much more rapid innovation taking place in an open environment," David B. Yoffie stated in a *New York Times* article with the illustrative title "Will Apple's Culture Hurt the iPhone?"[18] Rapid innovation is one thing, however, and no one really knows whether openness will prevail as a business strategy as it did during the PC era. As a matter of fact, the success with the controlled App Store indicates that openness as a key factor to digital development can be questioned.

The App Store is, no doubt, among the most policed software platforms in history, as Steven Johnson has argued. Yet "by just about any measure, the iPhone software platform has been, out of the gate, the most innovative in the history of computing." In one of the best articles on the matter, "Rethinking a Gospel of the Web," published in April 2010, Johnson has explained why "closed" in tech terms sometimes can be—or at least seems to be—preferred to "openness." Johnson asks what would have happened if Apple had loosened its restrictions. Would the iPhone ecosystem then have developed into something else, perhaps more innovative, even democratic? He suspects, however, that this view "is too simplistic. The more complicated reality is that the closed architecture of the iPhone platform has contributed to its generativity in important ways," a claim underscored by my interviews with app developers.

Hence, one might argue that most of the critique of Apple's closedness is misdirected. Rather, one needs to recognize that if external developers using a semiclosed platform such as Apple's iOS can produce hundreds of thousands of new programs in a few years, the platform must be regarded as generative, even if it is not essentially open. The iPhone development tools are a delight, and they have consequently been "a boon for small developers," as Johnson states. The economic model used by Apple, "one-click buying," has also helped nurture the ecosystem by making it easy and convenient for consumers to purchase apps impulsively. A third reason for the success, according to Johnson, has to do with Apple's hardware. The fact that all devices hooked up to the App Store run on iOS naturally helps developers since it means they have a "finite number of hardware configurations to surmount. Developers building apps for, say, Windows Mobile have to create programs that work on hundreds of different devices, each with its own set of hardware features." But developers who are building a game that uses an accelerometer, for example, know that every iOS device on the planet contains one. To be honest, Johnson does stress that the Apple ecosystem could, or perhaps would, benefit from a little more openness. And it does remain troubling to him that a single company can "veto any new application on a whim."[19] But then again, there remains no doubt, he believes, that the iPhone is a truly generative technology.

Mobile Strategies to Come

During late autumn of 2010, Mitch Kapor—founder of the Lotus Development Corporation and dubbed a veteran of the "PC-versus-Mac wars"—asserted that building a "tightly controlled ecosystem, which is what Apple has, is a large short-term advantage." But, he continued, it also means "a large long-term disadvantage. . . . The question is, how long is the short term?"[20] This statement generated a lot of responses on the Web. One commenter, in fact, wrote the firm answer that "the short term ends right around now." As innovative as Apple and the App Store might be, the argument went, its closed system would not win against an open system, especially in the rapidly changing smartphone market. "Android's openness will foster more innovation."[21]

In the United States, the iPhone remains the best-selling smartphone. According to Apple's first-quarter numbers for fiscal 2011, the company sold more than 16 million units.[22] Yet since the Android OS is used on many brands of smartphones, collectively those devices outsell the iPhone. There are naturally different corporate strategies that Apple could use to strengthen its market position. At the time of writing, for example, the major question is whether Apple will start using other network providers, such as Verizon, in order to attract people who might have avoided purchasing an iPhone simply because of AT&T's much criticized network. But the issue is also broader and hints at the question of how Apple perceives itself as a company—in short, what are its core products, and where does most of its profit come from? Increasingly strong sales of Mac computers suggest that mobile Internet devices—from iPhones to iPads—will perhaps not be Apple's main business (as many have guessed) in the years to come.

There have been a number of speculations that 2012 will be the year when mobile becomes the new default for the tech industry. Eric Schmidt, for example, recently confessed in the *Harvard Business Review* that as he thinks about Google's strategic initiatives, "I realize they're all about mobile. We are at the point where, between the geolocation capability of the phone and the power of the phone's browser platform, it is possible to deliver personalized information about where you are, what you could do there right now, and so forth—and to deliver such a service at scale."[23] Similar thoughts are also well represented within the blogosphere. Phil Wainewright has, for example, stated that "mainstream means mobile," basically predicting that a significant numbers of software enterprises will prioritize and develop for mobile first and desktop second. The corollary of this prediction, Wainewright writes, is that desktop interfaces will increasingly converge with mobile ones because "the mobile UI will be the bigger sibling that sets the standard for how other UIs behave."

According to Wainewright this shift will in turn influence the relative positions of iOS, Android, and Windows Mobile, giving the open standards an advantage in terms of new development. In short, what Wainewright suggests is that Apple's current leadership in the smartphone and tablet market will erode because the company does not pay enough attention to the Mac.[24] Major components of the Mac OS X, including the UNIX core, are open source, which is not the case at all with iOS. The App Store might be an "open platform," but the code regulating it cannot be altered.

Another blogger who has expressed similar ideas is Jean-Baptiste Soufron. Soufron argues that Apple's abandonment of open source with iOS on the iPhone (and iPad) is the first step of a corporate downturn and that during 2011 the company will be challenged by the open Android platform. "It's just a sad thing that Apple doesn't seem to put much effort into the development of OS X anymore," he states in blog post—and continues that to him Android was the OS X of 2010. "Being way more open than iOS, it's coming *en force* with . . . solid software, a nice interface, and the possibility to build upon it to innovate even more."[25] Naturally, the underlying code is one thing, and the programs running the OS another. The open-source-software community's immense pool of developers is an advantage for all open mobile operating systems, and the same goes for apps. Android's Market now has more than 400,000 apps, and it will likely overtake the App Store in the near future because of the vast number of developers.

Yet a comparison of coming mobile strategies requires a closer look at how the digital domain has developed in general. A core reason that Apple's App Store is such a success is that it offers a structured alternative to the open Web (a claim vividly expressed by most of the app developers interviewed for this article). It is simply a controlled digital space without viruses, malware, unsecure sites, or unstable programs: a gated community of code. And even if Google is doing a great job helping us find necessary information, there is also a feeling among the public (one might argue) that having access to everything on the Web means not being able to find anything. With an app, however, you instantly get what you want. The app universe, thus, could be considered a reaction to the openness of the Web. Like a newspaper, it is an edited space, and as much as we like to be free to read what we want, we also want the news to be delivered to us.

Compared to Android's open Market, the App Store is surely a walled garden, albeit one in which everything *always* works—which is hardly the case at the former. Of course, signed software is not an absolute guarantee that there is nothing malicious in the code, but there is (almost) no risk of trouble. All App Store apps function and are secure, stable, and constantly upgraded in the most simple way, which is important since most users are not particularly good at keeping their systems and software up to date.

The success of the iPhone and its subsequent App Store has not occurred in spite of the tight control over the software but rather because Apple is in command. Apple has constructed an enormously profitable market space as a structured alternative to the open Web, with public appeal on many levels. Customers might, of course, get annoyed if a single controlled outlet cannot meet *all* needs of *all* users, but as Steven Johnson put it, "sometimes, if you get the conditions right, a walled garden can turn into a rain forest."[26]

Notes

1. Lev Grossman, "Invention of the Year: The iPhone," *Time*, 1 November 2007.

2. Steve Jobs, "Third Party Applications on the iPhone" *Apple Hot News* 17 October 2007 – http://replay.waybackmachine.org/20071017221832/http://www.apple.com/hotnews/ (15 February 2011).

3. Grossman, "Invention of the Year."

4. See the page "iPhone" on Apple.com, http://www.apple.com/iphone/apps-for -iphone/ (15 February 2011).

5. Walt Mossberg, "Some Favorite Apps That Make iPhone Worth the Price," *Wall Street Journal*, 25 March 2009.

6. A Google search for "Apple open closed" in January 2011 generated almost 51 million hits.

7. Eric Schmidt, quoted in John Paczkowski, "If Google Is the Inverse of Apple, Then Is Eric Schmidt the Inverse of Steve Jobs?" *All Things Digital*, 29 September 2010, http://digitaldaily.allthingsd.com/20100929/google-the-inverse-of-apple/ (15 February 2011).

8. John Batelle, "Thursday Signal—Repeat After Me: Apps Are (Currently) Myopic (Or . . . We've Seen This Movie Before . . .)," blog post, 10 March 2010, http://battellemedia.com/archives/2010/03/thursday_signal_repeat_after_me_apps_are_ currently_myopic_orweve_seen_this_movie_before (15 February 2011).

9. Jonathan Zittrain, *The Future of the Internet—and How to Stop It* (New Haven, Conn.: Yale University Press, 2008), 2.

10. Jonathan Zittrain, quoted in Brian Baker, "A Killer Product—Will Closed De-vices Like Apple's iPhone Murder the Web?" *Newsweek*, 2 May 2008.

11. Zittrain, *The Future of the Internet*, 2.

12. See, for example, Jennifer Halbleib, "Apple Opens Up?" *Future of the Internet* blog, 28 September 2010, http://futureoftheinternet.org/apple-opens-up (15 February 2011).

13. Zittrain, quoted in Baker, "A Killer Product."

14. During late autumn and winter of 2010 I conducted a number of interviews with Swedish app developers. Some were done over e-mail with shorter questions, others in person at the enterprise in question. At three occasions longer interviews with CEOs at leading Swedish app firms where conducted: on 5 October 2010 with Anders Graffman, CEO Apegroup; on 21 October 2010 with Carl Loodberg, CEO Illusion Labs; and on 6 December 2010 with Johan Hemminger, CEO Monterosa.

15. "Glossary," *Future of the Internet* blog, http://futureoftheinternet.org/glossary (15 February 2011).

16. Zittrain, quoted in Baker, "A Killer Product."

17. Steve Jobs, quoted in Jason D. O'Grady, "D8 Interview: Steve Jobs Unfiltered," *ZDNet*, 1 June 2010, http://www.zdnet.com/blog/apple/d8-interview-steve-jobs -unfiltered/7067 (15 February 2011).

18. David B. Yoffie, quoted in Miguel Helft, "Will Apple's Culture Hurt the iPhone?" *New York Times*, 17 October 2010.

19. Steven Johnson, "Rethinking a Gospel of the Web," *New York Times*, 10 April 2010.

20. Mitch Kapor is quoted from Helft, "Will Apple's Culture Hurt the iPhone?"

21. Preston Gralla, "Five Reasons Android Will Beat the iPhone," *Computerworld*, 18 October 2010, http://blogs.computerworld.com/17179/five_reasons_android_will_ beat_the_iphone (15 February 2011).

22. "Apple Reports First Quarter Results," Apple press release, 18 January 2011, http://www.apple.com/pr/library/2011/01/18results.html (15 February 2011).

23. Eric Schmidt, "Preparing for the Big Mobile Revolution," *Harvard Business Review*, 21 January 2011, http://hbr.org/web/extras/hbr-agenda-2011/eric-schmidt (15 February 2011).

24. Phil Wainewright, "In 2011, Mainstream Means Mobile," *ZDNet*, 3 January 2011, http://www.zdnet.com/blog/saas/in-2011-mainstream-means-mobile/1235 (15 February 2011).

25. Jean-Baptiste Soufron, "In 2011 Apple Will Lose the Smartphone and the Tablet Market to Android Because They Forgot About OS X," Soufron.com, 4 January 2011, http://www.soufron.com/post/2559133301/in-2011-apple-will-lose-the-smartphone-and-the-tablet (15 February 2011).

26. Johnson, "Rethinking a Gospel of the Web."

III

The App Revolution

CHAPTER 11

The iPhone Apps

A Digital Culture of Interactivity

BARBARA FLUECKIGER

ATRICK COLLISON, who in his own words is a "hacker, pilot, student at MIT, cofounder of Auctomatic," and "lover of waffles," certainly can be seen as prototypical of certain first-generation developers of iPhone apps—the whiz kids.[1] Self-taught, he started to program software at an early age. When Patrick was seventeen, he founded his own company, Auctomatic, with his younger brother John and sold it two years later for an exorbitant sum to the Canadian company Live Current Media. During the winter of 2007 he programmed the iPhone app Encyclopedia, an offline version of Wikipedia that allows almost all of Wikipedia's online functions, including the use of links between different entries and in 2010 was offered in eighty-three languages, including Chinese, Hindi, and Vietnamese.

In a broad sense, Patrick Collison is an example of a "digital native." But he is more than that, given that "digital natives" need not, by definition, be creative in developing tools; they need only be highly literate in exploiting predefined structures. As I will argue, following the writings of the media philosopher Vilém Flusser, it would be a gross misunderstanding to believe that a technology brings forth mental structures or abilities. More often than not, as my investigations into the history of technological change have revealed, thought models develop in a wider cultural context before they result in new technologies, which in turn influence patterns of behavior and thus the "wiring" of thoughts. Accordingly, this chapter discusses aspects of the evolution and properties of a digital culture that led to the development of the iPhone as a multidimensional tool with functionalities far exceeding the making of phone calls. App development is a striking example of a technological achievement with a massive impact on the social and cultural structures that govern its use. After starting with some observations regarding the practice and history of iPhone app development, I will investigate the epistemological aspects of digital encoding in the main part of this chapter. At the end, I will connect these investigations and deduce certain general insights pertaining to the cultural and mental consequences of this new technology. This chapter addresses the role of iPhone apps, as well as their development and distribution, within the framework of a technological history of media development in the digital domain. The present study, like other studies of technological innovation I have conducted in the past, may be described with Frank Beau's term of "technobole": an analysis that focuses on a technology to extract from it an understanding of its position in culture and society. In this view, a technology is not the source of teleological change, as technological determinism would assume, but rather a node in a far reaching network of scientific knowledge and cultural artifacts. More broadly, my approach can be seen as related to the body of work often subsumed under the label of actor network theory, which represents an antiessentialist, pragmatic view of sociomaterial processes and the history of knowledge.

The Sweet Solution

At the June 2007 Worldwide Developers Conference, Steve Jobs presented the iPhone to an excited crowd.[2] The idea of third-party apps was already present: "We have been trying to come up with a solution to expand the capabilities of the iPhone so developers can write great apps for it, but keep the iPhone secure. And we've come up with a very. Sweet. Solution. . . . An innovative new way to create applications for mobile devices . . . it's all based on the fact that we have the full Safari engine in the iPhone." What Jobs and Apple's Scott Forstall were talking about were Web-based apps running on a browser, which limited their possibilities for development. At that time, Jobs and Forstall had a mere eleven apps that they presented over and over, including the calendar, the address book, and photos, apps that continue to constitute the core block of preinstalled apps on the iPhone. In March 2008 there were approximately 1,000 Web apps available, and the situation improved further after that when Apple launched its Apple SDK (software development kit) platform, which gave third-party developers a sound basis for the development of apps. According to Steve Jobs's keynote address at the June 2008 WWDC in, ninety-five days after its launch the SDK had 250,000 downloads and 25,000 registered developers.

With the SDK—which Scott Forstall introduced on the day of its launch in a presentation entitled "iPhone Software Roadmap"—external developers were given an application programming interface and a variety of tools to make use of the internal architecture of the iPhone and its built-in devices. These included, for example, the localizer, which triangulates the position of the iPhone and connects it to a Google map, and the accelerometer, a three-axis device for the positioning of the iPhone in space that adjusts the screen to its vertical or horizontal position and allows the iPhone to be used as a controller for games.

The API consists of four main architectural layers: the core operating system, iOS, an adapted version of Apple's OS X; core services, such as Core-Location for the development of location-aware apps (for example, to connect to nearby friends and find restaurants), the address book, and the SQLite database; media for the use of audio-visual content, core animation for the creation of layered animation, and the Open Graphics Library for Embedded Systems, a hardware accelerated interface for 3D graphics applications; and, finally, Cocoa Touch, the user-interface application framework that enables user control of content by touching the screen or by the use of the accelerometer or localizer. In addition, the SDK offered several tools, most importantly the Xcode integrated development environment to write code for a new project. This source code that controls a given application is usually hidden from users.[3]

Another tool is the Interface Builder, which facilitates graphic-interface design based on drag and drop. Developers can choose from a menu of predefined controls (buttons, switches, the wheel) or invent their own custom controls. "Cocoa Touch supports the model view controller paradigm of development," which also visually connects the view layer to the control layer. "Because it is a visual editor, you get to see exactly what your interface will look like at runtime," Forstall asserted in his "iPhone Software Roadmap" presentation.

The Interface Builder dictates standardized interfaces, providing a set of visual building blocks that ensures that every application developed by third parties fits into Apple's corporate design. All of these developer tools are supported by a range of extensions to test and debug applications, either by connecting the iPhone to a desktop computer or by running the apps on an iPhone simulator directly on a Mac. Yet first-generation developers such as Patrick Collison did not need such predefined structures. He wrote his Encyclopedia app six months before the App Store was even launched. As experienced hackers, these young people were able to gain their knowledge independently by investigating the iPhone and its operating system itself. As Collison put it in a private message, he "had to 'disassemble' the built-in apps to figure it out."

Binary Data Encoding and Digital Thinking

The term "digital" is often overused and overgeneralized; it does not differentiate the multifaceted phenomena that rely on digital code. Nevertheless, there is a basic property common to any form of digital representation, namely, the binary mode of data encoding. As a universal mode, this encoding process enables a variety of interactions with data that range from its transmission—the feeding of data in and to a variety of media—to its transformation—the processing of data by mathematical operations—and random access, which allows data to be accessed directly in a nonlinear fashion.

In 1988 Vilém Flusser published an essay called *Krise der Linearität* (*Crisis of Linearity*).[4] In my view, Flusser's essay remains the most valuable text for understanding the fundamental shift that digital data have brought about in our culture, society, and thought. Flusser's cryptic and idiosyncratically structured essay offers an analysis of the historical change in representing the world that has occurred through technologies ranging from the early cave paintings of Pech Merle to computer-generated images. Flusser addresses one of the most important aspects of representation, namely, the interaction between the underlying epistemological principles of a given representational technique—painting, alphanumerical texts, photographs, digital representations—and thought. While most scholars focus on the impact of technology on culture, Flusser turns this question upside-down and asks for the cultural foundation that arguably leads to a change in representational codes and in turn affects our thoughts, feelings, wishes, and imagination. While his observations mainly address digital representations, they also offer fundamental insights into the functions of digital data in general.

According to Flusser, painting emerged to orient a community toward future actions, such as organizing the chase of animals. Painting required the subject to stand back from the object not in terms of spatial distance but in terms of mental abstraction. To communicate a singular perception in an intersubjective way, the painter had to resort to his inner state—memory and imagination—to convey the outer world in a universal conventionalized language. In a second step the symbols that resulted from this technique were organized in a linear manner to move from the still ambiguous connotative meaning of pictures to the more denotative form of texts to satisfy the societal need for a more rational and thus more reliable communication. This change in encoding from a two-dimensional plane to a one-dimensional line brought a shift to linear thinking through a teleological model of development and rational cause-and-effect chains, and this shift remained at the center of Western culture for a long time. Yet the alphabetical code of texts still lacked a precise instrument to investigate imaginations and thus required an extension in the form of a numeric code. As Flusser establishes, the emerging alphanumerical code was in itself deeply contradictory: "While letters unravel the surface of an image into lines, numbers grind this surface into points and intervals. While literal thinking spools scenes as processes, numerical thought computes scenes into grains."[5]

If we follow this analysis, it is clear that binary code, which is fundamentally informed by its numerical and mathematical foundation, challenges traditional notions of linearity in the most radical manner not by representing the world as two-dimensional pictures or one-dimensional texts but by breaking down phenomena into clouds of zero-dimensional points. In contrast to the traditional forms of representation that produced effigies, which in turn served as models for future actions, synthesized digital images (i.e., computer-generated images) produce models that in turn might result in objects. That is, imagination predates perception, an observation for which Flusser introduced the German term *"Vorbilder"* to mean both models and "pre-images," or antetypes. One may describe Flusser's model of development as a cybernetic feedback loop in which cultural and technical forces enhance or correct each other. But this model still relies on a linear understanding of history, which in Flusser's view is based on the discovery of deficiencies in society that call for solutions. So he in fact combines an underlying teleological model with a circular or even dialectical structure.

Flusser's thoughts are clearly based on a materialist view that we may summarize best with Marshall McLuhan's catchphrase that "the medium is the message." Flusser's analysis shows its potential in relation to iPhone apps when we reflect on the impact on iPhone users' perceptions that the zero-dimensional pointlike mode of binary code and its deep roots in the mathematical domain of numbers will have. It is here that we can connect

Flusser's philosophical insights to the development and the distribution of iPhone programs.

Transformation and Mutation

In contrast to the hardware of established media technologies in the electromechanical domain—film, TV, radio, sound recordings—digital media comprise two layers: the hardware that houses the functions and the software that describes and thus generates the functions. While earlier analogue techniques involve an intricate connection between the flow of information and its material foundation, in the digital domain the two elements are completely separate, with the binary code defined arbitrarily by a protocol for encoding and decoding digital information. These complementary actions are at the foundation of every digitization and thus of every software program.[6] These insights go back to Nelson Goodman's distinction between autographic and allographic processes, a distinction central to William J. Mitchell's investigation of visual truth in the post-photographic era.[7] While autographic processes such as painting comprise only one stage from production to finished object, allographic processes such as musical notation systems require two stages, first, the writing of the notes on paper and, second, the notes' interpretation, which transforms the written text into a process accessible to the auditory system, for which it was intended from the beginning.

In a similar fashion, digital code or software is no more than a notation system for a future display in the planned domain. With the allographic system, however, comes another specific property of digital media objects. "Traditionally, musical scores, literary texts, and other specifications of allographic works have had final, definitive, printed versions," Mitchell notes. "The act of publication is an act of closure."[8] This does not apply to digital code as allographic because such code remains open to mutation. This openness blurs the distinction between producers and consumers since consumers may have access to the data, either directly on the level of the coding system or indirectly with the help of interpreting software that offers a graphical user interface. Transformation—and thus programmability—as well as interactivity are core properties of digital culture.

Both transformation and interactivity need an interface, and this is where Apple has a huge advantage in interface design based on the GUI and a developer-friendly API. In 1984, when using a computer still required active knowledge of computer code, Steve Jobs introduced the GUI into the

Macintosh universe. This GUI offered users a metaphorical surface consisting of graphical symbols that linked the world of computers to traditional office environments. It has become the industry standard since Microsoft's Windows operating system gained ascendancy in the 1990s. In fact, the GUI is the most important step for the spreading and democratization of home computers and—in their wake—of mobile devices such as laptops and now the iPhone, because it connects the opaque site of the binary encoding and control of the hardware with a transparent, intuitively accessible surface that is aesthetically pleasing.

Attempts have been made to simplify human-computer interaction since the beginning of computer history. A light gun was developed at MIT in the 1950s to allow the direct addressing of individual points on the cathode ray tube monitor of MIT's Whirlwind computer. Later in the same decade, the light pen was introduced as an input device to communicate with the computer. The single most important invention toward establishing a GUI was Ivan Sutherland's "Sketchpad." Presented in 1963, it was the result of his Ph.D. thesis at MIT and offered users possibilities to create, transform, and store objects on the computer. There was also a zoom feature to enlarge the view.[9] A few years later, Doug Engelbart from Stanford Research Laboratory developed the mouse and presented it to the scientific community. The mouse was easier to use than the light pen, and it spread in connection with the windows and icons metaphors that were to provide the building blocks of the GUI. At the Palo Alto Research Center of Xerox, Alan Kay then developed the windows style of the GUI even further—and from there it found its way into the Macintosh operating system.

When Steve Jobs presented the iPhone in 2007, usability and interface design were central to its potential success. The interface was key to differentiating the product from competing smartphones that—according to Jobs—were smarter than ordinary cell phones but not easy to use. There is, to draw again on the abstract theoretical discussion of transformation and mutation, an essential shift from systems dominated by hardware with mechanical buttons and controls, as in smartphones like the BlackBerry, to a system controlled in large measure by a flexible surface entirely open to any software design. In the two-stage allographic mode this means that the interpreter of the notation system has a much broader range of interaction open to his or her needs, provided by the vast possibilities of designing controls as pure graphical elements. With the touch screen operated by Cocoa Touch, this tiny computer taps the essence of transformation and mutability owed to basic binary encoding. The touch screen is also where the approximately 250,000 iPhone apps developed to date find their place to unfold myriad specific tools across an almost unlimited spectrum.

Steve Jobs thus seems to have been right when he stated in 2007 that with this design Apple was years ahead of its competition. Since 2007, most competitors have followed Apple's route—similar to how Microsoft adopted the GUI in the 1980s. Hardware-wise, the iPhone offers a variety of physical subsystems to which the apps can be connected, thereby further widening their range. In addition to the core processor there are many additional functionalities, such as the media processors for audio-visual content, the animation core for animated content, the Open Graphics Library, the accelerometer for the control of the iPhone itself in 3D space, and the localizer, which makes use of the GPS system, as well as the telephone and Internet-access capabilities and of course the touch screen. These hardware modules enable apps to connect these functionalities in individual ways, based on the transformation capabilities of the binary code and on random access.

An application can thus be understood as a translation device, enabling communication between the user interface and the hardware by a specific protocol. And this is where the second layer of interface comes into play, put into practice by Apple's SDK as the application programming interface. Much as Jobs had stressed the iPhone's touch screen, Scott Forstall said of the SDK that as a development environment it was years ahead of the competition in the mobile device market on its launch in 2008. In a Twitter post the same day, Patrick Collison agreed that this statement was not "marketing SPEAK"; instead, he stated that the SDK was the main advantage that would "cause them [Apple] to win the smartphone war" while at the same time bemoaning "the end of an era of reverse engineering. All those late nights spent pouring over . . . assembly."

Apple's primacy generally stems from the company's long history in the creation of various development interfaces. "They simply did a better job of creating the tools for allowing developers to create *good* software—that looks good, and works well. This is one of those things that I think people outside of the software world usually miss—the extent to which the nuance and tiny detail of implementations have a big impact in a way that's very hard to quantify," Patrick Collison told me in an e-mail in August 2010.

Random Access

A second, arguably even more important consequence of the pointlike structure of digital data is random access. Random access relies on digital code's distinct values to allow direct addressing of the individual numbers, thereby facilitating nonlinear connections between individual points in the data space to create network structures. A variety of practical applications arise from this. The first is the Internet, with billions of URLs that can be retrieved by billions of users. A second is the hypertext structure of Web-based documents, offering texts with layers to be navigated freely and hypermedia with text, graphics, and audiovisual media such as QuickTime files to be connected in myriads of individual ways. And a third application is the connection between surface elements such as graphic icons, the controls such as the touch screen, and the accelerometer with the hardware elements by means of software.

In this context one might recall McLuhan who—with startling prescience in 1964—predicted the emergence of the global village as a network structure in society that would implode space. To be sure, McLuhan attributed this change to electricity, not to the universality of digital code or to its point-like form of representation. McLuhan also confused the electric and the electronic. While light is electric, every device that implies a control of capacity or resistance or alters voltage or current, is electronic. Only electronic devices enable electric ones to become carriers of information, such as the radio. Electronic devices, in turn, have to be separated from digital ones, insofar as they still rely on an analogue relation between signal and encoding and thus do not employ binary coding. These distinctions are crucial as they separate different stages in the development of technology. Mechanical, electric, and electronic devices still belong to the domain of linearity as they produce processes that unravel in time. It is only with the digital that the mathematical form of representation shifts to spatially distributed spots that allow for random access. However, there were nonlinear systems even in the electro-mechanical age, such as card indices used in libraries to organize data. Even books can be used in a nonlinear manner based on an index that invites a nonlinear reading.

This historical irregularity accounts for the aforementioned observation that predecessors of a technological change can almost always be found. Furthermore, it documents a cultural need to overcome hard-edged linear or even nonlinear strategies and devices, which prompted Vannevar Bush to write his famous article, "As We May Think," in 1945, in which he states: "The human mind . . . operates by association. With one item in its grasp, it snaps instantly to the next that is suggested by the association of thoughts, in accordance with some intricate web of trails carried by the cells of the brain. . . . Man cannot hope fully to duplicate this mental process artificially, but he certainly ought to be able to learn from it."[10] Moreover, in his original definition of the term hypertext in the 1960s, Theodor H. Nelson proposed an interactive screen as an appropriate device for associative navigation.[11] Associative patterns, then, are at the very core of random access. We could even state that random access not only mirrors mental processes, as Bush noted, but also— by the very act of selection—breaks the world down into bits and pieces. Every fragment that emerges out of this process is a node in a new network built by the user. Associative mechanisms in thinking are thus perpetually enhanced and lead to change that challenges the traditional Western model of linear progress. Vilém Flusser embedded this notion in a broader cultural context when he identified modern conceptions of the world as proposed by quantum theory to be a precursor to this fragmented, nonlinear style of thinking. As a consequence, he saw the dissolution of the subject "in a col-lective psychic field, from which we emerge like temporary bubbles, acquire some information, process, share, to submerge again." Moreover, "we are immersed in an undulating field of culturemes, from which the individual cultures emerge through computation, just to blur again."[12]

Conclusion: Network Structures and App Development

The interactive culture of iPhone apps is in many ways intimately intertwined with the kind of network structures that Flusser calls the "collective psychic field." This holds true, of course, for every social activity on the Internet, including every Web 2.0 activity—from participation in forums to open knowledge sources such as Wikipedia to social networks. However, it is also a new phenomenon for a technological development to arise from this structure. Interestingly enough, it was exactly this vision that guided one of the masterminds of the Web, J. C. R. Licklider, a psychologist who pro-vided several ideas for the use of computers. In his 1968 paper "The Com-puter as a Communication Device" (written with Robert W. Taylor), Lick-lider proposed that "collaboration in creative endeavor [could gain] critical mass" by connecting people over computer-aided communication. "Take any problem worthy of the name, and you find only a few people who can con-tribute effectively to its solution. Those people must be brought into close intellectual partnership so that their ideas can come into contact with one another."[13]

This is exactly what happens in the programming of iPhone apps, where developers form a community to share ideas and get advice on solving indi-vidual problems. In this way, a company can outsource both its development work and the risk of failure that is intrinsic to every advance in technology. Companies can make use of masses of specialists all over the globe. Many developers come from countries such as Russia, India, or China and would likely have difficulties gaining access to institutionalized structures. The introduction of the SDK marked a shift from a free hacker culture in the first months of the iPhone's existence to a strictly formalized and institutionalized one. With the introduction of the App Store in June 2008, Apple gained maximal control over the distribution of apps and thus strengthened its influence further. While the first few months with the hacker system reflected possibilities of transformation and mutation in an innocent state, exploring in depth the native properties of the digital culture, the restrictions that followed had a severe effect on this free-floating state.

First of all, these restrictions implied a standardization of the apps as expressed in the Interface Builder. Second, and more importantly, these restrictions brought closure to an initially fully open system. This closure occurred on different levels, not least on the level of the text, that is, the software and its code for each individual app. Once an app has passed the strict evaluation process to be distributed in the App Store, it is closed and then is open to mutation only by the original developer and by hackers who use illegal ways to gain access. Marxist scholars such as Jean-Louis Comolli would argue that this is the classic story of the capitalist system appropriating innovations that come from the margins of society. Astonishingly, this view is also expressed in Chris Anderson's article, "The Web Is Dead: Long Live the Internet," published in *Wired*—a magazine hardly known for its critique of hegemonic ideology—which investigates the change of the Internet from an open web to a controlled distribution channel for proprietary apps. "This was all inevitable. It is the cycle of capitalism. The story of industrial revolutions, after all, is a story of battles over control. A technology is invented, a thousand flowers bloom, and then someone finds a way to own it, locking out others."[14] As Anderson argues, it is we who give these companies their power, because we prefer to get our software solutions from controlled sources and not from browsing unreliable download pages.

Does this form of institutional ownership imply that the idea of a digital culture of interactivity is dead? Yes, in part. While it is true that this step implies standardization and closure, the system is open to a broad movement of masses who could collaborate in this venture. Only with the launch of the App Store did it become possible for developers to become entrepreneurs. According to a survey from Flurry in March 2010 one in five developers are start-up enterprises.[15] These small companies were launched in order to develop either apps for mobile devices or independent software that could be transformed into apps.

Yet there are still independent individuals able to implement ideas based on their everyday experience, such as meeting up with friends, writing grocery lists, and controlling moods. In their spare time, individuals have even developed games and music-playing interfaces such as MooCowMusic. Some of the most successful apps, such as the music identification program Shazam or Loopt, a localization program based on GPS, also started their development long before the iPhone was introduced. One may wish to tell a story that follows the David versus Goliath narrative, with an individual hacker like Patrick Collison fighting the corporations. From an economic point of view, Apple is certainly a capitalist venture operating on a global scale. But beyond the exploitation of a mass of individual developers sharing their ideas and products, thus amplifying the iPhone's commercial success, the collaboration partly outweighs the capitalist pattern in operation. It is certainly indebted to the openness and universality of digital's binary encoding, with transformation and random access as its core properties.

NOTES

1. See http://collison.ie (15 February 2011).

2. Videos of these keynote speeches are available on iTunes at http://itunes.apple .com/us/podcast/apple-keynotes/id275834665 (15 February 2011).

3. See http://developer.apple.com/iphone/library/referencelibrary/GettingStarted/ URL_Tools_for_iPhone_OS_Development/index.html (15 February 2011).

4. Vilém Flusser, *Krise der Linearität* (Bern: Benteli, 1988). The English translation *Crisis of Linearity* is available at www.scribd.com/doc/26525368/Volume-1-Issue-1 (15 February 2011).

5. Ibid., 21.

6. See Nelson Goodman, *Languages of Art* (Indianapolis: Hackett, 1968); Malcom Le Grice, *Experimental Cinema in the Digital Age* (London: BFI, 2001); and Mark J. P. Wolf, *Abstracting Reality. Art, Communication, and Cognition in the Digital Age* (Lanham, Md.: University Press of America, 2000).

7. Goodman *Languages of Art*; Nelson Goodman, *Ways of Worldmaking* (Indianapolis: Hackett, 1976); and William J. Mitchell, *The Reconfigured Eye: Visual Truth in the Post-Photographic Era* (Cambridge, Mass.: MIT Press, 1992).

8. Mitchell *The Reconfigured Eye*, 51.

9. Ivan Sutherland, "A Man Machine Graphical Communication System," *Proceedings of the AFIPS Spring Joint Computer Conference* (Washington, D.C. 1963), 329–46.

10. Vannevar Bush, "As We May Think," *The Atlantic* (July 1945), http://www .theatlantic.com/magazine/archive/1969/12/as-we-may-think/3881/ (15 February 2011).

11. George P. Landow, *Hypertext 3.0: Critical Theory and New Media in an Era of Globalization* (Baltimore, Md.: Johns Hopkins University Press, 1992), 3.

12. Flusser, *Krise der Linearität*, 32–33.

13. J. C. R. Licklider and Robert W. Taylor, "The Computer as a Communication Device," *Science and Technology* 76 (April 1968): 29.

14. Chris Anderson, "The Web Is Dead. Long Live the Internet" *Wired*, 17 August 2010.

15. For a discussion, see www.appleinsider.com/articles/10/03/15/iphone_app_store_still_offers_level_playing_field_for_developers.html (15 February 2011).

CHAPTER 12

Slingshot to Victory

Games, Play, and the iPhone

MIA CONSALVO

I N ANNOUNCING THE creation of the iPhone, Steve Jobs proclaimed "every once in a while a revolutionary product comes along that changes everything." He went on to explain why the iPhone was being developed and what features it would offer, stating more specifically that "the killer app is making calls." Yet while the iPhone has been derided for its poor call quality and connectivity, it has met with unexpected success in another area—it has become a key global platform for digital games.[1] Even before the release of the iPhone, researchers had already been mapping out the ways that communication and media consumption were being changed by mobile phones. In 2001, Richard Ling concluded that mobile users had "a means of group communication, media content (entertainment, information, data, pleasure) and the ability to 'synchronise everyday life.'"[2] But the iPhone did do something else: it put a gaming platform in the hands of millions of people who had never considered (and likely will never consider) themselves gamers. And with the opening of the App Store in 2008, the iPhone began transforming smartphones into agents of play, reconfiguring how its users relate to a mobile technology.

Several years later, millions of iPhone owners across the globe now use their expensive, advanced technological devices to slice flying fruit (Fruit

Ninja), match multicolored jewels (Bejeweled 2), cut rope to release candy (Cut the Rope), trim a client's hair (Sally's Salon), and successfully land cartoon airplanes at a busy airport (Airport Mania). One of the most popular activities on the iPhone involves flinging cartoon birds through the air in order to crash through obstacles and destroy helmeted pigs. As the story transpires, the pigs have stolen the birds' eggs, and the birds are itching for revenge. The player determines an overall strategy and each bird's trajectory as she slingshots them toward the pigs, who hide underneath elaborate structures of wood, glass, and concrete. Such mayhem from the Finnish developer Rovio created the best-selling iPhone application for much of 2010 in more than sixty countries, including the United States, the United Kingdom, Canada, Germany, Sweden, Singapore, Chile, and Panama. The developers have sold more than 12 million copies of the game so far, across the iPhone, iPad, and other smartphone platforms, such as Android. Angry Birds is clearly a success for its developers as well as for Apple's App Store in general. And although no longer exclusively for the iPhone, Angry Birds is illustrative of games on the device as well as games on contemporary mobile phones.

This article takes Angry Birds as a case study of how games are played on the iPhone and how the platform has redefined the audience for games, created new forms of gameplay, and changed how games are marketed and sold. More broadly, Angry Birds and many other games like it have redefined our relationship with digital technologies, in this case mobile phones, as well as how we have incorporated play activities into our daily lives in an increasing and more pervasive manner.

From *Keitei* to Game Play

Early research on videogames was driven by social scientists, who studied the platforms and games available to them — starting with arcade games and then moving to home console systems such as the Atari VCS and Nintendo's NES and SNES systems. Researchers usually explored representations found in games, mostly focusing on violence and gender themes, and the games rarely appeared in a positive light. They also investigated the effects of games on individuals, usually concerned with the violence in games and how it might affect youthful players. Yet as game studies has evolved as a field, a broader variety of games and systems to play them on have appeared, and methods and approaches have likewise expanded. Researchers have started doing deep analyses of individual games, have investigated the preferences and practices of players, and have done important work studying the structures of the industry and its global presence. Yet the vast majority of that work has continued to focus on console and PC games, with mobile gaming a peripheral interest at best.

The earliest research mentioning mobile game players or games was often a minor part of broader studies of mobile phone use. Researchers were concerned to discover how mobiles fit into everyday life and tended to focus on societies with the greatest early adoption of mobiles—Japan and parts of northern Europe. Probably the best-known work on this subject is the edited volume *Personal, Portable, Pedestrian: Mobile Phones in Japanese Life*.[3] While helpful in conceptualizing how the mobile phone (or *keitei* in Japanese) has become a key mediating factor in diverse social situations and relationships in Japan, there is no discussion in the book of how games figure into mobile use. Speaking to mobile use more globally, Harvey May and Greg Hearn argue, "The mobile phone has begun to offer people entrenched in metropolitan lifestyles ways to expand limited leisure time."[4]

Even more recently, little attention continues to be paid to studying *play* in relation to mobile games, apart from a few highly specific areas. Most commonly, researchers have explored the use of mobile games for education—particularly health care and museums—and have written about mobile game designs as well as initial reception of those games. Likewise, researchers have studied how mobile devices can be used in the creation of urban games as well as hybrid-reality games that employ localized spaces as part of the game's space, objectives, and play. Generalized studies have concluded that playing mobile games is "an essential part of the mobile phone culture of teenagers" in Finland.[5] Likewise, other researchers found that for youth in the United States, Spain, and the Czech Republic, "visual appeal, perceived ease of use, escapism, and especially perceived convenience are major factors shaping widespread acceptance of mobile phone games."[6] Relative to the concept of play, Michal Daliot-Bul argues that during the mid-2000s in Japan, the *keitei* was transformed from a technological gadget into "a little friend that is an intensely personal part of users' lives and is an outlet for fun and play-thrills." Importantly, play was a central feature of that experience for users, contributing to what he saw as "the merging of play into everyday life." Play here is conceptualized broadly to include not only games but also nonserious applications such as ring tones, screen savers, horoscopes, and sports applications. And in addition to the normalized use of such applications, playfulness via mobile activity was key in inserting itself into "the in-between moments of everyday life, and their transformations into enjoyable, pleasurable breaks."[7]

Taking an industry perspective, Dean Chan has examined how Japanese game companies have adapted to the growing ubiquity of mobile use and tried to create a space in that use for games. During the early days of such activity, arcade classics were popular, forming "the backbone of casual mobile gaming." He details in particular how Square Enix expanded into the mobile market, bringing its well-known franchises Final Fantasy and Dragon Quest to the platform, primarily through ported versions of its early single-player titles, sold on preloaded handsets. He points out that such games not only engage current Square Enix players and fans but also broaden the market to "casual gamers who don't necessarily play console games," thus enlarging the player base for the entire franchise.[8]

Chan also reminds us that assumptions about the context of play must continually be challenged and kept in mind: for example, that the home is an increasingly popular space for mobile gaming, where previously consoles and personal computers were thought to be dominant. Likewise, while mobile games in South Korea might be crossovers with PC-based MMOGs such as Ragnarok Online, such games don't necessarily transfer well to Japan, where consoles remain much more popular as gaming devices than computers.

Thus although we know a bit about how mobile games are employed by youth, if not adults, there is still much to learn. Mobile games, as they have become more popular on phones, are merging with a technology already being used as a broad communications device and a media player. But with the iPhone, these games were introduced to a mass audience, leading to an explosion in the mobile game industry. Researchers are only now beginning to investigate what this means. For example, how might such devices transform the spaces we travel through, from the mundane to the playful, and, likewise, how might more of our interactions be mediated in a playful manner? There are no answers yet, but the iPhone is moving us in interesting directions.

The Mobile Game Industry

While research about mobile games has been scant, that's partly because mobile games are a fairly recent entrant into the larger digital games industry. Before 2002, only simple games such as Tetris were playable on mobile phones, and such games came embedded or preloaded onto phones at the time of purchase. The games that appeared were mostly ports of arcade classics or simple single-player games that could be played in short bursts of time.

After 2002, mobile developers began to experiment with different distribution models, allowing users to download games onto their phones or purchase and download games onto a PC and then transfer those games via cable or a sync connection to the phone. There were several problems with this model, however, that continued to slow the widespread adoption of games on mobile devices. Many mobile companies charged users for all air time used, meaning downloading games onto a phone incurred costs simply for the download itself, above any actual purchase cost for the game. Additionally, the market at the time featured a large number of phone models for each mobile company, and those companies usually employed their own pricing and use plans. Although there were some third-party sites, most phones could only access their provider's site for licensed games, thus ensuring walled gardens and limited choices. Developers also had to negotiate varying technological standards, including different screen sizes and display options, programming languages, and methods of payment for each mobile company. All of those challenges provided little incentive for game companies to try and create games for mobile devices and for consumers to try them.

In 2007, changes to the various infrastructures of the mobile industry led to wider opportunities for mobile game development and therefore player use. At that time, smartphones were becoming more widely available, in conjunction with mobile broadband connections with relatively flat data fees; the most important development, however, was the release of Apple's iPhone. Although it seems difficult to believe now, at launch in 2007 the iPhone did not allow users to download independent applications—or apps—onto their phones. The only apps available were created by Apple and featured no games at all. Yet by mid-2008 Apple opened its App Store and began allowing third parties to offer apps for download. Consumers downloaded more than 10 million individual apps in the first three days, and by November 2009, 100 million iPhone and iPod Touch apps were being downloaded each month. In January 2011, Apple announced that more than 10 million different apps had been downloaded across its various devices.

Such data show that games have played a significant role in the app explosion. Initially, games constituted more than three-quarters of all apps available, suggesting developers were finally seeing the potential for reaching a broader audience for mobile games. And data from 2010 suggest that games continue to be a hugely popular category for consumption, yet they do not dominate the app landscape as they previously have.[9] Overall, however, games are now considered a central part of the iPhone experience and feature regularly in the App Store's most popular and heavily downloaded offerings. As of January 2011, games were the second most popular app category (after books). And of apps submitted to Apple for approval, 14 percent of those for the month under review were games.[10] In January 2011, the top three Paid Apps (in the U.S. store) were all games—Angry Birds, Fruit Ninja, and Cut the Rope. The diversity of the offered games has evolved from simple 2D ports of older games to include original creations that fall into varied genres such as action, first-person shooter, role-playing, and adventure, as well as games that feature full 3D graphics, even if the best-selling games reflect simpler styles of play. Providing yet more choices, the App Store's section for games includes separate categories for educational, strategy, simulation, trivia, music, and other types of games.

Although games are a significant presence in the App Store as well as on many users' phones, their pricing model is still in flux, ranging from the more expensive titles such as Square Enix's Chaos Ring (US$12.99) to the more popular, cheaper games such as Fruit Ninja ($0.99), to games that cost nothing at all. Free games constitute a large portion of the games in the App Store, yet "free" can mean many things. The category includes fully free games, free games that are mainly demos or samplers for paid versions, and freemium games, which can be played for free but require payment to unlock various elements, such as additional levels, areas, items, or skills. There is still debate about which model is best for pricing and how much certain games should be priced at, with some developers worried that there is a "race to the bottom" of pricing that will result in declines in quality and opportunities for independent developers. Yet others argue that there are other ways to make a profit from mobile games, beyond a specific charge to buy the title. According to data about average prices for apps, the average game price in 2011 was $1.66, while the average app price was $4.07. This suggests that either games are popular because they are less expensive than other apps or that perhaps there is room for a price increase. Only greater experimentation among game developers will answer that question, however.

Thus, in only a few years, the iPhone went from being a games-free device to a platform that (along with the iPod Touch and the iPad) Apple now sees as a serious contender in the mobile gaming world.[11] Of course, simply offering games isn't enough to ensure they are purchased and played. Developers worked to build games that went beyond early ports and arcade classics and that specifically fit the context of use—mobility with a touch screen. And while multiple types of games featuring quite different play styles are available on the iPhone, some have been more successful than others in insinuating a particular type of gameplay into the domain of the everyday iPhone user. One such company is Rovio, via their game Angry Birds.

Angry Birds

The company that developed Angry Birds—Rovio—is based in Finland, and has been making games for various platforms since 2005; it is no newcomer to game development or to mobile games. The company has in the past made games for Nokia's N-Gage and other platforms, although nothing that generated the success of Angry Birds.

One of the challenges for iPhone game developers has been pricing. Rovio takes a common approach for Angry Birds: it offers both a free (limited) version of the game and a full version for ninety-nine cents. The free version serves as a demo for the full version, allowing players to try the game and see if they'd be willing to pay for more content. As of December 2010, Angry Birds had been downloaded (across all platforms) more than 42 million times, with about 25 percent of those downloads being the paid version.[12] Compared to conversion rates of 2 to 3 percent for downloadable casual games, such numbers point toward success. Yet it's likely the price point has been key—while other games can cost upward of ten dollars, most successful mobile games are either free or priced at ninety-nine cents.

Indie developers have noted their concern over this unwillingness by consumers to pay more for games—arguing that "it forces a lot of developers, specifically indies, to devalue their games to significantly increase the number of sales needed for developers to get back their investment."[13] Echoing that concern, the three games listed as top sellers for January 2011 all cost ninety-nine cents, and, indeed, all of the games listed in the top ten Paid Apps for this period (only two apps were not games) were priced the same. But although the price is a point of concern for developers, the majority of consumers have gravitated toward low- and no-cost games. Of course, price isn't their only concern—a game must be "good" in some way to succeed—and what makes a mobile game good is quite different from traditional console games. Examining the gameplay of Angry Birds makes this clear—the title has minimal story and basic graphics, yet gameplay is polished, is accomplishable in brief bursts, has multiple paths to success, and features mechanics and themes basic enough for almost any user to pick it up and play successfully.

Angry Birds has been described as a physics-based or platformer game that takes particular advantage of the iPhone's touch screen. The game has a nominal storyline (distracted birds have their eggs stolen by greedy pigs, at whom the birds then launch themselves for revenge via elaborate structures and bird-detonation choices) that plays as an introductory cut scene and offers the player a simple motivation for why one would want to fling birds at various structures. Each bird is launched via slingshot and has a special power—blue birds when tapped in midflight will multiply into three birds; yellow birds when touched will use a burst of speed; large red birds will drop a bomb, and so on. The birds are given to the player in a particular order, and the player must strategize how best to destroy each level's unique structure and thus reveal and destroy the pigs before running out of available birds. The player must also strategize her use of birds and where (at structures and pigs) they should aim and when.

The game's levels are arranged in chapters, and players must beat each individual level in order to advance. Levels are likewise scored, with the player receiving points for each pig that is destroyed, barricade elements that are demolished, and remaining birds left unused. Players can earn from one to three stars on a level but must clear the level in order to advance, even if only with one star. Each level can generally be played in under a minute, with levels varying in difficulty based on the challenges involved. The world of Angry Birds is a colorful one, with multihued birds and comical pigs that often wear helmets to keep themselves safe. Graphics are minimal, however, since the main point of the game is movement—figuring out the best trajectory for each bird and how best to use birds of various types—which part of a structure a bomb-dropping bird should target, as opposed to how best to launch an explode-upon-impact bird. The slingshot allows the player a fair amount of control over trajectory as well as speed, although simple force is never enough to clear levels and kill pigs. And while early levels are fairly straightforward and forgiving—almost any trajectory will work—later levels force players to strategize how to launch birds, where to detonate them, and how collateral damage can be used to add points as well as bump off a seemingly invincible pig.

The length of time it takes to play a level is key for a few reasons. First, clearing a level provides the playing of the victory theme, along with the player's score for the level, hopefully leading to gratification and a sense of accomplishment for the player. While easy levels can be easily dispatched and thus might pass in a blur, the endless barrage of levels is punctuated by the sounds of success every minute or so, giving the player short bursts of positive feedback. Likewise, if a player fails a level, it's over quickly and immediately available to retry—no long loading times or cut scenes to wade through. Levels can also be instantly interrupted and restarted. Thus if I know I need to use each bird in a particular way and one bird fails in its mission, I can quickly restart the level, rather than finish it knowing I will lose. The ability to replay and retry is a key element of the gameplay—normal, expected, and facilitated by the developers.

Another reason for short levels is to accommodate the varying nature of mobile gaming. Although mobile games are increasingly played in the home, in a person's bedroom, they are also ubiquitous in public places. At the time of this writing, Angry Birds is probably currently being played on buses and subways, in grocery store and bank lines, while waiting for friends and relatives to be ready, and in many other interstitial spaces and times. A level can be completed in as little as ten seconds. Yet once started, those quickly accomplished levels, as well as the annoyingly difficult levels, can also lead players to a "just one more" mindset, allowing gameplay to balloon outward in time, sometimes spilling over into and interrupting the events the game was supposed to help one get to or past.

Another way that Angry Birds finds success with the market is through its varied play style. While for some players it may be effort enough to progress from one level to another and unlock new birds and chapters, Rovio also built in elements for those desiring different experiences. For example, each level must be completed to advance, but players can earn from one to three stars for completion. Stars are awarded based on points earned via destruction of pigs and structures, and via conserving the birds allotted to the player. Those desiring perfect scores can thus replay levels to achieve full stars, which can also unlock special bonuses in the game. The final element is the addition of leader boards and achievements. These are not an overly obvious part of the game but do figure into its success. Players can compete against a worldwide population or against friends. Likewise the game awards for certain achievements that the player unlocks. For players desiring to compete or earn visible recognition of their Angry Birds scores, these add to the pleasure of the game. Finally, the game is regularly updated by the developers, who add new levels and birds to keep the game from growing stale. All of these elements combine to give different types of players multiple paths to play through and enjoy without requiring all of them.

Those multiple options and simple form of play ultimately help us take games along with us more easily throughout our days. Although dedicated gamers have always had the option of mobile game systems such as the Nintendo Game Boy (or more recent 3DS) and Sony's PSP to move gaming out of the home or away from a stationary arcade, games on the iPhone make games more accessible for many more people. Games are being democratized and destigmatized—the app for Angry Birds sits quite easily beside it's owners Facebook app, weather app, and Nike+ app. The owner doesn't need to purchase a dedicated gaming system to engage in some playful activity. Games are thus normalized, becoming part of the everyday landscape that is an iPhone owner's screen. That sharing of screen space indicates the banality of games just as it signals their move—quite literally—into pedestrian life and their resulting mainstream acceptance.

Conclusion

Although mobile games existed before the iPhone, the device created a common platform that developers could exploit to reach more players and widen their potential audience. The large number of games available upon the opening of the App Store to third-party developers indicates some of that pent-up demand finally being released. Developers now have a sizable, preinstalled base of potential customers and have worked to create games that fit the portable, tactile, motion-sensitive device. Likewise, consumers were eased into buying games through the iTunes storefront and have made games one of the most profitable segments of app development.

One of the greatest successes of that system is Angry Birds, although many other games have also developed similar styles of play and reached many people who otherwise do not play games. What's key about Angry Birds (and the games like it) is its success in normalizing *play* in the everyday lives of a growing segment of society. While consoles are still seen as being for "core gamers" and thus a smaller, more easily identified demographic group, iPhone game players defy categorization. They likely do not even identify themselves as game players or, worse (to them), as *gamers*. Games are simply more apps on their phone—to use to pass the time, avoid interactions, relax and unwind, compete, or learn. As previous researchers found in Japan, iPhone users more broadly have incorporated play as a nonexceptional activity into their lives and thus normalized the practice. In part thanks to the iPhone, now no one is a gamer—instead, we are all players.

NOTES

1. Andrew Honan, "Apple Unveils iPhone," *MacWorld*, 9 January 2007, http://www.macworld.com/article/54769/2007/01/iphone.html (15 February 2011).

2. Harvey May and Greg Hearn, "The Mobile Phone as Media," *International Journal of Cultural Studies* 8, no. 2 (2005): 200.

3. For a discussion, see Mizuko Ito, Daisuke Okabe, and Misa Matsuda, *Personal, Portable, Pedestrian: Mobile Phones in Japanese Life* (Cambridge, Mass.: MIT Press, 2005).

4. May and Hearn, "The Mobile Phone as Media," 196.

5. Virpi Oksman and Jussi Turtiainen, "Mobile Communication as a Social Stage," *New Media and Society* 3 (2004): 319–39.

6. Shintaro Okazaki, Radoslav Skapa, and Ildefonso Grande, "Capturing Global Youth: Mobile Gaming in the US, Spain, and the Czech Republic," *Journal of Computer-Mediated Communication* 13 (2008): 827–55.

7. Michal Daliot-Bul, "Japan's Mobile Technoculture: The Production of a Cellular Playscape and Its Cultural Implications," *Media, Culture, and Society* 6 (2007): 945–71.

8. Dean Chan, "Convergence, Connectivity, and the Case of Japanese Mobile Gaming," *Games and Culture* 1 (2008): 13–25.

9. G. De Prato et al., "Born Digital/Grown Digital: Assessing the Future Competitiveness of the EU Video Games Software Industry," in *JRC Scientific and Technical Reports* (Luxembourg: Publication Office of the European Union, 2010).

10. "Apple iTunes App Store Metrics," *148apps.biz*, 9 January 2011, http://148apps .biz/app-store-metrics (15 February 2011).

11. Christian Nutt, "Analysis: Apple Heading Toward a Gaming Collision Course," *Gamasutra*, 1 September 2010, http://gamasutra.com/view/news/30224/Analysis_ Apple_Heading_Toward_A_Gaming_Collision_Course.php (15 February 2011).

12. Ben Parr, "Angry Birds Hits 42 Million Free and Paid Downloads," *Mashable. com*, 8 December 2010, http://mashable.com/2010/12/08/angry-birds-hits-42-million -downloads/ (15 February 2011).

13. Andrew Webster, "Finding the Sweet Spot: Pricing for Independent Games," *Gamasutra*, 12 Janury 2010, http://www.gamasutra.com/view/feature/4241/finding_ the_sweet_spot_pricing_.php (15 February 2011).

CHAPTER 13

Reading (with) the iPhone

GERARD GOGGIN

At Xerox PARC, to spur interest in high culture cum computers,
I made a slide presentation about a wonderful technology called Basic
Organization of Knowledge (B.O.O.K.) It was solid state; held
several megabytes . . . weighed only a few pounds; had low power drain;
had a high resolution, high contrast readable display that was highly
legible in daylight; and had the capacity to represent the most important
segments of the world's knowledge. "Yes, folks," I used to say, "the
B.O.O.K. will revolutionize our culture, lead to better forms of politics
and technology, and bring about a new kind of modern world."
—ALAN C. KAY, *"A Review Article: Dynabooks: Past, Present, and Future"*

Ebooks promise to revolutionize the way the world reads.
—BILL GATES, *"Beyond Gutenberg"*

It doesn't matter how good or bad the product is, the fact is that
people don't read anymore. . . . Forty percent of the people in the U.S.
read one book or less last year. The whole conception is flawed at the
top because people don't read anymore.
—STEVE JOBS, 2008

The book . . . just turns out to be an incredible device.
—JEFF BEZOS, 2007

THE USE OF handheld electronic devices—recently termed e-books or
e-readers—for reading has a relatively long history, spanning at least four
decades. There were many experiments, prototypes, commercial developments, and some early reader fascination. In the 2010s, mobile phones and
media have become well positioned as important forces in contemporary
reading. New genres associated with text messaging and "cell-phone novels"
(popular notably in Japan) are already well established. Moreover, the advent
of smartphones promised to offer new applications to make the mobile a
reflex technology for reading.

It is fair to say, however, that neither the market for e-readers nor their extensive use really coalesced until 2007. A key reason that e-reading finally started to capture the wider public imagination, in Western countries at least, was the appearance of the iPhone. It was the iPhone that really catalyzed the potential of mobiles to be full-fledged reading devices with its new affordances—haptic manipulation of text, ductility of the handset, characteristics of its screen resolution—and, of course, the fertile possibilities of iPhone apps. For many users, the iPhone really became a flexible, cheap, relatively easy-to-use reader, competing with the e-readers still languishing in their infancy, such as Sony's e-reader. Consequently, this chapter argues that if we wish to understand the dynamics and contours of the iPhone, its social functions, historical "moment," and cultural implications, then reading is an important part of its story. Conversely, if we are interested in contemporary reading practices, then our itinerary takes us through the iPhone—indeed, a notable stop on such an exploration.

In this chapter, I reprise the iPhone's career as one of the first viable e-readers. First, I briefly sketch the prehistories of electronic reading that shaped the iPhone, including types of reading on mobile phone devices. I then look at the design of the iPhone and what Apple imagined as the reading possibilities for the technology. I consider how users, the people formerly known as readers, took up the iPhone, discussing the kinds of reading practices they devised—and also what kinds of reading apps were developed and became popular. I place the development of reading on the iPhone in the wider scene of the digital transformation and politics of reading and publishing. Here I consider the advent of Amazon's Kindle and the panoply of e-readers around the world and where the iPhone fits into these dynamics. Finally, I look at Apple's third device, the one in the middle between the laptop and smartphone, as CEO Steve Jobs famously described the iPad at its January 2010 launch. With the iPad making a trio of the duo of laptop and smartphone, not to mention, in point of fact, many other kinds of devices and shades in between, reading becomes a full-fledged part of the moving data and personalization of media that the iPhone moment represents.

Prefiguring iPhone Reading

The history of reading is a large, rich topic, with much recent research, theorizing, and revisionary discussion. There is a wealth of work on the closely related topics of writing, authorship, and publishing but also on the relatively new research area of the history of the book. We also have a substantial literature on technologies of reading, especially electronic and digital technologies and books.[1] Until comparatively recently, however, these discussions on the history of online reading, e-books, and digital technologies have tended to focus on the computer and online media, such as hypertext and the Internet—rather than mobiles. However, an interesting aspect about attempts to grapple with the iPad, especially, has been the way that commentators, notably in the tech press and blogs, have had recourse to popular, available histories of computing and portable technologies—and how these figured in new notions of reading and writing.

The most obvious precursor device for the iPad is the Dynabook, devised by Alan C. Kay in the late 1960s and described as a protoype in a famous 1972 paper.[2] Reflecting on the Dynabook thirty years later, Kay wrote:

> I proposed a notebook-sized 'Dynabook' ('Dynabook: A Personal Computer for Children of All Ages') that would act as a new kind of electronic book for content of all kinds—especially dynamic and high content—and could also serve as a supermedium for authoring a wide range of ideas in new and important ways . . . it struck me that a children's computer had to be mobile (just like them) and should look more like a notebook than a time-sharing terminal on a desk (an Aldus book vs. a Gutenberg Bible). . . . [Children] needed to be able to read about important ideas of all kinds and to 'write' in a variety of media to make the ideas their own. This meant that the display had to be really readable (not just decipherable).[3]

Extolling its virtues in 1972, Kay suggested that:

> 'Books' can now be 'instantiated' instead of bought or checked out. . . . The ability to make copies easily and to 'own' one's information will probably not debilitate existing markets, just as easy xerography has enhanced publishing (rather than hurting it as some predicted), and as tapes have not damaged the LP record business but have provided a way to organize one's own music. Most people are not interested in acting as a source of bootlegger; rather, they like to permute and play with what they own. A combination of this 'carry anywhere' device and a global information utility such as the ARPA network or two-way cable TV, will bring the libraries and schools (not to mention stores and billboards) or the world to the home.[4]

In his study of the Dynabook, John Maxwell comments: "If the invention of the digital computer can be compared with the invention of the printing press, then it follows that there is an analogous period following its initial invention in which its role, function, and nature have not yet been worked out. In the history of printing, this period was the late 15th century, commonly called the incunabula, when early printers experimented with ways of conducting their craft and their trade."[5] Maxwell's observation is a telling one for the field of electronic books, as well as personal computers, to which Kay and his colleagues at Xerox PARC made such significant contributions.[6] The parallels between the Dynabook and the iPad have been remarked on by several commentators, among them the tech writer Wolfgang Gruener. Gruener interviewed Alan Kay about the similarities, and Kay told the following story:

> "When Steve [Jobs] showed me the iPhone at its introduction a few years ago and asked me if 'it was good enough to criticize,' which is what I had said about the Mac in 1984, I held up my Moleskine notebook and said 'make the screen at least 5"x8" and you will rule the world," Kay said. . . . "Of course, I meant do more than just that, but it was clear the iPhone was going to be really appealing and very useful for most people," Kay said. "When I saw the iPhone, I figured that they had already done a tablet version, which is easier to make work than the iPhone, so I was partially joking with Steve."[7]

In the years between the Dynabook and iPad, the personal computer developed enormously. Much reading of documents, texts, and books was actually done on desktop computers until portability became possible with laptops, notebooks, and tablets. Yet the personal computer does not appear to be directly conceived via the metaphor of the book. By this I mean that while the computer certainly was the subject of much experimentation, habituation, and discussion as a new kind of reading device—a catalyst for innovations in both reading and writing—its materiality was quite different from existing books, their forms, tactility, associations, and affects. Rather, the concept of an e-book developed—twinning the portability of a book with its ability to contain and represent words, writing, and texts. The origins of this "dream of electronic books"[8] has been traced to Vannevar Bush's famous paper "As We May Think," where he proposes a device dubbed a "memex" that operates, like the human mind, by association. "Consider a future device for individual use, which is a sort of mechanized private file and library," Bush wrote. "It needs a name, and to coin one at random, 'memex' will do. A memex is a device in which an individual stores all his books, records, and communications, and which is mechanized so that it may be consulted with exceeding speed and flexibility. It is an enlarged intimate supplement to his memory. . . . Wholly new forms of encyclopedias will appear, ready-made with a mesh of associative trails running through them, ready to be dropped into the memex and there amplified."[9] One trajectory from Vannevar Bush obviously leads through hypertext narrative and writing and the World Wide Web—and now through the contemporary visions of social media. Another trajectory neglects the emphasis Bush puts on imagining a new associative technology and realizes, even if only as an intermediate goal, the idea of storing and retrieving books. This later trajectory is largely what commercially available e-books have followed, since the term become widely used in the late 1990s. As Terje Hillesund explains:

> In the broad sense e-books have been around for several decades. In the Gutenberg Project thousands of books, mostly classic and public domain literature, have been made available for free as digital documents since the 1970s. . . . Before the term e-book came around in the late 1990s it was not unusual to talk about electronic books in terms of files collected in the Gutenberg Project or books formatted on compact discs. There were also early unsuccessful attempts at making reading software for computers. . . . [In 2001] the term e-book refers to digital objects specially made to be read with reading applications operating on either a handheld device or a personal computer. This modern concept of e-books came into common use after Martin Eberhart and Jim Sachs both started their own companies and developed Rocket eBook and SoftBook, the first two handheld e-book reading devices.[10]

Some commentators talk of the first generation of e-book readers, including the Sony Data Discman (1990), the Franklin Bookman, and the early Rocket eBook and Softbook. The second generation—with "modem capabilities, greater memory, better screen resolution, and a more robust selection of available titles"[11]—included the SoftBook Reader (1998), Libruis Millenium device, and Everybook Dedicated Reader. In 1998, an organized effort began to create a common standard, and the Open eBook Structure was produced the following year. It became a precursor to the standards now produced by the International Digital Publishing Forum. Sensing the mood of the late 1990s, Bill Gates—promoting Microsoft's development of the font-display technology "Clear Type" as well as the corporation's involvement in the open e-book standard—declared that "e-books promise to revolutionize the way the world reads. Whereas paper books are stand-alone entities, e-books can include hypertext links to additional content, whether it is in other books, databases or web sites." Gates also stressed that "you will also be able to customize e-books by adding your own notes, links and images. In a paper book, content is fixed; with e-book technology it is flexible. Finally, you will be able to get sound and moving images to support the text, creating an entirely new multi-medium."[12]

Despite the enthusiasm shown by large booksellers, computer companies, and e-book technology developers, the road still remained bumpy.[13] Standards remained a problem, especially with e-books, whereas some types of proprietary software, such as Adobe PDF, were gaining acceptance and portability across devices, amounting to de facto standards.[14] Moreover, the affordances of the devices themselves were underwhelming. In reviewing available e-books, no less than Alan Kay himself judged that "little of what is good about books and good about computers was in evidence."[15] The metaphor of generations is, of course, too pat, but if it does hold, this can be seen to commence in 2005, when Sony launched its e-book reader—the "Sony Librie"—using E-Ink technology for its screen. I will return to the Sony e-book reader shortly, but for the present I want to depart from the history of e-books, as they were regarded from the late 1990s through 2005, to consider cellular mobile phones and reading.

Cellular mobile phones were launched commercially in the late 1970s, and for their first decade and a half were principally associated with portable voice telephony and communications. With the advent of second-generation digital mobile phone standards, notably the Global Standard for Mobile, various kinds of writing and reading became possible and popular. The most distinctive textual feature of mobile phone culture was text messaging. Text messaging commenced as a form of subcultural exchange of messages and witnessed the development of abbreviated language and even argot among users. The possibilities for messages, letters, and even longer texts soon became something that attracted experimentation and even a genre of literature based on text messaging. There were different varieties of such writing—especially based around sending of messages as installments, epistles, or parts of dialogue. Most prominently, however, cell phone novels emerged in a number of countries, first Japan (in 2003), then other countries in Asia, Europe, and Africa. The largest Japanese cell phone novel site, Maho i-Land, attracted considerable attention in English-language press, especially notable as a gendered form:[16] "The cell-phone novel, or *keitai shosetsu*, is the first literary genre to emerge from the cellular age. For a new form, it is remarkably robust. Maho i-Land . . . carries more than a million titles, most of them by amateurs writing under screen handles and all available for free." According to the figures provided by the company, the site, which also offers templates for blogs and home pages, is visited three and a half billion times a month.[17] The phenomenon of the mobile phone novel highlights the potential of these portable devices to go beyond simply functioning as useful document readers.

With the availability of Windows Office, Adobe PDF, and other software on mobiles, especially smartphones—to compete with the PDA market— more computer-screen-like reading on mobiles began to occur. A French company, Mobipocket, founded in 2000, became the leader in e-book read- ing on mobile devices. Mobipocket is one of the three main e-book formats based on the Open eBook standards, focusing on offering book titles for reading on PDAs or a range of mobile-device operating systems (Windows Mobile, Blackberry, Symbian, and so on). Acquired by Amazon.com in 2005, Mobipocket promotes its e-books under rubrics such as "Did you ever try to read a book one handed?," "Did you ever try to read in the dark?," and "Read everywhere":

> Reading on a phone? What a funny idea . . . the screen is too small and I don't even read PDF documents! This is what I thought before trying, but . . . 5 minutes to kill? I always have a phone in my pocket. Packed sub- way? There is always enough room to pop out my phone. On vacation? I've my entire library with me. It's dark? It's cool to have a backlight. The screen is too small? Of course not, I like to read on my phone.[18]

Similarly, the resurgence of mobile Internet from after 2006 (it had been introduced but flopped in the late 1990s), also saw many kinds of online read- ing familiar from computer and laptop screens migrating to mobiles. These developments continued, but a new direction emerged with the appearance of the iPhone.

Reading with the iPhone

When Apple first launched its iPhone to rapturous reviews and strong sales, its capabilities as a reading device were not well-publicized. Apple's first of- ficial media release announced:

> Apple® today introduced iPhone, combining three products—a revo- lutionary mobile phone, a widescreen iPod® with touch controls, and a

breakthrough Internet communications device with desktop-class email, web browsing, searching and maps—into one small and lightweight hand-held device. iPhone introduces an entirely new user interface based on a large multi-touch display and pioneering new software, letting users control iPhone with just their fingers. iPhone also ushers in an era of software power and sophistication never before seen in a mobile device, which completely redefines what users can do on their mobile phones.[19]

In the early flush of enthusiasm for the iPhone, Apple emphasized music, maps, browsers, touch, and the device's sensors, without any mention of reading books. In its early advertising, however, Apple did focus upon newspapers. A 2008 advertisement for the iPhone on the Apple website prominently featured a page from the *New York Times* to show the ease of browsing on the device. News on mobile media devices had been in development since the mid-1990s offering alerts, information, messages with breaking headlines, premium mobile services, and, with better mobile Internet, reading newspapers via their online websites.[20] So the promotion of the iPhone as a news- and newspaper-reading device should be seen as a significant development in this trajectory. (It is interesting to note here that the *New York Times* has been a prominent sponsor and partner in many Apple events to promote the iPad.)

Apple seemed to devote little or no effort to promoting e-books and e-reading, apart from news; less than two years later, however, the iPhone was forging ahead in the e-book market, apparently without even trying, according to a much-quoted article in *Forbes* magazine:

> It's official: The iPhone is more popular than Amazon.com's Kindle. And not just in the obvious categories like listening to music, browsing the Web or the other applications where Kindle barely competes. Now, the iPhone is also muscling into Amazon's home turf: reading books. Stanza, a book reading application offered in Apple's iPhone App Store since July, has been downloaded more than 395,000 times. . . . By comparison, Citigroup estimates Amazon will sell around 380,000 Kindles in 2008. . . . Sony's Reader [it is estimated] will sell only a fraction of that number. In other words, Apple may have inadvertently sold more e-readers than any other company in the nascent digital book market.[21]

One year later, the iPhone had been hailed as a genuine force in the e-reader market. "One of the most popular e-reader devices on the market could soon be the iPhone," an article in *eWeek* stated. "'In October [2009] one out of every five new apps launching in the iPhone has been a book,' said Peter Farago, Flurry's vice president of marketing. . . . 'Publishers of all kinds, from small ones like Your Mobile Apps to megapublishers like Softbank, are porting existing IP [intellectual property] into the App store at record rates.'"[22] It is unclear what Apple's corporate strategy was for e-reading on the iPhone in the initial launch; little or nothing is evident in the publicly available documentation. Thus, the popularity of the iPhone as a reading device appears to have occurred because of apps as a platform or arena for innovation.[23]

At its launch, the iPhone did not allow third-party developers to offer applications, a heavily criticized move.[24] Once it released its Software Developers Kit and Apps Store, the results were impressive—a wide range of apps including various e-readers. The two that initially became popular on the iPhone were Stanza and eReader, a piece of software with a pedigree on mobile devices: "Fictionwise's eReader has a long and glorious history as the e-book software for the Palm OS. And it was right there the first day iPhone apps became available. . . . Fictionwise's extensive experience in the field shows in eReader's many well-thought-out interface choices."[25]

Various other e-reader apps followed. These included the Classics app, which featured a stylized wooden bookshelf: "Escape into some of the greatest stories ever written and experience a revolutionary new reading platform, only for iPhone and iPod Touch. . . . We care deeply about these books. That's why we've spent countless hours working on making them look just right on the screen, with included illustrations when available, and even our own, custom cover designs."[26] There is nothing fancy about the Classics app, but it assumed its place of honor on the iPhone, as *PC Magazine* stated:

> Other iPhone e-book readers take pride in how many books they offer and how much they let you futz with fonts and display. Not so Classics. The selection of books you can read is limited to what the software vendors consider worthy great literature [*sic*], and the formatting is painstakingly designed—and immutable. . . . [But] Classics is a worthy addition to any bibliophile's iPhone owner's stable of apps. The program's aesthetic is much like Apple's own: You get only one choice, but it's beautifully executed.[27]

Pioneering e-reader apps on the iPhone, such as Stanza and eReader, allowed readers to tap into the existing stock of e-books in different formats, built up over some time. In February 2009, Google made its public-domain books available through a mobile website for both iPhone and Android users—with readers using their browsers, as is customary with Google

Books. Best-selling titles were gradually made available via e-reader apps for the iPhone, including popular genres such as romance, fantasy, science fiction, and so on. In the meantime, "classics" were heavily featured in the Classics app. In early 2011, the Classics website featured titles such as *Alice in Wonderland*, *Robinson Crusoe*, *Gulliver's Travels*, *Paradise Lost*, *Pride and Prejudice*, and *Treasure Island*: "Some of the greatest stories ever written." Beyond the cultural legitimacy offered by these choices, a practical reason is that classics are typically out of copyright (unless copyright resides in a particular recent edition). So machine-readable e-texts are widely available at little cost, not the least via projects such as Gutenberg, even if, as the case is with Classics, the company spends "countless hours working on them to look just right on the screen." Ultimately, iTunes was not so much a way to offer books for purchase as to make the apps themselves available—and then to provide a way for users to load, transfer, and organize their book purchases or existing free books via iTunes. A more adventurous development occurred in the modification or creation of interactive books as apps for the iPhone. These included genres such as children's books, with titles such as *Princess Dress-Up: My Sticker Book*, Dr Seuss's *Fox in Sox*, *Winnie the Pooh Puzzle Book*, and *True Ghost Stories from Around the World* (with new stories regularly added). Children's books had long had different kinds of interactivity, users expectations, and play (pop-ups, tactile features, tear-offs, stickers, and so on), so iPhone apps provide a new medium for realizing these features.

No sooner had the iPhone established itself as a handy medium of choice for many readers through the unexpected user-driven success of e-reader apps then the real battle in the economy of reading began. In November 2007, Jeff Bezos launched Amazon's much awaited Kindle e-reader device. *Newsweek* called the event the "reinvention of the book":

> Though the Kindle is at heart a reading machine made by a bookseller—and works most impressively when you are buying a book or reading it—it is also something more: a perpetually connected Internet device. A few twitches of the fingers and that zoned-in connection between your mind and an author's machinations can be interrupted—or enhanced—by an avalanche of data. Therein lies the disruptive nature of the Amazon Kindle. It's the first "always-on" book.[28]

Quickly adopted by readers, particularly in the United States, because of its potential for easy purchase and wireless and mobile download of books—but also because of the well-known Amazon brand—the device proved so

popular that it eclipsed the early-to-market Sony e-Reader. The Kindle became the first dedicated e-reader to gain wide adoption in the consumer market. This presented both a challenge and an opportunity for Apple's iPhone.
On the one hand, Apple, by dint of the e-reader apps available for the iPhone,
had become popular for reading, echoing its popularity in the games and
music markets. Kindle also was forced to create an app for iPhone because
of its popularity—and the need to ensure that Amazon, rather than Kindle
per se, was represented on the iPhone platform. On the other hand, the Kindle was a worthy, if not formidable competitor to the iPhone because its
larger format, customized for reading, was a preferred reading experience
for many. And the Kindle opened the door directly to the vast trove of Amazon's book wares, quite an advantage given that Amazon was the leviathan
of online book retailing. Kindle also departed in important respects from the
iPhone and other smartphones because it was, after all, a device centered on
book lovers. Its early versions were anomalous in this regard: it was devoid
of Web surfing and e-mail capabilities, and its wireless feature functioned
as a delivery mechanism rather than something the user could configure or
customize.

At the end of 2009, the bricks-and-mortar U.S. book giant Barnes & Noble launched its own e-reader, the Nook. With the Nook, Barnes & Noble
claimed to offer access to more books, newspapers, and magazines than Amazon, and also, via its Wi-Fi, free in-store browsing of complete e-books.[29] The
Canadian Kobo e-reader launched in May 2010, a venture in which Indigo
Music and Books holds the majority interest and has partnered with Borders
to offer the device in Hong Kong and Australia.[30] At the same time, Kobo
launched its software, which works on other e-reader devices, such as laptops,
smartphones, and tablets, and allows access to a Kobo account for purchasing
e-books, audiobooks, and other materials.

The launch of the iPhone in the United States, and especially as it slowly
rolled out in the rest of the world, occurred only a little before the e-reader
market gained a great deal of energy and consumer acceptance. Although
Apple was not lacking for business and profitability with the great success of
its iPhone, the device still unexpectedly won them a toehold in the e-reader
market. Of course, Apple, with its reputation for secrecy, was doubtlessly
developing its e-reader strategies in private.[31] Yet the furious incubation of
e-readers all around the world after late 2007—including in countries like
China, which have received little notice from the Anglophone world—also
posed serious challenges for Apple's directions in smartphones and its next
gambit—the reinvention of the tablet.

Apple's First (Official) Reader: the iPad

Gossip about Apple's plans to develop a tablet device, perhaps called the iTablet or iSlate, was rife for some years before the iPad premiered. The press release announcing the iPad outlined its main selling points:

> Apple® today introduced iPad, a revolutionary device for browsing the web, reading and sending email, enjoying photos, watching videos, listening to music, playing games, reading e-books and much more. . . . Apple also announced the new iBooks app for iPad, which includes Apple's new iBookstore, the best way to browse, buy and read books on a mobile device. The iBookstore will feature books from major and independent publishers.[32]

When Jobs unveiled the iPad, he also touted the iBooks app, claiming that it would be a breakthrough in e-reading. Apple deliberately targeted the publishing community and actively began to negotiate deals.[33] Unlike the iPhone, however, in which e-reading grew "unofficially," the "official" iBook app and the iBookstore were slow to develop—especially in countries other than the United States. "When Steve Jobs launched the iPad this year, he predicted its iBooks app would be the way forward for publishing, purchasing and reading e-books. But the months since the tablet's launch in Australia have been frustrating as Apple concentrated on setting up US and British markets, leaving merely out-of-copyright classics in the local iBookstore."[34] Even toward the end of 2010, the Apple iBookstore lacked titles, compared to its chief competitors: Kindle, Nook, and Kobo. With the ease of use and features of these e-reader apps, and others, there was no compelling reason for iPad users (including this author) to wait for Apple to finally offer comprehensive offerings through its iBookstore.

Apple's iPad had a slow start as an official, authorized, and self-proclaimed entrant into e-books. Yet in other respects, the iPad built upon the achievements of the iPhone in becoming a reading technology, extending upon the smartphone's features and uses. As a tie-in—rhetorically, at least, if not materially significant yet—with Rupert Murdoch's News Corporation's publishing interests and his drive to find a "pay wall" solution for his newspapers, the iPad has been used by the press to experiment with iPhone apps. Many newspapers were quickly available in iPhone apps for a modest monthly subscription of a few dollars or bundled in with the regular hardcopy newspaper delivery. These newspaper iPad apps were as much prototypes as mature software, as much an innovation—or incunabula—as online news websites were in the 1990s (and indeed to the present day).

The iPad has also become the e-reader and document reader of choice of many of its early adopters because of its size, resolution, and compatibility with other Apple computers and e-reader software. This is surprising in one sense, but there are many difficulties in using the iPad as a versatile computer or e-reader: its operating system is not easily accessible; unless hacked (voiding the warranty), software can only be installed via the app store; it has no ports; and available software for document reading was still clunky when this article was written (I have made do with Documents to Go, an unsatisfactory, but workable solution). The user finds all these poor design aspects of the iPad and its apps (Apple's and those of third-party developers) curious for a corporation praised for its hip design achievements. Some of these issues are likely to be addressed with the iPad 2. However, they underscore how the iPad is skewed toward consumption of media content, reading included. The iPad certainly has had its success and become a necessary complement (or supplement) to the computer for many, including those who would rarely choose to read a long PDF or other document or book on-screen if the more amenable version for the tablet is available.

Phoning in the Future of the iBook

The Apple iPhone represents a surprising development in the technologies of reading. As I have argued, its achievement, thus far at least, is in many ways accidental—or, to put it another way, coeval with other features of the iPhone that have made it a striking development in mobile personal media. It is obvious that Apple's genius, as received by, appropriated by, and cocreated with its users, does not lie solely in the technical, social, cultural, or imaginative breakthroughs of a Vannevar Bush, Theodore Nelson, or Alan C. Kay. Nor does it stem from a longstanding engagement with, say, the roots of contemporary online and electronic reading and writing in hypertext narrative and systems (associated with Mark Bernstein's Eastgate Systems in the 1990s), nor from a deep research and development immersion in e-reading, e-ink, and so on of the likes associated with Sony or various other pioneering corporations. Rather, Apple is able to bring together various inventions and capabilities; combine them, with an eye to attractive design, good user interfaces, and new navigation concepts; and, with particular classes of devices, thematize an area of media—whether computing (Macs), music (iPods), games, telephony, messaging, maps, and e-mail (iPhone), and digital consumption of convergent media, news, and other people's e-readings (iPad, after the iPhone).

Apple's iBookstore may well start to make headway against its vertically integrated e-reader competitors. If it does not yet have the know-how or cultural capital possessed by other booksellers, nor solid relationships with major publishers, what it does have is a simple, well-established advantage: iTunes. With business models and billing systems for digital goods under development since the mid-1990s, and still changing, Apple's iTunes gives the corporation a handy advantage—apparent in the recently launched Mac App Store. The many consumers of Apple computers, iPods, iPhones, and iPads are accustomed to using iTunes for purchasing music, games, videos, apps—and, eventually, audio and e-books. Indeed, it is difficult to overstate the importance of iTunes as the backbone for the distribution platforms that undergird all of Apple's devices. Consumer acceptance of iTunes in terms of security and ease of use is strong, and payment requires only a credit card or purchase of iTune vouchers or credit. From iTunes Apple gets a significant advantage, not only over its competitors in the smartphone, e-reader, tablet, computer, and other device markets but also vis-à-vis suppliers of content, distribution, and billing systems.

Yet it seems that reimagining reading is something that Apple still struggles with. A sign of this lies in the dull image of the iBook app itself. It is simply a wooden bookshelf, one of the most obvious figures of books and reading. Indeed, it rather resembles the image chosen by the Classics app, a similarity for which Apple has been accused of copying without attribution or appropriate acknowledgment.[35] Probably the best thing that Apple has done so far in its adventures in reading was to open itself up to the wide range of software of its third-party apps developers and, despite its efforts at control, the unauthorized and permissible acts of domestication, hacking, modification, and innovation by its millions of everyday iPhone and iPad users. In all other respects, however, when it comes to reading futures, we still await the magic and revolution Apple has promised.

NOTES

1. On the history of reading, see Lucien Febvre, *The Coming of the Book: The Impact of Printing, 1450–1800* (London: New Left Books, 1976); and Alberto Manguel, *A History of Reading* (London: Harper Collins, 1996). On the history of the book,

see Frederick Kilgour, *The Evolution of the Book* (New York: Oxford University Press, 1998); Simon Eliot and Jonathan Rose, eds., *A Companion to the History of the Book* (Malden, Mass.: Blackwell, 2007); and Gabrielle Watling and Sara E. Quay, eds., *Cultural History of Reading* (Westport, Conn.: Greenwood Press, 2009). And on reading technologies, see, for instance, Phillip Hills, ed., *The Future of the Printed Word: The Impact and the Implications of the New Communications Technology* (Westport, Conn.: Greenwood, 1980); Jay David Bolter, *Writing Space: The Computer, Hypertext, and the History of Writing* (Hillsdale, N.J.: Lawrence Erlbaum, 1991); Ziming Liu, *Paper to Digital: Documents in the Information Age* (Westport, Conn.: Libraries Unlimited, 2008); Bill Cope and Angus Phillips, eds., *The Future of the Book in the Digital Age* (Oxford: Chandos, 2006); Peter L. Shillingsburg, *From Gutenberg to Google: Electronic Representations of Literary Texts* (Cambridge: Cambridge University Press, 2006); Ray Schreibman and Susan Siemens, *A Companion to Digital Literary Studies* (Malden, Mass.: Blackwell, 2007); Sherman Young, *The Book Is Dead, Long Live the Book* (Sydney: University of New South Wales Press, 2007); Marilyn Sutherland and Kathryn Deegan, *Transferred Illusions: Digital Technology and the Forms of Print* (Farnham, U.K.: Ashgate, 2009).

2. For a discussion, see Alan C. Kay, "A Personal Computer for Children of All Ages," paper presented at the National Conference Proceedings of Association of Computing Machinery, Boston, 1972, http://www.mprove.de/diplom/gui/Kay72a .pdf) (15 February 2011).

3. Alan C. Kay, "A Review Article: Dynabooks: Past, Present, and Future," *Library Quarterly* 3 (2000): 385–95.

4. Kay, "A Personal Computer."

5. John Maxwell, "Tracing the Dynabook: A Study of Technocultural Transformations," Ph.D. diss., University of British Columbia, 2006, http://thinkubator.ccsp.sfu .ca/Dynabook (15 February 2011).

6. As well as Maxwell's thesis, forthcoming as a book, other histories of the personal computer include D. K. Smith and R. C. Alexander, *Fumbling the Future: How Xerox Invented, Then Ignored, the First Personal Computer* (New York: Morrow, 1988); M. M. Waldrop, *The Dream Machine: J. C. R. Licklider and the Revolution That Made Computing Personal* (New York: Viking, 2001); and M. A. Hiltzik, *Dealers of Lightning: Xerox PARC and the Dawn of the Computer Age* (New York: HarperBusiness, 1999).

7. Wolfgang Gruener, "Did Steve Jobs Steal the iPad? Genius Inventor Alan Kay Reveals All," *Tom's Hardware*, 27 April 2010, http://www.tomshardware.com/news/ alan-kay-steve-jobs-ipad-iphone,10209.html (15 February 2011).

8. Larry Press, "From P-books to E-books," *Communications of the ACM* 5 (2000).

9. Vannevar Bush, "As We May Think," *Atlantic Monthly* (July 1945), http:// www.theatlantic.com/magazine/archive/1969/12/as-we-may-think/3881/4/ (15 February 2011).

10. Terje Hillesund, "Will E-books Change the World?" *First Monday* 6, no. 10 (2001): http://131.193.153.231/www/issues/issue6_10/hillesund/ (15 February 2011).

11. Nancy K. Herther, "The Ebook Reader Is Not the Future of Books," *Searcher*, no. 8 (2008).

12. Bill Gates, "Beyond Gutenberg" (1999), http://www.microsoft.com/presspass/ ofnote/11–19billg.mspx (15 February 2011).

13. Nancy K. Herther, "The E-Book Industry Today: A Bumpy Road Becomes an Evolutionary Path to Market Maturity," *Electronic Library*. no. 1 (2006).

14. Philip Barker, "The Future of Books in an Electronic Era," *Electronic Library*, no. 3 (1998).

15. Kay, "A Review Article."

16. Larissa Hjorth, "Cartographies of the Mobile: The Personal as Political," *Communication, Politics, Culture* 42, no. 2 (2009): 24–44.

17. Dana Goodyear, "I Heart Novels: Young Women Develop a Genre for the Cellular Age," *New Yorker*, 22 December 2008.

18. "Why eBooks," Mobipocket, http://www.mobipocket.com/ (15 February 2011).

19. "Apple Reinvents the Phone with iPhone" *Apple*, 9 January 2007 – http://www.apple.com/pr/library/2007/01/09iphone.html (15 February 2011).

20. For a discussion, see Gerard Goggin, "The Intimate Turn of News: Mobile News," in *News Online: Transformation and Continuity*, ed. Graham Meikle and Guy Redden (London: Palgrave Macmillan, 2010).

21. Andy Greenberg and James Erik Abels, "iPhone Steals Lead Over Kindle," *Forbes*, 2 October 2008.

22. "Apple's iPhone Could Become Next Hot EReader Says Report," *eWeek*, 2 November 2009.

23. Harmeet Sawhney and Seungwhan Lee, "Arenas of Innovation: Understanding New Configurational Potentialities of Communication Technologies," *Media, Culture, and Society*, no. 27 (2005): 637–60.

24. Jonathan Zittrain, *The Future of the Internet—and How to Stop It* (New Haven, Conn.: Yale University Press, 2008).

25. Michael Muchmore, "eReader Predates the iPhone, but Does That Experience Translate Into the Best Piece of Software for Transforming Your Apple Device Into a Kindle?" *PC Magazine*, 23 December 2008.

26. "Classics Redefined," http://www.classicsapp.com/ (15 February 2011).

27. Michael Muchmore, "Classics (for iPhone): Made Famous in an Apple TV Commercial . . ." *PC Magazine*, 20 February 2009.

28. Steven Levy, "The Future of Reading," *Newsweek*, 17 November 2007.

29. "Amazon Drops Price of Kindle eReader," *eWeek*, 23 October 2009.

30. Susan Krashinsky, "Kobo Takes a Page from the Kindle," *Globe and Mail*, 25 March 2009.

31. Omar El Akkad, "Behind Apple's Iron Curtain: After years of secrecy and speculation, Steve Jobs may finally reveal the iSlate," *Globe and Mail*, 15 January 2010.

32. "Apple Launches iPad: Magical and Revolutionary Device at an Unbelievable Price," Apple, 27 January 2010, http://www.apple.com/pr/library/2010/01/27ipad.html (15 February 2011).

33. Calvin Reid (with Jim Milliot), "Apple iPad Invades Digital Book World," *Publishers Weekly*, 1 February 2010.

34. Jason Steger, "Local E-Book Market 'Chaos,'" *Age*, 4 November 2010.

35. Brian X. Chen, "Apple's Tablet e-Book App Rips Off Indie Dev Creation," *Wired*, 27 January 2010.

CHAPTER 14

Ambient News and the Para-iMojo

Journalism in the Age of the iPhone

JANEY GORDON

THERE ARE PIVOTAL moments that identify a change in the way that our societies function far beyond the significance of the event itself. For example, when Heinrich Hertz detected radio waves, he dismissed the phenomena: "I do not think that the wireless waves I have discovered will have any practical application."[1] However, when Hertz died in 1894—and his obituaries summarized his work—Guglielmo Marconi, who was then nineteen years old, is said to have read one obituary and realized the possibilities that Hertz's work presented. Naturally, Marconi could not have foreseen the far-reaching effects that wireless technologies would have on our lives in the twenty-first century.

A similar key event in the timeline of communication technology and its relationship with journalism took place on 15 January 2009, when Janis Krums, a nutritionist, was travelling on a ferry across the Hudson River in New York. Along with many others, including the local Coast Guard, he witnessed the emergency landing of a passenger jet on the river and the successful evacuation and rescue of all its passengers and crew. Significantly, Krums used his iPhone to take a picture, which he sent to the social networking site Twitpic with the comment, "There's a plane in the Hudson. I'm on the ferry going to pick up the people. Crazy."[2]

Krums's use of his iPhone to take a picture and disseminate it with a short textual comment and without reference to other media organizations testified

FIGURE 14.1. Miracle on the Hudson. Photo by © 2009 Janis Krums. Used with permission from the photographer and Twitpic.

to a sea change in news gathering, and the dissemination and consumption of news, that was already taking place but was crystallized in this event and its reporting. Over the last two to three years, scholars from the areas of media and journalism, along with news activists, professional journalists, and news organizations, have been engaged with the converging technologies that the iPhone encapsulates. They are seeking to explore, theorize, and understand what its impact is—and will be in the future as smartphone technology develops. The online services sent from news providers were the initial frontier of these changes. Web feeds and SMS texts send news headlines and targeted news to individual subscribers and give specific information that they wish to receive, for example, on sport or financial matters. More recently, smartphones, including the iPhone, have begun to bring users a full news service. However, this is simply dissemination from the news industry. More extraordinary is the contribution of the news consumers who, given the ability to record and upload pictures, sounds, videos, and text via their mobile handsets, are doing so and becoming a part of the generation of news and its coverage.

This chapter attempts to give a snapshot of the current relationship between news journalism and the new media technologies common on the iPhone and other smartphones. It begins by identifying the technologies that may be embedded in smartphones that both professional journalists and amateur news creators are using. I then discuss current terms and concepts in order to draw together and try to pin down activities of current news production. The chapter concludes by suggesting some bad news and some good news in the era of the iPhone journalist and news consumer.

Smartphone News Technologies

During a televised sports event, an outside broadcast unit can usually be seen housed in several large caravans outside the stadium. But these days, a journalist with a smartphone in his pocket effectively has a miniature outside broadcast unit with similar abilities. The handset can send a live commentary via a phone call; a live video stream using facilities such as Qik or Bambuser; capture both still and moving images; record sound; or be used to type and file a report or a brief update. Crucially, all these feeds can be sent directly from the phone handset to a mainstream news provider, a group of like-minded contacts, a few friends, or another individual.

Besides transmitting material, the mobile handset can also receive and exchange information and search and select data, including data from GPS services. Many smartphones have a number of these attributes, but the iPhone developed the "killer app." Its screen behaves and looks, to some degree, the same as a screen on a desktop computer. Smartphone users can do more than make phone calls and send text messages; they can use voice-over-Internet protocols such as Skype; read, write, or respond to a blog or e-mail; use Facebook to chat with more personal contacts; or send a Tweet to a large group of other Tweeters as Janis Krums did. Since the iPhone's release in 2007, social-networking sites have developed rapidly. Twitter's growth from its beginnings in 2006 to the 100 million daily messages at the time of writing would appear to owe much to the growth of smartphone use.[3] Twitter's 140-character messages are an obvious tool for mobile phone users, and by September 2010, 62 percent of users accessed Twitter on a mobile handset, 8 percent using their Twitter for iPhone app and 7 percent Twitter for Blackberry.[4] Since its inception Twitter has been used to disseminate a number of stories that would traditionally been labeled "news." The death of the singer Michael Jackson in June 2009 is a well known case where many people first became aware of the event on Twitter and then spread the news to their own groups of friends and contacts. But can these users be termed journalists?

The many uses of a smartphone are available to almost any user, not just a professional journalist. Journalists who rely heavily on their mobile phones to collect and file stories have been nicknamed "Mojos." The term is fluid and used to describe stringers or freelance or professional journalists who spend much of their time on their mobile handsets, and it is associated with a particular set of journalistic practices.[5] MoJo was also the name used by Nokia to describe an initiative it had with Reuters, which it tested with Reuters journalists and further field-tested with students in South Africa. Indeed, a number of African nongovernmental organizations and activists were early adopters of mobile journalism. For example, the Voices of Africa project started in 2006 and set about training journalists who complied and filed their reports using mobile handsets.[6] It is difficult to assess the number of professional journalists using iPhones, although the use of a smartphone seems ubiquitous. However, iPhone apps and other kits specifically designed for journalists are widely available, for example, the Poddio, a sound- and video-editing app that is a part of the iPhone 4 package.

What Is News?

"News" is viewed as a prime good in society, and a healthy press is regarded as a measure of the democratic nature and active citizenship of that society. James Curran and Jean Seaton summarize the traditional liberal view of the press as "the agency through which private citizens are reconstituted as a public body, exercising informal supervision of the state."[7] This view also enshrines the concept that the news media educates citizens and champions the individual against the abuse of power. The ability to publicly chart events, issues, and developments in society and open these to debate and discourse is viewed as a crucial element of a healthy society. Article 19 of the U.N. Universal Declaration of Human Rights, for example, states: "Everyone has the right to freedom of opinion and expression; this right includes freedom to hold opinions without interference and to seek, receive and impart information and ideas through any media and regardless of frontiers."[8] Some countries have the freedom of the media enshrined in their constitutions or laws, for example, the First Amendment of the U.S. Constitution. Other countries, such as China, impose a high level of media censorship. The Chinese government even imposed a news blackout on their citizen Liu Xiaobo's winning the Nobel Peace Prize in 2010.

There is little agreement on what constitutes news. If the definition comes from a journalistic background it tends to concern information that is fresh and important to society in that the event or action may influence or cast a shadow over society in some way. So politicians, war, crime, financial matters, and health and well-being get a high level of coverage by professional news personnel. But a cursory glance at a news outlet demonstrates that this is merely a small part of news and certainly of journalistic interests. Tony Harcup and Deirdre O'Neill's study of U.K. newspapers in 2001 found that a large part of professional news includes much that may be better regarded as gossip concerning the lives and actions of those already in the public view. Further areas of news include much that may be considered to be lifestyle journalism, which details fashions, entertainment, hobbies, and activities and is often aimed not at participants but at spectators, sports coverage being a notable example. There are specialist periodicals and websites for sports *participants*, for example, *Sport Diver* or *Runners World*, but mainstream news coverage is for the sports spectators. Harcup and O'Neill's study was conducted using printed newspapers, and, by 2001, both the British news consumers that they studied and the wider global public were more commonly getting news from broadcast sources. However, in the last decade there have been declines in both newspaper readership and the viewing of TV news, and numerous commentators point to an increase in lightweight leisure journalism and a decline in serious professional news journalism.[9] It is clear from a number of different studies that by 2010 large sections of the population in the developed world were getting their news from websites. In addition, there has been a growth in the use of RSS news feeds to mobile handsets, including the iPhone, which accounts for three-quarters of the mobile visits to U.K. newspaper websites. It seems inevitable that the news agenda is changing with the changing patterns of its dissemination and the reporting of factual news providing the catalyst for comment from professionals and the wider public on blogs and Internet forums.

The Professional and Amateur Mojo

Although the news stories disseminated on mobile phones are selected and written by journalists, the content is limited, with little room for comment or editorial. This is provided by links to other web pages or to journalists' blogs. Professional journalists provide informed and researched comment rather than necessarily giving the first report of the story, and it is now regarded as de rigueur for a professional journalist to have a blog, which may give a more extended and personal account of a news story. Paul Bradshaw has even suggested that professional journalists ought to be adept and active on Twitter to keep abreast of stories, pick up on unpredictable events, and look out for the amateur mojo's contributions to the news agenda.[10] The news agenda that Edward S. Herman and Noam Chomsky once felt was being manipulated by governments and commercial interests undoubtedly still remains, but, increasingly, local, national, and international events are being given an extra dimension by those who are physically present.[11] These are the amateur mojos who collect material via their mobile smartphones and upload this to websites, to social-networking sites, or as user-generated content to mainstream media providers. The material may still be subject to editorial control, although the roles of news creators, news curators, and news consumers are becoming increasingly blurred.

As a consequence, user-generated content is now a feature of most mainstream news websites. Some are recent entrants to this field, and other news services were early providers. For example, the BBC website was an early adopter of UGC; it encourages the public, particularly after a major incident, to upload photographs, videos, and written accounts. A notable case that received international attention was Alexander Chadwick's picture taken on his mobile phone in a smoke filled London underground tunnel on 7 July 2005 after the terrorist bombings. His picture of the passengers walking through the blackened tunnel became one of the iconic images of that day and was used by professional news media. Less well known is the poignant account he also uploaded onto the BBC's website:

> Smoke was everywhere so we were a little concerned about fire but it soon became clear that there was none so we just stayed put and waited

for someone to tell us what to do! No one in my carriage panicked which is quite surprising as the smoke was really thick and nasty, everyone was breathing through shirts and tissues. We were stuck on the train for about 25 minutes before an official came and told us what was going on, and we evacuated quite calmly. I don't know what happened up at the front of the train though.

What Chadwick's photograph lacks in technique it makes up for in poignancy and a narrative about the behavior of people that day in London. There is no blood, hysteria, or colorful movement. Those involved are walking through darkness in an orderly way toward a light. Chadwick's Nokia picture captured a moment that was expressive, moving, and important to Londoners and others. He told the story of Londoners' restrained response to the events, which was not what the international media expected to hear.[12]

So can Chadwick and Krums claim to be mojos, or could they be "citizen journalists"? The word "citizen" confers rectitude, but can an opportunist witness be termed a journalist? Surely the job of the journalist is inherently a professional one, with ethical values and certain skills associated with it. The

FIGURE 14.2. Underground tunnel. Photo by © 2005 PAI. Used with permission from the copyright holder.

term "citizen journalist" is in common use but is problematic. Professional journalists are likely to be citizens of the country where they live or work, yet asylum seekers, refugees, and displaced populations and individuals seeking sanctuary well away from the locale claiming them as a citizen may be practicing journalism. They may do this as contributors to forms of media that John Downing summarizes as "alternative media, citizens' media, community media, tactical media, independent media, counter-information media, participatory media, Third Sector media, social movement media,"[13] with each sector having associated journalists and journalistic techniques to provide it with material. These individuals have been termed activist, public, community, civic, and hyper-local journalists. Each term gives a slightly differing angle, but all suggest a canon of reportage outside the commercial or established media authorities.

It is likely, however, that neither Krums nor Chadwick considers himself to be a journalist of any sort. They witnessed events and used the technologies available to them on their mobile phones to provide immediate eyewitness material, which was quickly taken up by the mainstream media as user-generated content. Alfred Hermida uses the term "para-journalism" to describe Krums's and Chadwick's actions, borrowing the term from "paralegal" and "paramedic," although both these groups are professionals. Para-journalism may be thought of as content collected by individuals who are not full-time journalists but who alert others to situations and events. They augment and enrich mainstream coverage. Hermida argues that "new para-journalism forms such as micro-blogging are 'awareness systems', providing journalists with more complex ways of understanding and reporting on the subtleties of public communication."[14] These new forms merge para-journalism with smartphone mojos, and there have been a number of recent dramatic examples of a para-mojo with an exceptional view of a news story that professional journalists did not have access to. Hermida also describes the idea of "ambient news," that the public is receiving news almost constantly even if not aware of it. He suggests that the growth of micro-blogging services such as Twitter and Facebook is providing "ambient journalism," where news consumers can be almost constantly alerted to and aware of events and can contribute to the dialogue if they wish.[15] Alex Burns furthers the discussion by suggesting that ambient journalism is not simply something that the para-journalist contributes to or that the active news consumer absorbs. Professional news institutions that rely on high skill levels are a key part of the ambient journalistic world and are constantly scanning a range of news sources in order to continually update and refresh the ambient news environment.[16]

New(s) Consumers

As news consumers we use an array of platforms to obtain our news, including newspapers (actually on paper), TV, radio, and Internet and mobile Web feeds. But we are also a part of its dissemination. In 2010 more than 2.3 million visits to U.K. newspaper sites came via a phone handset—1.7 million were from an iPhone. A Pew Research Center study conducted in the United States in early 2010 found that although news consumption generally was steady, 27 percent of mobile Internet users surveyed had received news on their mobile phone the previous day.[17] Stories accessed on mobiles and the Internet also get passed among consumers using social networking sites: journalists' blogs are responded to; curious or momentous incidents may be recorded and uploaded to another social networking site or a mainstream or specialist news curator; and day-to-day actions are recorded on a micro-blog.

Care must be taken when generalizing internationally from country-specific statistics. However, as figures from the International Telecommunication Union note, the adoption of mobile telephony is growing globally and the adoption of smartphones is leapfrogging simpler formats in developing countries. By the end of 2010, there were an estimated 5.3 billion mobile cellular subscriptions, corresponding to 76 per 100 inhabitants globally (116 per 100 in developed countries and 68 per 100 in developing countries). The report further stresses that "people are moving rapidly from 2G to 3G platforms, in both developed and developing countries. In 2010, 143 countries were offering 3G services commercially, compared to 95 in 2007."[18] These figures indicate where global mobile phone use is likely to be heading.

Conclusion

The Bad News

A consequence of these changing news patterns is that the days of the newshound reporter, press pass in hatband, nobly putting himself at risk to defend society from the excesses of the ignoble politician or wealthy autocrat, are long gone. The professional journalist's role sometimes seems to have been demeaned to that of the purveyor of gossip about the sexual doings of minor celebrities and those seeking fifteen minutes of fame. The technologies available to us embedded in our smartphones can offer almost unlimited gossip on inconsequential matters.

Is the old ideal of the "scoop" relevant either? Does it really matter which Web feed has a second or two lead time? With the development of smartphones and their ability to access the Internet, it is inevitable that individuals who find themselves a witness to or participant in a critical event will record and share their experiences rapidly, scooping the professionals who can only parachute in later to provide factual comment. Surely anyone can be a para-mojo and have pictures and text up on the Internet in seconds? The ambient news consumer may be aware of a dramatic news story before the professional newshound has donned his trilby. The problem for both curator and consumer is how to judge the veracity of the Tweet, the intelligence of the blog, or the indications as to what this might mean to society at large.

As we enter the second decade of the twenty-first century, the news consumer has a relatively high level of media literacy and is weary and wary of the news being used to "spin" politics or the manipulation of the news agenda by public relations companies. Publicity stunts by extremist groups or those seeking to promote their own activities, views, or commercial businesses have eroded confidence in the objectivity of the news and its relevance to our lives and society at large. A further erosion of confidence in news values stems from the fact that an obsession with the dramatic has led to the orchestration of tragic and extreme events by those who would use violent actions to gain publicity and force reprisals. Furthermore, although it is felt that news is important in our society, we are reluctant to pay much for it, and informed, quality reporting that requires research and consideration is expensive. The professional news services have to redefine how they sell news.

The Good News

The good news for ambient mobile news consumers, however, is that there is a multiplicity of news sources available on their mobile handsets to suit their own community and interests. These services may be from the major providers and mainstream news services or smaller, niche-news providers that are nevertheless run in a professional manner. Alongside these are the professional bloggers and Tweeters, often skilled journalists, who give added value to their published news stories by the rich detail of user-generated content coming in via blogs, micro-blogs, or social media. UGC may come from a fixed-line source or from a para-mojo such as Alexander Chadwick. It may be uploaded to an open-access site or a curated site. These sites may be deliberately aiming for or devoted to UGC, as is Jasmine News in Sri Lanka. For the news creators and professional mojos there is a similar multiplicity of news alerts and tip-offs. A professional mojo can find eyewitnesses to an event via Twitter or respond rapidly with a piece of dramatic coverage.

In countries where news services are tightly controlled by the state, the mobile phone has, in addition, become a method of comparing actual events and factual information from witnesses and those involved, who upload material to blogs and micro-blogs and get information to the outside world that would otherwise not be available. Arguably, the richness and ease of news sourcing and dissemination is a social good. However, the sifting, editing, and verifying of all this material may still need the attention of skillful news curators.

And Finally

It is evident that we are currently in a transitional period with regard to news journalism and its creation, curation, and consumption. Much of this has come about because about 5.3 billion people on the planet now carry around varying degrees of their own mobile news service and news desk. In particular, as smartphones such as the iPhone have a greater penetration into the mobile phone market, it is likely that the definitions of "news" will continue to change. Both Alexander Chadwick's and Janis Krums's pictures tell personal stories that added to our understanding of the events that they were a part of. The difference between them is that whereas Chadwick's picture was uploaded to a curated website that used it as user generated content, Krums became one of the first para-iMojos by sending his iPhone picture directly to Twitpic without any intermediary. It seems likely that the role of the professional journalist will increasingly be to provide verification of events along with informed analysis and comment, rather than be first with a scoop at the scene. But ambient news journalism is in our pockets, and news consumers will need to expect to pay for quality sources of information and accuracy.

Notes

1. The 1888 quotation from Heinrich Hertz is taken from the biographical entry, "Heinrich Rudolf Hertz," http://www-groups.dcs.st-and.ac.uk/~history/Biographies/Hertz_Heinrich.html (15 February 2011).

2. Janis Krums's message can be read at http://twitpic.com/135xa (15 February 2011).

3. For a discussion, see Douglas MacMillan, "Twitter Aims to Get One Billion Users, Matching Facebook Target," *Bloomberg News*, http://www.bloomberg.com/news/2010-10-12/twitter-aiming-to-get-1-billion-users-matching-rival-facebook-s-target.html (15 February 2011).

4. "The Evolving Ecosystem," Twitter blog, 2 September 2010, http://blog.twitter.com/2010/09/evolving-ecosystem.html (15 February 2011).

5. Gerard Goggin, "The Intimate Turn of News: Mobile News," in *News Online: Transformation and Continuity*, ed. Graham Meikle and Guy Redden (London: Palgrave Macmillan, 2010), 107.

6. For a discussion, see Christian Kreutz, "Mobile Activism in Africa: Future Trends and Software Development," in *SMS Uprising: Mobile Activism in Africa*, ed. Sokari Ekine (Oxford: Pambazuka Press, 2010), 135–60.

7. James Curran and Jean Seaton, *Power Without Responsibility: The Press and Broadcasting in Britain* (London: Routledge, 1991), 277.

8. United Nations, "Declaration of Human Rights" (1948), http://www.un.org/en/documents/udhr/index.shtml (15 February 2011).

9. It is worth noting that in the United Kingdom, radio listening has hardly changed. See http://www.rajar.co.uk/listening/quarterly_listening.php (15 February 2011).

10. Paul Bradshaw, "Ten Ways Journalism Has Changed in the Last Ten Years (Blogger's Cut)," 6 March 2008, http://onlinejournalismblog.com/2008/03/06/ten-ways-journalism-has-changed-in-the-last-ten-years-bloggers-cut/ (15 February 2011).

11. For a discussion, see Edward S. Herman and Noam Chomsky, *Manufacturing Consent: The Political Economy of the Mass Media* (New York: Pantheon, 1988).

12. The story in the international news the following day was that Londoners were going back to work. CNN confessed that they had expected to be reporting the deserted saddened streets and found that many Londoners were going about their business.

13. John Downing, "Uncommunicative Partners: Social Movement Media Analysis and Radical Educators" (2008), http://eprints.lse.ac.uk/21559/ (15 February 2011).

14. Alfred Hermida, "Twittering the News: The Emergence of Ambient Journalism," *Journalism Practice* no. 3 (2010): 297–308.

15. Alfred Hermida, "From TV to Twitter: How Ambient News Became Ambient Journalism," *M/C Journal* 13, no. 2 (2010): http://journal.media-culture.org.au/index.php/mcjournal/article/ view/220.

16. Alex Burns, "Oblique Strategies for Ambient Journalism," *M/C Journal* 13, no. 2 (2010): http://journal.media-culture.org.au/index.php/mcjournal/article/view/230.

17. Pew Research Center, "Americans Spending More Time Following the News: Ideological News Sources: Who Watches and Why" (2010), http://people-press.org/2010/09/12/section-2-online-and-digital-news/ (1 October 2011).

18. ITU, "The World in 2010, ICT Facts and Figures" (2011), http://www.itu.int/ITU-D/ict/statistics/index.html (3 June 2011).

CHAPTER 15

Party Apps and Other Citizenship Calls

ANU KOIVUNEN

"I just tweet; that's just the way I roll."
—SARAH PALIN

G IVEN THE 2008 publicity surrounding Barack Obama's affection for his Blackberry and the news in 2009 about the decisive role of social media in the Norwegian parliamentary election, it is no wonder that some radical change in campaigning methods was expected in the Swedish parliamentary election in 2010. News about "Obama's social media advantage" and Norwegian prime minister Jens Stoltenberg's "hyper-active" and "teenage-like enthusiasm for facebooking, blogging and tweeting" circulated across Swedish media.[1] "E-readiness" is important to the Swedish self-image, and Sweden tops three recent global indexes relating to information and communications technology access, use, and skill. Eighty-four percent of Swedes have Internet access at home; half of Swedes are members of social networks; and 1.5 million make status updates. While the Internet is predominantly accessed from home, the use of the mobile Internet is increasing with wireless broadband and the explosion of smartphones, especially among young people between the ages of twenty-six and thirty-five.[2] Furthermore, blogs played a major role in the 2009 European elections in Sweden, and the Pirate Party, lobbying for more free content on the Internet, sensationally won 7.1 percent of the vote and a seat in the European parliament.[3]

Against this background, it seems a given that the nature of the media would be one of the major questions during the election campaign. Indeed, it seemed in 2009 and spring 2010 that social media was outlined as one of the protagonists of the election. To paraphrase a general feeling: "This year's election campaign, much more than any before it, will take place on the Internet." Many headlines supported this notion: "Social media becomes an election platform," "Social media ever more important in politics," "Parties are now gearing up for visibility in the social media," and "The web is the new market place."[4] This rhetoric, however, was short-lived. By July 2010, two months before the election, a newspaper headline claimed, "Social media will not play any role," and a week before the election a major newspaper finally declared that social media had become "a flop in the election campaign."[5] In fact, not only were social media deemed a nonfactor, but political issues involving the Internet in general were largely absent from the election agenda.[6] File sharing, for example, which had been intensely debated in Sweden in 2009, not the least because of the international trial of the Pirate Bay, was almost totally forgotten. Immediately after the elections, scholars and analysts published research results that showed that the election was not, after all, a breakthrough for social media and net-based issues and that old media outshone social media. For large electorates, they concluded, television, radio, and newspapers still matter the most.[7] In the Swedish elections, then, one candidate—the social media—lost.[8]

However, I argue that the election campaign provided momentum and a framework for both political parties and the established media to imagine political citizenship in the age of a changing media landscape, amid fears about democratic deficits, weakened interest in political participation, and a decreased connection to the public.[9] For the parties, the continuous process of mediatization is a major challenge. With media as an important—for many, the most important—"bearer of democracy's political communication," political parties increasingly not only adapt themselves but also internalize the media logics of newsworthiness. On the other hand, political campaigns have become increasingly professionalized in Sweden and have sought to gain independence from the media.[10] As for the traditional media, while their status as providers of political information is still strong, their importance, especially for young people, is in question, as is their future as providers of a sense of public connection.[11] For political actors and media, the question remains, to quote Peter Dahlgren, "where we find the center of gravity for political dynamics in late modern society," that is, how and where the future civic cultures will emerge and operate.[12]

Notably, the 2010 election campaign in Sweden coincided with the introduction of smartphones on the European mass markets. Sweden has a population of some 9 million people, and some 2 million now own a smartphone. Among smartphones, Apple's iPhone has enjoyed high media visibility, and the streets of Stockholm are sometimes resemble a kind of "Apple country," as a journalist noted, where a "trip in the Stockholm metro can easily give one the impression that every other Swede owns an iPhone. Many people sit immersed, gazing the small screens, rolling their fingers frenetically over the digital menus."[13] According to media market research companies, in summer 2010 more than 700,000 people in Sweden owned an iPhone, and many more intended to acquire one within a year. Analysts estimated that in Sweden every second mobile sold would be a smartphone by the end of 2010, and smartphones would therefore soon account for 50 percent of the mobile market.[14] In the Swedish media, the iPhone enjoyed special attention and was repeatedly referred to as a "success." Interestingly and notably, its popularity was first envisioned as and later compared to a "popular movement," in other words, a community comparable to a political party. In any case, it was narrativized as becoming the telephone for "the ordinary Swedish."[15]

It is therefore no coincidence that a number of political iPhone apps were released during the summer of 2010 by different parties before the Swedish elections. In doing so, Swedish parties kept up with an international trend. In the U.S. presidential elections in 2008, various Web, Facebook, and iPhone applications were introduced as campaign devices. In the 2010 midterm elections, smartphone apps were deemed "a must," and 2010 was described as "the year of the election app." In British parliamentary elections in 2010, several parties (Labour, Conservative, the Liberal Democrats, the Greens, and the UK Independence Party) launched apps as part of their e-campaigns. And in Germany, for instance, the Christian Democratic Union and the Green Party (Die Grünen), have launched national and regional election apps.[16] At the same time, media companies in the United States and United Kingdom but also in Sweden have released iPhone apps that serve as gateways to their offerings in general or are designed specifically for elections. In Sweden, both the commercial network television TV4 and the two public-service companies, Swedish Television (SVT) and Swedish Radio (SR), launched apps before the election campaigns. Also, *Svenska Dagbladet*, the independent right-wing newspaper, and *Aftonbladet*, the Social Democrat tabloid paper, launched an app in cooperation.

Through discussing three different cases—first, the iPhone apps released in Sweden by the two political blocs and three parties; second, the iPhone apps of the public television and radio networks and the commercial national television network; and, third, the story of social media as a protagonist in the elections in Swedish print journalism[17]—this article will focus on the explicit (or implicit) framing of personalized, social media and smartphones as a major new gateway for political citizenship. In the absence of definite empirical findings about the importance of either social media or iPhones for political agency or engagement in the public sphere, I will look at the discursive constructions of citizenship evoked in the three cases.

Party Apps and Political Citizenship

When a number of Swedish political party secretaries, communications officers, and election managers were questioned in June 2010 about the importance of social media in the upcoming election, their responses were unanimous: social media would play an important role but not a decisive one. They all saw social media as a way to mobilize supporters and, especially, as a key device for those involved in personal campaigning, still a rarity in Swedish elections.[18] Social media was outlined as one of many strategies to engage in a dialogue with the voters. As part of this e-campaigning, in late August and early September several political apps were released by the right-center Alliance for Sweden (consisting of the Moderate Party, the Liberal Party of Sweden, the Christian Democrats, and the Centre Party), the Christian Democrats and Centre Party acting on their own, the Red-Green Coalition, and the Social Democratic Party. The apps were fairly simple and can be regarded as ways to make headlines during the final stretch of the campaigns. Yet all of them also made an attempt to frame the parties and political alliances as e-ready, as modern and up-to-date. Moreover, all of them entertained a notion of political citizenship in the age of the iPhone.

Three of the apps, those by the Christian Democrats, the Centre Party, and the Alliance, evoked a notion of the citizen as a gamer, albeit in different ways. The two small Alliance parties published apps built around the personas of their party leaders. The Centre Party app featured political communication through the audio book of *Ett land av friherrinnor* (A country of baronesses), the autobiography and vision of Sweden by Maud Olofsson, who was the party leader at the time. The app further asked the user to take a quiz on "How much Maud are you?" The quiz, while playful in tone, featured an array of multiple-choice questions and resulted in a verdict delivered by Olofsson. The app also offered links to party websites. In contrast, the Christian Democrat app sidestepped political agendas altogether in favor of presenting the party leader Göran Hägglund as a kind of stand-up comedian. The app,

Göran Says, offered itself as a fan device, featuring quotes or humorous expressions from Hägglund: "WTF is going on, dude?", "Red-green smog," "It is cool," and so on. These quotations were meant to be enjoyed repeatedly, and the app offered links to Hägglund's Twitter and Facebook accounts for more live comments. Also, the app offered links to YouTube videos, as well as to Hägglund's favorite music list on Spotify. This app won Hägglund much publicity as it was discussed in broadcast media and newspapers as an example either of political campaigning becoming more entertainment oriented or of the increasing personalization of politics in Sweden, where people primarily vote for party lists. In general, however, Hägglund's public image was discussed in favorable terms.

The Alliance app, representing the four right-wing and center parties, has a more sober tone and employed conventional political rhetoric. It presented itself as "an app that listens," thus reflecting the political coalition's platform of "giving all people, independent of their background, equal opportunities to grow and develop out of their own dreams and their own desire." Repeating key phrases in the Alliance's campaign rhetoric, the app declared: "We want our iPhone application to listen rather than talk." In practice, the app offered the user the ability to build complete sentences with refrigerator-magnet words. Despite the rhetoric of interactivity and the emphasis on increased user participation, the app served to disseminate a strategically chosen vocabulary, a carefully directed political language. Available sentences begin "In my Sweden . . . ," and the user can choose among several words, some of which display in orange. These are called "value words" and are underlined as "extra important for the Alliance." Such words included names of well-known and much-debated policies such as "tax reduction for the employed," "primacy of employment," "tax reduction for renovations on the home," and "tax deduction for services performed in the household." Moreover, the value words included nouns such as "choice, work, enterprise, tax, economy, energy, freedom, care of the elderly, childcare, welfare, health care, safety, school, integration, period of mandate, pensioner, tax, and climate." These words could be combined with an array of others, including the names of the participating parties, the first names of party leaders, qualifiers ("little, young, big, best, historic, happy, pleased, high, lower, right-wing, left-wing"), nouns ("day, mother, quality, desire, thank, responsibility, night, allowance, outsider ship, weekend, wage-worker, entrepreneurship"), verbs ("fix, vote, give, work, meet, will have time, seek, meet, create"), markers of time and space, markers of opinion, and various fill-in words ("like, or, for, on, as, how, with, your, your, to, what, through, together"). The vocabulary thus made it possible for the user to repeat, with some variation, arguments for Alliance policies and to criticize the Red-Green opposition and its leader. Finally, the user was offered the possibility to save the finished sentences as a photo in one's phone or to share them by Facebook or Twitter. Interestingly, while addressing the viewer as somebody to be listened to and somebody whose thoughts are important, this app first and foremost made visible the political nature of language and the potential for manipulation.

For the political opposition, the citizen was explicitly envisioned as a seeker of arguments and information. The Red-Green coalition app, For the Whole of Sweden, does not feature any game or play moments but instead addresses the user as a potential campaign worker in need of political weaponry. The app features a poster of the four opposition-party leaders as a background and a menu with five different channels: First, "The Red-Green vs. the Alliance," an opportunity to compare political messages across various issues. Second, the app summarizes critical claims by the Alliance and offered counter-arguments to these. Third, the app features a blog, linking to a webpage, and, fourth, a link to an e-mail application enabling the user to post questions that the coalition promises to answer within one day. Finally, users were invited to engage and register as election workers. In line with this information-oriented approach, the Social Democratic Party released an app of its own dedicated to election information, "Vote 2010," featuring Google maps and guidance about where and when one could vote before and on Election Day. The app includes links to YouTube and other visual campaign material, such as posters and logos, but otherwise did not contain political information.

In contrast with the more playful or outright entertainment-oriented Alliance apps, these opposition products did not risk any ambiguous readings. Instead, they sought credibility by underlining information while also forcefully marketing the key issues, arguments, and appropriate language for those engaged in campaigning. In line with the classic notion of political communication, the Red-Green app attempted to arm its users with tools and weapons for engagement, deliberation, and argumentation. Unlike the Alliance app's veiled rhetoric of "value words," the Red-Green app's mode of address was explicitly ideological and antagonistic.

The National Network Media Goes App

Most current discussion of apps tends to focus on either their business potential or the fears of monopoly and censorship, but the tone was different in the initial stages of the Swedish election campaign. The public radio channel, Sveriges Radio, had released its first iPhone application in 2008, and the two national television networks were competing in December 2009 to get their apps launched. TV4 Play was released in December 2009, and SVT Play in early February 2010. SVT Play, the app from the public television network, was launched with a much-publicized campaign, "Dear Steve Jobs."[19] In this campaign, all Swedes were addressed as allies and asked to "help convince Steve" to hurry the approval and launching process of the SVT app. The online petition, "Come on Steve, Sweden is waiting," gained 407,074 signatures, and the campaign actually got wide publicity when representatives clothed in Swedish national costumes demonstrated outside the Apple headquarters in California.

The national emphasis of this campaign, evoking the atmosphere of a major sporting event, can be interpreted as a strategic move against European Union media policies that question the limits of public networks. Commercial media companies have criticized public-service companies as distorting and threatening competition.[20] For Sweden, innovations such as SVT Play on the Internet—which, along with the BBC iPlayer, is arguably one of the best ways that European public television has upgraded itself and as a consequence become hugely popular—and apps that provide free content are cases that probe the limits of the public-service remit under EU regulations. In this light, the SVT campaign for its app reads not only as yet another claim from "old media" for its centrality but also as an offensive push into a larger battle over national media policies.[21] The campaign provided an opportunity to frame Swedish public television as a national matter, not a political interest. At the same time, however, the campaign also contributed to the image of the iPhone as a default media device and as an issue of national importance, echoing the media framing of it as a "popular movement."[22]

Swedish Television (SVT), Swedish Radio (SR), and the commercial "quality channel" TV4 all made special efforts to cover the election and to engage viewers and listeners with it—and they extended these efforts to the Internet. While TV4 Play provided access to the channel's regular news programming and clips from its elections coverage, the company also launched a special poll device, Mentometer, that enabled smartphone users to participate in polls during its final debate programs and elections coverage.[23] Both public companies, again, used their license-funded resources for launching extensive thematic sites for the 2011 election and tailoring them to app users. The SVT and SR applications offered first-page entries to "Election 2010" ("Valet 2010," SVT) or the "Election Pod" ("Valpodden," SR), featuring video and audio clips as well as journalism. With these special channels, the networks underlined the force of the election's presence, heightening its immediacy for the fully informed citizen and media consumer. Notably, SVT enacted the principles of its public-service remit in offering both information and entertainment, aiming both to represent the complexity of the election issues and to seek broad, popular legitimacy for this endeavor.[24] Balancing the same line as the political parties with their iPhone apps, SVT imagined the political citizen as hungry for both debates and comic programming. Hence, SVT created a convergence between politics and popular culture, combining political involvement and participation with an explicit notion of fun, albeit in the traditional format of political satire.[25] Alongside extensive links to interviews, hearings, and debates, the site offered access to comic clips and satiric commentaries, often specially produced for Internet users, whether stationary or mobile. While the SVT and SR websites were primarily created to gather and organize their election coverage—both national and regional, as well as catering to special groups (young people, disabled, linguistic minorities)—they tailored much of this for mobile users as well.

Other old-media outlets entered the app field. Crossfire (Korseld), created by two Stockholm-based dailies, *Svenska Dagbladet* and *Aftonbladet*, was the only election app that users had to pay for. Structured, as the title implies, around a debate between two opposing political standpoints, the app exemplifies a crossover between the personalization of political journalism and a strict issue-focused political discussion. In the app, the user was offered a range of political questions and offered two different viewpoints by two editorial-page journalists, Sanna Rayman of the right-wing *Svenska Dagbladet* and Katrine Kielos of the Social Democrat *Aftonbladet*. The user was also offered access to a series of questions to leading politicians. In setting up an antagonistic approach between two opposing views, the app both reflected and contributed to the new shape of Swedish politics, where the voter is offered a choice between two political alliances. Here, the interdependence of media and the political system became visible, as did the limits of media independence: the framing of the debate is bound to political realities.

The Re-Mediation of the Center

The staging of social media as one of the "parties" participating in the election—something to be appropriated and assessed—was by and large productive for media, politicians, and political parties alike. Social media in its various upgraded forms became an opportunity to put parties and media or-

ganizations on the agenda by participating in this narrative. As Nick Couldry
has argued, "the myth of the centre" and "the myth of the mediated centre"
are fundamentally connected. The notion of a society's center is naturalized
by media, but at the same time it supports the media representing themselves
as *the* frame of that centre.[26] A concrete manifestation of this convergence is
the annual week of Swedish politics in Almedalen on the island of Gotland,
where Swedish political and media elites and lobby organizations mingle. In
July 2010, social media was one of the major topics for seminars and discussions. Journalists and politicians tweeted and updated Facebook from the
event, and as a consequence numerous politicians were photographed working on their iPhones or other smartphones.[27] In this context, as in central
Stockholm, smartphones were presented as necessary accessories.

Beyond discussing the relative importance and success or failure of
e-campaigning in 2010, the treatment of social media by Swedish print media testifies to a process of "domestication."[28] In discussing "new media" or
social media, the "old media" introduced Facebook and Twitter, provided
guidelines and advice for their use—for both politicians and voters—and engaged in critique of them. All of this is indicative of the old media's desire and
attempt to hold on to the center. For the purposes of introduction and civic
education, print media published lists of blogs, Twitter accounts, YouTube
channels, and Facebook groups "worth" following or joining, hence assign-
ing themselves the role of gatekeeper.[29] National and local media presented
individual politicians as engaged actively and successfully in this sphere.[30] At
the same time, media consultants published guidebooks for politicians and
parties and were recruited by the old media to evaluate the efforts and success of different parties.[31] Notably, then, while the old media allied with the
political elite in establishing a myth of the mediated center, when discussing
social media and the election, they allied with educators, consultants, and the
imagined political citizen, the voter, to criticize politicians for deficient skills
in "doing" social media. Media consultants and journalists alike criticized
politicians for a number of deficiencies: being too passive; using Twitter or
Facebook for one-way communication, as "megaphones" for PR; having bad
judgment; and reducing the medium to meaningless chatter.[32]

The narrative of the failure of social media to meet expectations in the
2010 Swedish election—as if it indeed had been a popular movement—can
thus also be read in relation to the myth of the mediated center. This narrative
delivers an assurance that old media did maintain its importance and primary
status in the election and, by implication, its role as "the center." Unsurprisingly, Martin Gelin, the e-campaign manager for the Red-Green coalition

protested against this narrative of failure and countered such claims by referring to moments in which social media overtook the old media:

> Facebook especially has contributed to a new political discussion. We had 55,000 who used our Red-Green Facebook application. 36,000 Swedes shared the link to the blog update by Emelie Holmquist on her mother's problems with social insurance. 120.000 saw on YouTube the Red-Green rally speech by Stellan Skarsgård, ten times the amount who were there. Yesterday, a seventeen-year-old girl managed, within a couple of hours, to get 7,000 people to join her on Sergel Torg in a protest against Sweden Democrats. Those who say that digital media have not influenced Swedish politics do not know what they are talking about.[33]

In this counter-narrative, Gelin notably singles out moments in social media when the celebrity factor, moral outrage, or political protests became highly visible in the national public sphere, i.e., the old media. Five days before the election, the blogosphere and social media users significantly influenced the political debate: a blog post by Emelie Holmquist about how her mother, suffering from a rare hormonal disease, had been treated by the Swedish Social Insurance Agency received 2,000 comments and was shared by 14,000 Facebook-users.[34] This case was widely discussed in television debates, radio programs, and newspaper reports. Whether this event had influenced the election result is impossible to know. Of significance, however, is the implied convergence between an entertained citizen—with personalization and dramatization being the key features—and the increase in "public connection."[35] The political potential of mobilizing affect in social media is, notably, the key feature of the US Tea Party app, featuring "the outrage of the day." Inciting outrage is an important strategy for such politicians as Sarah Palin, whose "just tweeting" is framed as direct communication with her followers, beyond the gatekeepers of traditional media.[36]

After the election in Sweden, social media was seen to have brought about change in one sense. A new effect of social media and personalized, networked media is an increase in manifestations of political identities: the visibility of likes and dislikes. On Facebook, for example, 60,000 people stamped their profile images to wish for a Red-Green government. On the other hand, 18,680 people "liked" the page "We who consider moving abroad if Mona Sahlin is elected prime minister." In the old media, this was framed as the "vote coming out of the closet."[37]

Conclusion

It remains to be seen whether political citizenship in the age of personalized media feeds into a reinvigoration of political citizenship beyond the classic and clichéd divide between information and entertainment or whether personalized media is doomed to feed into what Jodi Dean has termed "communicative capitalism," where networked communication and information technologies "capture" and "reformat" political energies, turning "efforts at political engagement into contributions to the circulation of content, reinforcing the hold of neoliberalism's technological infrastructure."[38] The fantasies of abundance, participation, and wholeness that Dean attributes to "communicative capitalism" were in operation both in the Swedish election coverage and in the political apps and other investments in social, personalized media. In the rhetoric of e-campaigning, citizens were called upon as participants, messages were coded as contributions, clicks were framed as input, a sense of flow was enhanced, and a rhetoric of interaction and dialogue was highlighted. The narrative of failure can partly be understood as reflecting the unrealistic promises of this rhetoric. In the convergence of election campaigns and personalized and social media, several critical trajectories overlapped. The obvious question of who is going to win the election was supplemented with two interlinked questions about the future of democracy and media. Both the old media and political parties were fighting for an increase in public connection—and indirectly for their roles at the center of society. No new civic cultures emerged, but the efforts, hopes, fears, and disappointments articulated by both media and the political parties testify to the complexities of citizenship and the media matrix in an age of personalized media.

NOTES

1. See, for example, Martin Jönsson, "Medievalet," *Svenska Dagbladet*, 8 June 2008; Martin Jönsson, "YouTube—valets vinnare," *Svenska Dagbladet*, 8 June 2008; Fredrik Wass, "Den sociala valrörelsen," *Internetworld*, 30 October 2008; Lova Olsson, "Sverige vill lära av segraren," *Svenska Dagbladet*, 6 November 2008; Björn Jansson, "Obamametoden till Sverige," *Computer Sweden*, 8 December 2008; Björn Jansson, "Vi måste finnas där människor finns," *Computer Sweden*, 8 December 2008; Hanna Dunér, "Alliansens nya byrå ska inte härma Obama," *Svenska Dagbladet*, 5 May 2009;

Björn Lindahl, "Sociala medier avgjorde valet," *Svenska Dagbladet*, 15 September 2009; Tobias Brandel, "Obamas valstrateg i Sverige," *Svenska Dagbladet*, 225 May 2010.

2. Olle Findahl, "Swedes and the Internet," Stiftelsen för internetinfrastruktur, 26 January 2010, 15, 37–39, *www.iis.se/docs/soi2010_eng_web.pdf (15 February 2011)*.

3. See, for example, Lena Hennel, "Riksdagspartierna ska locka väljare på nätet," *Svenska Dagbladet*, 7 April 2009; Anders Tiger, "Sociala digitala medierna sänker politiska tröskeln," *Kristdemokraten*, 13 May 2009; Magnus Krantz, "Nätet blev valets vinnare," *Gotlands Tidningar*, 9 June 2009; "Obama-effekt på EU-valet," *Tidningarnas Telegrambyrå*, 8 June 2009; Susanne Claesson, "Valet då digitala strategier slog igenom," *Kristianstadsbladet*, 11 June 2009.

4. Tobias Brandel, "Sociala medier blir ny pr-kanal," *Svenska Dagbladet*, 4 January 2010; "Sociala medier allt viktigare i politiken," *Västerbottens Folkblad*, 2 January 2010; Tobias Brandel, "Facebook blir valplattform," *Svenska Dagbladet*, 9 January 2010; Janne Sunding, "Bloggosfären är rödgrön. Nu laddar partierna för att synas i de sociala medierna," *Resumé*, 4 February 2010; "Nätet är ett nytt torg," *Göteborgs-Posten*, 22 March 2010.

5. Brit Stakston, "På väg mot flopp för sociala medier i årets valrörelse?" JMW Kommunikation, 17 July 2010, http://www.jmw.se/2010/07/17/pa-vag-mot-flopp-for-sociala-medier-i-arets-valrorelse-valrorelsen-2010-del-13/ (15 February 2011); Tobias Brandel, "Sociala medier spelar ingen roll. Riksdagspartierna utnyttjade internet dåligt i Almedalen," *Svenska Dagbladet*, 17 July 2010; Kristoffer Örstadius, "Sociala medier en flopp i valrörelsen," *Dagens Nyheter*, 12 September 2010; Mats Olofsson, "Vart tog valgenomslaget för sociala medier vägen?" *Västerbottens-Kuriren*, 15 September 2010.

6. Tomas Zirn, "Inget parti orkar lyfta it-frågorna under valkampanjen," Compusweden.se, 3 September 2010.

7. Göteborgs Universitet, "Valrörelsen 2010: Inget genombrott för de sociala medierna," Göteborgs Universitet, 22 September 2010, http://www.jmg.gu.se/Aktuellt/Nyheter/fulltext/valrorelsen-2010-inget-genombrott-for-de-sociala-medierna .cid954688 (15 February 2011); Anders Orrenius, "Gammelmedia utklassade sociala medier i valrörelsen," *Riksdag & Departement*, 22 October 2010; "Så har sociala medier påverkat valrörelsen," SVT Rapport, 19 September 2011; Britt Stakston, "Forskare visar att sociala medier var marginella i valrörelsen," JMW Kommunikation, 19 November 2011, http://www.jmw.se/2010/11/07/sociala-medier-marginella-i-valrorelsen/ (15 February 2011).

8. The relative importance of social media for younger voters is briefly mentioned but not analyzed in the otherwise extensive analysis of media in the 2010 elections. See Kent Asp, "Mediernas prestationer och betydelse. Valet 2010," Institutionen för journalistik, medier och kommunikation, Göteborgs universitet, http://www.jmg.gu.se/digitalAssets/1335/1335825_63-mediernas-prestationer-och-betydelse.pdf, 21–22 (20 June 2011).

9. For an extensive discussion, see Pippa Norris, *Democratic Deficit: Critical Citizens Revisited* (Cambridge: Cambridge University Press, 2011).

10. Peter Dahlgren, *Media and Political Engagement: Citizens, Communication, and Democracy* (Cambridge: Cambridge University Press, 2009), 2–3; Jesper Strömbäck

and Lars W. Nord, "Media and Politics in Sweden," in *Communicating Politics: Political Communication in the Nordic Countries*, ed. Jesper Strömbäck, Mark Ørsten, and Toril Aalberg (Gothenburg: Nordicom, 2008), 103–4, 117–18; Jesper Strömbäck, "Four Phases of Mediatization: An Analysis of the Mediatization of Politics," *The International Journal of Press/Politics* 13, no. 3 (2008): 235–36.

11. Nick Couldry, Sonia Livingstone, and Tim Markham, *Media Consumption and Public Engagement: Beyond the Presumption of Attention* (Houndmills: Palgrave Macmillan, 2007), 147–48.

12. Dahlgren, *Media and Political Engagement*, 52.

13. Olle Zachrison, "Iphone—Svenssons nya mobiltelefon," *e24*, 15 February 2010, http://www.e24.se/business/it-och-telekom/iphone-svenssons-nya-mobiltelefon_1865013.e24 (15 February 2011).

14. The official sales figures for iPhone are not public knowledge. For media market analyses, based on surveys, see IT Research, "Sverige, mobiltelefoner, andra kvartalet, Kv-2–2010," IT Research press release, http://www.itresearch.se/Document Archive/63522.doc (15 September 2011); Mediavision, "Iphone—fortsatt framgång i Sverige," Mediavision Press Release, 14 September 2009, http://www.mediavision.se/Templates/News1.aspx?PageID=31b349db-b00a-4b24-ba9b-198c12ff79e5 (15 February 2011); Lena Holmberg, "Snart 50 procent smartphones," *Telekomidag.se*, 14 October 2010, http://www.telekomidag.se/nyheter/artikel.php?id=32912 (15 February 2011); Christina Lindqvist Sjöstöm, "Många vill prata smart," *Svenska Dagbladet*, 23 December 2010. For a warning against the different publicized figures, see Zachrison, "Iphone—Svenssons nya mobiltelefon."

15. Olle Cornéer, "Apple tar över världen," *Veckans affärer*, 18 December 2008; Olle Zachrison, "Iphone—Svenssons nya mobiltelefon."

16. Carol Pinchefsky, "7 Essential iPhone Election Apps," *MacLife*, 31 October 2008, http://www.maclife.com/article/feature/political_apps_roundup (15 February 2011); Caroline McCarthy, "Invasion of the Election Apps," *CNET News*, 31 October 2008, http://news.cnet.com/8301-13577_3-10080171-36.html (15 February 2011); Brian Ries, "Killer Election Apps," *The Daily Beast*, 21 October 2010, http://www.thedailybeast.com/blogs-and-stories/2010-10-21/midterm-elections-killer-smartphone-apps/# (15 February 2011); Tim Difford, "6 iPhone Apps to Help You Track the UK General Election," *The NextWeb.Com*, 9 April 2010, http://thenextweb.com/uk/2010/04/09/uk-general-election-iphone-apps-roundup/ (15 February 2011).

17. Based on searches in Mediearkivet (2007–2010), a full-text archive indexing major Swedish print and online media.

18. "Veckans fråga: Vilken betydelse får sociala medier i valrörelsen," *Riksdag & Departement* (June 2010).

19. See, for example, "Dear Steve Jobs," http://212.247.38.181/beforeapproval/ (15 February 2011); SVT, "Webbkampanjen Dear Steve Jobs prisbelönad," 15 December 2010, http://svt.se/2.125349/1.2267392/dearstevejobs.com (15 February 2011).

20. On the application of Article 86(2) of the EC Treaty to state aid in the form of public-service compensation granted to certain undertakings entrusted with the operation of services of general economic interest, see European Commission, "Communication on State Aid to Public Service Broadcasters," 2 July 2009, http://ec.europa

.eu/competition/state_aid/legislation/specific_rules.html#broadcasting (15 February 2011).

21. For a discussion of the media systems, see James Curran, Shanto Iyengar, Anker Brink Lund, and Inka Salovaara-Moring, "Media System, Public Knowledge, and Democracy: A Comparative Study," *European Journal of Communication* 24, no. 1 (2009): 5–26.

22. Olle Zachrison, "Iphone—Svenssons nya mobiltelefon."

23. Anders Pihlblad, "Mentometer: 14 000 har laddat ner TV4:s app," *Politikerbloggen*, 15 September 2010, http://www.politikerbloggen.se/2010/09/15/36898/ (February 15, 2011).

24. Cf. Laurie Ouellette, *Viewers Like You? How Public TV Failed the People* (New York: Columbia University Press, 2002).

25. Liesbet van Zoonen, *Entertaining the Citizen: When Politics and Popular Culture Converge* (Lanham, Md.: Rowman & Littlefield, 2005).

26. Nick Couldry, *Media Rituals: A Critical Approach* (London: Routledge, 2003), 45–46.

27. Brit Stakston, "Program för socialmediakuten och daglig JMW-talkshow i Almedalen," JMW Kommunikation, 6 June 2010, http://www.jmw.se/2010/06/06/program-for-socialamediakuten-och-jmw-talkshow-i-almedalen/ (15 February 2011); Stakston, "På väg mot flopp för sociala medier i årets valrörelse?"

28. Cecelia Tichi, *Electronic Hearth: Creating an American Television Culture* (Oxford: Oxford University Press, 1991).

29. Tobias Brandel, "Populära sociala medier inför valet. Bloggar, Twitter, Youtube and Facebook växer i politisk betydelse," *Svenska Dagbladet*, 7 March 2010.

30. Maria Sköld, "Schyman twittrar mest," *Göteborgs-Posten*, 12 August 2009; Tobias Brandel, "SD dominerar sociala medier," *Svenska Dagbladet*, 26 April 2010; Karin Pettersson, "Så segrade Mona kampen i nätet," *Expressen*, 2 May 2010.

31. Per Ström, *Sociala medier: Gratis marknadsföring och opinionsbildning* (Malmö: Liber, 2010); Paul Ronge, *Sociala medier: En halv sekund från ord till handling* (Sundbyberg: Optimal förlag, 2010); Brit Stakston, *Politik 2:o: Konsten att använda sociala medier* (Göteborg: Beijbom Books, 2010).

32. Tobias Brandel, "Sociala medier blir ny pr-kanal," *Svenska Dagbladet*, 4 January 2010; Tobias Brandel, "Risk för nya valskandaler," *Svenska Dagbladet*, 17 March 2010; Niklas Orrenius, "Konsten att släppa megafonen," *Sydsvenska Dagbladet*, 17 May 2009; Anders Mildner, "Sociala medier som valstrategi," *Corren*, 13 March 2010; Hanna Grahn Strömbom, "Få politiker vill lära om sociala medier," *Borås tidning*, 10 May 2010; Kenny Genborg, "Mest struntprat i sociala medier," *Göteborgs-Posten*, 15 May 2010; Kenny Genborg, "Svärmen kan styra politikern," *Göteborgs-Posten*, 16 May 2010; Anders Mildner, "Samtal pågår," *Kvällsposten*, 25 May 2010; Tobias Rydegren, "Sociala medier fungerar sämst i en valrörelse," *Resumé*, 6 May 2010; Jenny Kallin, "Monolog i megafon när politiker twittrar," *Dagens Nyheter*, 12 September 2010; Emanuel Karlsten, "En plågsam och pinsam digital valrörelse," *Same Same But Different*, 17 September 2010, http://samesamebutdifferent.se/2010/09/17/en-plagsam-pinsam-digital-valrorelse/ (15 February 2011); Sofia Mirjamsdotter, "Partierna misslyckades med sociala medier," *Metro Teknik*, 20 September 2010.

33. Martin Gelin, quoted in Fredrik Thambert, "Vet inte vad de pratar om," *Resumé*, 21 September 2010.

34. See blog post by Emelie Holmquist, "Sveket," *Klamydiabrevet*, 15 September 2010, http://klamydiabrevet.blogspot.com/2010/09/sveket (15 February 2010). For a self-reflexive analysis, see "Where Does Democracy Take Place?" *Journalism 3:0: Media Ecology and the Future*, Sveriges Radio, 28 February 2011, http://sverigesradio.se/sida/artikel.aspx?programid=4042&artikel=4317587 (1 March 2011).

35. Van Zoonen, *Entertaining the Citizen*, 45; Couldry, Livingstone, and Markham, *Media Consumption and Public Engagement*, 5–6.

36. Robert Draper, "The Palin Network," *New York Times*, 17 November 2010.

37. Kristoffer Örstadius, "Nu visar vi var vi stär," *Dagens Nyheter*, 25 September 2010.

38. Jodi Dean, "Communicative Capitalism: Circulation and the Foreclosure of Politics," in *Digital Media and Democracy*, ed. Megan Boler (Cambridge, Mass.: MIT Press, 2008), 101–21; Jodi Dean, *Democracy and Other Neoliberal Fantasies* (Durham, N.C.: Duke University Press, 2009), 31–32.

39. Dean, *Democracy and Other Neoliberal Fantasies*, 25.

CHAPTER 16

The iPhone's Failure

Protests and Resistance

OLIVER LEISTERT

T HE MASSIVE WORLDWIDE roll-out of mobile phone technology has been accompanied by the development of a specialized practice of mobile media within various protest movements. Reports of massive mobile-media use in different protest situations show up daily—and the list of scholarly publications on the topic is growing as well. Events in Iran in 2008—and in 2011 in Tunisia and Egypt—have made mobile technologies pertinent for protesters. Yet one needs to remain critical about the extent to which these protests and demonstrations have been empowered by mobile media. In addition, keeping mobile media available and sustainable is becoming increasingly difficult for protesters since regimes have learned about their empowering capacities—and how to limit them.[1] "All mobile operators in Egypt have been instructed to suspend services in selected areas," as an Egyptian Vodafone statement in late January 2011 read. "Under Egyptian legislation the authorities have the right to issue such an order and we are obliged to comply with it. The Egyptian authorities will be clarifying the situation in due course."[2] Cases of harsh repression based on cyber-surveillance abound. Hence, it would be insufficient to praise the powers of liberation granted by mobile communication technology because this fails to acknowledge retaliatory effects. Mobile media are, in fact, a technology of governing—and as such they easily may be switched from a liberal to a reprimanding mode.

Technically, the iPhone is invested with all common necessary features to support its use in active, autonomous protests as it provides Internet connectivity on the road and a myriad of communication tools. Hence, iPhones could potentially be omnipresent at political protests today. Yet there are a number of reasons that this is not the case. And while the iPhone is in wide use in many areas of modern life, in this article I will argue that despite all the innovation hype, it has largely failed to "revolutionize" revolutions proper, the key reason being that the iPhone is too expensive and mostly sold in combination with a post-paid plan. During my extensive research on mobile media, social movements, and surveillance, comprising numerous interviews with social activist worldwide, none of these subjects turned out to be an iPhone owner. One might conclude that the iPhone is for the wealthy only, whose interest in, say, a more just world seldom leads to active street protests. Yet there are a variety of reasons that do not relate to the costs the iPhone entails, and it certainly would be simplistic to assume that wealth equals political opportunism, as such a statement would rest on a notion of class that neglects the inherent multidimensionality of power relations, thus echoing the neoliberal doctrine that individuals are activated only in the pursuit of their own economic benefit. Rather, I want to begin my article where all mobile communication begins—at the level of infrastructures—and I will conclude by elaborating on the technically most basic, but enormously widespread tool that mobile media provide social movements with: short messaging. The purpose of the article, then, is to show that the iPhone fails as a protester's device for reasons related to Apple's closed-source culture and because the needed tools are coming with other platforms and phones. Apple's license politics and closed-source culture appear to be among the biggest obstacles, and, indeed, the iPhone is well known for its ultra-rigid method of application and content delivery, including the first successful DRM strategy, while other mobile media platforms, such as those based on Android or Maemo/MeeGo, take advantage of the productivity of their own community and continue to blur the distinctions between user/recipient and developer/producer.[3]

Why Open Source Matters in a Proprietary Surrounding

Mobile media generally have their closest connection to open-source and hacker culture within the domain of application development for activist purposes. Within these circles, Apple is hardly the preferred brand. "The iPhone is cool and it is completely locked. The possibilities there are limited," states

"Yossarian," a developer for the activist portal Indymedia.[4] At the same time, however, the iPhone has also spurred and generated a mobile media culture that might change how activists behave, as one of my interviews with application developer Nathan Freitas revealed:

> I have . . . recently looked at higher end smartphones . . . the android operating system, the HTC g models. . . . Things with better keyboard and cameras, iPhone-type devices. And just thinking about a year or two from now and the next big upgrade comes and everyone has, like we have seen it in America, everyone seems to have an iPhone. It changed how much media have been produced. So, looking at that, the high-end Nokias and what happens if that trickles down into Africa or Asia in the way the basic Nokias are there now.

The hope of 3G phones "trickling down" into poorer regions might remain illusory. Still, what Freitas addresses applies to an increasing number of people, and thus he certainly is right in welcoming efforts to develop 3G phone applications that meet the criteria for anticensorship campaigns in, say, China or Burma. "One of the reasons why I like Android is that you can replace the applications, you can replace the dial, the text-messaging application, saying this is the default." When open-source and Linux-based phones entered the arena, one prevalent barrier fell that had made any mobile phone, including the iPhone, an untrustworthy device. Seen from Freitas's perspective, open-source software is a necessary preliminary step for secured communication.[5] Not that every individual compiles from source, fixes bugs, or reads crypto-algorithms, but everyone *might* do that. Freitas has, for example, taken advantage of these features when developing a number of Android applications tailored to the demands of anticensorship activists in China and Burma, such as anonymous Internet usage via Tor or encrypted and password-protected file systems on the phone, encrypted telephony and SMS, and steganographic use of MMS. These are features that might affect the well-being of activists and are available only because of the open-source culture enabled in Android. Again, Apple's iPhone cannot be deployed for the development of such applications because of its closed-source and centralized deployment regime.

Freitas's efforts naturally also echo the problem of mobile-phone infrastructures generally. Client to client encryption is, for instance, a measure taken because the pathway in between—the infrastructure—remains untrustworthy. The matter can only be bypassed if there is a possibility for everyone to develop and distribute applications free from the producer or distributor of the phone itself, which is difficult in case of the iPhone. Mobile telephony networks, thus, differ significantly from the Internet. The latter is based on open standards and so encourages development while the mobile phone infrastructure can only be reverse engineered, that is, understood by analyzing input and output functions and operations without access to the processes running inside. Security issues about GSM, the Global System for Mobile Communications, for example, are only slowly being disclosed to the general public, a concern emphasized by a number of my social-activist interviewees, such as software developer Daniel Kahn Gillmor:

> The other thing is the issue of control over communications. As a free software developer I do think (despite my caveats) that there is a potential for emancipatory change in a global communications network; but it can only happen when people are actually in control of their own communications. That is one of the reasons why free software is important. Mobile phones in the communications world have been our adversaries in this particular struggle. The idea of making myself dependent on a machine that has so many layers of inaccessible proprietary control is really unacceptable for me.[6]

To both iPhone and Microsoft users, such statements may sound fancy. Control over means of communication, nevertheless, is the driving force for hacker and free-software developer communities. These demands stem from a critical perspective on proprietary, closed-source information and communication technologies—and not from an affirmation of technology. They can be traced back to the demands of ownership over means of production and thus link to an old heritage of work struggles. Seen from this perspective, mobile-phone infrastructure is complicated by telecommunication companies having full control, leaving phone users passive and dependent and the infrastructure itself a black box, sealed by various nondisclosure agreements signed before getting access to critical information on closed-source applications. Any public disclosure is then prohibited, which naturally produces distrust within the tech-savvy community and among activists.

These concerns in their most radical form have lead to proposals and concrete attempts to rebuild the mobile infrastructure from the ground up, as in the case of local message delivery. As mobile telephony was shutdown in Egypt during the protests in early 2011, for instance, device-to-device connectivity via Bluetooth regained importance for communication on the streets.

Regarding wireless protocols disseminated on a larger scale, one of my interviewees named "Startx" stated that he had always been

> fascinated by the idea that people have these sophisticated devices they carry around everyday: their telephones. And they hardly use any of the possibilities of it. They have a recording device, a video camera, a photo camera. All the mobile phones of the last years have a wireless device with Bluetooth, but nobody is using all this stuff. Everybody has it and is carrying it around. So our idea was to start with Bluetooth because it is the most common and most spread kind of wireless protocol.[7]

Using Bluetooth, wireless devices can be merged into a network where clients also act as routers. Radical developers such as Startx are envisioning a return to decentralization (or even distributed systems) in response to pressing issues of surveillance, and responding also to high prices for basic services such as SMS. Setting up wireless networks that cover parts of London, for instance—based on protocols that encourage distributed topologies—one responds to the unjustified high costs for local mobile-phone telephony. The idea of a Bluetooth-based messaging service thus becomes a real challenge to the untenable scenarios set up by various telecoms. As a consequence, the call for open standards and open source are integral parts of an attitude developed within the open culture of the Internet and in clear contradiction to proprietary mobile communication standards such as GSM. While the iPhone relies on GSM (or UMTS, the Universal Mobile Telecommunications System) like other phones, it has from the start failed to provide preliminary necessities to reliably circumvent this problem: open-source code base, decentralized application distribution, and autonomy from its producer. For commercial reasons, Apple keeps the iPhone tied tightly to its own distribution channels and thus reduces it deliberately to a consumer device instead of a tool for emancipatory personal communication.

Phone Activism

In spite of the persistent struggle for control over the means of mobile communications, mobile phones have become an integral part of the activist toolkit. The contradiction of not having control over one's own means of communication while using it is an activist tool is agonizing: almost every interviewee expressed the discomfort with this situation. Here, the exposed position of such activists sheds light on the unsolved issues discussed above. Being under surveillance because of one's activities marks a watershed of sorts: on the one side, surveillance remains an undirected default activity with unknown outcome, and, on the other side, surveillance is explicitly targeted as both a means of repression and as a means of establishing fear and paranoia. "Blax," a media activist from Oaxaca, Mexico, reports on how to contain surveillance:

> In the context of the social repression here in Oaxaca . . . human rights activists were trained in the use of mobile phones to try to contain the surveillance because the surveillance was declared as a permanent reality. So, we can not fight it, we can not stop it, but we can try to contain it and we have to live with it. The use of the phone, not saying a lot, not saying delicate parts of your life. As media activists, we were trying to help people use encryption for their communication.[8]

Living under heavy surveillance raises questions about how one should use mobile phones. Yet these are also multipurpose tools, and mobile media are used in many ways. Cameras and microphones, especially, have been employed by my interviewees in places such as Pakistan, India, or Brazil. Even simple mobile phones nowadays provide cameras to capture evidence. Low-resolution pictures and films and mono recordings can fulfill these tasks even better as their transmission to the Internet has become significantly faster.

"Roberto" is a member of the Cooper Gliceria, a collectors' self-organized cooperative in São Paulo, which developed as a response to the unorganized and thus more vulnerable social status of the paper and cards collectors in the city.

> Once the city police was arresting the cards. With the cell phone I was able to take a picture of it and then make a denouncement. And this eventually stopped the police action. It changed the way the police acted towards the collectors. And secondly: whenever we have meetings with authorities, with the major and secretary and something like that, we can record with the cell phone and so have their voices on tape and claim our rights on the agreements made because it is on tape.[9]

The mobile phone thus serves as a tool for reclaiming rights where the power relation has become so asymmetrical that without documented evidence the stronger party could simply renege on an agreement and the weaker party would have no recourse. Of course, this is basically not a new practice or strategy, but it is the mobile phone that for the first time brings a recording machine or a simple camera to many people, such as in the autonomous Mexican region of Chiapas, when the Mexican military tried to control the streets in a remote area, as reported by "Olinca," from the Association for Progressive Communications member Laneta in Mexico City: "In Chiapas, people send images through mobile phones, when they have pictures of the military transports or movements, they send the picture to other areas to put them very fast in circulation, so the military can not surprise them anymore. Some communities also send these pictures to San Cristóbal. Sometimes also to the Internet."[10]

The mobile phone and its camera become tools of intelligence service for those who are commonly the targets of intelligence operations. I also visited Lahore, Pakistan, to talk with lawyers and activists about mobile media during the peak of the lawyers' movement that lead to the reinstallation of the Pakistani chief of justice, and thus an independent judiciary, in 2008, as well as the forced resignation of the dictator Pervez Musharraf. Internet access has never made it to the common people here but remains a tool of the upper and middle classes. Although the lawyers and activists who were at the heart of the lawyers' movement are from the wealthier part of the society, the use of basic SMS services became the main means of communication and organizing.

Hamid Zaman is the president of the Concerned Citizens Society of Pakistan (CCP), a group of citizens mostly with a high education and wealthy background, which joined the lawyers' efforts early and which were able to mobilize on short notice whenever necessary:

> All our messages used to go out by mobile phone because a very small percentage of people have email and internet, out of the people that were with us maybe 20 percent. And so the mobile phone was the most effective way of mobilizing, because you are always carrying a mobile and so I can send you in the morning a message for demonstration in the evening and you would read it some time in the day. So all messages used to be sent via mobile phones. Any directions and instructions that needed to be given. We had a CCP number, one central phone, so that any person who wanted to send back feedback would send it to that number. That number was monitored by a secretary all day. It could be used for people to send comments.[11]

Here the core issue of mobile media is their capability to gather people on short notice. This power has been confirmed by almost all interviewees, independent of origin. As the CCP people had a wealthy background, they also used other technologies at their disposal. They could bridge the gap to the Internet to reach out to overseas Pakistanis, who could not follow the issue via the mass media since media reports were strictly censored during the emergency phase. This is where social networking sites in combination with mobile phones jumped in and, according to "Mr. Kahn," another member of CCP, thus helped, for instance, to raise money for the imprisoned lawyers:

> Video recording and picture taking, besides SMS, was important. We were able to move images very fast into the web. Especially the students exploited this feature. The people overseas were constantly being updated, so someone studying overseas was able to move that information back and forth, that did put a lot of pressure on the media. That was to me the most phenomenal thing. I could take a picture and put it on Facebook while I was there. We had a CCP group on Facebook. Social networking is now connected to the phone.[12]

These features could have been supported by iPhones very well. But I have to admit: during my whole stay in Lahore, I did not notice any iPhone in use, not even among the wealthy CCP people.

The Rule of the Mobile

But what happens to those excluded from electronic communication? Interestingly, even in countries such as India, exclusion from political participation on grounds of unavailable mobile-phone technology is a concern for a constantly decreasing number of people, as an activist from Bangalore nicknamed "ManasaSarovara" tells us: "The maximum people that we are connected with are not on the internet, many people are not even literate. But they have a phone. The main demographic that we are relating to, like the fisher people, all these people are not on the internet, maybe one person, some leaders. But all the others are not. But they all have phones. Everyone. It is only at 2000 rupees."[13] This statement is seconded by Madhuresh Kumar from Delhi, who works on the mobilization of social movements that travel from rural areas to the capital to protest:

Mobile phones are very useful in a country like India, because many of these movements work in places where electricity is unreliable or absent and no access to internet is available. The emails are only for the urban situation, but for the rural it is the mobile where you can communicate . . . using voice but also the SMS, which became useful in the way that if anything happens anywhere in the country you create a text message and send it across the country to all supporters in the villages and the cities, and it is easy and quick to organize support.[14]

Without electricity, mobile phones win over other infrastructural measures. Kumar's comments also point us toward the nondetachable integration of these devices into social movements' practices. As mentioned above, paranoia and fear of repression through use of mobile media were addressed by nearly all interviewees, and nonetheless nearly everyone had embraced the comfort and change in agency brought by the new tools.

iGovern

After discussing the tool function of mobile media for political protests, we also need to take into account the disempowering aspects of mobile media, their dark side, so to speak. I would like to argue that mobile media can be understood as a governmental technique, spreading around the globe to enhance productivity—the main task of governing, as Foucault convincingly has laid out. Although a liberal regime as such is not present in all countries, I suggest that where mobile media exist, there also is some sort of liberal rule; the technology allows the population to communicate in relative independence from the state. When it comes to surveillance issues, on the other hand, understanding mobile media from its illiberal governmental side helps to understand that this dark side of mobile media indeed is systemic: governing is always an undertaking involving the two sides of the same coin, the production of economic freedom but at the same time, securing that freedom against possible threats. Liberal rule necessarily depends on social exclusion by exertion of illiberal, disciplinary, and sovereign measures.

The dark side of mobile media became notorious when many protestors in Teheran were arrested after being identified via a state-of-the-art Nokia-Siemens Telecommunications Surveillance infrastructure for mobile phones. This anti-emancipatory interpretation of mobile media gains dominance when liberal rule, enacted by the massive roll-out of mobile media, turns into illiberal or even sovereign rule: mobile devices turn themselves against their users as technologies of repression. Whether the regime is a formal democratic one or not, whether it has an oligarchic structure or a strong middle-class base, it tries to withstand, incorporate, or reject a grassroots, bottom-up pressure that can trigger illiberal or sovereign rule. Because activists understand the dangers they are dealing with when they use data streams for such purposes (e.g., with every SMS they send), it is the activists themselves who constantly define and redefine the qualities that mobile media bear in socially contested fields. They are constantly testing borders. Acts of self-censorship, such as switching off the mobile during meetings or using code words, are not deliberately chosen means but responses to scenarios of threat and, as such, part of a specific mobile-media rationality that informs subjectivation. Liberal governmental subjectivation then provokes its counter-subjectivation: switching off the phone is the most drastic activity an individual can engage in. Stopping the flow of information, connectivity, and reachability echoes the blockage invoked by sovereign rule.

As surveillance is a one-way, asymmetric, and opaque operation, fear and paranoia are governmental factors in this rationality. This is the reason that it is promising to elaborate on the subjectivities produced in these contested fields and speculate on the role of mobile media—beyond the ideological promise of unlimited communication and access—as direct propagators of freedom, wealth, and democracy. The iPhone can be understood as a governmental supersymbol because it was one of the first mobiles that provided a constant stream of information, the large-scale integration of e-mail, chat, Twitter, Facebook, and other social media in one device. But in protest cultures and well-organized resistance, such factors are regarded with ambivalence at best. The interviewees all have expressed their general discomfort about this 24/7 online setting not because it is not useful but rather because the liberal promise of mobile media lost its plausibility once the illiberal or sovereign mode of mobile media has been experienced firsthand.

Conclusion

As the iPhone is sealed off more than other phones for software distribution, it fails to become a phone of interest for developers of protest software, who are driven by a noncommercial spirit. People who have experienced the dark side of mobile media are naturally interested in minimal data traces. The iPhone stands in opposition to minimal data traces since by default it sends out regular valid and precise position and communication act details on a scale that *no* state legislation demands. For instance, a common activist practice is to remove a phone's battery to ensure no microphones or cameras can be activated. The iPhone does not even allow the user to do this without loss of warranty. Considering costs, the closed source, centralized software channels, and the lack of any feature that makes it particularly more useful than other phones, the iPhone's irrelevance in protests becomes evident. The iPhone is not a tool deliberately chosen by activists and social movements. While the iPhone occasionally is present where protests happen, more often than not it is rejected by activists in favor of other mobile media devices.

NOTES

1. Throughout the article, the term "mobile media" is used for any highly portable device capable of wireless communications. The term "smartphone" implies a difference from other phones that can not be justified by technology alone. Thus, the evidence transported in the term "smart-" blurs what the device is actually used for and what this practice adds up to. Using the term "mobile media" instead of "smartphone," and resisting the lures of ever-newer technologies, is an attempt to avoid both rosy delusions about technology, on the one hand, and technological determinism, on the other.

2. See "Vodafone Egypt Statement," 27 January 2011, http://www.vodafone.com/content/index/press.html (15 February 2011).

3. DRM stands for "digital rights management," and its goal is corporate control over content and applications for computing devices, mainly in the realm of intellectual property enforcement and thus the reinstallation of the regime on analog media circulation. Although historically DRM refers to different strategic technologies, Apple's regime implements DRM both conceptually and in practical effect. Jailbreaking the iPhone might be a possible solution for circumvention, but this is considered a breach of warranty and thus the iPhone cannot be described in the same manner as Android.

4. "Yossarian," interview by the author, London, 6 April 2009.

5. Nathan Freitas, interview by the author, New York City, 12 August 2009.

6. Daniel Kahn Gillmor, interview by the author, New York City, 11 August 2009.

7. "Startx," interview by the author, London, 6 April 2009.

8. "Blax," interview by the author, Oaxaca, 2 September 2009.

9. "Roberto," interview by the author, São Paulo, 30 July 2009.

10. "Olinca," interview by the author, Mexico City, 1 September 2009.

11. Hamid Zaman, interview by the author, Lahore, 27 October 2009.

12. "Mr. Khan," interview by the author, Lahore, 27 October 2009.

13. "ManasaSarovara," interview by the author, Bangalore, 14 October 2009. Two thousand rupees is approximately forty U.S. dollars.

14. Madhuresh Kumar, interview by the author, Delhi, 17 October 2009.

IV
Mobile Lives

CHAPTER 17

I Phone, I Learn

ANNE BALSAMO

FROM THE CLICK wheel of the first iPods to the touch-sensitive screens of the iPads, Apple has redefined the way we communicate with our devices. As Steve Jobs, CEO of Apple, made clear in several interviews, the company's approach to design was never simply about the look of the device; it was about *how* the devices worked. This concern with the "how" extends well beyond the domain of device affordances into the realm of "how" the devices are woven into the lifestyles of intended users and consumers. With the iPhone, Apple launched a product that is implicated within a matrix of cultural changes that concern not simply how we communicate but also how we live, play, affiliate, work, and learn in a digital age.

These changes—spread across domains—rest on a reconfigured relationship between bodies and devices. Where is the interface—that liminal place—between my phone and myself? Just as I know my hand to be a part of myself, so, too, I behold my iPhone. Where the Web made the multiplication of spaces a function of my ten-fingered hands—keyboarding and clicking—the iPhone requires only one or at most two fingers to move between spaces of the ear, the voice, the eye, and the mind. Like the iPod before it, the iPhone has become an icon of the smart device that presents the user not simply with a GUI (graphical user interface) but more tellingly with a NUI (natural user interface) that privileges touch, gesture, and voice recognition. I incorporate it as a prosthetic extension of my corporeal being. Not merely an extension of my ear, as McLuhan would have argued, it is me. My body/myself—my iPhone/myself. I become the cyborg I always wanted to be.

Me and My iPhone

I grew up in an age of designer phones available in different colors to complement the décor of every room. Thus, I was generationally prepared to welcome the iPhone as a prosthetic device that would subtly but surely reconfigure my corporeal sense networks. Tumors might form, we hear, from the low level microwaves used to send and receive signals. Nonetheless, I keep my iPhone near me at all times, reluctantly letting go only in the presence of transportation security scanners or the shower. I am exceedingly anxious when it is out of my sight.[1] I wear it more frequently than I wear my corrective eyeglasses. In many senses, the iPhone is the first ubiquitous wearable computational device. While it is true that all mobile phones could be considered prototypes of wearable computing, the iPhone, coupled with the wide-scale interest in the development of IOS apps, made it the platform of choice for wearable prototypes. As early as 2008, developers were exploring ways to attach the device to a set of glass frames to produce a rudimentary version of virtual reality goggles.[2] In the time since, the use of eyeglass frames has been set aside in favor of the development of applications that allow an iPhone user to access augmented-reality experiences. We finally understand, perhaps, that we don't need to "wear" the iPhone on the bridge of our noses for it to be wearable. We see with it in the palm of our hand.

My usage history maps my imagination and announces at every turn that I "was here" and "here" and "here." My iPhone always knows where I am, even when I don't. Even when no one can find me, the information I seek always does. These personal geographies mean that I am always potentially at home in the world. I can never be lost—even when my signal drops, my phone still functions as a homing beacon. Moreover, my iPhone use testifies to the productivity of consumption as the active appropriation of signs, symbols, and codes. In using it, I insert myself into the flow of media, images, voices, sounds, and data from which I activate an elaborate, media-rich communication network where all sorts of transactions take place that have as their common objective the compulsive reproduction of symbolic plentitude. My iPhone is a personalized read/write culture machine.

From that symbolic plentitude, I assemble a sense of self, aggregated from the bits and pieces I retrieve from various media flows. In so doing, I participate in what Manuel Castell describes as "mass self-communication"[3]—the one-to-many communication modality that floods network traffic. But what I communicate is not a preassembled "self" but rather my self that is itself an assemblage of my travels through various networks. Like the Internet more broadly, the media flows I access with my iPhone are discontinuous narrative spaces. My assembled self provides a weak narrative framework for my travels through these virtual flows. But interestingly, as I leave traces of myself wherever I go in the form of passwords, purchases, downloads, texts, tweets, images, and end-user license agreements signed but not read, these traces are fed back to me in subsequent sessions in the form of personalized advertisements for what I once went looking for. My desires are mirrored back to me with uncanny precision. My self-in-formation is fixed by the way the network writes over me.

The entire purpose of the iPhone is, hence, to reflect me back to myself. As a looking glass onto my digitally distributed self, it mirrors to me my favorites, my friends, my landscapes, my adventures, my comforts, my hopes, my world that I have molded to perfectly suit me. As the key interface for my BAN (body area network), it ensures my preferred interaction style is always at hand.[4] Its presence comforts me, not only because of the connection information it archives of my contacts but also because it has become my most intimate personal digital companion. It is more consistently present for me and with me than any human could ever be. It amuses me, informs me, reassures me, educates me, surprises me, hijacks me, soothes me, angers me, delights me, amplifies me, connects me, reflects me. As a device, it is the ideal techno-embodiment of the perfect mother.

This ideal has animated the imagination of science fiction writers for decades. One of the most evocative narratives to explore the promises and consequences of such a technology was conjured by Neal Stephenson in his novel, *The Diamond Age* (1995). In the year the novel was published, DVDs had just been invented, Google had just launched the beta version of its famous search site, and the first e-book readers were still three years from market. Manifesting the prescience that makes him one of the most fascinating twenty-first-century science fiction authors, Stephenson invents a technology called "The Young Lady's Illustrated Primer," which looks like a standard book but isn't, of course. The Primer is a piece of advanced nanotechnology that uses interactive paper to create a book with special properties: through a process of imprinting, the book bonds with its owner/reader to serve her as a lifelong, individually attuned learning portal.

'As we discussed, it sees and hears everything in its vicinity,' Hackworth said. 'At the moment, it's looking for a small female. As soon as a little girl picks it up and opens the front cover for the first time, it will imprint that child's face and voice into its memory.'

'And thenceforth it will see all events and persons in relation to that girl, using her as a datum from which to chart a psychological terrain, as it were. Maintenance of that terrain is one of the book's primary processes. Whenever the child uses the book, then, it will perform a sort of dynamic mapping from the database onto her particular terrain.'

'The Illustrated Primer is an extremely general and powerful system capable of more extensive self-reconfiguration than most. Remember that a fundamental part of its job is to respond to its environment.'

As is typical for science-fictional devices, the wonders of the Primer are many. As envisioned by the main character, the Primer was created for use as an educational device for young boys and girls starting at the age of four. Indeed, for Nell, the beleaguered young girl character who receives a purloined Primer as a consequence of her brother's petty theft, the book proves to be life transforming. She learns over time that the Primer will help her learn: "She did not know all the words, but she knew a lot of them, and when she got tired, the book would help her sound out the words or even read the whole story to her, or tell it to her with moving pictures just like a cine." The fables narrated by the book change over time, providing Nell with important lessons about deception, self-defense, and justice.

We eventually discover that the Primer is actually a mixed-reality device that makes use of the services of anonymous "ractors"—people who work as paid actors who perform voiceovers and provide synchronous vocal instruction for digital applications. Miranda, the ractor for Nell's Primer narrates life lessons pitched perfectly for Nell's stage of development. What begins as a set of media-rich fairytales (revolving around Princess Nell and her magical companions) evolve into a set of dynamic virtual adventures (all narrated by Miranda) designed to teach Nell everything she needs to know to survive in her increasingly violent and hostile world. Over the course of the novel Miranda's and Nell's fates become intertwined as the Primer serves not only as a learning platform but also as an object of affiliation for the two characters. "'The woman you seek is named Miranda,' he said. All thoughts of crowns, queens, and armies seemed to vanish from Nell's mind, and she was just a young lady again, looking for what? Her mother? Her teacher? Her friend?"[5] And indeed, at the end of the novel, the characters meet for the first time when Nell saves Miranda's life by designing a new nanotechnology that counteracts the devastation wrought by blood-based nanomotes that infect her.

As much as it is an entertaining work of science fiction, *The Diamond Age*, is an evocative fable about learning in a digital age. The Primer encompasses key features we yearn for in new learning devices: network access, configurable data delivery, customizable information aggregation, imaginative expansion capacity (that grows along with the user), and a recommender system to connect the user with other people (known or not) who have something to teach. If we squint, we see these specifications evident in our most sophisticated smartphones. For everything that it is—wearable computer, mirror of myself, techno-mother—the iPhone also signals the development of a new platform for learning in a digital age.

Learning designers and educational technologists are using smartphones and other mobile technologies in different ways. Some are building educational activities specifically designed to expand the range of phone users. For example, the Madrid-based company BabySkool creates iPhone and iPad applications to teach young children (infants to five-year-olds) basic language skills; in spring 2010 they released a new app called My First Words in Spanish.[6] Such efforts to build programs for young children have led critics to ask if the development of mobile learning applications isn't really a marketing ploy designed to grow the consumer base of the future.[7] These critics notwithstanding, the promise that excites educators and designers is the use of smartphones as an ubiquitous interaction device that could transform the physical world into a space of annotated exhibits by enabling users to access information embedded in physical environments. Whether as mobile classroom or ubiquitous joystick, many educators are betting on the iPhone and other mobile devices to reawaken wonder in technologically jaded students by designing learning activities to open eyes and ears to the scenes all around us that have something to teach.

Learning on the Go

Not only does the iPhone allow access to digitally augmented spaces, but the multiplication of spaces *in* my hand is the iPhone's magnum opus. This has a profound impact on the place of learning. Since the advent of the World

Wide Web, the physical place of school has given way to a proliferation of online educational places that represent entirely new spaces for learning. For many young people, school is no longer bound to a brick and mortar building: it is better understood as a distributed learning ecology.[8] With the use of such smartphones, students traverse these learning spaces while they simultaneously traverse geographic spaces as well. No longer do they need physical access points; the infrastructure of learning on the go includes the digital connections among physical places, virtual environments, and mobile practices of access and interaction.

Michel de Certeau once made a poetic distinction between "space" and "place" when he stated that "a space is a practiced place."[9] A place has stable boundaries and a fixed location; a space is created in time through actions and practices. In this sense, school is a place, and learning is a spatial practice. This insight is not merely theoretical. It captures something important about the nature of learning in a digital age. Outfitted with their smartphones, as young people physically travel from home to school then on to after-school programs, they may have also virtually traveled through a dozen other learning sites: online virtual environments (such as Whyville), social networking sites (Facebook), and cultural portals (Youth2Youth).[10] For all their differences in actual access to technology and tools, the spaces of learning have multiplied for this generational cohort, and the movement among them has become seamless, a matter of clicks rather than the transport of bodies by school buses.

Memes are cultural concepts that circulate through media of communication: verbally (through language), physically (through bodily habits and fashion), and technologically (through symbols and codes). As a meme machine, the iPhone enables the wide circulation and rapid dissemination of cultural genetic material. Members of the born-digital generation understand themselves as just-in-time learners, confident that when they need to know something they'll know where to find it. These young people understand how to mine their networks, both digital and social, for their information needs. Many of them treat their affiliation networks as informal Delphi groups (a structured communication technique relying on a panel of experts.) The statistical phenomenon of Delphi groups demonstrates that even when each person does not know a factual piece of information, the aggregate mapping of responses from group members tends to cluster around the correct answer. For these youth, the process of thinking now routinely—and in some cases, exclusively—relies on social-network navigation. As they navigate intersecting digital networks, they are exposed to different learning communities:

those of peers, popular pundits, parents, media shills, and formal educators. Each community offers different data sets: opinions, recommendations, enticements, and requirements. In short, data mining from different information sources and media flows has become a crucial component of learning in a digital age.

But memes are not memories, and culture is not the simple accumulation of data, tweets, or links. Data do not equate to knowledge, and knowledge does not equate to insight. What is required to transform data mining into insight is the creation of learning activities that structure pattern recognition. The ability to apprehend patterns among data and to construct narratives that provide context for the meaning of memes results in the creation of knowledge and insight. Exploring this concern has resulted in the development of location-based learning applications that use the iPhone's connection to the global positioning system to provide the context for a specific activity. While museums have been at the forefront of the use of location-based applications for the purposes of informal learning, the idea of using smartphones as an interface for context-specific learning activities has generated considerable enthusiasm among educators.[11] The idea is to explore the concept of "situated learning" by bringing learning activities to students as they venture forth from classroom into broader environments. While the enthusiasm is high, as of late 2010 there are few examples of situated learning applications to review.[12] But things are moving swiftly. For example, in October 2010, the GLS Mobile Learning Team (at the University of Wisconsin–Madison) released the Augmented Reality and Interactive Storytelling application for the iPhone. ARIS is an open-source tool that enables learning designers "to create location-based educational games, stories, tours and data collection activities for place based learning curriculum and mobile citizen science projects."[13] One of the activities created with ARIS, called Dow Day, allows middle-school students to view "situated" video footage of Vietnam War protests that took place on the University of Wisconsin campus. As they walk through the current campus landscape they can see the historical footage overlaid onto the view of the current scene. With tools such as ARIS now available, the situation is ripe for the development of a rich array of situated-learning activities.

Building Learning

Benjamin Bratton has argued that the iPhone is unique not because it is the best or the first mobile communication device but because it is "the first to put it all together in a way that changes how a critical mass of consumers could envision a new genre of computing: interaction in the wild." The wild, in Bratton's view is the digital city, which is best understood as "a shared nervous system" whose membranes have been breeched by the proliferation of digital information networks.

The foremost infrastructural projects of our generation have been the planetary proliferation of digital information networks, and now another moves that infrastructure from an embedded *sous*-terrestrial network to a pervasive in-hand circuit of body and information cloud. Computation evolves from a rare, expensive national asset to a cheap ubiquitous vapor. That stream's orifice is the handheld phone, PDA, homing beacon, Geiger counter, magic antenna, virtual goggles, scanning X-ray filter, field recording microphone, and camera that makes hidden wisdom appear; the device becomes a window onto the hidden layers of data held in or about the user's immediate environment.[14]

As Bratton goes on to elaborate, the iPhone—as the trendiest version of the phone as "orifice"—made interaction with locative media an everyday reality for city dwellers. While his concern is the implication of this technocultural development for architects and urban environment designers, others are exploring a wider range of applications that imagine new sorts of interactions between residents and buildings equipped with dense, computational sensor nets. In these experiments, it is not simply that the user or student learns from a computationally rich "situated" place but that the place itself learns as well. These learning activities make use of the mobile devices to collaborate on the creation of knowledge not simply with other users/students (who may be physically present or not) but also with elements in the built environment.

Applications such as Google Maps, Flickr's geotagged images, and even Twitter are part of the mobile ecology that enable cocreation and the sharing of knowledge among people who are distant from one another in both time and place. Users enjoy instant access to a vast accumulation of data and distributed intelligence regardless of their time or their place. To date, museums have been among the first cultural institutions to actively engage in the use and development of new tools and platforms that make use of mobile devices for educational purposes. For example, our recent research on "the distributed museum" itemizes the innovative ways that public museums and libraries in the United States have embraced mobile media practices.[15] These institutions are using technologies of mobility not only to connect to new audiences (the "born-digital" generation, for example) but also to extend the time and place of the museum itself. These mobile experiences have moved beyond the use of the traditional handheld audio guide to feature cell phone tours that include not simply audio but also image-based annotations. For example, the Walker Art Center in Minneapolis, Minnesota, offers a program titled Art on Call. When visitors dial a central number, they hear multiple voices offering interpretations of the artwork on display. Not only does the curator have a say, but so do visitors who can leave audio comments. Because the Walker Art Center also sponsors several public art installations and events throughout the city of Minneapolis, the Art on Call program also enables art visitors to connect to the museum from remote locations. In this way, the reach of the museum is extended beyond its brick and mortar buildings into the spaces of the city itself.

The use of mobile media for informal education offers important insights for the use of such devices for formal education as well. At the very least, these programs and experiences suggest the rich possibilities of actively engaging the user/visitor/learner in the creation of content not simply for the purposes of demonstrating "learning" (for the teacher or instructor) but also, and more interestingly, for the benefit of other learners. But perhaps one of the more intriguing vectors to explore based on these experiments in the use of mobile media for informal learning is the idea of learning on the go. Here we are encouraged to think creatively about how learning happens in and through the engagement with distributed networks of mobile computational devices.

If the original tag line for the iPod promised "a thousand songs, in your pocket," a kinship tagline for the iPhone might suggest "a million stories, in your hand." This sentiment is evident in a project by the Mobile Environmental and Media Lab at the University of Southern California called the Million-Story Building. Led by Scott Fisher, MEML explores the development of location-specific spatial storytelling. The Million Story Building project uses the iPhone to interact with a campus building to experiment with the notion of "ambient storytelling." Through the use of the iPhone application, building visitors and residents are immersed in "an emergent, responsive environment of collaborative storytelling." The experience is designed to encourage building inhabitants to develop a relationship with the built space. The building used in the project houses the USC School of Cinematic Arts; on its walls are dozens of posters from films that have involved USC students. The MEML research team created an activity called Movie Tagger that invites users to tag movie clips. Next to each film poster is a QR (quick response) code. When a user scans the QRC, the Movie Tagger application not only provides information about the film (and the alum's role in its production) but also engages the user by asking her to tag a clip from the film (displayed on a nearby screen). If the user agrees, Movie Tagger guides the user to the screen and prompts further input.

Additionally, as inhabitants begin to interact with the building and provide the requested information, a digital archive of all the collected videos, images, tagged movie clips, and other data is created. The resulting database will be useful to the School of Cinematic Arts not only as a way of developing a living history of the new building but also as a tool to harvest the collective expertise of the building's inhabitants for the purposes of enhanced pedagogy. For example, as more movie clips are collaboratively tagged, professors and students will be able to access the database simply by using keywords to retrieve film clips: every classroom becomes an on-demand film library and archive.[16]

This project takes advantage of the sensor nets embedded in the building and the unique character of the learning environment: as home to the School of Cinematic Arts, the building is occupied by many knowledgeable film students and professors. The result is an enduring relationship between inhabitants and objects in the built environment, where each encounter contributes to the evolution of an unfolding story of learning and collaborative knowledge making. This discipline- and building-specific approach to crowdsourcing makes it a practice of everyday life lived within a media-rich and responsive architectural environment. As an example of interactive architecture, the project suggests that learning on the go is not simply about information acquisition but, more importantly, about contributing to the stories that make the built world meaningful.

The Million Story Building project is only one of several early experiments in creating new learning experiences using the affordances of emergent networks of mobile media. Interest in this topic is exploding in the United States. A new (2011) open-scholarship project called *Learning Through Digital Media: Essays on Technology and Pedagogy*, edited by Trebor Scholz, offers a online collection of essays that considers the learning opportunities of a wide range of new media, ranging from blogging applications such as Wordpress to the use of Second Life, Tumblr, and YouTube.[17] This project enacts its own mission—readers are invited to comment on drafts of each of the essays. The results of these online asynchronous conversations will be disseminated under a Creative Commons license as a printed book and free download for various e-readers. Taken together, the essays perform a collaborative assessment of the learning affordances of new digital media.

While the iPhone is not the privileged object of these analyses, it certainly maintains a central position within the learning ecology created through the use of new digital media.

Living the Singularity

Just as the iPhone has emerged as the first ubiquitous wearable computer, Twitter might be reasonably anointed as its most stylish accessory. Communication in the twenty-first century is seamless, informal, and immediate; microblogging is the genre of choice. Life now is a series of 140-character Twitter moments. A minor earthquake in northern California may go unnoticed physically but not socially. David Talbot reported that after a January 7, 2010, earthquake, the Twitter website recorded "quake related tidbits coursing through the company's servers at the rate of 296 per minute."

> In the first seconds and minutes after the quake, anyone tapping 'earthquake Mountain View' (or the name of any other nearby municipality) into Google's search field found that the only hits pertaining to the new quake were . . . tweets. While the Google results page included direct information feeds from the U.S. Geological Survey and a slick Google Maps display of recent tremblors [sic], none reflected the latest event. Official USCG-confirmed data on the quake wouldn't shop [sic] up until 10:20 am [ten minutes after the quake]. But at 10:12 am, the sixth-highest search return was a rolling scroll of tweets posted 'seconds ago': '*Wow, that was an earthquake jolt in Mountain View!*'.[18]

Taken together, the iPhone and Twitter are the killer apps of the "singularity." The term "singularity" was popularized by science fiction author Vernor Vinge to describe a time when the pace of technological change outstrips not only our human capacity to apprehend the transformation but also to do anything about it. Theorists react in different ways to the notion and its implications in a networked society. Pessimists fear the day the machines and the networks they form turn against us; optimists focus on the development of the network as a superhuman form of intelligence. Common to most visions of the singularity is the belief that human intelligence is undergoing a profound transformation as our interactions with networked cybernetic systems get more complex and extensive. The most hopeful version asserts that the consequence of networked human-machine encounters will result in the explosion and expansion of human intelligence. Intelligent amplification, rather than artificial intelligence, is the promise of the singularity.

This vision is well represented among those who see the iPhone as the technological (and stylish) extension of the human body. Few (if any) commentators lament the unplugged "natural" body. The iPhone-augmented body has been thoroughly naturalized; it frames the vision of how things will and should unfold in the future. Five years ago, campaigns to develop computer-based education were met with severe criticism based on the uneven distribution of computer access. These criticisms have all but disappeared in the discussions about the future of mobile learning applications. With more than 5 billion mobile-phone subscribers on the planet, including two billion who live in developing countries, the issue of access doesn't hold the same rhetorical sway it once did. The meaning of the term "digital divide" must be reconsidered. Given the ubiquity of mobile-phone use and the increasing interest in the development of educational applications and platforms the diagnosis of the structure of (persistent) disempowerment cannot be based solely on a reading of the availability (or not) of technology. While this issue is beyond the scope of this essay, suffice it to say that the cultural and political implications of technological access across the globe have changed significantly with the proliferation of mobile media. This is not to say that the use of mobile devices is without a downside: all technologies have multiple and contradictory consequences. The challenge is how to imagine the range of these consequences while gripped by enthusiasm for augmenting positive intentions and safeguarding others.

When considering the use of iPhones and other mobile devices as platforms for learning, I wonder about the logics of mobility that they foment. As these devices enable network connections on the go, they promote a belief in unrestricted movement through space and time. But in light of the tightening of national borders and the increasing surveillance of people in the name of national security, the mobility offered by these devices is more a characteristic of the information conveyed than of the people who use the technologies. And this is what I worry about: that these devices will lure users into believing that mobility is more available than it really is. This is what cultural critics might refer to as the ideological work of mobile technologies. By providing an illusion of mobility, experienced as a user travels virtually from site to site and portal to portal, these devices draw attention away from the conditions and exercise of power through which the physical movements of users in time and space are increasingly managed and curtailed. For all that is promised by the advocates of these devices to make the world come alive as a media-rich learning environment, they are also the means whereby individuals can be tracked and tethered to a particular time and place. I raise this issue at the end of this essay not to cast a pall over the promise of our new mobile devices but to signal the ongoing paradox of our technological fascinations. We love our devices; they comfort us, provide pleasure, structure our hopes and aspirations. But at the same time, they are implicated in the ongoing consolidation of power, the institutionalization of governmentality, and the reproduction of inequality. The challenge for educators, tool/platform developers, and cultural critics is how to think complexly about the multiple and contradictory meanings and possibilities of these objects of desire. They are both/and. Even as I crave them as desirable consumer commodities—with all that that implies ideologically—I also want them to serve the greater social good: to augment learning, to enable access to collective intelligence, to sustain humane social networks. This is a lot to ask of a simple device. But as I suggested in the beginning, this device is not all that simple. It is a part of me and an extension of me. So in the end, what *it* accomplishes and what *it* fails to do will be a matter of my will, my agency, and my creative performances. This is what it means to be a cyborg in the twenty-first century.

NOTES

1. I am not alone in this anxiety. Jan Chipchase, the former chief of usability research at Nokia, now at Frog Design, described the emotional bonds that people form with their mobile phones in his TED talk in March 2007. To ease such separation anxiety, a company called Zomm makes the "Zomm Monitor"—a type of digital leash that registers the signal strength of a Bluetooth connection with the phone and alerts users when they get too far away from it.

2. David Becker, "Turn Your iPhone Into 3D Virtual Reality Goggles," *Wired*, 10 March 2008.

3. Manuel Castells, *Communication Power* (New York: Oxford University Press, 2009), 58.

4. While much of the research on the creation of body area networks (BANs) focuses on the application of wireless sensor networks to monitor health and real-time body functioning, designers and engineers are exploring the use of BANs as the infrastructure for wearable computing. For a discussion, see Clive van Heerden, Jack Mama, and David Eves, "Wearable Electronics," in *New Nomads: An Exploration of Wearable Electronics by Philips*, ed. Stefano Marzano et al. (Rotterdam: 010 Publishers, 2001), 36–56.

5. Neal Stephenson, *The Diamond Age; or, A Young Lady's Illustrated Primer* (New York: Bantam Books, 1995), 106, 107, 151, 492.

6. There are two main product lines: the My First Words collection offers activities to enable children to learn important words in several languages. For further information see http://www.babyskool.eu/en/iphone.html (15 February 2011).

7. Anya Kamenetz, "A is for App," *FastCompany*, April 2010.

8. I describe the emergent cultural formation of school as a distributed learning ecology in my book *Designing Culture: The Technological Imagination at Work* (Durham, N.C.: Duke University Press, 2011).

9. Michel de Certeau, *The Practice of Everyday Life* (Berkeley: University of California Press, 1984), 117.

10. Balsamo, *Designing Culture*.

11. The Tate Museums in Britain have prototyped several mobile informal learning activities.

12. Bryan Alexander, "Going Nomadic: Mobile Learning in Higher Education" *Educause Review* 39 (2004): http://www.educause.edu/EDUCAUSE+Review/EDUCAUSEReviewMagazineVolume39/GoingNomadicMobileLearninginHi/157921 (15 February 2011).

13. The GLS Mobile Learning Team has prototyped several augmented-reality learning games using ARIS, including one called STEEL that locates virtual "mines" throughout downtown Madison, which are accessed by reading QR codes. Students learn about mining minerals as they collect metals by downloading information about the mines they discover: http://arisgames.org (15 February 2011).

14. Benjamin Bratton, "iPhone City," *Architectural Design* 26 (2009).

15. Anne Balsamo et al., "Report on the Project: Inspiring the Technological Imagination: The Future of Museums and Libraries in a Digital Age," May–July 2009, http://dmlcentral.net/resources/3854 (15 February 2011).

16. Jennifer Stein, Scott S. Fisher, and Greg Otto, "Interactive Architecture: Connecting and Animating the Built Environment with the Internet of Things," paper presented at The Internet of Things Workshop, 2010.

17. For further discussion, see *Learning Through Digital Media: Essays on Technology and Pedagogy* (Media Commons Press 2010–), http://mediacommons.futureofthebook.org/mcpress/artoflearning/ (15 February 2011).

18. David Talbot, "Can Twitter Make Money?" *Technology Review* (March/April 2010).

CHAPTER 18

EULA, Codec, API

On the Opacity of Digital Culture

LANE DENICOLA

F THE ECSTATIC virtues of speed and risk are among the hallmarks of modernity, complexity has reasonably been posed as another dimension of
that order. The everyday life of urban environments is awash in ever-greater
tides of information, and this is popularly recognized as an advantageous
firmament for civic participation and universal convenience. Yet at the same
time it is often experienced as a frustrating source of distraction or fragmentation, the sign of a problematic fascination with information at the expense
of knowledge. There is a growing understanding that the "power" of information technology is as much about its ability to judiciously *filter out* some
information streams, its ability to help us assimilate data and ease cognitive
load, as it is about accessing new streams and accruing greater quantities of
data. Powerful digital technologies, that is, are as much about *selectivity* as
they are about *speed, capacity,* or *sensitivity*. It is in the midst of that popular
recognition that the iPhone (and perhaps the Apple brand in general) has
emerged as an icon. The conventional wisdom that it "just works"—its in-
teroperability and functional resilience, the intuitive design of its interface,
its visual and tactile harmonies—ameliorates a gnawing mass anxiety rooted
in complexity. A growing diversity of social and discursive terrains, it seems,
are just beyond the limits of our own cognitive limits, yet—if we are truly

moderns, truly individuals engaged with our communities and the world—these are the terrains we are compelled to inhabit.

It is all too easy, however, to omit from such phenomenological observations the more obscure components of the iPhone as not just an apparatus but an *assemblage*, a nexus of social, institutional, and material relations "made concrete." The physical artifact that is the iPhone itself is of course worthless without, for example, the vast infrastructure of the Internet for communications routing and media distribution. The iPhone's use and cultural meaning is shaped not only by its interface design and form but by a dizzying constellation of material and immaterial technosocial amalgams: data formats, compression algorithms, connection standards, network transfer protocols, spectrum allocations, copyrights, proprietary standards, licensing agreements, and so on. It is undoubtedly the common experience of its immanent surfaces that has catapulted the device into the stratosphere of popular consciousness, but what are we to make of these other dimensions of the iPhone as a locus of apparatus, technique, culture, and law? What proportion of the cost of the iPhone (real or effective, externalized or otherwise) is incurred not in the labor of its production and design or the raw materials of its physical components but in its attendant "intangibles"—licenses, intellectual property, storage capacity, and bandwidth? Does the widening gulf between our pedestrian experience of such devices and their arcane "insides"—arguably, some of the very complexities they are designed to alleviate—warrant analytic or political concern? Further, what is the *cultural* significance of this "iceberg" quality, the fact that a growing proportion of our everyday experience is opaque to the casual observer, residing "beneath the surface" of lay scrutiny and held fast within a dense technosocial matrix?

An Anthropological Consideration of the iPhone

This article considers these questions through what in many ways is a quite traditional anthropological approach: an examination of "the Other," that is, the peripheralized or subordinated populations whose position within some prevailing imaginary is defined largely in reference to the dominant population. Adopting an approach in this fashion is unavoidably partial and approximate, "anthropomorphizing" a technical system and attaching to it certain conceptual "baggage" that risks clouding rather than clarifying. Yet the advantages offered to an analysis of the iPhone are manifold. Within the tradition, analytic acuity is gained through comparison, through a forced decentering or reordering in which the "situated perspective" of the Other is at least tentatively accorded the status of privileged insight. The "primitive," the colonized, or the disenfranchised become "experts," key interlocutors who have in some ways a deeper understanding of dominant cultures than the latter do of the former. In the case of the iPhone, a naïve metaphorical construction of such an Other might point to its principal competitors, those devices from other manufacturers purporting similar features but arguably failing to orchestrate them with quite the same potency (and empirically failing to garner equivalent market share or brand resonance).

This construction, however, misses the more incisive difference of the "user" embedded in the design of such devices. Sherry Turkle has described how since the early days of the "computer revolution" the term "transparency" underwent an illuminating transformation. In the now dominant meaning of the term, a "transparent" device is one whose use is highly intuitive, employing an interface that rapidly disappears from our perception.[1] In the earlier meaning of the term, a "transparent" device was one whose inner workings were visible and accessible, a device amenable to functional understanding and rapid appropriation. The iPhone is nothing if not an exemplar of "transparency" in the more recent sense—insofar as the vast bulk of its hardware, software, and content is patented, trademarked, licensed, or copyrighted as proprietary. Even the use of the term "iPhone" is provided its own set of guidelines, backed by the regulatory grammar of trademark law.[2] Beyond technically shallow customizations, many types of (technically quite feasible) modifications that a user might desire would render the device's warranty or other attached agreements null and void. In some assessments, this is the cost of "just working." The design innovation and attention to detail required to ensure such simplicity is compensated for by the revenue generated from a deeply proprietary user-artifact relationship.

From the standpoint of material culture and the paradigm that "things make people as much as people make things,"[3] this dyadic concept of "transparency" provides a more useful basis on which to construct an Other that reveals the "persons" presumed by the iPhone. If the iPhone is designed to reduce the complexity or "opacity" of *use*, its Others would be designed instead to reduce the complexity or opacity of *function*, the barriers to causal understanding and deep modification. Perhaps the most salient comparison is to be found with the growing array of devices, systems, and services that bear a strong functional similarity to those that constitute the iPhone but distinguish themselves as being built on open source, open standards, open content, and alternative licensing. The analysis entailed here begins with this exploratory stance in an effort to answer the questions of "occluded culture" with which we began.[4] In particular, I consider three artifacts of digital culture and their realization within the iPhone and its Others: the "end-user licensing agreement," or EULA; the coder-decoder, or "codec"; and the "application programming interface," or API. Constituting wholly distinct facets of the typical "digital multimedia device," they serve to illustrate the social and political relevance of the immaterial and the opaque.

EULA

Before the predominance of digital culture, when a person purchased a book or a piece of recorded music, the first-hand experience of that purchase entailed the acquisition of a material commodity, the book itself, a long-playing record album, a cassette tape, or even (in later years) a compact disc. While the legal framework governing the use of this object by (for example) publishers or radio broadcasters bore noteworthy significance for their activities, in the mind of the typical consumers they now "owned" that book or recording, and the uses to which they put it—sharing it, reading it aloud, reselling it—were constrained principally by technical and economic feasibility. While illegal copying or "bootlegging" during this period certainly occurred, low reproduction quality and other limitations of the physical apparatus involved made such practices comparatively uncommon. In the digital era, consumer technologies for rapid, high-quality text and audiovisual reproduction are inexpensive, portable, and widely available. Moreover, the entrenchment of the Internet as a common domestic utility has made global distribution available to all, and, in many instances, it has virtually eliminated the artifactual component of book and music purchase. The same transformation can be noted for software in its rapid transition from punch cards to magnetic tapes and so on (though of course this occurred in the more esoteric environments of scientific and technical research laboratories rather than in the mass-consumer market). When the "texts" that are the digital instantiations of such productions are downloaded directly from one hard disk to another, it is only a highly abstracted numeric pattern that is exchanged.

Particularly within cultures that valorize the sharing of cultural productions, this presents something of a paradox to the average consumer. Lawrence Lessig has lucidly explained how "theft" as traditionally understood is a problem less because it makes the stolen thing accessible to people who have no right to it, than because it limits or eliminates access to that thing by its rightful owner.[5] In the case of digital texts, even massive distribution of illicit copies introduces no such constraints on the legitimate owner. Instead (so the argument goes), it is the "theft" of prospective revenue that is at issue in digital "piracy," whether the profits of the producers, the distributors, the marketers, or the authors or artists themselves. Yet so compelling was the attachment between physical artifact and "reading/listening experience" that the result of its recent erasure has yielded a social and economic calamity in the eyes of such industry trade groups as the Recording Industry Association of America, the Business Software Alliance, and the Entertainment Software Association.

The "end-user licensing agreement," or EULA, is an immaterial artifact of digital culture that lies precisely at this juncture of commercial "producers," individual users, and the state (through its regulatory capacities). When today's consumer purchases copyrighted software and digital content, they do not acquire "rights of ownership" at all, whether to physical artifact or numeric pattern. Instead they purchase a "license," a legal agreement binding the "licensor" and the purchaser and articulating what each party is thereby entitled to do (and must not do). Enunciated in the arcane, hybridized language of legal and technical documents, the EULA is often first encountered some time *after* software is purchased—a so-called contract of adhesion—and presents as a lengthy page of inscrutable prose with a simple yes-or-no acceptance choice. Just as common is the conventional wisdom that no one actually reads the EULA and fewer understand its meaning or real-world impact. As with credit card agreements, insurance policy declarations, and the vast galaxy of banal textual forms moderns routinely encounter, the arcane text of the EULA is experienced less as a text than as an obligatory, ritualized point of passage that rhetorically positions the state as interlocutor between "user/consumers" and "designer/producers."

Codec

Digital content—particularly textual, graphic, or audiovisual content—can be stored and displayed using a variety of techniques. Some of these techniques are optimized for their display or replay fidelity; others offer advantages in the storage capacity they require or the economy of their transfer over digital networks. Conventional wisdom among computer scientists has it that in comparison with innovations in *technological artifacts* or their production (microminiaturization, the capacity and throughput of storage media, the energy density of chemical batteries), innovations in *computational technique* (e.g., algorithms for compression, graphical rendering, encryption, sorting) have provided an order of magnitude greater increase in the capability of information systems over the last four decades. It is these algorithms, in fact, that are often at the heart of a given "technology." For example, the Moving Picture Experts Group standard Audio Layer 3 (typically referred to with the more manageable "MP3"), whose industry ubiquity is illustrated in the use of the term "MP3 player" to refer to portable digital music players in general, is popularly understood first and foremost as a common file format for digital audio. It also comprises an audio "codec," or coder-decoder, however, a scheme for encoding and decoding an audiorecording by eliminating aural components that are outside the perceptual range of the average human being. Industry standardization and other technosocial factors aside, the value of this compression algorithm was that it dramatically increased the amount of music that could feasibly be stored within the limited storage capacity of a portable device. Similarly, the GIF (Graphics Interchange Format) and JPEG (Joint Photographic Experts Group) so common today are not only data formats but also image-compression algorithms. The less commonly known RSA (after Rivest, Shamir, and Adleman, its inventors) is a cryptographic algorithm that makes a significant portion of today's financial transactions over the Web possible.

The prevailing paradigm that algorithms—essentially recipes, techniques—can be "owned" as intellectual property has a convoluted history and has not been without its detractors. Important in that discussion is the distinction between algorithms and software. Software straddles a conceptual line between text and machine, disrupting the ontology that allowed copyright law and patent law to remain distinct. Yet algorithms are more abstract than either in that a single algorithm can have many distinct "implementations" in code or mechanism. If software is akin to a "text" written in code, algorithms are more akin to a "plot" or "character," representable as a mathematical or logical procedure. Even some proponents of software as intellectual property question the legitimacy of algorithmic ownership, and while the algorithms of RSA and JPEG are now within the public domain, those of MP3 and GIF remain patented as of this writing (and all have been involved in protracted corporate litigations).

In key ways the codec is the bridge between digital artifact (data, a file) and human experience (of a song, a photo, an exchange).[6] Without the codec, data are essentially inert. Typically, when a consumer purchases a communications or multimedia device such as the iPhone, a portion of the cost to the consumer covers the licensing fees paid by the manufacturer to the patent holder of every algorithm that the device employs. If the iOS, for example (the iPhone's operating system), is capable of reading, writing, and playing/displaying MP3s or GIFs, the software developer is legally required to have purchased a license to have it do so. The effect of this mandate is that the consumer may well have to pay for *the content* he or she acquires (music, e-books, feature films), but that transaction does not necessarily include *the experience* of that content. The techniques he or she needs to employ in order to *listen to*, *read*, or *watch* the purchased content entail a separate commercial transaction. In a growing array of examples, in fact, commercial models of "ownership" are giving way entirely to models centered on the consumption of "experience." Streaming media services such as Spotify, for instance, permit the purchase of advertising-free listening time. Rather than purchasing a song or album (in material or immaterial form), consumers purchase a predetermined amount of time during which they have access to the entirety of the vast online library of music. For my purposes here, the question this yields might be framed as follows: How are people's practices and posture toward cultural forms such as songs, novels, and films—practices including the production, expression, and exchange of those cultural forms—transformed under this shift from commodity ownership to commodified experience?

API

A significant proportion of consumer-level software is not organized as a single monolithic text but takes the form of bundled "libraries" of preexisting components with specialized functions, stitched together for a specific application. Ideally, these libraries are highly modularized, focused on a well-defined set of tasks (e.g., the reading, manipulation, and writing of JPEG files, or communication with other proximate devices using the Bluetooth wireless standard). It may be that these get manipulated or interacted with by the average consumer as a single piece of "software" (when an update is performed, say, or a fresh installation is attempted), but to those interested in modification or new development, access to this software as a bundle of libraries is typically of much greater utility. Well-organized software libraries represent the "wheels" that the programmer need not reinvent, and without them the task of software development would entail a significantly greater complexity and effort. While software may be "commercial" or "free" (conventionally meaning "sold for a fee" or "free of charge"), it can also be "proprietary" or "open source." In the former (proprietary) case, software is sold as a "black box," an "executable" file that performs valuable functions but whose internals are not easily accessible by a person, while in the latter case the source code for the software is published publicly in human-readable format (and sometimes distributed along with the executable versions). All permutations of these are possible; both commercial and free software may be either proprietary or open source.

In order to capitalize on software libraries, to suture them together in novel and useful ways, the programmer must be able to "call upon" the functions they provide from within his or her own code. This interface between new code under development and the prefabricated code of libraries is generically known as an "application programming interface," or API. In a sense the API is quite similar to the "user interface" that software users are so familiar with, with the difference that instead of mapping the gestures and actions of the user to specific functions, the API maps the calls and output of the programmer's code to the specific functions of the library. Further, just as a user interface may require documentation explaining its use, the API for a given library must be documented in order for a programmer to make substantive use of it. Such documentation typically includes the library's ontological framing, the precise names of specific functions, the inputs they require and outputs they provide, and perhaps a synopsis of the more complex techniques they employ. Often this documentation is provided with the library itself, and both may be included as components of a "software development kit," or SDK.

This is the pedestrian reality of a programmer's interface with software, but what is its relevance to the typical user? Certainly the libraries folded into a piece of software (and as a corollary the code itself) are unlikely to be of any interest whatsoever to the majority of its users; it is in fact the "black-boxing" of such details that in large part they are willing to pay for. To a degree, however, it is the very dichotomization of designer and user that is at issue, the inculcation of a paradigm that entrenches or even intensifies the two populations as necessarily distinct. Such a paradigm forecloses the possibility that even a quite large population of individual users could draw on the expertise of a tiny minority within their own numbers—interaction is constrained to the commercial. More incisively, a dichotomized paradigm of this sort naturalizes the idea that *access* to mechanism is entirely distinct from *ownership* of that mechanism. Our rights to the software we buy and our consumption of that software in no way entail access to or modification of its internals, even if we do care about such things and have the requisite programming skills. As a consumer, within this paradigm we are given rights only to the *effects* of software, not to the software itself. Often programmers (both professional and amateur) will praise the release of the API for a given application, and this is primarily because it allows them to incorporate a generically useful set of functions into applications of their own design. Many of the services offered by Google, for example, including their premier Web search service, have a publicly documented API available at no cost. While not every user is a software developer, everyone could be. This is less a philosophical dichotomy than a spectrum of attitudes toward the user/designer (and consumer/producer) relationship.

Others of the iPhone

It is useful at this point to consider more specifically the iPhone and some of its Others as resolved through the lens of the EULA, the codec, and the API as cultural phenomena. As mentioned above, the operating system for the iPhone is iOS, which incorporates some open-source components but as a package is itself proprietary and covered by an Apple-specific EULA. Android, in contrast, is a mobile operating system derived from Linux (a popular open-source operating system), developed independently at first but purchased by Google in 2005. Currently the best-selling mobile operating system worldwide, Android is open source and covered by the Apache Software Foundation's free software license. Many aspects of the iPhone's interface are designed (unsurprisingly) to steer consumers of software and multimedia toward Apple's App Store and iTunes Store. Taken as a whole, these online marketplaces are dazzling in their speed and simplicity and the fluidity of their interfaces, and copyrighted content, digital rights management, and proprietary EULAs and codecs are de rigueur.

By contrast, Android steers consumers toward the Android Market for software, but for music, films, games, and so on it is comparatively agnostic. Online music sources that foreground alternative licensing models and public-domain materials (e.g. Jamendo, Magnatune, the Internet Archive) are no more or less occluded than the iTunes Store. In terms of the operating systems themselves, originally only Apple developers and their contractors could modify or develop new software for the iPhone, but since late 2007 an SDK with a documented API has been available for anyone who wishes to develop applications or "apps" for the iPhone (though the source code for iOS remains unavailable). The full body of Android's source code, on the other hand, has been available online since 2007 and is backed by the Open

Handset Alliance, a consortium of more than seventy telecom companies with an interest in the promotion of open standards for mobile devices.

While the concept of "open source" has begun to slip into vernacular usage (sometimes erroneously), the same principles can be applied to hardware as easily as software: the adoption of open standards, the easy availability of interface documentation, the virtuous coding of "accessibility," and a design philosophy centered on repurposing and appropriation by users are all characteristic of "open" hardware. The Neo FreeRunner is an illustrative case and perhaps the quintessential iPhone Other. Developed under the Openmoko project (another Linux-derived smartphone operating system) and built by the Taiwanese computer manufacturer FIC, the Neo FreeRunner is a touch-screen smartphone with many of the same basic functions of the iPhone but designed around full user access. Buyers receive the device itself, which can be opened and probed using standard electronic test equipment. A specialized "debug board" is available for more detailed modifications and troubleshooting. Schematic diagrams for its electronics are publicly available, and it can run a variety of operating systems (including Android and other Linux-variants). While highly experimental, the FreeRunner has been commercially available in the United States since 2008, and a community of hackers/phreaks has adopted it as an exemplar of fully open devices that nonetheless offer significant commercial opportunities.[7]

Conclusion

A number of open-source advocates and hacking observers have suggested that "DIY culture" and technosocial movements such as Students for Free Culture have been catalyzed in recent years by the proliferation of inexpensive video-production capability and the ubiquity of the Internet and vernacular media forms and forums. Some perceive the phenomenon as a simple outgrowth of frugality, individualism, domesticity, and the availability of leisure time among an expanding middle class. A subset of those communities, however, purport an explicitly political dimension to their activities, perceiving DIY culture and related phenomena as a collective response to corporate malfeasance, the prioritization of short-term profit over sustainability in design, highly centralized media control, and the broadly proprietary colonization of a cultural landscape rightfully held in common. Take, for example, an article published in *Make* magazine, a periodical devoted to tinkering and DIY and published both in print and online. The article, "Owner's Manifesto," suggests abstractly that "if you can't open it, you don't own it" and outlines "a Maker's Bill of Rights to accessible, extensive, and repairable hardware":

Meaningful and specific parts lists shall be included.

Cases shall be easy to open.

Batteries should be replaceable.

Special tools are allowed only for darn good reasons.

Profiting by selling expensive special tools is wrong and not making special tools available is even worse.

Torx is OK; tamperproof is rarely OK.

Components, not entire sub-assemblies, shall be replaceable.

Consumables, like fuses and filters, shall be easy to access.

Circuit boards shall be commented.

Power from USB is good; power from proprietary power adapters is bad.

Standard connecters shall have pinouts defined.

If it snaps shut, it shall snap open.

Screws better than glues.

Docs and drivers shall have permalinks and shall reside for all perpetuity at archive.org.

Ease of repair shall be a design ideal, not an afterthought.

Metric or standard, not both.

Schematics shall be included.[8]

This has since become something of a slogan for this loose federation of makers, routinely echoed on websites, e-mail signatures, and t-shirts. Of most significance here is the explicit disruption it represents to the prevalent norm that when we purchase a device, we are purchasing only access to its "surfaces," a transient experience of use divorced from either internal mechanism or the particulars of production. In many ways this parallels the historical shift in automobile ownership, which over the last six decades has resulted in automobiles that are more technically complex, less amenable to owner maintenance and repair, and less customizable (except in their surface features).[9]

To return to the questions this article began with, I first propose an analytical framing I will refer to here as "dark culture," akin to the "dark matter" hypothesized by astrophysicists. Dark matter is something of a theoretical placeholder, a temporary stand-in necessary to buttress prevailing cosmological theory. Its effects on visible matter and background radiation are manifest and so its existence is inferred, but direct observation through any orthodox method (e.g., using the light it emits or reflects) has so far eluded astronomers. Most significantly, all available evidence seems to suggest that 80 percent of the matter in the universe is this so-called dark matter. In contrast to dark matter, we are routinely able to observe dark culture, such as the forms I have explored here: the EULA, the codec, and the API. Yet we have little in the way of an ordered understanding of its effects, its influence on how we construct meaning. What makes it "dark," invisible to routine scrutiny, is not simply that it demands highly specialized fluencies (legal or technical) or that it is cloaked by the constraints of sovereignty (copyright and other aspects of the regulatory apparatus accorded the state) but its intrinsic *immateriality*, its *complexity*, and its *liminal status* in mediating people, the state, and the built world. Though dark culture is undeniably artificial—of human construction—and can profoundly shape the envelope of our daily experience and interaction, it typically creeps into the awareness of the vast majority of us only rarely or indirectly. As the manifold technologies we employ to connect with one another and to mediate our environments continue to proliferate, the proportion of culture that is "dark" will only increase.

There is a tendency in discussions of new media and information technologies to cast consumer technologies such as the iPhone as symptomatic of escalating technological dependence, the erosive force of mediated experience, alarming crises of "literacy," and a widening digital divide that spreads the socioeconomic spectrum across the equally wide spectrum of technical capacities. There are well-reasoned arguments to be found behind some of these claims, but it hardly seems that the resolution of those issues is to be found in the rote rejection of digital technologies (if such a thing is even possible). Instead, the problem should be analyzed in terms of cultural opacity, the roles presumed by technologies such as the iPhone, and the moves by users, designers, and scholars toward a reflexive study of "dark culture."

Notes

1. Sherry Turkle, "Seeing Through Computers: Education in a Culture of Simulation," *The American Prospect* 8 (1997): 76–82.

2. Apple Legal Team, "Copyright and Trademark Guidelines," 2011, http://www.apple.com/legal/trademark/guidelinesfor3rdparties.html (15 February 2011).

3. Christopher Tilley, *Handbook of Material Culture* (London: Sage, 2006).

4. From the perspective of the social scientist, the study of aspects of culture occluded in this way is tricky proposition. They may well be pervasive dimensions of a given culture yet simultaneously bound within languages and practices that are known

only to a tiny elite or minority (e.g., the place of witchcraft or sorcery within some Micronesian villages). In the anthropological study of "modern technoculture," code, technical terminology, and disparate information networks may be substituted for potions, incantations, and the spirit world, but the challenges of its analysis largely remain.

5. Lawrence Lessig, *Free Culture: The Nature and Future of Creativity* (London: Penguin, 2005), 83.

6. There is an important distinction here between codecs and algorithms. In these discussions, the former is downloadable, a realization of the latter in code. Both can be made "proprietary," though the intellectual property status of one is not necessarily coupled to that of the other.

7. "Phreak" is a slang term referring to people who study and tinker with tele-communications systems such telephone networks, more as a hobby than as part of their gainful employment. In its original meaning, "hacker" referred to mischievous individuals who attempted to disrupt computer networks or profit somehow from their infiltration. More recently the term has been applied to amateur programmers, electronics hobbyists, DIY enthusiasts, and others without the connotations of malicious intent.

8. Mister Jalopy, "Owner's Manifesto" *Make*, no. 4 (2005):   http://makezine .com/04/ownyourown/ (15 February 2011).

9. Some might argue that many of the improvements seen in today's automobiles — in fuel efficiency, reduced emissions, safety — would have been impossible without the introduction of significant technical complexity (and thus the need for more specialized servicing equipment). One counterargument is that this fails to see user maintainability (and its alleged societal benefits) as an engineering challenge of as great a magnitude as greater power-to-weight or fuel efficiency.

CHAPTER 19

The Back of Our Devices Looks Better than the Front of Anyone Else's

On Apple and Interface Design

LEV MANOVICH

REAT DESIGN IS as important as great technology—this has been the underlying philosophy of Apple from the first Mac in 1984 to the latest iPhone today. Underlining the importance of design has made Apple into the world's most valuable technology company and its first iPhone (2007) a prototype for what to come. Strikingly different from the phones available at the beginning of the decade, the iPhone offered a rich and nuanced aesthetic experience as opposed to pure functionality.

The shift from functionality to design experience in turn forms but one example of a larger technological trend, which I have called "aesthetization of information tools," a process that Apple has likewise fueled and dominated.[1] This trend, which reaches back to the launch of the first iMac, may be seen in the context of larger socioeconomic shifts in the world, such as the democratization of design and the rise of branding as responses to an increased competition in the global economy and the dramatic increase in the size of the middle class during the 1990s. For example, in 1996 *Wallpaper* magazine was launched, and Collete, the first store for hip design products, opened in Paris. In 1997, the new Guggenheim Museum in Bilbao became an icon for the city; in 1998, the design-centered iMac went on sale. At that time Apple famously declared that "the back of our computer looks better than the front of anyone else's," a hyperbolic ad notion that would guide much of the praised Apple design in years to come.

While the aestheticization of technology certainly parallels such larger developments, I think that its main raison d'être is something else. Aestheticization relates to the shift in the role of computers in society. Until the mid-1990s, only people working in office jobs would spend (basically) all their work hours interacting with computerized information. These interactions were limited to work spaces and times; they did not spill over into leisure and other nonwork activities.

In the next ten years, however, the systematic adoption of computers and computer-based devices in every profession greatly increased the proportion of people whose work revolves around manipulating information. At the same time, interacting with information via computers and computer-based devices gradually became part of people's everyday lives. Because of their inherent multifunctionality and expandability, the computer—and gadgets such as the iPhone, which basically are built on top of it—came to be used for all kinds of nonwork activities: entertainment, culture, social life, or communication with others. Consequently, work and nonwork, the professional and the personal, met within the same information-processing machines, the same physical objects, the same hardware and software interfaces—and in some cases even the same software. It is enough to think of how Web browsers are equally work tools and leisure tools.

As these machines came to be redefined as consumer objects to be used in all areas of people's lives—a development which starts with Steve Job's new vision of a personal computer as a home media center, an idea that took shape after he came back to Apple in 1997—their aesthetics were altered all together. The associations with work and office culture and the emphasis on efficiency and functionality came to be replaced by new references and criteria. These included being friendly, playful, pleasurable, expressive, fashionable; computers now signified cultural identity, were aesthetically pleasing, and were designed for emotional satisfaction. Accordingly, the modernist design formula "form follows function" came to be replaced by a "form follows emotion" approach, which subsequently was adopted by companies such as the world-famous Frog design (which designed the first Macintosh computers).[2] In the remainder of this article, I will analyze this shift in information-technology design that took place between 1998 (the first iMac) and 2007 (the first iPhone).

Interface Experiences

In the 1980s and 1990s, the design of user interfaces was often governed by the idea that the interface should be invisible. A successful interface was considered to be one that the user did not notice. This paradigm prevailed until the end of the 1990s—that is, it dominated during a period when, outside of work, people used information devices on a fairly limited basis. What happened when the quantity of these interactions greatly increased and information devices, such as iMac, iPod, iPhone, and iPad, became intimate companions of people's lives? Naturally, the more you use a smartphone, a media player, a tablet or another personal information device, the more you interact with the interface itself.

Today the design of user interaction reflects this new reality. Designers no longer try to hide the interface. Instead, the *interaction is treated as an event* rather than a nonevent as in the previous invisible interface paradigm. Using personal information devices is now conceived as a carefully orchestrated *experience* rather than a means to an end. The interaction explicitly calls attention to itself, with the interface engaging the user in a form of play, asking her to devote significant emotional, perceptual, and cognitive resources to the very act of operating the device. With the iPhone, for instance, frequently praised for its innovative interface design and quickly copied by all other major players on the mobile market, most of the input takes place through a touch screen. Instead of pushing buttons, a user employs multitouch gestures—swapping, pinching, tapping, swiping—thus "playing" the device. Swiping the finger to unlock the iPhone is part of this game, a way to enter the space where a user's fingers take on magical powers.

Today a typical information device such as a smartphone provides two kinds of interfaces. One is the physical interface consisting of buttons and the phone body (which can communicate through vibration). The second is a media interface: graphical icons, menus, and sounds. The new paradigm that treats interaction as an aesthetic experience, an "event," applies equally to both types of interfaces. The most dramatic example of the historical shift in how interfaces are understood concerns the differences in user-interaction design between the successive generations of the operating system used in Apple computers—OS 9 and OS X. Released in October of 1999, OS 9 was the last version of Mac OS still based on the original system that came with the first Macintosh in 1984. Its look and feel—the strict geometry of horizontal and vertical lines, the similarly restrictive palette of grays and white, simple and businesslike icons—speaks of modernist design and the ideology of form following function. It also perfectly fits with grey suites, office buildings in international style, and twentieth-century office culture in general.

OS X, introduced in 2001, came as a radical departure to that approach. Its new user interface was called Aqua. Aqua's icons, buttons, windows, cursor, and other elements were colorful and three-dimensional. They used shadows and transparency. The programs announced their start by opening their windows via an animation. The icons in Dock playfully increased in size as the user moved a cursor over them. And if in OS 9 default desktop backgrounds were flat single-color monochrome, the backgrounds that came with Aqua were much more visually complex, more colorful and assertive—drawing attention to themselves rather than attempting to be invisible.

In OS X, the interaction with the universal information-processing machine of our time—the personal computer—was redefined as an explicitly aesthetic experience. This experience became as important as the functionality (or, in technical terms, usability). "Aesthetics" is commonly associated with beauty, but this is not the only meaning that is relevant here. Under OS X, the user interface was aestheticized in a sense that it was now to explicitly appeal to and stimulate *senses*—rather than only users' cognitive processes.

Aesthetic Integration

The transformation of Apple from a hardware and software company to a world leader in consumer-product design—just think of all the design awards won by iMacs, Powerbooks, iPods, and other Apple products—is in itself the most striking example of what I am calling the aestheticization of information tools. It is relevant here to recall a more classical meaning of aesthetics: the coordination of all parts and details of an artwork or design—lines, forms, colors, textures, materials, movements, sounds. (I am referring to classical aesthetics because twentieth-century art has often aimed at opposite effects—shock, collision, and the establishment of meaning and aesthetic experience through montage rather than the unification of parts.) The critical and commercial success of Apple products and the truly fanatical feelings they invoke in many people have much to do with the degree of this integration, which had not been seen before in commercial products in this price range. In each new product or version, the details were refined until they all work together to create a rich, smooth, and consistent sensorial whole. This also applies to the way hardware and software work together. For example, think of the coordination between the circular movement of the user's finger on the track wheel of the original iPod and the corresponding horizontal movement of menus on the screen (which borrows from OS X column view.)

In the beginning of the new millennium, other consumer-electronics companies gradually began to follow Apple in putting more and more emphasis on the design of their products across price categories. Sony started using the "Sony Style" phrase. In 2004, Nokia introduced its first line of "fashion phones," declaring that personal technology can be an "object of desire." By investing in the industrial design of its consumer products, Samsung was also able to move from an unknown supplier to a top world brand. Even companies whose information products were almost exclusively used by professionals and business users started to compete by dressing their products in an Apple-like design. The 2006 version of the BlackBerry smartphone so popular with business people and professionals was, for instance, introduced with the slogan: "BlackBerry Pearl—Small, Smart, and Stylish." Nevertheless, if other companies tried to copy Apple's design strategies, Apple still was able to stay ahead at least until the end of the millennium's first decade by repeatedly launching products that came to define entire new market categories: powerful, media-rich smartphones (iPhone, 2007) and media tablets (iPad, 2010).

One way that Apple is able to do this is by systematically expanding the idea of the integration between different experiences into new spaces—in the process redefining the economics of the PC and consumer-electronics industries. With iTunes, released in 2001, the seamless integration between a physical device and its media interface was extended to include an online store selling, first, songs and, later, TV programs, feature films, and games—and eventually even software applications. Apple's iPhone was, arguably, the smartphone that started this. The phenomenally successful App Store redefined the economics of mobile computer devices, prompting all other major players to follow Apple in creating their own ecologies (or platforms) consisting of devices and their unique operating systems and apps markets, such as the Android market. Early in 2011 Apple announced that in less than four years, 10 billion apps had been downloaded from the App Store, which is greater than the numbers of songs downloaded from iTunes in its ten years of operation.

Interaction and the Experience Economy

In retrospect, it is quite apparent that the aestheticization (or perhaps, theatrization) of user interfaces with laptops, smartphones, cameras, and other mobile technology, which took place approximately between 2001 and 2005, had been conceptually prepared in previous decades. Based on work done in the 1980s, Brenda Laurel published a groundbreaking book, *Computers as*

Theatre, in 1991.[3] She described the interface as an expressive form and compared it to theatrical performances. By using Aristotle's *Poetics* as her model, Laurel suggested that interaction should lead to "pleasurable enjoyment."

The notion of interaction as theater brings an additional meaning to the idea I put forward in the beginning of this article, namely, that a smartphone interface engages its user in a kind of game or play. Since about 2005, new phones began to respond to user action in a surprising and often seemingly exaggerated manner. This applies to both physical and media interfaces. For example, pressing the cover of a Motorola PEBBLE opens the phone in an expected and unique way. The buttons on the LG Chocolate suddenly begin glowing in red when the phone is switched on; when you select an option the LG device confirms your selection by replacing the current screen with a new graphic screen.

Understanding interaction as theater helps us come to terms with another dimension of these playlike features. In some phone models, such as the LG Chocolate, various sensorial effects that the phone generates in response to user actions often come not as single events but rather as sequences of effects. As in a traditional theater play, these sequences unfold in time. Various sensorial effects play on one another, and it is their contrast as well as the differences between the senses being addressed—touch, vision, hearing—that add up to a complex dramatic experience. In 1991, when Laurel published her book, the use of technology products was still limited to particular professions, but as designers of the iMac soon clearly recognized, at the end of the decade these products were becoming mainstream items of the consumer economy, which was undergoing a fundamental change. In their 1999 book, *Experience Economy: Work Is Theatre and Every Business a Stage*, Joseph Pine and James H. Gilmore famously argued that the consumer economy was entering a new stage where the key to successful business was delivering experiences. This new stage followed the previous stages centered on goods and, later, services. To be successful today, the authors argued, "a company must learn to stage a rich, compelling experience."[4] If Laurel evoked theater as a way to think about the particular case of human-computer interaction, Pine and Gilmore suggested that the theater may work as a metaphor for understanding the interaction between consumers and products in the new economy.

The aestheticization of hardware design and user interfaces that gradually took place throughout the industry in the decade following Pine and Gilmore's book fits very well with the idea of the "experience economy." Like any other interaction, *interaction with information devices became a designed experience*. In fact, we can say that the three stages in the development of user interfaces—command-line interfaces of the 1970s (Unix), graphical user interfaces of the 1980s and 1990s (Mac OS), and the new sensual, highly aestheticized interfaces of the post–OS X era—can be correlated to the three stages of consumer economy as a whole: goods, services, and experiences. Command-line interfaces "deliver the goods": that is, they focus on pure functionality and utility. GUIs, in turn, add "service" to interfaces. And at the next stage, interfaces become "experiences."

The concept of the experience economy works particularly well to explain how the physical interaction with technology objects—as opposed to their physical forms and screen interfaces—turned into a stage for delivering rich sensorial and often seductive experiences. For instance, early mobile phones did not have any covers. Screens and keys were always there and always visible. Around 2005, the profane act of opening a mobile phone or pressing its buttons turned into veritable micro-plays: short narratives complete with visual, tactile, and three-dimensional effects. In the short history of mobile phones, the examples of particular models whose commercial and critical popularity can to a significant degree be attributed to the innovative sensorial narratives of interaction with them are the Motorola RAZR V3 (2004), the already discussed LG Chocolate (2006; the actual model number is LG VX-8600) and, of course, the iPhone (2007), with its uniquely staged transitions between application screens.

The Aesthetics of Disappearance

As the iMac (1998) and OS X (2001) have demonstrated, the aestheticization paradigm was applied equally to designs of information products and their user interfaces—i.e., both hardware and software. In fact, although released at different times, the first iMacs, OS X, and the iPhone iOS share similar aesthetic features: bright clear colors, the use of transparency or translucency, and rounded forms. And while all aim to remove the standard twentieth-century associations of information technology—cold, indifferent to human presence, suited only for business—at the same time they cleverly exploit their technological identity. Both the translucency of iMac's plastic case, the Dock magnification and Genie effects in the Aqua interface, and iPhone's iOS all similarly stage technology as magical and almost supernatural.

Along with this rich and colorful aesthetics, Apple chief designer Jonathan Ive also developed another approach. His hardware designs for Apple products in the 2000s—from PowerBooks to iPads—have adopted different, minimal aesthetics. According to his aesthetics the technological object wants to disappear, fade into the background, and become ambient rather than actively attracting attention to itself and its technological magic like the first iMac. Consciously or not, these minimalist designs communicate, or rather foretell, the new and developing identity of personal information technology—the eventual disappearance of specific technological objects as such as their functions become fully integrated into other objects, surfaces, spaces, and cloves.

This, in fact, is the stage of ubiquitous computing in which a technological fetish is dissolved into the overall fabric of material existence. The actual details of this potential future dematerialization will most probably be different from how it is imagined today, but the trend is clearly visible. But how to stage this future disappearance using technology available today? The minimalist designs of Apple's hardware in the 2000s can all be understood as responses to this challenge. Historically, its particular aesthetics occupies an intermediate, transitional stage: between technology as a designed lifestyle object (exemplified by 1998 iMac and Nokia's 2004 Fashion collection of mobile phones) and its future stage as an invisible infrastructure implanted inside other objects, architectural forms, and human bodies.

In 1998, Hans Ibelings published an influential book, *Supermodernism*, in which he identified a similar "aesthetics of disappearance" in the architecture of the 1990s, as exemplified by the Foundation Cartier in Paris or the French National Library. According to Ibelings, this supermodern aesthetics "is characterized mainly by the absence of distinguishing marks, by neutrality." This aesthetics stands in opposition to previous architectural aesthetics of the 1980s and early 1990s. As Ibelings notes, "whereas postmodernist and deconstructivist architecture almost always contain a message, today architecture is increasingly conceived as an empty medium."[5]

Ibelings was looking only at architecture and not at computers. However, just a few years later, Jonathan Ive and his team used a similar supermodern aesthetics in designing Apple products. To achieve this aim, the designers employed many techniques: newly developed materials and finishes; the flat, largely empty surfaces uninterrupted by multiple buttons or screws; the monochrome appearance that visually emphasizes the shape as a whole; the rounded corners; the glow of the Apple logo, which creates a three-dimensional effect; the simplicity of the overall 3D form. All these techniques work to create a powerful impression that an object is about to fade and completely dissolve. Apple designs also create a different spatial experience equaling the "new spatial sensibility" that Ibelings found in supermodern buildings, a "boundless and undefined space" that, however, "is not an emptiness but a safe contained, a flexible shell."[6]

Ibelings speculated about the reasons for supermodern aesthetics in architecture. In the case of personal information technologies, the spatial form, which is simultaneously boundless, undefined, and also flexible, seems a perfect spatial metaphor for the values these technologies are supposed to communicate, as imagined by industry leaders attuned to lifestyle and cultural trends: Apple, Nokia, Samsung, LG, Sony, and others. These values include mobility, flexibility, adaptability, and the lack of predefined boundaries and limits. The last concept also happens to define a modern computer in theoretical terms—a universal simulation machine that, via software, can simulate an unlimited number of other machines and tools and, again via software, is infinitely expandable. But how do you find a visual or spatial expression for such a metamachine? This is one of the challenges of contemporary aesthetics. The supermodernist aesthetics of Apple products as designed by Ive and his team has so far been one of the more successful solutions to this fundamental challenge.

NOTES

1. For a discussion, see Lev Manovich, "Interaction as an Aesthetic Event," *Receiver*, no. 17 (2007): http://dm.ncl.ac.uk/courseblog/files/2011/03/Manovich_InteractionAs AestheticEvent.pdf (15 February 2011). This article is an expanded and updated version of the former essay.

2. For a discussion, see the interview, "Getting Emotional with . . . Hartmut Esslinger," *Design & Emotion*, 15 August 2006, http://www.design-emotion. com/2006/08/15/getting-emotional-with-hartmut-esslinger (15 February 2011).

3. Brenda Laurel, *Computers as Theatre* (Reading, Mass.: Addison-Wesley, 1991).

4. Joseph Pine and James H. Gilmore, *Experience Economy: Work Is Theatre and Every Business a Stage* (Cambridge, Mass.: Harvard Business Press, 1999).

5. Hans Ibelings, *Supermodernism: Architecture in the Age of Globalization* (Rotterdam: NAI Publishers, 1997), 88, 62.

6. Ibid, 62.

CHAPTER 20

Playing the iPhone

FRAUKE BEHRENDT

H OW TO PLAY an iPhone? You can talk, sing, or blow into the microphone; shake, stroke, or spin the device; use the camera; touch the screen and any of the built-in sensors, just to name a few ways. You can build on existing acoustic or electronic instruments, experiment with individual and group performances, explore public and private performance contexts, and push all the way beyond the boundaries of what a mobile phone is meant to be used for.

Artists and musicians have been exploring the use of mobile devices such as mobile phones, the walkman, or the iPod for musical interactions since the early 2000s, especially at the Mobile Music Workshop Series and at the New Interfaces for Musical Expression, held since 2004 and 2001, respectively.[1] Yet mobility in use has never been a constitutive element of mobile-phone musical instruments, as most of them allow for musical interaction indoors as much as outdoors, in the privacy of the home as much as in public, on the go as much as in stationary environments. Similar to other mobile devices for producing sounds (including your guitar or ghetto-blaster), the iPhone—or for that matter, any mobile phone—can be played on stage, around the campfire, at home, alone, or in a group. The interesting difference with conventional instruments is, rather, that music comes as an added function to an already existing device that accompanies us everywhere we go.

Consumer media have been turned into musical instruments previously; just think of turntables and boom boxes, for instance, or at the ways game controllers and mobile gaming consoles such as the Game Boy have been refashioned as musical devices, becoming important predecessors to mobile-phones-turned-musical-instruments before the smartphone "revolution" set in. Still, the popularity of the iPhone has made the experimental niche pursuit of playing your mobile into a mainstream leisure activity, notably through the Ocarina app. This chapter focuses on those interfaces and applications that have been developed specifically for the mobile phone and on the sonic interaction paradigms designed for the mobile. Mobile versions of more traditional computer music applications will not be considered because their design paradigm treats the mobile phone as miniature computer, with the software often being nothing more than a downsized versions of already existing studio software. Neither will I consider those works where the mobile acts as some sort of remote control, often in conjunction with other hard- and software, using data from the phone (such as the camera stream) as an input for Max/MSP, to give just one example.

From Dialtone Symphonies to Daisyphone Loop Music

Before taking a closer look at the Ocarina app for the iPhone, a brief survey on mobile phone music will help to understand its significance. Since the early 2000s, I was able to collect and document hundreds of examples of mobile music projects and mobile sound artworks.[2] In some of these contexts, mobile phones were treated as expert instruments to be played by one or several trained musicians, while in other cases, more accessible mobile phone instruments were developed for amateur use. Many mobile music projects were social experiments featuring an ensemble of networked and mobile devices within a group of people who collaboratively produced music either in the same space or at the same time (i.e., without being colocated). Artists have used traditional musical forms such as the symphony, the opera, or the musical in their mobile phone works. They also have experimented with a variety of locations for mobile phone music, inviting mobile phones into locations of traditional musical performance, such as the concert hall, or, alternatively, taking performances out into the streets.

Golan Levin has to be credited for pioneering the idea of using mobile phones in a concert setting in 2001, when he invited the audience and their mobile phones to form an orchestra, conducted by the artist on stage, to perform his "Dialtones: A Telesymphony." Before the event, audience members had to register their phone numbers and ringtones and then received seating assignments. Using a database fed with all this information, Levin was able to call up to 200 audience phones at once, creating a symphony out of monophonic ringtones, structured by themes and movements and joined by soloists on stage. Levin's performance skillfully played with the juxtaposition of traditional musical form, the then still relatively recent proliferation of mobile phones, and the taboo of ringing them in an art context.[3] Elsewhere, orchestras have performed ring-tone inspired pieces such as the "New Ring Cycle" (at the Cheltenham Music Festival 2002) or "Spring Cellphony" (in Jerusalem 2001). Mobile-phone-transmitted heartbeats have been used to generate a choir score and to drive a sound installation in "Kadoum" (Berlin 2000), and a distributed musical instrument involving 144 mobile phones and a local radio station has performed a radio concert entitled "Wählt die Signale" (Hamburg 2003). Newly founded ensembles include the Handy-Dandy, a mobile-phone rock band, or the MoPho mobile-phone orchestra.[4]

Mirroring these attempts to bring mobile phones into traditional art venues and concert halls, artists and musicians have taken traditional forms of musical performance out into the city. For instance, during the performance of "Cellphonia: In the News" (2006), callers were invited to join the chorus of a location-based karaoke opera, singing parts of the libretto into their phones, with the collaborative musical performance shared via conference call. In turn, "Mandala 3 and Mandala 4" by Greg Schiemer (2006) involved performers spinning a mobile phone—in a pouch attached to a string—overhead in the middle of the street, using the Doppler shift to produce microtonal music. The phones also were used to change and control the sounds played by each device.[5] Gamelike features and playful approaches have also been key elements of mobile phone music, as with "Schminky" (2003), a musical game running on PDAs (as mobile phones were not smart enough at the time), or the "Daisyphone" (2006), which featured as an "interface for remote group music improvisation and composition" drawing from collaborative gaming aesthetics.[6] The 2007 "Pophorns," finally, were a family of musical applications that could be installed on mobile phones, playfully engaging a variety of communities around the world in public performances.[7]

All the projects mentioned in this brief survey were marked by an avant-garde ethos and launched in the nonmainstream context of media art festivals, academic conferences, or within the research and development labs of mobile phone corporations. The arrival of the iPhone, however, and the introduction of Ocarina, in particular, completely changed this situation, making mobile music applications a part of the redefinition of mobile media entertainment.

The iPhone Ocarina

Every iPhone user knows the Ocarina: it is an application that allows users to play their phones like a traditional ocarina, blowing into the iPhone's microphone while fingering notes using the four holes of the instrument emulated on the display. Familiarity with the ocarina means people intuitively understand how to use the microphone as a mouthpiece and the graphics on the touch screen as "finger holes." Ocarina thus merges the features of an ancient wind instrument with those of a new mobile device,[8] based on its (and the iPhone's) sensitivity to breath, touch (via a multitouch interface mimicking the four-hole English pendant ocarina), and movement (a dual axis accelerometer controls vibrato rate and depth).[9] In addition, the app allows a user to listen in on the songs being played by other phone users simultaneously around the globe. Ocarina, in other words, fuses the networked capabilities of the mobile phone with the experience of lay music. In the words of its designer, Stanford professor Ge Wang, it thus can be seen as "a unique social artifact," since it "allows its user to hear other . . . players throughout the world while seeing their location—achieved through GPS and the persistent data connection on the iPhone."[10] The networked element is even complemented by a Web portal where players are able to share scores and other information (http://ocarina.smule.com/).

Despite these innovations, attention so far has mostly been devoted to Ocarina's developing company, Smule, to Smule's marketing strategies, and to the commercial success of the app, rather than to how Ocarina has turned the iPhone into a new musical instrument. Within four days of its release in 2008, the app reportedly became a best-selling item in the App Store, and by end of November 2008, it arguably had been played on more than one million iPhones, making it the epitome of Apple's "All-time top 20 Apps" in summer 2009 and ever since.[11] Newspapers, magazines, and online media have discussed Ocarina by repeatedly pointing to the "sound of serious money," as *The Observer* put it.[12] "Released in November, 'Ocarina' racked up 400,000 downloads in less than a month," *Newsweek* reported. "Smule, which originally set a goal of taking in $100,000 in revenue this year, instead will end up making closer to $1 million."[13] *USA Today* discussed the finances of Smule and its founders, Ge Wang and Jeff Smith: "Smith raised $5.5 million from local investors and says his target was to do $100,000 in the first six months. Instead, Smule did $500,000. The sales target for the first year was $1.6 million, and Smith says that will be exceeded, too."[14] By and large, the press attributed Smule's success in 2009 to its new marketing strategies. Wang "focused on working the social Web via YouTube, Twitter and Facebook," as one commentator observed: "If you see some person holding a phone like a sandwich and have sound coming out, you get it."[15] Ocarina and other Smule applications also were featured widely on U.S. and international media, including television (CNBC, Fox News), newspapers—as a front page feature in *USA Today*—and a plethora of online magazines and blogs. Smule applications have certainly also benefited from exposure through Apple, as underlined by its listing in the "best app" category or by inviting the company to speak at a presentation of the iPhone software update.

A more pertinent question is, however, how the designer of the Ocarina app actually envisioned its integrating music making into people's everyday lives, and how people actually perform music using Ocarina. In an interview, Wang once stated that he believes "that everyone is inherently creative; and we want to unlock that creativity in everyone." Wang's expressed hope was that applications like Ocarina could "bring the vision of computer music to a much wider audience," thus allowing the app "to combine music with technology, where anybody can play. You don't have to spend 10 hours in a practice room learning how to play. With the iPhone, anyone can do it."[16] Yet despite its extraordinary download figures and Smule's success as a commercial enterprise, the Ocarina app never reached out to a wider audience since the iPhone remains one of the most expensive smartphones on the market. Nor do such figures tell us if—and how—people play their iPhones and how they share the Ocarina app in music making.

There are, however, more significant indications of Ocarina use. Ratings in the App Store at least testify to thousands of people taking the time to write a comment. YouTube videos showing iPhone users playing the Ocarina are even more indicative, with searches generating more than 100,000 hits and videos such as "iPhone App by Smule: Ocarina [Zeldarian]" having been watched almost 2 million times. Ocarina has also been featured in several public events and concerts, such as a concert with the San Francisco Symphony. Not least, anytime the app starts (which now runs on the iPad as well), there are other players performing at the same time. In fact, it is the Ocarina forum and its many active contributors that illustrate how active the community is in negotiating the best practices of Ocarina playing (http://ocarina.smule.com/forum/). For if one does not like the performance one is listening to, one can easily skip to the next. Or as one blogger put it: "You'll probably be using this button often, as many of the people playing are awful."[17] The forum gives an indication of the number of people who are performing for others and also those listening and voting. Finally, in December 2009 an Ocarina contest opened, with YouTube working as a main platform to distribute the videos of those participating.

One more critical question concerns how long and how intensively people actually engage with applications like Ocarina and how the educational effect of the app should be measured. After the initial hype in 2009, usage actually appears to have dropped, at least by measures of Web exposure. The app is, of course, in all likelihood more of a gimmick to most people and is marketed accordingly in the App Store as an entertaining iPhone add-on for "blowing away your friends and family with your new talent." Still, the educational potential of mobile phone instruments cannot be overestimated, and one might in fact argue that this potential has only just begun to be seriously explored. Mobile phones are ubiquitous, and music making, listening, remixing, and sharing through an app such as Ocarina offer new forms of access to culture for people without computers and broadband connections. Exposure to the iPhone Ocarina reportedly has inspired people to learn to play the analog ocarina, resulting in a flourishing ocarina community.

Social Mobile Music

After releasing the Ocarina app, Smule continued developing similar apps. Over the last two years, the company has created top-selling social music apps for iOS, including the Magic Piano, I Am T-Pain, Glee Karaoke, and the Magic Fiddle. According to the company web page, "Users of Smule products have now performed more than 132 million songs around the world." In 2011, the company announced it was doubling its staff, and a press release stated that the

> new Magic Piano App for iPhone and iPod touch has been downloaded from the App Store more than 2.7 million times in its first four weeks. During this brief period of time, users of Magic Piano have played more than 31 million songs including such works as Lady Gaga's "Poker Face" and Robert Schumann's "Von fremden Ländern und Menschen." Magic Piano

App users have also used their iPhone or iPod touch to play over 13 billion musical notes, or over 300,000 notes per minute.[18]

It still remains to be stressed that the quality of music performances on these different apps is not what makes them interesting. What is relevant about these mobile phone musical instruments is how people who do not consider themselves musicians take up playing music, how music is performed in new contexts, and how phone users engage in social musical interactions, such as listening to others' performances or sharing their own compositions. These social aspects of musical interaction are not taking place in one and the same location, as it would be the case with more traditional musical collaboration such as band performances or classical concerts. Remote collaborative music making such as networked music has often focused on desktop computers and laptops. But with mobile phones, these networked music experiences extend well beyond the desk or the sofa, to take place in any possible space. That is, although mobile music does not depend on mobility in use, it is the *mobility of the device* that opens up new social and physical realms of collaborative music making. Given the unprecedented spread of mobile phones around the globe, networked music making is brought to a much wider audience than traditional desktop appliances would have had. Accessible and playful musical activities such as iPhone Ocarina performances thus have taken networked music making from a niche pursuit of electronic musicians and academics into mainstream culture — promoting a redefinition of what constitutes "high" and "low" culture.

The social aspects of the iPhone Ocarina thus remain key and vital for this instrument's success. Playing, listening, evaluating, and sharing related information such as scores happen in networked, social situations. One might argue that the success of the iPhone Ocarina as a phenomenon of popular culture also builds on the popularity of musical console games such as Guitar Hero, for which sociomusical interaction is crucial. The iPhone Ocarina is, in short, a *web phenomenon* of pop culture in that it uses the entire telephone network and not only the device itself.

Analyzing the iPhone Ocarina has, hence, enabled me to explore how a device that those of us who can afford it own and carry around can be turned into an highly innovative musical instrument. Highlighting the mobile phone's accessibility, ubiquity, and familiarity, this chapter has briefly pointed to the technological interactions of mobile phone instruments (pressing buttons or tilting the device, for instance), how these instruments are embedded within social contexts (playing for a remote audience or a small group performance, for example), and how they make use of their physical environments (such as public places or the private bedroom)—all vital for an understanding of how mobile musical instruments are performed. With the arrival of the iPhone in 2007 and the subsequent release of Ocarina and a vast number of other musical iPhone applications, such as Guitar Hero, Bloom, Beatmaker, Looptastic, TonePad Pro, and RjDj, mobile music has become a part of today's mainstream media culture.

NOTES

1. See www.mobilemusicworkshop.org and www.nime.org (15 July 2011); and Nicolaj Kirisits et al., eds., *Creative Interactions—the Mobile Music Workshops, 2004–2008* (Vienna: University of Applied Arts, 2008).

2. See http://mobilesound.wordpress.com/ as well as Frauke Behrendt, "Mobile Sound: Media Art in Hybrid Spaces," Ph.D. diss., University of Sussex, 2010. A PDF can be found at http://sro.sussex.ac.uk/6336/ (15 June 2011). See also Frauke Behrendt, *Handymusik: Klangkunst und "Mobile Devices"* (Osnabrück: Epos, 2004).

3. Golan Levin, "Project Report for Dialtones (a Telesymphony)," http://www.flong.com/storage/pdf/reports/dialtones_report.pdf (15 June 2011).

4. Ge Wang et al., "Do Mobile Phones Dream of Electronic Orchestras?" paper presented at the International Computer Music Conference, Belfast, Northern Ireland, 2008.

5. Greg Schiemer and Mark Havryliv, "Pocket Gamelan: Swinging Phones and Ad Hoc Standards," paper presented at the Mobile Music Workshop in Amsterdam, 2006.

6. Nick Bryan-Kinns and Patrick Healey, "Daisyphone: Support for Remote Music Collaboration," paper presented at the New Interface for Musical Expression in Hamamatsu, Japan, 2004.

7. See Erik Sandelin and Magnus Torsensson, "Pophorns," http://www.pophorn.net/ (15 June 2011).

8. Gil Weinberg et al., "Zoozbeat: A Gesture-Based Mobile Music Studio," paper presented at the International Conference on New Interfaces for Musical Expression in Pittsburgh, 2009.

9. Ge Wang, "Designing Smule's Ocarina: The Iphone's Magic Flute," paper presented at the International Conference on New Interfaces for Musical Expression in Pittsburg, 2009.

10. Ibid.

11. Jefferson Graham, "Ocarina, Leaf Trombone Lead Big Parade of Iphone Apps," *USA Today*, 21 April 2009. "The remarkable 'Ocarina' app . . . transforms this most up-to-date of contraptions into an instrument that dates back 12,000 years by harnessing the iPhone's built-in features in a wonderfully creative way," as *PC Magazine* stated, and David Pogue of the *New York Times* declared in 2009, "It's one of the most

magical programs I've ever seen for the iPhone, and probably for any computer. . . . It's a brain-frying experience to know that you're listening to someone else playing 'Ocarina', right now, in real time, somewhere else on the planet. (And then you realise that someone, somewhere might be listening to *you*!)." See Michael Muchmore, "Ocarina (for Iphone)," *PC Magazine*, 9 December 2008, http://www.pcmag.com/article2/0,2817,2336513,00.asp (15 June 2011); and David Pogue, "So Many Iphone Apps, So Little Time," *New York Times*, 5 February 2009 (15 June 2011).

12. John Naughton, "The Iphone Ocarina Is the Sound of Serious Money," *The Observer*, 8 February 2009.

13. Daniel Lyons, "There's Gold in Them Iphones," *Newsweek*, 18 December 2008.

14. Graham, "Ocarina, Leaf Trombone."

15. Graham, "Ocarina, Leaf Trombone."

16. Graham, "Ocarina, Leaf Trombone."

17. Jason Kincaid, "Smule's Ocarina: This Is How You Build a Great Iphone App," http://www.techcrunch.com/2008/11/07/smules-ocarina-a-textbook-example-of-how-to-build-a-great-iphone-app/ (15 June 2011).

18. "Smule's Magic Piano App for iPhone and iPod Touch Reaches 2.7 Million Downloads in First Month," Smule press release, 7 June 2011, http://www.smule.com/news/magicpiano-first-month (15 June 2011).

CHAPTER 21

Mobile Media Life

MARK DEUZE AND THE JANISSARY COLLECTIVE

A S LIFE GETS experienced not with but rather in media, the global shift toward mobile and haptic connectivity is not just a step toward natural user interfaces but also toward an increasingly seamless integration among human beings, nature, and technology. This chapter explores the key components of a media life as lived through the iPhone, showing that the profound power of media can only be found in their invisibility and, ultimately, disappearance. Today's mobile phone in general—and the iPhone in particular—can arguably be seen as the ultimate device when it comes to communication and conversation, especially as it includes modalities of other media, such as television and film, games, photography, and the computer. Access to mobiles is so much more widespread than usage of the World Wide Web that James Katz, for example, suggests the device deserves the subtitle of "the real world's Internet."[1] Considering the near-universal adoption of mobile communication and the rapid growth of wireless broadband connectivity (especially in developing countries), a certain mobility afforded by small portable artifacts can be considered to be at the heart of what it means to live a media life.

Although the mobile phone as we know it has been in development for at least fifty years, and (trans-)portable phones were used by telephone companies in the United States and in the British army in the South African Anglo-Boer War (1899–1902), only since the 1980s have the devices become widely available.[2] Gerard Goggin describes how during the mid-twentieth century the combination of computer code automating many aspects of the communication process, a shift to organically shaped cells (specific areas around a transmitter tower) to send and receive mobile communication signals, and reducing otherwise rather bulky features of the artifacts involved laid the groundwork for mobile telephony.[3] In terms of size, the world's first mobile telephone call was made in 1973 with what is called the Brick: a 1,134 gram analog model manufactured by Motorola.[4] With the switch to digital networks, a new generation of mobile phones emerged: much smaller and smarter, at least according to industry rhetoric. All that intelligence refers to the contemporary cell phone's ability to learn just about everything from and about its user and how the industries catering to it—telecommunications companies, ISPs, software studios, marketing and advertising agencies, and all kinds of other businesses—can adapt their products and services accordingly.

Over the past thirty-five years, the bulky and solo-use mobile phone has transformed into a sleek and multifaceted device; the iPhone 4 in fact only weighs 136 grams. This transformation continues as the mobile device morphs from a distinct technological phenomenon to an artifact of increasingly seamless media and everyday life integration. As mobile media advance, previous technologies and practices are remediated. The journey of the mobile phone's integration into modern society has left in its wake a myriad of bypassed and remediated devices. Shortly after the publication of Charles Darwin's *On the Origin of Species* (1859), the British novelist Samuel Butler, for example, responded with a satirical op-ed piece for the New Zealand newspaper *The Press*, titled "Darwin Among the Machines," published in mid-June 1863. In this piece, Butler wonders out loud about the direction of mechanical evolution, or what he calls "mechanical life," awestruck as he is "at the gigantic strides with which it has advanced in comparison with the slow progress of the animal and vegetable kingdom." Applying the principle of natural selection to machines, Butler notes how the ongoing diminution in the size of technological devices attends their development and progress toward ever-increasing independence from humans. To Butler, the emergence of wristwatches is an example of how smaller technologies may replace larger ones—clocks—and thus render them extinct.[5]

Digital (R)evolution

Today, most college freshmen consider wearing a wristwatch unnecessary. Different research has found that many digital devices, from laptops to MP3 players, are a serious threat to the wristwatch industry. As mobile phone sales continue to increase, wristwatch sales have remained flat or are in decline. In fact, digital devices may eventually change how wristwatches are designed, and Apple's devices do—as in 2010, when Apple released a wristwatch version of the iPod Nano. High-end, designer wristwatches may never fade away because of their function as a status symbol, but the days of the affordable Casio may soon be coming to an end. Another timekeeping device also feeling the repercussions of advanced mobile technology is the alarm clock. It, too, is being evolved out of place by features on mobile phones. Numerous polls suggest that over half of people who own a mobile phone use it as an alarm clock. Rightmobilephone.co.uk, for example, polled nearly 1,500 people, of whom 82 percent owned a mobile phone, and over half of these reported to waking up to its alarm in the morning. Beyond telling the time and sounding the alarm, mobile media in general, and smartphones such as the iPhone in particular, are in a position to swallow up other technologies and uses in their design: the (digital) camera, the credit card (to check in at airports or pay for your coffee), and so on. The iPhone and the Android smartphone have already replaced numerous gadgets—from common features such as the calculator and stopwatch, to lesser known novelties like the builder's level and instrument tuner, the functionality of these devices can now fit in the palms of our hands.

As technology continues to advance at what seems to be a blistering pace, we are constantly reminded of just how quickly it is happening. The generation that saw the emergence of the World Wide Web as one of the greatest advances in human history is followed by an era of individuals who have always experienced the personal computer to be online. The ubiquity of mobile technology is quickly advancing to reshuffle both the analog and digital artifacts of modern times. As mobile technology continues to integrate the functions of our daily lives, one might argue that mobile devices like the iPhone will no longer be considered devices at all but simply an accepted and invisible part of our natural environment. The transition is happening so quickly that even technologies that can be considered to be part of the digital (r)evolution are in danger of being subsumed by the mobile device, lending further credence to Samuel Butler's nineteenth-century concerns. If technologies have the potential to render one another obsolete, and their evolution moves at a pace far beyond that of nature, Butler proceeds in his article, "we refer to the question: what sort of creature man's next successor in the supremacy of the earth is likely to be." Ultimately, "man will have become to the machine what the horse and the dog are to man. He will continue to exist, nay even to improve, and will be probably better off in his state of domestication under the beneficent rule of the machines than he is in his present wild state." The solution to this evolutionary conundrum, according to Butler, is to wage "war to the death" with machines.[6]

Butler's advice may sound ridiculous, but he has a point: considering the qualities of mobile media in terms of their "lifelike" ubiquity, pervasiveness, and remediation of older and new modalities of communication and conversation brings us a bit closer to a mindset of, as Martin Heidegger would say, turning any media device from a thing we just use (and thus is "ready-to-hand") into an artifact that is open to questions about what is the matter with it. However, we tend to question media only when they stop working or do not work the way they are supposed to. The laptop only becomes a machine one thinks about when it fails to boot up; an iPhone ceases to be an extension of people's life- and workstyle when they forget to pay the monthly bill; and a book only becomes a book when it's missing a page at a crucial part of the story. In other words: only when media are destroyed—when we first wage war with them—can we meaningfully address what is the matter with media.

Continuing this line of thought, Friedrich Kittler constructs his philosophical media project around the realization that we have become blind to our media to the extent that even when we try to say something meaningful about media, we need media to express it. Generally speaking, when we use media we tend to be unaware of the structuring power of the particular media used to make a point about them. To Kittler, "this crazy coincidence of forgetfulness with technological change" that pervades the history of media directly relates to "the exclusion of physical and technical media from questions of ontology." Once we start articulating more precisely what media are and how media fit into our everyday lives, we come to the inevitable conclusion that media are not "external and extensive objects" that we can switch on or off and therefore control. Media, "on the one hand and man on the other are inseparably linked by an endless feedback loop." In Kittler's history of communication media, this feedback loop accelerates with each stepping stone—from writing and printing via telegraphy and analog media to digital media. He predicts that ultimately media technologies will overhaul one another to evolve beyond the essential intervention of humans, returning us safely and securely back in the warmongering arms of Samuel Butler.[7]

Technology Fading Into Our Lives

The process toward the media we know today was not necessarily linear or uncontested—yet, as Gerard Goggin notes, the key to the future of cell phones seems their irrevocable (and inevitably messy) metamorphosis into mobile media, "infiltrating into and reworking all sorts of old and new media forms."[8] With that, argues Paul Levinson, comes a process whereby new media devices "become even smaller and lighter than they are now, following Buckminster Fuller's 'dymaxion principle', which holds that new technologies get ever smaller and more powerful."[9] In the original prescient words of Fuller—an early-twentieth-century American inventor, architect, and futurist—his size-based standard is "an attitude and interpretive principle . . . of doing the most with the least in consideration of a mobilizing, integrating society."[10] The architect would probably be thrilled about current attempts to reduce the size and integrate the multimodal connectedness of technologies even further.

And indeed, the iPhone seems not just to be taking over other technologies but to be entering into all kinds of reciprocal relationships with the way we live, organize, and give meaning to our lives. Summarizing the situation in the United States in 2009, the *Pew Internet and American Life Project* concludes that "mobile connectivity is now a powerful differentiator among technology users. Those who plug into the information and communications world while on-the-go are notably more active in many facets of digital life."[11] This digital life is to a large extent based on a mobile lifestyle, according to market research based on international comparative studies of attitudes and behaviors related to wireless devices and communication. Or, as one such report claimed in 2002, "constant awareness of wireless finally wanes when people are truly living a mobile lifestyle," ultimately seamlessly integrating wireless in everyday life "where people find it difficult to live a life without wireless."[12] Combining qualitative and quantitative data from Asia, Europe, and the United States, numerous researchers have mapped a globally emerging mobile communication society where what people do with mobile technology serves to reinforce, maintain, and create collective identity while at the same time functioning as an expression of a distinctly personal style and way of life. How far this process plays out in everyday life is evident in the work of media anthropologists, such as Daniel Miller, studying the various roles social and mobile media play in the lives of a variety of groups in society: students, migrant workers, and the homeless. Miller and Mirca Madianou conclude that people around the world, coming from a wide variety of social and economic backgrounds, increasingly live in a situation of "polymedia": exposed to a plurality of media that change the relationships between communication technology and society by the mere fact of their omnipresence and seemingly effortless integration into the social and emotional realm of people's everyday existence.[13] As they state in their work, for Filipino and Caribbean people living in London and Cambridge and the families they have left behind, media are their "technologies of love." In his fieldwork, Miller finds that people spend so much time living with media that media become their life, in effect treating media as their home.[14] This results in typical "home" idioms being translated into media contexts, for example, by incessantly decorating one's online social network profile or by constantly rearranging and tidying up the files, applications, and icons of one's personal computer or smartphone. Just as the home gets infused with (and reshaped through) media, our media become domesticated spaces typified by a mass personalization effort: customized ringtones, individualized screensavers and wallpaper, fine-tuned arrangements of favorite websites and television stations, tailor-made carrying pouches and various forms of wearable media.

The central role of the mobile phone in processes of personal transformation toward greater individualization and transnational connectivity reveals its nature as a "charismatic" technology; it was originally designed for work and business but changed identity quickly as it entered the domestic sphere. Once inseparable from that sphere, the telephone in general and mobile media in particular become part of the day-to-day coordination of both family and personal life. In doing so, media add a certain dynamism and mobility to the daily rhythm of life while at the same time they should be seen as extending or even amplifying existing networks and ways of doing things. With the iPhone, boundaries between media and life blur beyond meaningful distinction. Yes, we are overtly aware of the latest and greatest in devices and apps. At the same time, our lived experience with ubiquitous, always-on, mobile media makes these same technologies, paradoxically, disappear into our lives.

Computer scientists have long emphasized this vanishing. As Mark Weiser put it in 1991, the ideal-typical goal for engineers should be "to conceive a new way of thinking about computers, one that takes into account the human world and allows the computers themselves to vanish into the background."[15] Considering our haptic (iPhone) and kinetic (Wii and Kinect) intimate technologies today, this mission indeed seems accomplished. Weiser and his colleagues, then at the Xerox Palo Alto Research Center, envisioned devices that fit the human environment, not devices that force humans to enter mediated worlds. Next-generation tablet and smartphone technologies point to ways that the technology is indeed fading into our lives. Readers may already own an iPhone that either includes or works in harmony with other personalized machines in our lives—the refrigerator, the washer and dryer, the television, the automobile, the coffee maker.

The idea that our selves can extend into devices and "be" even when "we" are not there is by now familiar. Facebook, Twitter, and other Web-based awareness tools allow us to present multiple selves online that connect and share statuses with others (and ourselves). Today, these cherished tools prompt engagement by posing questions like *what are you doing?* and *what's on your mind?* And we oblige with a passion for sharing that has driven awareness tools to the forefront of the mobile Web. What if we could ask of our devices, *what should I do?*—or maybe even, *what should I think?* That capability is more than hypothetical. Among the darlings of Silicon Valley right now are social question and answer services. Such "answer sites" flourish around the world, providing a form of information discovery that is social and potentially more personalized than search engine results. Social Q&A sites like Quora and ChaCha thrive on mediated communities built around information sharing. The appeal is hard to deny: instead of a keyword search on a search engine, answer sites allow us to express information needs as questions and answers are provided in narrative form, rather than as a list of documents, as in search engine results.

The iPhone Alive

Apple's April 2010 acquisition of Siri, a mobile personal assistant, signals the direction of next-generation Q&A for the iPhone. Siri emerged from Stanford Research Institute International, the Menlo Park research institute that is contracted by global governments and corporations. Siri drew initial funding from the Defense Advanced Research Projects Agency under its Personalized Assistant That Learns program. The goal: build a smart assistant that seamlessly shares our media life, learns from it, and guides us. Much of the interest swirling around Siri and other so-called cognitive assistants focuses on speech recognition and voice-activated search, not on the learning, bonding, and co-creative decision-making capabilities. Siri and its cohort are capable of developing what could prove to be a tantalizing intimacy with us. Additionally, one could consider the rising prominence of augmented-reality applications for the iPhone and Android platforms, which are charismatically changing how we view and interact with the world around us. Programs like the Dutch system Layar or Google's Goggles digitally overlay a multitude of information about the contents of the camera view of a smartphone in real time. The iPhone's Type'n'Walk application allows the user to literally never avert her attention from the screen by providing a camera view of the surroundings while texting or e-mailing.

Scientists working for Apple, Facebook, Google, Microsoft, and other media giants push the limits of mobile search, bringing haptic and audiovisual connectivity together with dynamic artificial intelligence. It is in this context perhaps unsurprising that a famous book on the evolution of a global artificial intelligence by George Dyson carried as its title the same name as Butler's original essay: *Darwin Among the Machines* (1998).[16] As Dyson assumed, humanity, nature, and technology coevolve. In his 2009 work *The Nature of Technology*, Brian Arthur similarly suggests that nature and technology coevolve to the point of not just mirroring but even subsuming each other—while indeed also citing Butler's thesis.[17] Given the developments in multimodal convergence, life- and workstyle integration, social-media tools (including answer sites, mobile personal assistants, and augmented-reality applications), as well as broader trends toward human-machine osmosis, it is not too far-fetched to suggest that the iPhone is alive. Its materiality draws on the power of social and artificial intelligence. It learns from experience. It reasons. It gets to know us. It follows commands. And, if we want the iPhone to, it issues commands.

It is striking to find in many of these accounts of the history and adoption of mobile media a certain seamlessness; a way of describing and analyzing the technology strictly in terms of its success as defined by market penetration and its gradual reworking from a presumably lifeless machine into a generally reproductive yet potentially transformative social tool. Such a perspective reflects a barely implicit emphasis on how media become life—where "becoming" refers to media extending the communication and conversation capabilities of their users, embedding themselves physically with people through forms of wearable computing, and finally becoming part and parcel of every aspect of daily life and one's sense of self.

Considering the ubiquity of mobile communication and increasing migratory behaviors of people and things worldwide, researchers (such as John Urry) have made a rallying cry for a "mobility turn" in our thinking about (media and) life today. In a less ambitious but similar vein, Rich Ling and Jonathan Donner advocate the adoption of what they call a "mobile logic" as determined by mobile and increasingly ubiquitous devices around the world. The implications of such a logic governing people in their daily life, they suggest, are that individuals compartmentalize and apportion "their activities to a greater extent than previously possible," which also means that we interlace "multiple tasks with multiple actors and multiple venues, competing and jostling for time and attention." All of this seemingly frantic activity is premised, according to Ling and Donner, on permanent reachability or the expectation thereof. At the heart of such mobility-inspired considerations of the contemporary human condition are concerns about the structure and consequences of constant communication, and the public/private-boundary-erasing activities associated with the portability of mobile media. Mobile devices and wireless access enable constant communication, making people instantly accessible and therefore burdened with the expectation of availability. There is no alternative to the "always-on" paradigm of media life, or so it seems.[18]

Urry goes as far to consider mobile devices "lifelines" as the loss of a cell phone could throw a person into "a no-man's land of nonconnectivity."[19] Considering the widespread popularity of "Lost My Cell Phone—Give Me Your Number" groups on social networking sites like Facebook, he certainly has a point. Given the charismatic nature of media in our lives, it is perhaps safe to say that the passing of a mobile device does not just inspire the need to reclaim one's electronic address book but extends feelings of loss to the safety of one's home and community, and therefore in a very real way affects people's sense of belonging. For all their technological groundlessness and rootlessness, mobile media provide us with a space where we in effect feel connected, planted firmly in a community of peers—a sense of communal living based on our own terms and biographized experiences. Mobility in general and mobile media in particular do not necessarily uproot but, more exactly, continuously repot the plants of communal life.

Conclusion

An archaeology of mobile media suggests that these technologies, their uses, and how they fit into the daily lives of people around the world amplify media life's complexity in two directions. On the one hand, today's tiny yet quietly powerful mobile media can be seen as "intrinsically solipsistic" technologies, enabling the ongoing retreat of people into quasi-autonomous "personal information spaces."[21] On the other hand, this individualized mobile immersion instantly and haptically connects people with people anywhere else, thus turning their own societal bubbles of space into a fully mediated space of global coexistence. This space—or mediaspehere, to use Peter Sloterdijk's term—forms an invisible electronic shell around us whereby our entire experience of others becomes mediated. Yet life in a mediasphere can also leave people blind to coexistence.

Considering the evolution of portable communication technologies it is perhaps better to replace the "soundscapes" of cell phones with the "media-

scapes" of mobile media more broadly conceived. Arjun Appadurai introduces the concept of mediascapes by way of suggesting how media are central
to constituting shared imagined worlds by people and groups spread around
the globe. Appadurai's analysis brings home the connection among media,
daily life, and issues that world society faces on a daily basis by stressing how
an ongoing deterritorialization of people through global labor and family migration contributes to the production and maintenance of symbolic ties with
"imagined" homelands through media.[22] Such diasporic communities get
sustained through local networks as well as transnational media connections;
meeting fellow expatriates at the downtown community center while calling
family members back in the homeland on the way over. The mobile phone
in particular is a powerful instrument for maintaining close ties within and
across otherwise geographically dispersed communities, considering their
widespread popularity and the abundance of relatively cheap international
calling rates. At the same time, all this mediated global connectivity does not
exclude or necessarily limit local interactions. In fact, media above all seem to
contribute to a process of ongoing "glocalization" of communities.

To some extent this explains the growth and success of diasporic media in
general and "new" or mobile media in particular, while this conclusion at the
same time amplifies concerns about speed, scale, and volume in the transnational circulation of images and ideas. A glocalized world society is provincial
in the sense of Sloterdijk's assumptions about people turning increasingly to
the inner world of a modern individuality, supported by a complex media
environment, while it is also markedly part of Appadurai's observations of an
accelerating global flow of "people, machinery, money, images, and ideas."[23]
The same information and communication technologies support and super-
charge these seemingly different trajectories. What remains at the heart of our
mobile media life—unless we wage war on it—is the gradual disappearance of
media from our awareness. With media, we become invisible, perhaps both
to others as to ourselves.

As the iPhone and mobile media in general pervade people's lives, such devices are rapidly being transformed from cutting-edge gadgets into a seamless
integrated and multifunctional necessity of everyday life. Perhaps the most
telling facet of devices contributing to this transformation is the ever-increasing ease of interaction between the technology of the device and the user.
The general trend of mobile technology has been towards a haptic interface,
and one cannot contest the ease with which touch-screen technology can be
manipulated. In the case of the iPhone, one can navigate a dizzying maze
of icons giving way to even more icons; one page sliding away to reveal yet

another page—in short, a myriad of applications all accessible with simple taps and flicks of the finger.

An irony of the trend toward hapticity is these devices' loss of their tactile qualities. From the inception of the cellular phone, mobile technology has functioned via the presence of plastic or rubber keys used to navigate the device, the physical depression of the buttons and the ever-present *clacking* of the keys providing assurance to the user that her command is being processed. This tactile interface is rapidly becoming obsolete as it makes the user acutely aware of the device's presence by drawing attention to its form. Considering our earlier observations, the popularity of and corresponding shift toward ubiquitous computing, natural user interfaces, and an overall increasingly immersive engagement with our media can possibly be explained by the realization of how media both operate as a McLuhanian extension of our bodies and must be seen as altogether fused with bodies. By drawing less attention to itself, the transition from physical keypads via touch screens to kinectic interfaces allows users to become immersed in their devices (and what they do with them). Assuming for a moment how hapticity and kinectivity will benchmark lived experience in media, this trend necessitates the assumption that for people in everyday contexts, the channel of communication evaporates.

The current and potential influence mobile media possess in how we socially and culturally navigate our environment point toward their existence as what Jean Baudrillard famously called a "simulacrum to hyperreality." As discussed earlier in this chapter, there is a veritable laundry list of artifacts, activities, and arrangements that become fused in mobile media life. As reality shrinks into the palm of our hand, augmented by applications such as Layar and Goggles, mobile media amplify our bodies into a state of complete mediation. We become media, and media become us. This insight was originally voiced quite literally by the French physician Julien Offray de La Mettrie in his essay "L'homme machine" (translated as "Man a Machine" or "Machine Man"), written in 1748, where he argued against Descartes's distinction between matter and soul, instead suggesting that our bodies are like machines in that they influence the way we think and express ourselves. In his essay, La Mettrie suggests that our expressions in (and use of) media not only set us apart from primates but also introduce an element of plasticity into our lives—making ourselves and our experience of reality malleable. Before Butler's prescient take on media's (r)evolution, short stories such as E. T. A. Hoffman's "Der Sandmann" (published in 1816) and Edgar Allen Poe's "The Man That Was Used Up" (first published in 1839) explored the potential consequences of real-time man-machine fusion. Poe describes in his work an encounter with a "singularly commanding" and "remarkable man—a very remarkable man": Brevet Brigadier-General John A. B. C. Smith. After thoroughly investigating the source of Smith's unrivaled perfection and enthusiasm for "the rapid march of mechanical invention," he eventually is confronted in terror with Smith as nothing but "a large and exceedingly odd-looking bundle of something," with arms, legs, shoulders, bosom, eyes, tongue and palate mechanically attached. Inspired by such work—and in particular with the uncanniness exemplified by the confrontation with a real that seems not to be—Sigmund Freud navigates similar territory in his essay "Das Unbehagen in der Kultur" (translated as "Civilization and Its Discontents" and published in 1930). In this piece (and with direct reference to Hoffman's tale about a man falling in love with what turns out to be a mechanical doll), Freud considers man a "prosthetic" God, inventing and deploying all kinds of tools and appliances that overcome the imperfections of man's own body and mind. In doing so, human beings surround themselves with technologies that put them at farther removes from direct, unmediated experience. The lived experience of being both what Freud calls "a feeble animal organism" as well as some kind of "prosthetic God" can therefore be seen as filled with ambivalence and uncertainty—necessary byproducts of life's newfound plasticity (or what Zygmunt Bauman would describe as our liquid modern lifestyle of being "permanently impermanent").

This exploration of the iPhone in the context of a perspective of life as lived *in* rather than *with* media, thus, allows us to wage war on our machines, even though our machines are us. It is a way to look at media differently while at the same recognizing that they become (like) us more and more and through our immersion in them we become like (our) media. We are concurrently confronted with real or perceived expectations of being connected at all times (and costs), constantly changing (and upgrading), instantly reachable yet always on the move, qualities we tend to anticipate in our media. Seen as such, the iPhone can be considered to be the embodiment of our life as we experience it now.

NOTES

The Janissary Collective is Mark Deuze, Watson Brown, Hans Ibold, Nicky Lewis, Peter Blank.

1. James Katz, ed., *Handbook of Mobile Communication* (Cambridge, Mass.: MIT Press, 2008), 434.

2. The blog *Webdesigner Depot* has an excellent overview of cell phone design between 1983 and 2009: http://www.webdesignerdepot.com/2009/05/the-evolution-of-cell-phone-design-between-1983-2009 (15 February 2011).

3. Gerhard Goggin, *Cell Phone Culture: Mobile Technology in Everyday Life* (London: Routledge, 2006).

4. See http://en.wikipedia.org/wiki/Motorola_DynaTAC (15 February 2011).

5. Samuel Butler, "Darwin Among the Machines," *The Press* (New Zealand), 13 June 1863.

6. Ibid.

7. Friedrich Kittler, "Technologies of Writing," interview, trans. M. Griffin and S. Herrmann, *New Literary History* 27, no 4 (1996): 731–42.

8. Goggin, *Cell Phone Culture*.

9. Paul Levinson, *New New Media* (New York: Allyn & Bacon, 2009), 191.

10. Buckminster Fuller, *Nine Chains to the Moon* (1938; Philadelphia: Lippincott, 1964), 340.

11. See http://www.pewinternet.org/Reports/2009/5-The-Mobile-Difference-Typology.aspx (15 February 2011).

12. Report available at http://www.contextresearch.com/context/study.cfm (15 February 2011).

13. See http://blogs.nyu.edu/projects/materialworld/2010/09/polymedia.html.

14. Daniel Miller and Mirca Madianou, *Migration and New Media. Transnational Families and Polymedia* (London: Routledge, 2011).

15. Mark Weiser, "The Computer for the Twenty-first Century" (1991), available at http://www.ubiq.com/hypertext/weiser/SciAmDraft3.html (15 February 2011).

16. George Dyson, *Darwin Among the Machines: The Evolution of Global Intelligence* (New York: Helix Books, 1998).

17. Brian Arthur, *The Nature of Technology: What It Is and How It Evolves* (New York: Free Press, 2009).

18. Rich Ling and Jonathan Donner, *Mobile Phones and Mobile Communication* (Cambridge: Polity Press, 2009), 28–29.

19. John Urry, *Mobilities* (Cambridge: Polity Press, 2007), 178.

20. David Morley, *Media, Modernity, and Technology: The Geography of the New* (London: Routledge, 2007), 211; Mark Deuze, *Media Work* (Cambridge: Polity Press, 2007), 30.

21. Arjun Appadurai, "Disjuncture and Difference in the Global Cultural Economy," in *Global Culture*, ed. Mark Featherstone (London: Sage, 1990), 295–310.

22. Ibid.

V

Coda

CHAPTER 22

The End of Solitude

DALTON CONLEY

WHEN I WAS eighteen, I did what many middle-class American college students have done as a rite of passage ever since air travel became accessible to a broad cross-section of the public: I backpacked through Europe on a rail pass. Much cheap wine was consumed. Many hard-earned savings were spent at discotheques. My buddies and I spent most of the time together, but on occasion we split up to travel through different cities with plans to rendezvous back together in northern Italy—at a particular American Express office where we would leave messages.

During my time alone, I slept on the beach in Spain, in a public park in Genova, and on the marble floor of the fascist-built Milan train station. I read Dostoevsky. Most of the time I was on my own, I was miserable. I self-consciously hurried through meals. I sat in public parks and wrote in my journal. And I only occasionally made new acquaintances at the hostels. Meanwhile, I spoke to my parents perhaps once a week—at most—from the cabin of a public phone bank. I hurriedly told them I was alive and made sure everyone back home was, too. The whole conversation took less than five minutes and that was pretty much it when it came to communication. After all, there were better things to spend my money on.

The first day I arrived—in Paris—I stood in a patisserie, my stomach grumbling, as person after person ordered their baked goods, while I practiced my request in my head—"Je voudrais un baguette s'il vous plait . . . Je voudrais un baguette s'il vous plait . . ."—over and over, until finally, I swallowed and spoke the words aloud—but not loud enough, evidently, since I was ignored in favor of other patrons. It took twice as long for me to try again—since it took twice the courage to speak up even louder. Again I was ignored. I finally gave up and slunk out of the shop. To my back, I heard the baker shout: "Je voudrais *une* baguette! *Une*! C'est féminine, la baguette!"

It was the most powerful French lesson I would ever endure—complete with the Pavlovian reward of the delicious, still warm loaf of bread. How was I to know the sex of a baguette? I had no iPhone translation app to tell me that "baguette" was feminine. There was no Google to google. And I was alone.

My story is by no means unique. The American version of the aboriginal "walkabout" has long been a rite of passage in our culture of rugged individualism. It may be summer in Europe. Or it could be a hike on the Appalachian Trail or a bike trip down the coast. It doesn't matter how far you go, just as long as you disconnect, cut the umbilical cord, get lost, and have stories to tell your kids someday (edited for public consumption, of course, and perhaps exaggerated just a tad). Whether physically alone on the side of a mountain or psychically alone in a the public square of a new city, time away from our social networks is necessary to figure out who we are, review and process the social interactions we have experienced, create and innovate, and even become fully individual.

But, as of late, this tradition of finding ourselves in the social wilderness is being eroded by omnipresent connectivity—a.k.a the mobile telecommunications device. Without time to be disconnected, the great American tradition of individualism will wither. Without solitude, we will be, ironically, less connected to our intimate relations and families. Without loneliness, our society will innovate and create less. While collaboration is often important to creativity, so is solo incubation and processing time. After all, necessity may be the mother of invention, but boredom is its father.

This tradition of "finding ourselves" in the vast American landscape by losing our social network ties for a while extends all the way back to Thoreau and Walden Pond. In fact, the pastoral tradition—the romanticization of the lone shepherd; the revitalizing influence of losing ourselves in a natural landscape—goes all the way back to Virgil, the great Roman poet, though it should be said that America as a new, uncivilized continent played a special role in this myth's story line. The cultural critic Leo Marx tells us that America was, on the one hand, a Garden of Eden where the fruits of the Earth abounded and life was idyllic. But, he argues, in his 1960 classic *The Machine in the Garden*, it was simultaneously the forbidding jungle full of dangerous savages, where the comforts of civilization were lacking.

Thomas Jefferson, it seems, was so taken by the imagery of the yeoman farmer, functioning independently, needing nothing but his own plot of land, that his entire vision of a functioning democracy rested on the notion of the individual (white, male) farmer tending his garden alone, coming to the public square only occasionally (and reluctantly) to do the nation's business—again, harking back to Roman imagery, in this case Cincinnatus and his plow. Forty acres and a mule (and a plow) were all a man needed for self-reliance—that is, subsistence farming. This formula became the basis of radical Republican cries for "forty acres and a mule" as reparations to make the former slaves truly free and whole during the early postwar years of Reconstruction. Individual self-sufficiency was still seen as key to liberty. Alas, it was not to come to pass; the dependency relations of sharecropping would become the dominant form of economic life for most black Americans of the late nineteenth century. Common to Virgil's lone shepherd, the American farmer, the Western cowboy, and even the college backpacker was the notion that he was one place—in the pastoral landscape—and civilization was somewhere else. Then in 1829, Leo Marx tells us, everything changed.

The locomotive, which had first been deployed in 1829 in the United States, did more than link cities across the North American expanse. The railroad brought the city into the pastoral—the machine into the garden, so to speak. By 1844, Nathaniel Hawthorne finds his solitude in Sleepy Hollow—not far from Walden Pond—rudely disrupted by a train whistle, which, in turn, conjures images of sweaty urban businessmen; coal shovelers; and various other unpleasant associations of civilization. He cannot escape; his solitude has been shattered.

The consequences of railroads—from the need for standardized time keeping to the stitching together of regions into a national identity—have been well documented elsewhere. Here, I introduce the railroad as only the first step along an almost 200-year path to the iPhone and the almost complete erasure of solitude and its associated virtues. Whereas the railroad merely reminded Hawthorne of "that other place" teeming with people (and, of course, allowed some of those people to escape the Dickensian cities of industrializing America), the telegraph and telephone socially connected the garden and the city in real time.

At least those technologies required a physical wire. The metaphoric importance of the telephone wire lay in the explicitness of the connection—like two cans and a piece of string—between the social cacophony of the city and the solitude of the countryside. By liberating us from the wire, mobile phone and WiFi technology has, in a sense, collapsed space in a qualitatively distinct way. We can, of course, be anywhere; the distance from our interlocutor is no longer of much importance—the way it was when in the 1980s I called my grandparents from California on a scratchy, transcontinental line. Now what matters is how far the conversers are from their cell phone towers. Yes, there are still dead spots in North America, but not for much longer. More importantly, the expectation that we carry our phone numbers on our person at almost all times—and especially when we travel to some remote place where we fear getting a flat tire—means that we can never truly be alone. Bye, bye solitude. Bye, bye individualism.

Solitude and individualism do not just go together for political and economic reasons, however. Solitude, ironically, is what is necessary not just for individualism but also for intimacy. Allow me to elaborate. The early-twentieth-century social psychologist George Herbert Mead argued that the self emerged from a splitting of the "me" (the object) from the "I" (the subject). This ability to perceive oneself from the point of view of others emerged in stages. First, we learn to take the role of one other person in one social situation through play. Think peek-a-boo: at first, a baby thinks that if she covers her eyes, you can't see her. She is only able to mimic. But soon she learns through one-on-one games to take the role of another player vis-à-vis herself. Playing house, playing go fish, playing any simple game forces the child to think about how—in that specific, structured situation—she is perceived by the other player. Then she moves up to an ability to take the role of multiple others but still within a highly constrained social situation. Team sports are a good example. If you've ever seen a pack of four year olds play soccer, it's abundantly clear that they have not mastered the notion that there are multiple players all reacting differently given their particular roles (i.e., positions). Eventually the kids get it and can play a given position and anticipate multiple players' reactions given their knowledge of roles and scripts for particular positions in specific situations.

Complete, true selfdom—the split between the "I" and the "me"—is only reached when we are able to see ourselves as the "generalized other" perceives us. The generalized other, according to Mead, is the abstracted reactions of many others in many situations. Situations, even, that we may never have encountered. (If you've seen the film *Borat*, you can see how well the generalized other functions: Even when a pair of naked pseudo-journalists enter the elevator with folks, most know to still stare at the numbers.) So it appears to be all a social process—from imitation to play to games to our encounters with Borat. However, in order to see ourselves as the generalized other sees us, we need to spend time alone, disconnected, to incubate the reactions we have gotten, review the videotape, so to speak, and to integrate across all the social interactions in the same way we need sleep to filter and process the day's learning.

We also need a backstage, to borrow the term Erving Goffman used in his 1963 classic, *The Presentation of Self in Everyday Life*. The backstage is exactly what it sounds like: the safe, private space where we explicitly don't have to worry about the generalized other watching us, where we can let our hair down, practice our new social routines, and where we can strike back against the indignations of life in the public square—where, in other words, I could curse the damn French baker for humiliating me. The backstage, is where our "true" self resides, as distinct from the front stage self that we present at the office, in a restaurant, at the doctor's office, or just walking down the street.

And herein lies the connection between solitude and intimacy: Until we have (and can protect) that private self, we cannot be intimate with anyone. For intimacy, to extend Goffman's dramaturgical metaphor, is like giving backstage passes to a select few. It rests on the private self remaining distinct from the public self so that you have something to offer in exchange for peeks behind the curtains of your BFFs. But besides leaving us precious little time to develop that authentic self—to develop a relationship between the "I" and the "me"—the cell phone in the garden erodes that private space through the way it transforms our very social interaction itself.

Recently I found among my Facebook feeds the announcement that a professional colleague I had never met in person (but whose work I admire and who friended me) was getting divorced. It was all going to be OK, he told me and 368 other "friends," since a shared-custody arrangement had been arrived at and his ex and he were going to remain friends. My generalized other kicked into action, and I felt squeamish for having read this painful, personal information that I really shouldn't know. But more and more of our interactions take place in broadcast mode—i.e., front stage. By definition, if you are tweeting something to all your followers or your Facebook buddies, then you are on front stage. Or are you? The whole metaphor breaks down online as privacy is turned inside out, and perhaps the best policy is to hide in plain sight. And yes, as our parents join Facebook, perhaps we will migrate to another site or create other aliases on Twitter for our real BFFs. But without that clear curtain to retreat to, that physical door to close to make sure none else is listening, it gets pretty hard to have a private cohesive self and, by extension, intimacy.

If the locomotive as "machine in the garden" was the nineteenth-century metaphor for the tension between the pastoral and the industrial, then the iPhone becomes the relevant image for the lone cowboy and his ambivalent relationship to the new, social economy of Facebook, LinkedIn, Twitter, and a thousand apps yet to be born in the minds of Silicon Valley venture capitalists. For the train was not just a link to the factory; it was a linchpin to the steel and coal economy, linking once-distant markets as its smoke poured out across the virginal skyscape of North America. Likewise, the iPhone is not just a link to the social economy; it is its principle instrument of trade.

But what makes the smartphone all the more pernicious is its fetishizing of the social. While fetishizing has taken on myriad connotations as of late (mostly sexual), the original meaning as offered by Karl Marx (no relation to Leo) is worth recalling. Fetishizing occurs when an object is imbued with such power as to exert a social force over the individual. Marx claimed that this happened when social relations were monetized and the products we created—through the division of labor—were more complicated than one lone craftsman could comprehend. In this way—through factory work on the assembly line—the person was no longer dominant over the tool or product he created. Rather, the product is larger than any lone individual can conceive and produce himself and instead comes to dominate him.

The same process can be said to be happening with respect to social life. Slowly, slowly, face-to-face interaction, unmediated by technology, is being eclipsed by mediated communication. From smoke signals to papyrus to moveable type to the telegraph to instant messaging, the means of production of communication have become more elaborate and obscured from the user to the point that the medium—the iPhone—has truly become the message, to appropriate Marshall McLuhan's famous quote. Or if not having "become" the message, it has at least come to dominate the message.

Acland, Charles. "Curtains, Carts, and the Mobile Screen." *Screen* 50, no. 1 (Spring 2009): 148–66.

———. *Screen Traffic: Movies, Multiplexes, and Global Culture*. Durham, N.C.: Duke University Press, 2003.

Agamben, Georgio. "What Is an Apparatus?" In *What Is an Apparatus? And Other Essays*, 1–24. Stanford, Calif.: Stanford University Press, 2009.

Agar, Jon. *Constant Touch: A Global History of the Mobile Phone*. Cambridge: Icon, 2004.

Anderson, Chris. *The Long Tail: Why the Future of Business Is Selling Less of More*. New York: Hyperion, 2006.

———. "The Web Is Dead. Long Live the Internet." *Wired*, 17 August 2010.

Andrejevic, Mark. *iSpy: Surveillance and Power in the Interactive Era*. Lawrence: University of Kansas Press, 2007.

Appadurai, Arjun. "Disjuncture and Difference in the Global Cultural Economy." In *Global Culture*, ed. Mike Featherstone, 295–310. London: Sage, 1990.

———. *Modernity at Large: Cultural Dimensions of Globalization*. Minneapolis: University of Minnesota Press, 1996.

Arthur, Brian. *The Nature of Technology: What It Is and How It Evolves*. New York: Free Press, 2009.

Baker, Brian. "A Killer Product—Will Closed Devices Like Apple's iPhone Murder the Web?" *Newsweek*, 2 May 2008.

Balsamo, Anne. *Designing Culture: The Technological Imagination at Work*. Durham, N.C.: Duke University Press, 2011.

Baudrillard, Jean. *Simulacra and Simulation*. Ann Arbor: University of Michigan Press, 1981.

Baudry, Jean-Louis. "The Apparatus: Metapsychological Approaches to the Impression of Reality in the Cinema." In *Narrative, Apparatus, Ideology*, ed. Philip Rosen. New York: Columbia University Press, 1986.

——. "Ideological Effects of the Basic Cinematographic Apparatus." In *Narrative, Apparatus, Ideology*, ed. Philip Rosen. New York: Columbia University Press, 1986.

Becker, David. "Turn Your iPhone Into 3D Virtual Reality Goggles." *Wired*, 10 March 2008.

Behrendt, Frauke. *Handymusik: Klangkunst und "Mobile Devices."* Osnabrück: Epos, 2004.

Beniger, James R. *The Control Revolution: Technological and Economic Origins of the Information Society*. Cambridge, Mass.: Harvard University Press, 1986.

Benjamin, Walter. "The Work of Art in the Age of Its Technological Reproducibility." Second version. In *The Work of Art in the Age of Its Technological Reproducibility, And Other Writings on Media*, ed. Michael W. Jennings, Brigid Doherty, and Thomas Y. Levin, 19–55. Cambridge, Mass.: Belknap Press of Harvard University Press, 2008.

——. "The Work of Art in the Age of Mechanical Reproduction." Third version. In *Selected Writings*, vol. 4, ed. Marcus Bullock and Michael W. Jennings, 251–83. Cambridge, Mass.: Belknap Press of Harvard University Press, 2003.

Bleeker, Julian, and Jeff Knowlton. "Locative Media: A Brief Bibliography and Taxonomy of GPS-Enabled Locative Media." *Leonardo Electronic Almanac* 14, no. 3 (2006): http://www.leoalmanac.org/journal/vol_14/lea_vi4_no3–04/jbleecker.html.

Bolin, Göran. "Notes from Inside the Factory: The Production and Consumption of Signs and Sign Value in Media Industries." *Social Semiotics* 15 (2005): 289–306.

——. "Symbolic Production and Value in Media Industries." *Journal of Cultural Economy* 2, no. 3 (2010): 345–61.

——. *Value and the Media: Cultural Production and Consumption in Digital Markets*. Farnham: Ashgate, 2011.

Bolter, Jay David. *Writing Space: The Computer, Hypertext, and the History of Writing*. Hillsdale, N.J.: Lawrence Erlbaum, 1991.

Bolter, Jay David, and Richard Grusin. *Remediation: Understanding New Media*. Cambridge, Mass.: MIT Press, 1999.

Brucker-Cohen, Jonah. "Art in Your Pocket: iPhone and iPod Touch App Art." *Rhizome.org*, 7 July 2009, http://rhizome.org/editorial/2009/jul/7/art-in-your-pocket (6 January 2011).

——. "Art in Your Pocket 2: Media Art for the iPhone, iPod Touch, and iPad Graduates to the Next Level." *Rhizome.org*, 26 May 2010, http://rhizome.org/editorial/2010/may/26/art-in-your-pocket-2 (6 January 2011).

Bull, M. "To Each Their Own Bubble: Mobile Spaces of Sound in the City." In *Media/Space: Place, Scale, and Culture in a Media Age*, ed. Nick Couldry and Anne McCarthy. London: Routledge, 2003.

Burns, Alex. "Oblique Strategies for Ambient Journalism." *M/C Journal* 13, no. 2 (2010): http://journal.media-culture.org.au/index.php/mcjournal/article/view/230 (15 June 2011).

Bush, Vannevar. "As We May Think." *The Atlantic* (July 1945), http://www.theatlantic
.com/magazine/archive/1969/12/as-we-may-think/3881/ (15 February 2011).

Campbell, Heidi A., and Antonio C. La Pastina. "How the iPhone Became Divine: New Media, Religion, and the Intertextual Circulation of Meaning." *New Media and Society* 12, no. 7 (2010): 1191–1207.

Cannon, Robert. "The Legacy of the Federal Communications Commission's Computer Inquiries." *Federal Communications Law Journal* 55 (2003): 167–206.

Casetti, Francesco. "Back to the Motherland." *Screen* 52, no. 1 (2011): 1–12.

——. "Filmic Experience." *Screen* 50, no. 1 (Spring 2009): 56–66.

——. "The *Last Supper* in Piazza della Scala." *Cinéma & Cie* 11 (Fall 2008): 7–14.

——. "L'esperienza filmica e la rilocazione del cinema." *FataMorgan* 4 (April–May 2008): 23–40.

Castells, Manuel. *Communication Power*. New York: Oxford University Press, 2009.

——. "Informationalism, Networks, and the Network Society: A Theoretical Blueprint." In *The Network Society: A Cross-Cultural Perspective*, ed. Manuel Castells, 3–45. Northampton, Mass.: Edward Elgar, 2004.

Chan, Dean. "Convergence, Connectivity, and the Case of Japanese Mobile Gaming." *Games and Culture* 1 (2008): 13–25.

Classen, Constance. "Museum Manners: The Sensory Life of the Early Museums." *Journal of Social History* 4 (2007) 895–914.

Cooper, G. "The Mutable Mobile: Social Theory in the Wireless World." In *Wireless World: Social, Cultural, and International Issues in Mobile Communications and Computing*, ed. B. Brown, N. Green, and R. Harper, 381–410. London: Springer, 2002.

Cope, Bill, and Phillips Angus, eds. *The Future of the Book in the Digital Age*. Oxford: Chandos, 2006.

Couldry, Nick. *Media Rituals: A Critical Approach:* London: Routledge, 2003.

Couldry, Nick, Sonia Livingstone, and Tim Markham. *Media Consumption and Public Engagement: Beyond the Presumption of Attention*. Houndmills: Palgrave Macmillan, 2007.

Cubitt, Sean, Robert Hassan, and Ingrid Volkmer. "Does Cloud Computing Have a Silver Lining?" *Media, Culture, and Society* 33, no. 1 (2011): 149–58.

Curran, James, Shanto Iyengar, Anker Brink Lund, and Inka Salovaara-Moring. "Media System, Public Knowledge, and Democracy: A Comparative Study." *European Journal of Communication* 24, no. 1 (2009): 5–26.

Curran, James, and Jean Seaton. *Power Without Responsibility: The Press and Broadcasting in Britain*. London: Routledge, 1991.

Dahlgren, Peter. *Media and Political Engagement: Citizens, Communication, and Democracy*. Cambridge: Cambridge University Press, 2009.

Daliot-Bul, Michal. "Japan's Mobile Technoculture: The Production of a Cellular Playscape and Its Cultural Implications," *Media, Culture, and Society* 6 (2007): 945–71.

Dawson, Max. "Television Between Analog and Digital." *Journal of Popular Film and Television* 38, no. 2 (2010): 95–100.

Dean, Jodi. *Blog Theory: Feedback and Capture in the Circuits of Drive*. London: Polity Press, 2010.

——. "Communicative Capitalism: Circulation and the Foreclosure of Politics." In *Digital Media and Democracy*, ed. Megan Boler, 101–21. Cambridge, Mass.: MIT Press, 2008.

——. *Democracy and Other Neoliberal Fantasies:* Durham, N.C.: Duke University Press, 2009.

De Certeau, Michel. *The Practice of Everyday Life.* Berkeley: University of California Press, 1984.

De Lange, Michiel. *Moving Circles: Mobile Media and Playful Identities.* Rotterdam: Erasmus University Rotterdam, 2010.

De Prato, G., et al. "Born Digital/Grown Digital: Assessing the Future Competitiveness of the EU Video Games Software Industry." In *JRC Scientific and Technical Reports.* Luxembourg: Publication Office of the European Union, 2010.

Deuze, Mark. *Media Work.* Cambridge: Polity Press, 2009.

Du Gay, Paul, et al., eds. *Doing Cultural Studies: The Story of the Sony Walkman:* London: Sage, 1997.

Dyson, George. *Darwin Among the Machines: The Evolution of Global Intelligence.* New York: Helix Books, 1998.

Ekström, Louise, and Helena Sandberg. "Reklam funkar inte på mig." In *Unga, marknadsföring och Internet.* Copenhagen: Köp publikation, 2010.

Eliot, Simon, and Jonathan Rose, eds. *A Companion to the History of the Book.* Malden, Mass.: Blackwell, 2007.

Elsaesser, Thomas. "Early Film History and Multi-Media: An Archaeology of Possible Futures?" In *New Media, Old Media: A History and Theory Reader,* ed. Wendy Hui Kyong Chun and Thomas Keenan. New York: Routledge, 2005.

——. "New Film History as Media Archaeology." *Cinémas* 14, no. 2–3 (2003): 75–117.

——. "'Where Were You When . . . ?'; or, 'I Phone, Therefore I Am.'" *PMLA* 118, no.1 (2003): 120–22.

Fanchi, Mariagrazia. "Metamorfosi, divinazioni e presagi." In *Terre Incognite. Lo spettatore italiano e le nuove forme dell'esperienza del film,* ed. F. Casetti and M. Fanchi. Rome: Carocci, 2006.

——. *Spettatore.* Milan: Editore Il Castoro, 2005.

Febvre, Lucien. *The Coming of the Book: The Impact of Printing, 1450–1800.* London: New Left Books, 1976.

Feldman, Erich. "Considérations sur la situation du spectateur au cinéma." *Revue Internationale de Filmologie* 26 (1956).

Florida, Richard. *The Rise of the Creative Class: And How It's Transforming Work, Leisure, Community, and Everyday Life.* New York: Perseus, 2002.

Flusser, Vilém. *Krise der Linearität.* Bern: Benteli, 1988. English translation, *Crisis of Linearity,* www.scribd.com/doc/26525368/Volume-1-Issue-1.

Fortunati, Leopoldina. "The Mobile Phone Between Orality and Writing." Paper presented at the e-Usages conference, Paris, 12–14 June 2000.

Frieden, Rob. "What Do Pizza Delivery and Information Services Have in Common? Lessons from Recent Judicial and Regulatory Struggles with Convergence." *Rutgers Computer and Technology Law Journal* 2 (2006): 247.

Fuller, Buckminster. *Nine Chains to the Moon.* 1938. Philadelphia: Lippincott, 1964.

Giardina, Carolyn. "Consortium of Studios, Manufacturers Throws Weight Behind UltraViolet Management System." *The Hollywood Reporter,* 6 January 2011.

Gillan, Jennifer. *Television and New Media: Must-Click TV.* New York: Routledge, 2011.

Gitelman, Lisa. *Always Already New: Media, History, and the Data of Culture*. Cambridge, Mass.: MIT Press, 2008.

Goggin, Gerard. "Adapting the Mobile Phone: The iPhone and Its Consumption." *Continuum*, no. 23 (2009): 231–44.

——. *Cell Phone Culture: Mobile Technology in Everyday Life*. London: Routledge, 2006.

——. "The Intimate Turn of News: Mobile News." In *News Online: Transformation and Continuity*, ed. Graham Meikle and Guy Redden. London: Palgrave Macmillan, 2010.

Goodman, Nelson. *Languages of Art*. Indianapolis: Hackett, 1968.

——. *Ways of Worldmaking*. Indianapolis: Hackett, 1976.

Gordon, Andrew. "E.T. as Fairy Tale." *Science Fiction Studies* 10, no. 3 (1983): 293–305.

Gray, Jonathan. *Show Sold Separately: Promos, Spoilers, and other Media Paratexts*. New York: New York University Press, 2010.

Graser, Marc. "Biz Mad for iPad Apps." *Variety*, 5 April 2010, 1.

——. "Hollywood Clicks with Ultraviolet Digital Locker." *Variety*, 5 January 2011.

——. "Mobile Video Use Overestimated, Report Says." *Variety*, 20 January 2011.

——. "99-Cent Store; Apple TV Revamp Dives into Rentals." *Variety*, 2 September 2010, 1.

Grossman, Lev. "Invention of the Year: The iPhone." *Time*, 1 November 2007.

Grosz, Elisabeth. *Time Travels: Feminism, Nature, Power*. Durham, N.C.: Duke University Press, 2005.

Hayles, N. Katherine. *How We Became Posthuman: Virtual Bodies in Cybernetics, Literature, and Informatics*. Chicago: University of Chicago Press, 1999.

Hebdige, Dick. *Subculture: The Meaning of Style*. London: Methuen, 1979.

Hennion, Antoine, and Sophie Dubuisson. *Le design: L'object dans l'usage*. Paris: Les Presses de l'École des Mines, 1996.

Herman, Edward S., and Noam Chomsky. *Manufacturing Consent: The Political Economy of the Mass Media*. New York: Pantheon, 1988.

Hermida, Alfred. "From TV to Twitter: How Ambient News Became Ambient Journalism." *M/C Journal*, no. 2 (2010): http://journal.media.culture.org.au/index.php/mcjournal/article/ view/220 (15 June 2011).

——. "Twittering the News: The Emergence of Ambient Journalism." *Journalism Practice*, no. 3 (2010): 297–308.

Hills, Phillip, ed. *The Future of the Printed Word: The Impact and the Implications of the New Communications Technology*. Westport, Conn.: Greenwood, 1980.

Hiltzik, M. A. *Dealers of Lightning: Xerox PARC and the Dawn of the Computer Age*. New York: HarperBusiness, 1999.

Hjorth, Larissa. "*Cartographies of the Mobile: The Personal as Political.*" *Communication, Politics, and Culture 42, no. 2 (2009)*: 24–44.

Hjorth, Larissa, and Gerard Goggin. *Mobile Technologies: From Telecommunications to Media*. New York: Routledge, 2009.

Holt, Jennifer. *Empires of Entertainment*. New Brunswick, N.J.: Rutgers University Press, 2011.

——. "Which Way to the Mothership? New Directions for Television Distribution." Unpublished manuscript, 2011.

Holt, Jennifer, and Alisa Perren, eds. *Media Industries: History, Theory, and Method*. Oxford: Wiley-Blackwell, 2009.

Huhtamo, Erkki. "Time Traveling in the Gallery: An Archaeological Approach to Media Art." In *Immersed in Technology: Art and Virtual Environments*, ed. Mary Ann Moser, 233–70. Cambridge, Mass.: MIT Press, 1996.

Ibelings, Hans. *Supermodernism: Architecture in the Age of Globalization*. Rotterdam: NAI Publishers, 1997.

Ito, Mizuko, Daisuke Okabe, and Misa Matsuda. *Personal, Portable, Pedestrian: Mobile Phones in Japanese Life:* Cambridge, Mass.: MIT Press, 2005.

Jacob, Christian, and Edward H. Dahl, eds. *The Sovereign Map: Theoretical Approaches in Cartography Throughout History*. Chicago: University of Chicago Press, 2006.

Jenkins, Henry. *Convergence Culture: Where Old and New Media Collide*. New York: New York University Press, 2006.

Jessop, Glenn. "A Brief History of Mobile Telephony: The Story of Phones and Cars." *Southern Review* 38, no. 3 (2006): 43–60.

Katz J., ed. *Handbook of Mobile Communication*. Cambridge, Mass.: MIT Press, 2008.

——, ed. *Machines That Become Us: The Social Context of Personal Communication Technology*. New Brunswick, N.J.: Transaction, 2003.

Kay, Alan. "A Review Article: Dynabooks: Past, Present, and Future." *Library Quarterly* no. 3 (2000): 385–95.

Kay, Alan, and Adele Goldberg. "Personal Dynamic Media." *Computer*, no. 10 (1977): 31–41.

Kilgour, Frederick. *The Evolution of the Book*. New York: Oxford University Press, 1998.

Kittler, Friedrich. "Technologies of Writing." Interview. Trans. M. Griffin and S. Herrmann. *New Literary History* 27, no 4 (1996): 731–42.

——. "Towards an Ontology of Media". *Theory, Culture, and Society* 26, no. 2–3 (2009): 23–31.

Kline, Stephen, Nick Dyer-Witheford, and Greig de Peuter. *Digital Play: The Interaction of Technology, Culture, and Marketing*. Montreal: McGill-Queen's University Press, 2003.

Kompare, Derek. "Publishing Flow: DVD Box Sets and the Reconception of Television." *Television and New Media* 4 (2006): 335–60.

Kreutz, Christian. "Mobile Activism in Africa: Future Trends and Software Development." In *SMS Uprising: Mobile Activism in Africa*, ed. Sokari Ekine, 135–60. Oxford: Pambazuka Press, 2010.

Kirisits, Nicolaj, et al., eds. *Creative Interactions—the Mobile Music Workshops, 2004–2008*. Vienna: University of Applied Arts, 2008.

Landow, George P. *Hypertext 3.0: Critical Theory and New Media in an Era of Globalization*. Baltimore, Md.: Johns Hopkins University Press, 1992.

Laurel, Brenda. *Computers as Theatre*. Reading, Mas.: Addison-Wesley, 1991.

Le Grice, Malcom. *Experimental Cinema in the Digital Age*. London: BFI, 2001.

Lessig, Lawrence. *Free Culture: The Nature and Future of Creativity*. London: Penguin, 2005.

Levinson, Paul. *Cellphone: The Story of the World's Most Mobile Medium and How It Has Transformed Everything*. New York: Palgrave, 2004.

——. *New New Media*. New York: Allyn & Bacon, 2009.

Licklider, J. C. R., and Robert W. Taylor. "The Computer as a Communication Device." *Science and Technology* 76 (April 1968): 21–31.

Ling, Rich. *The Mobile Connection: The Cell Phone's Impact on Society*. San Francisco: Morgan Kaufman, 2004.

Ling, Richard, and Jonathan Donner. *Mobile Phones and Mobile Communication*. Cambridge: Polity Press, 2009.

Liu, Ziming. *Paper to Digital: Documents in the Information Age*. Westport, Conn.: Libraries Unlimited, 2008.

Lotz, Amanda. *The Television Will Be Revolutionized*. New York: New York University Press, 2007.

Lüders, Marika. "Conceptualizing Personal Media." *New Media and Society* 10 (2008): 683–702.

Madianou, Mirca, and Miller, Daniel. *Technologies of Love: Migration and the Polymedia Revolution*. London: Routledge (forthcoming).

Manguel, Alberto. *A History of Reading*. London: Harper Collins, 1996.

Manovich, Lev. "Interaction as an Aesthetic Event." *Receiver*, no. 17 (2007): http://dm.ncl.ac.uk/courseblog/files/2011/03/Manovich_InteractionAsAestheticEvent.pdf.

——. *The Language of New Media*. Cambridge, Mass.: MIT Press, 2001.

——. "The Poetics of Augmented Space." *Visual Communication* 5, no. 2 (2006): 219–40.

Marks, Laura U. *The Skin of Film: Intercultural Cinema, Embodiment, and the Senses*. Durham, N.C.: Duke University Press, 2000.

——. *Touch: Sensuous Theory and Multisensory Media*. Minneapolis: University of Minnesota Press, 2002.

Mascheroni, Giovanna. *Le comunità viaggianti. Società reticolare e mobile dei viaggiatori indipendenti*. Milan: FrancoAngeli, 2007.

Maxwell, John. "Tracing the Dynabook: A Study of Technocultural Transformations." Ph.D. diss., University of British Columbia, 2006. http://thinkubator.ccsp.sfu.ca/Dynabook (15 February 2011).

May, Harvey, and Greg Hearn. "The Mobile Phone as Media." *International Journal of Cultural Studies* 8, no. 2 (2005): 195–211.

Mazo, Gary, Martin Trautschold, and Kevin Michaluk. *Crackberry: True Tales of Blackberry Use and Abuse*. New York: APress, 2010.

McCarthy, Anna. *Ambient Television: Visual Culture and Public Space:* Durham, N.C.: Duke University Press, 2001.

——. "From Screen to Site: Television's Material Culture and Its Place." *October*, no. 98 (2001): 93–111.

McLuhan, Marshall. *Understanding Media: The Extensions of Man*. New York: McGraw-Hill, 1964.

Michaud, Philippe-Alain. Introduction to *Mouvement des images: The Movement of Images*. Paris: Centre Pompidou, 2006.

Miller, Daniel. *Tales from Facebook*. Cambridge: Polity, 2011.

Mitchell, William J. *The Reconfigured Eye: Visual Truth in the Post-Photographic Era*. Cambridge, Mass.: MIT Press, 1992.

Mittell, Jason. "TiVoing Childhood: Time-Shifting a Generation's Concept of Television." In *Flow TV: Television in the Age of Media Convergence*, ed. Michael Kackman et al., 46–54. New York: Routledge, 2011.

Morley, David. *Media, Modernity, and Technology: The Geography of the New*. London: Routledge, 2007.

——. "What's 'Home' Got to do with It? Contradictory Dynamics in the Domestication of Technology and the Dislocation of Domesticity." *European Journal of Cultural Studies* 6, no. 4 (2003): 435–58.

Nakahata, John T. "Regulating Information Platforms: The Challenge of Rewriting Communications Regulation from the Bottom Up." *Telecommunications and High Technology Law* 1 (2002): 98–99.

Netherby, Jennifer. "Digital Cloud's Dark Lining." *Variety*, 2 November 2009.

Norris, Pippa. *Democratic Deficit: Critical Citizens Revisited*. Cambridge: Cambridge University Press, 2011.

O'Grady, Jason D. *Apple Inc*. London: Greenwood Press, 2009.

Okazaki, Shintaro, Radoslav Skapa, and Ildefonso Grande. "Capturing Global Youth: Mobile Gaming in the US, Spain, and the Czech Republic." *Journal of Computer-Mediated Communication* 13 (2008): 827–55.

Oksman, Virpi, and Jussi Turtiainen. "Mobile Communication as a Social Stage." *New Media and Society* 3 (2004): 319–39.

Ouellette, Laurie. *Viewers Like You? How Public TV Failed the People*. New York: Columbia University Press, 2002.

Parks, Lisa. "Flexible Microcasting: Gender, Generation, and Television-Internet Convergence." In *Television After TV: Essays on a Medium in Transition*, ed. Lynn Spigel and Jan Olsson, 133–62. Durham, N.C.: Duke University Press, 2004.

Patterson, Mark. *The Senses of Touch: Haptics, Affects, and Technologies*. Oxford: Berg, 2007.

Pedersen, Isabel. "'No Apple iPhone? You Must Be Canadian': Mobile Technologies, Participatory Culture, and Rhetorical Transformation." *Canadian Journal of Communication* 3 (2008): 375–84.

Perren, Alisa. "Business as Unusual: Conglomerate-Sized Challenges in the Digital Arena." *Journal of Popular Film and Television* 38, no. 2 (2010): 72–78.

Pine, Joseph, and James H. Gilmore. *Experience Economy: Work Is Theatre and Every Business a Stage*. Cambridge, Mass.: Harvard Business Press, 1999.

Rheingold, Howard. *Smart Mobs: The Next Social Revolution*. Cambridge: Basic Books, 2002.

Richardson, Tim. *Sweets: A History of Temptation*. London: Bantam, 2003.

Riegl, Aloïs. "Late Roman Art Industry" (1901). In *Art History and Its Methods: A Critical Anthology*, ed. Eric Fernie. London: Phaidon, 1995.

Robins, J. Max. "The Iger-Pod." *Broadcasting and Cable*, 17 October 2005, 5.

Rodowick, David N. "Dr. Strange Media, or How I Learned to Stop Worrying and Love Film Theory." In *Inventing Film Studies*, ed. Lee Grieveson and Haidee Wasson, 374–98. Durham, N.C.: Duke University Press, 2008.

Rogoff, Irit. "Regional Imaginings." In *Unleashed: Contemporary Art from Turkey*, ed. Hossein Amirsadeghi. London: TransGlobe, 2010.

Rose, Frank. *The Art of Immersion: How the Digital Generation Is Remaking Hollywood, Madison Avenue, and the Way We Tell Stories:* New York: Norton, 2011.

Rosi, M., and F. Giordano. "Applicazione per iPhone: tra film interattivo e gioco." In *Il film in tasca: Videofonino, cinema e televisione*, ed. M. Ambrosini, G. Maina, and E. Marcheschi. Ghezzano (PI): Felici Editori, 2009.

Sawhney, Harmeet, and Seungwhan Lee. "Arenas of Innovation: Understanding New Configurational Potentialities of Communication Technologies," *Media, Culture, and Society*, no. 27 (2005): 637–60.

Schmidt, Eric. "Preparing for the Big Mobile Revolution" *Harvard Business Review*, 21 January 2011.

Schreibman, Ray, and Susan Siemens. *A Companion to Digital Literary Studies*. Malden, Mass.: Blackwell, 2007.

Schroeder, R. "Mobile Phones and the Inexorable Advance of Multimodal Connectedness." *New Media Society* 12, no. 2 (2010): 75–90.

Scifo, Barbara. *Culture mobili. Ricerche sull'adozione giovanile della telefonia*. Milan: Vita e Pensiero, 2005.

Shillingsburg, Peter L. *From Gutenberg to Google: Electronic Representations of Literary Texts*. Cambridge: Cambridge University Press, 2006.

Sloss, Robert. "Das drahtlose Jahrhundert." In *Die Welt in hundert Jahren*, ed. Arthur Brehmer, 27–50. Berlin: Buntdruck, 1908.

Smith, D. K., and R. C. Alexander. *Fumbling the Future: How Xerox Invented, Then Ignored, the First Personal Computer:* New York: Morrow, 1988.

Sobchack, Vivian. *The Address of the Eye: A Phenomenology of Film Experience*. Princeton, N.J.: Princeton University Press, 1992.

——. *Carnal Thoughts: Embodiment and Moving Image Culture*. Berkeley: University of California Press, 2004.

Staiger, Janet, and Sabine Hake, eds. *Convergence Media History*. New York: Routledge, 2009.

Stephenson, Neal. *The Diamond Age; or, A Young Lady's Illustrated Primer*. New York: Bantam Books, 1995.

Stewart, James B. *DisneyWar*. London: Simon & Schuster, 2008.

Steyerl, Hito, *Die Farbe der Wahrheit. Dokumentarismen im Kunstfeld*. Vienna: Turia+Kant, 2008.

Stiernstedt, Fredrik. "Maximising the Power of Entertainment: The Audience Commodity in Contemporary Radio." *The Radio Journal* 6 (2008): 113–27.

Stockton, Kathryn Bond. *The Queer Child, or Growing Sideways in the Twentieth Century*. Durham, N.C.: Duke University Press, 2009.

Strauven, Wanda. "The Observer's Dilemma: To Touch or Not to Touch." In *Media Archaeology: Approaches, Applications, Implications*, ed. Erkki Huhtamo and Jussi Parikka, 148–63. Berkeley: University of California Press, 2011.

Striphas, Ted. *The Late Age of Print: Everyday Book Culture from Consumerism to Control*. New York: Columbia University Press, 2009.

Strömbäck, Jesper. "Four Phases of Mediatization: An Analysis of the Mediatization of Politics." *The International Journal of Press/Politics* 13, no. 3 (2008): 228–46.

Strömbäck, Jesper, and Lars W. Nord. "Media and Politics in Sweden." In *Communicating Politics: Political Communication in the Nordic Countries*, ed. Jesper Strömbäck, Mark Ørsten, and Toril Aalberg. Gothenburg: Nordicom, 2008.

Sturken, Marita, and Lisa Cartwright. *Practices of Looking: An Introduction to Visual Culture*. New York: Oxford University Press, 2001.

Sutherland, Ivan. "A Man Machine Graphical Communication System." In *Proceedings of the AFIPS Spring Joint Computer Conference*, 329–46. Washington, D.C., 1963.

Sutherland, Marilyn, and Kathryn Deegan. *Transferred Illusions: Digital Technology and the Forms of Print*. Farnham: Ashgate, 2009.

Thompson, John B. *The Media and Modernity*. Cambridge: Polity, 1995.

Thorburn, David, and Henry Jenkins, eds. *Rethinking Media Change: The Aesthetics of Transition*. Cambridge, Mass.: MIT Press, 2004.

Tichi, Cecelia. *Electronic Hearth: Creating an American Television Culture*. Oxford: Oxford University Press, 1991.

Tilley, Christopher. *Handbook of Material Culture*. London: Sage, 2006.

Townsend, Anthony. "Locative-Media Artists in the Contested-Aware City." *Leonardo* 39, no. 4 (2006): 345–47.

Tryon, Chuck. *Reinventing Cinema: Movies in the Age of Media Convergence*. New Brunswick, N.J.: Rutgers University Press, 2009.

——. "Redbox vs. Red Envelope, Or, What Happens When the Infinite Aisle Swings Through the Grocery Store." *Canadian Journal of Film Studies* 20, no. 2 (Fall 2011).

Turkle, Sherry. *Alone Together: Why We Expect More from Technology and Less from Each Other*. New York: Basic Books, 2011.

——. "Seeing Through Computers: Education in a Culture of Simulation." *The American Prospect* 8 (1997): 76–82.

Turow, Joseph. *Niche Envy: Marketing Discrimination in the Digital Age*. Cambridge, Mass.: MIT Press, 2006.

Tuters, Marc, and Kazys Varnelis. "Beyond Locative Media: Giving Shape to the Internet of Things." *Leonardo* 39, no. 4 (2006): 357–63.

Ulin, Jeff. *The Business of Media Distribution: Monetizing Film, TV, and Video Content*. New York: Focal Press, 2010.

Uricchio, William. *Media, Simultaneity, Convergence: Culture and Technology in an Age of Intermediality*. Utrecht: Universiteit Utrecht, 1997.

Urry, John. *Mobilities*. Cambridge: Polity, 2007.

Vaidhyanathan, Siva. *Copyrights and Copywrongs: The Rise of Intellectual Property and How It Threatens Creativity*. New York: New York University Press, 2001.

Van Buskirk, Eliot. "Netflix for iPhone Is Coming, Subject to AT&T's Data Caps." *Wired*, 7 June 2010.

Van Couvering, Elizabeth. "The History of the Internet Search Engine: Navigational Media and the Traffic Commodity." In *Web Search: Multidisciplinary Perspectives*, ed. Amanda Spink and Michael Zimmer, 177–208. Berlin: Springer, 2007.

Van den Boomen, Marianne, et al., eds. *Digital Material: Tracing New Media in Everyday Life and Technology*. Amsterdam: Amsterdam University Press, 2009.

Van Heerden, Clive, Jack Mama, and David Eves. "Wearable Electronics." In *New Nomads: An Exploration of Wearable Electronics by Philips*, ed. Stefano Marzano et al., 36–56. Rotterdam: 010 Publishers, 2001.

Van Zoonen, Liesbet. *Entertaining the Citizen: When Politics and Popular Culture Converge*. Lanham, Md.: Rowman & Littlefield, 2005.

Venegas, Cristina. *Digital Dilemmas: The State, the Individual, and Digital Media in Cuba*. New Brunswick, N.J.: Rutgers University Press, 2010.

Verhoeff, Nanna. "Screens of Navigation: From Taking a Ride to Making the Ride." *Refractory* no. 12 (2008), http://refractory.unimelb.edu.au/2008/03/06/screens-of-navigation-from-taking-a-ride-to-making-the-ride/ (15 June 2011).

——. "Theoretical Consoles: Concepts for Gadget Analysis." *Journal of Visual Culture* 3 (2009): 279–98.

Vogelstein, Fred. "The Untold Story: How the iPhone Blew Up the Wireless Industry." *Wired*, 1 September 2008.

Völker, Clara. *Mobile Medien: Zur Genealogie des Mobilfunks und zur Ideengeschichte von Virtualität*. Bielefeld: Transcript, 2010.

Waldrop, M. M. *The Dream Machine: J. C. R. Licklider and the Revolution That Made Computing Personal*. New York: Viking, 2001.

Wallenstein, Andrew. "Why Apple Rental Plan Alienated Most Studios." *Hollywood Reporter*, 2 September 2010.

Watling, Gabrielle, and Sara E. Quay, eds. *Cultural History of Reading*. Westport, Conn.: Greenwood Press, 2009.

Wark, McKenzie. *Gamer Theory*. Cambridge, Mass.: Harvard University Press, 2007.

Weiser, M. "The Computer for the Twenty-first Century." *Scientific American* 265, no. 3 (1991): 94–104.

Wellman, B., and C. Haythornthwaite, eds. *The Internet in Everyday Life*. Oxford: Blackwell, 2002.

Williams, Raymond. *Culture and Society, 1780–1950*. Harmondsworth: Penguin, 1958.

——. *Television: Technology as Cultural Form*. New York: Schocken, 1974.

Wilken, Rowan, and John Sinclair. "'Waiting for the Kiss of Life': Mobile Media and Advertising." *Convergence* 15 (2010): 1–19.

Winthrop-Young, Geoffrey. *Kittler and the Media*. Cambridge: Polity Press, 2011.

Wolf, Mark J. P. *Abstracting Reality: Art, Communication, and Cognition in the Digital Age*. Lanham, Md.: University Press of America, 2000.

Woodman, Oliver J. "An Introduction to Inertial Navigation." In *Technical Report UCAM-CL-TR-696*. London: University of Cambridge Computer Laboratory, 2007.

Wright, Charles. *Mass Communication: A Sociological Perspective*. New York: Random House, 1959.

Wu, Tim. *The Master Switch: The Rise and Fall of Information Empires*. New York: Knopf, 2010.

Young, Sherman. *The Book Is Dead, Long Live the Book*. Sydney: University of New South Wales Press, 2007.

Zielinski, Siegfried. *Audiovisions: Cinema and Television as Entr'actes in History*. Amsterdam: Amsterdam University Press, 1999.

Zittrain, Jonathan. *The Future of the Internet—and How to Stop It*. New Haven, Conn.: Yale University Press, 2008.

Žižek, Slavoj. *Looking Awry: An Introduction to Jacques Lacan Through Popular Culture*. Cambridge, Mass.: MIT Press, 1992.

Anne Balsamo is a professor with joint appointments in the Interactive Media Division, School of Cinematic Arts, and the Annenberg School of Communication and Journalism, University of Southern California, Los Angeles. Her most recent book, *Designing Culture: The Technological Imagination at Work* (2011) examines the relationship between cultural reproduction and technological innovation (see also www.designingculture.net/blog/).

Jennifer M. Barker is assistant professor in the Department of Communication at Georgia State University. She is the author of *The Tactile Eye: Touch and the Cinematic Experience* (2009) and a number of essays on cinematic spectacle, ethnographic documentary, and feminist experimental film.

Frauke Behrendt is senior lecturer in media studies at the University of Brighton. She is leading the EPSRC-funded research project "Smart E-bikes" and is on the steering committee of the European COST Action on "Sonic Interaction Design" and of the International Workshop of Mobile Music Technology. She is the author of a book on mobile phone music (2005, in German).

Göran Bolin is professor in media and communication studies at Södertörn University in Stockholm, Sweden. He has worked in (and headed) research projects on violence in the media, youth and cultural production, entertainment television, and mobile phone use. His latest book is entitled *Value and the Media: Cultural Production and Consumption in Digital Markets* (2011).

Kristopher L. Cannon is a Ph.D. candidate in moving image studies at the Department of Communication at Georgia State University. His research examines new media, film, and other visual artifacts that lend to various visions, versions and manifestations of bodies.

Francesco Casetti is professor of film and media at Yale University. He is author of *Inside the Gaze: The Fiction Film and Its Spectator* (1999); *Theories of Cinema, 1945–1995* (1999); and *Eye of the Century:Film, Experience, Modernity* (2008). He taught for thirty years in Italy, serving as president of the Association of Film and Television Teachers.

Dalton Conley is the dean of social sciences and professor of the social sciences at New York University. His most recent publications include *The Pecking Order: A Bold New Look at How Family and Society Determine Who We Become* (2004) and *Elsewhere, U.S.A: How We Got from the Company Man, Family Dinners, and the Affluent Society to the Home Office, BlackBerry Moms, and Economic Anxiety* (2009).

Mia Consalvo is a visiting associate professor in the comparative media studies program at MIT and associate professor in the School of Media Arts and Studies at Ohio University. She is the author of *Cheating: Gaining Advantage in Videogames* (2007) and coeditor of the *Blackwell Handbook of Internet Studies* (2011, with Charles Ess).

Lane DeNicola is lecturer in digital anthropology at the Department of Anthropology, University College London. He is the author of *The Clickwheel Cargo Cult: Reading the iPod as Cultural Artifact* (2011) (see also: http://digitalcargo.wordpress. com).

Mark Deuze is associate professor in the Department of Telecommunications at Indiana University. His published work comprises seven books, including *Media Work* (2007) and *Media Life* (2012) (see also: http://deuze.blogspot.com/).

Barbara Flueckiger is a professor in the Department for Cinema Studies at the University of Zurich and a research fellow at Harvard University and had an earlier professional career as a location sound engineer in feature film production. She is the author of the pioneering books *Sound Design* (2001) and *Visual Effects* (2008) (see also www.zauberklang.ch/).

Gerard Goggin is professor of media and communications at the University of Sydney. He researches new media and their social, cultural, and policy implications. His most recent book publications include *Cell Phone Culture* (2006), *Mobile Phone Cultures* (2008), and *Global Mobile Media* (2011).

Janey Gordon is a principal lecturer in the School of Media, Art, and Design and a media undergraduate field chair and associate and fellow for the Centre of Excellence in Teaching and Learning at the University of Bedfordshire. Her research interests and publications are in the areas of community radio, mobile phones, and media pedagogy. She is the editor of *Notions of Community: A Collection of Community Media Debates and Dilemmas* (2009).

Jennifer Holt is assistant professor of film and media studies and the codirector of the Media Industries Project at the Carsey Wolf Center, University of California, Santa Barbara. She is the author of *Empires of Entertainment* (2011) and the coeditor of *Media Industries: History, Theory, and Method* (2009, with Alisa Perren).

Anu Koivunen is associate professor in the Department of Media Studies, Stockholm University. Her research focuses on questions of television history, popular culture, feminist media studies, queer theory, and national cinema. She is the author of *Performative Histories, Foundational Fictions: Gender and Sexuality in Niskavuori Films* (2003).

Oliver Leistert is a research fellow at the Centre for Media and Communication Studies at Central European University Budapest. His research focuses on online, social, and mobile media and especially on cybersurveillance and mobile protest media. He recently coedited *Generation Facebook* (2011, with Theo Röhle).

Lev Manovich is professor in the Department for Visual Arts at the University of California, San Diego, director of the Software Studies Initiative at California Institute for Telecommunications and Information Technology, and professor at European Graduate School. He is the author of *The Language of New Media* (2001), *Soft Cinema: Navigating the Database* (2005), and *Software Takes Command* (2008) (see also manovich.net).

Alisa Perren is associate professor in the Department of Communication at Georgia State University. She is currently completing a manuscript tracing the evolution of Miramax during the 1990s and is the coeditor of *Media Industries: History, Theory, and Method* (2009, with Jennifer Holt) (see also: www.themediaindustries.net/).

Karen Petruska is a Ph.D. candidate in the Department of Communication at Georgia State University.

Sara Sampietro is a Ph.D. candidate at the Università Cattolica del Sacro Cuore of Milan.

Alexandra Schneider is associate professor at the Media Studies Department of Amsterdam University. Her research interests include media archaeology, nontheatrical film, and transnational cinema.

Pelle Snickars is head of research at the National Library of Sweden. His recent book publications include the coedited book *The YouTube Reader* (2009, with Patrick Vonderau) (see also: http://pellesnickars.se/).

Jennifer Steetskamp is a Ph.D. candidate at the University of Amsterdam. Her research focuses on installation art and media history, exploring the multiple relationships among cinema, media history, and the arts from a media archaeological perspective.

Chuck Tryon is assistant professor of film and media studies at Fayetteville State University. His book, *Reinventing Cinema: Movies in the Age of Digital Convergence*, was published in 2009 (see also: http://chutry.wordherders.net/wp/).

Nanna Verhoeff is associate professor in comparative media studies at Utrecht University. She is currently preparing a book entitled *Mobile Screens: The Visual Regime of Navigation* (see also www.nannaverhoeff.net/).

Patrick Vonderau is associate professor in the Department of Media Studies, Stockholm University. His most recent book publications include *The YouTube Reader* (2009, with Pelle Snickars) and *Films That Work: Industrial Film and the Productivity of Media* (2009, with Vinzenz Hediger).